Public Administration in World Perspective

Public Administration in World 🌐 Perspective

Edited by **O. P. DWIVEDI** and **KEITH M. HENDERSON**

IOWA STATE UNIVERSITY PRESS / AMES

O. P. DWIVEDI is Professor and Chairman, Department of Political Studies, University of Guelph.

KEITH M. HENDERSON is Professor of Political Science, State University of New York College at Buffalo.

© 1990 Iowa State University Press, Ames, Iowa 50010
All rights reserved

Composed and printed in the United States of America
⊗ This book is printed on acid-free paper.

Library of Congress Cataloging-in-Publication Data

Public administration in world perspective / edited by O. P. Dwivedi and Keith M. Henderson.
    p.   cm.
  ISBN 0-8138-0154-0 (alk. paper)
    1. Public administration. 2. Comparative government. I. Dwivedi, O. P. II. Henderson, Keith M., 1934–
JF1351.P8182   1990
350–dc20   90–10712

Contents

3   Internationalization

Preface

THE IDEA FOR THIS BOOK of essays in comparative public administration originated in an exchange of correspondence between the two editors from their home bases several years ago and continued to be developed from such unlikely locations as Papua New Guinea and Adana, Turkey. Both editors felt the need for a useful set of original essays emphasizing the importance of public administration in world perspective, and for a supplement to the one comprehensive textbook in the field—then and now—Ferrel Heady's *Public Administration, A Comparative Perspective,* 3d ed. (New York: Marcel Dekker, 1984). Further, the editors are aware of the fact that most of the comparative public administration books consist of essays written on different countries by Western specialists; thus in this book, we have, perhaps for the first time, brought indigenous experts together to provide perspectives from their own points of view. In a sense, this has been a truly international endeavor.

Comparative public administration—the study of administration in various countries around the globe—changed dramatically in the 1980s. It no longer remains a predominantly American enterprise concerned with problems of comparison, transfer of technical assistance, and elimination of "cultural blinders." It acquired a worldwide perspective with many—we are tempted to say *most*—of its contributions coming from non-American experts. It has moved beyond isolated case studies to systematic attention to common variables but has retreated from the model-building preoccupations of the 1960s. Along with its "protégé," development administration, it has revived the interest in administrative phenomena not merely as a by-product of political or economic changes but as a unique focus deserving greater attention.

By choosing administrative growth and change—including administrative reform—as a framework, along with policy developments in recent years, the editors have attempted to provide a common denominator for the various country and regional studies. Each contributor has had the freedom to interpret his country/region from his own expert perspective but with common benchmarks. In addition, selections on the field as a whole and its dilemmas and training opportunities are provided.

We wish to acknowledge the forbearance and support of our family members as well as our colleagues and the press editorial staff. We are also indebted to specialists in the field for their helpful comments and suggestions.

1

Perspectives
on Comparative
Administration

1

Introduction

FERREL HEADY

COMPARATIVE PUBLIC ADMINISTRATION is continuously trying to reconcile two tendencies that seem at first to be in competition, but that on further consideration turn out really to be complementary.

The first is the urge to generalize by making comparisons that are as inclusive as possible and by searching for administrative knowledge that transcends national or regional boundaries. These efforts are inspired by forces such as the search for a science of administration with principles that have generalized applicability, the desire to encompass in the range of comparison all existing national political entities, and the movement to foster global or international capabilities for making comparative studies in administration.

The second tendency emphasizes separatism. It has even older and stronger roots. Public administration as an academic discipline or specialization has focused primarily on a particular national system of administration, with only scant attention, or none at all, to foreign experience. Educational institutions offering programs for the training of future public administrators have emphasized the task of producing professional administrators for the nation or state fostering the institution. Administrative structures and procedures developed domestically are normally given a higher value and priority than those derived from an outside source. Finally, the impression is widespread that administrative characteristics must and should vary from one national or cultural setting to another, making borrowing risky and study of other systems unnecessary.

The basic thrust of the comparative administration "movement" of the last three decades has been to support the first tendency. Specific indications of this include the activities of the older CAG (Comparative Adminis-

3

tration Group) and the newer SICA (Section on Comparative and International Administration) affiliated with the American Society for Public Administration; the contributions of both general systems and middle-range theorists as to how comparative studies should be conducted; the technical assistance programs in public administration (particularly those aimed at the establishment of Third World centers for study and training); and the arguments frequently made that by now public administration as a discipline or field of study must be viewed as global in scope, with American, Soviet, or Brazilian public administration appropriately viewed as only subfields of interest (Heady 1984).

The second separative tendency has not only been persistent but is also currently being reenforced. Even in the United States, where the postwar initiative in comparative public administration was centered, both the literature of public administration and the curricula of educational programs in public administration continue to concentrate primarily on American public administration. The volume of officially sponsored assistance and interchange in public administration across national boundaries is on the decline rather than increasing. Although more attention is being given to techniques for project implementation, increased scepticism is being expressed as to the predictability of positive results. Privatization is advocated frequently as preferable to governmental action for the attainment of public policy goals, often with insufficient attention being given to the necessity of a solid public administration infrastructure as a precondition for success in privatization efforts (ACIPA 1986; Moe 1986).

Another development is that social science research is now devoting greater attention to the impact and importance of factors that are nationally specific rather than more generalized. This is true of much of the work in the analysis of public policy in a variety of functional fields. The significance of cultural characteristics in understanding and explaining administrative institutions and behavior receives more and more sophisticated treatment. Concepts such as "political culture," "bureaucratic culture," and "organizational culture" suggest guidelines that are potentially useful for this purpose. The political culture of a nation is supposed to identify its particular distribution of patterns of orientation toward political matters, subdivided into cognitive, affective, and evaluational aspects (Almond and Verba 1963). Building on this foundation, Nachmias and Rosenbloom developed a model to study orientations toward the public bureaucracy as a specific unit of political systems, and used it in a study concentrating primarily on Israel. Retaining the cognitive, affective, and evaluative subtypes of orientations, they concentrated on two dimensions—orientations of citizens or the general public toward the public bureaucracy, and orientations of the bureaucrats toward the bureaucracy. They also were interested in assessing the congruence of these two sets of orientations. Out of this analysis, they arrived at typologies of orientations toward public bureaucracies by groups of citizens, on the one hand, and by bureaucrats, on the other. Theoretically this bureaucratic culture model offers a means of systematically profiling characteristics of different national systems of public administration in a way that might be potentially useful for decisionmakers assessing prospects for success in cross-cultural transfers (Nachmias and Rosenbloom 1978). More recently, attempts have been made, at the more restricted level of specific organizations, to use the concept of "organizational culture" for the exploration of relationships between organizations and their environments. Used primarily so far in the study of private organizations (Frost et al. 1986), organizational culture analyses of public entities should be of equal value.

Other scholars have focused particularly on differences caused by cultural factors. Rogerio F. Pinto (1981) has forecast the emergence of a field of "cross-cultural organizational socio-psychology" based on the proposition that "human behavior varies with culture and, therefore, significant differences — rather than similarities — are to be expected as one moves from one culture to another." Wesley E. Bjur and Asghar Zomorrodian have recently suggested a conceptual framework for developing "context-based, indigenous theories of administration," recognizing that every cultural context "presents a different mix of value 'allies' and 'enemies' in the administrative pursuit of efficiency" (Bjur and Zomorrodian 1986:396).

In the study of comparative and development administration, elimination of either the tendency toward generalization or the tendency toward separatism would be a mistake. So would excessive emphasis on either one of them. The temptation from focusing on the first tendency is to be overly optimistic about prospects for success in the transfer of administrative knowledge and techniques across cultures. The danger of concentrating unduly on traits that are culturally specific is that this will discourage mutual interchanges that may be both desirable and possible.

If these comments are valid, materials offered for use by students of comparative public administration and development administration should try to strike a balance between these two competing but complementary tendencies. This volume edited by Professors Dwivedi and Henderson succeeds in meeting this objective. The essays of the editors and of the other contributors are designed to and should convey to the reader an appreciation both of the peculiarities of different national and regional systems of public administration and of the underlying similarities that make comparisons intellectually stimulating and also worthwhile as a practical means of advancing the science and art of public administration around the world.

Most of the contributors to this volume have authored studies concentrating on their own native countries or regions. These chapters are devoted almost equally to the "developed" and "developing" areas of the world. As a group, these studies illustrate convincingly the reality of the "globalization" of comparative public administration (Heady 1983). It is no longer necessary in most cases to rely on scholars from the developed West to produce studies of public administration in Third World countries and regions. This has the distinct advantage that the view is always one "from the inside" rather than "from the outside." Chapter by chapter, here is a source for up-to-date information on a wide range of contemporary politico-administrative arrangements provided by experts intimately familiar with their subject matter. At the same time, the simultaneous publication of a series of studies planned and written according to a common plan offers unusual opportunities for comparative analysis. The differential impact on the operation of a variety of administrative systems of such environmental factors as historical background, culture, religion, economic circumstances, and political regime characteristics can be examined under promising circumstances.

Preceding and following these country/regional studies are several more comprehensive efforts to review the past, examine the present, and peer into the future of comparative and development administration.

The editors, in a "state of the art" essay, review briefly the evolution of both comparative public administration and what they refer to as its "protégé," development administration, but they are mainly concerned with dilemmas confronting the combined comparative-development administration field. They encourage the globalization process, and emphasize the desirability already mentioned of developing local expertise. They deplore, as has often been done before, the lack of a paradigmatic consensus, with the consequent likelihood that proliferation of studies may not result in aggregation of knowledge, but they do not respond to this dilemma beyond providing a common framework to guide the country/regional study contributors to this volume. They touch upon the uneasy and ambiguous relationship between comparative public administration and comparative public policy, and worry about a resulting tendency to subordinate administrative to policy concerns. My reaction is that what differentiates the two fields is in essence this contrast in emphasis, and that a policy emphasis by some does not preclude an administrative emphasis by others, or diminish the importance of exploring the policy-administration interface. They properly endorse the long-standing urge of comparativists to be relevant. "Ultimately," they state, "the test of comparative public administration is its usefulness in development administration." I agree that this is one criterion for evaluation, but doubt that it is as exclusively important as their language implies. This volume itself will serve other well-justified purposes, including the education of future public administrators who may not be primarily engaged in what are commonly regarded as careers in development administration.

The thrust is toward the future in the concluding essay by Gerald Caiden and Naomi Caiden, but they start with a look back at the comparative administration movement and an assessment of its shortcomings. This is done perceptively and evenhandedly, reflecting their long record of participation in the movement they describe and evaluate. Unlike the authors of many earlier critiques, they do not hesitate to spell out in considerable detail what needs to be done to rectify the shortcomings identified.

Recognizing that "comparative analysis is probably the most difficult part of the study of public administration," the Caidens have no illusions about easy solutions, but they do lay out what seem to me to be helpful suggestions as to problems and priorities. Without claiming that they or anyone else can discover *the* comparative approach, they offer a list of what is required for *any* appropriate comparative approach.

As to future prospects, the Caidens are basically optimistic that a revitalization of comparative administration is possible and is indeed already occurring. As they perceive the situation, there is no dearth of comparative material with which to work. The question is what matters deserve priority attention. They conclude by making ten suggestions as to areas "ripe for comparative treatment," without putting them in any particular order of importance.

The suggestions on the Caidens' list are obviously not of equal weight and comprehensiveness, and some will be easier to tackle than others. Readers will make their own judgments as to priorities and interrelations among them. My reaction is to seek a blend that will include both the separatist and generalist tendencies already discussed. Hence from this list I would emphasize such matters as the identification of administrative cultures and the connections between cultural traits and public sector productivity, which focus on differences from system to system, and such topics as the configuration of the administrative state and education and training for public service, which are more likely to highlight similarities. In the long run, nothing on the Caidens' list is apt to be more crucial than public service education and training. They end with the optimistic observation that the future of comparative administration seems to be in good hands. If this is now and continues to be an accurate statement, it will be due to sustained attention to educational and training needs in a variety of national settings. This collection of essays, together with an impressive array of other contemporary publications already published or on the way, gives a basis for encouragement that this need is getting the recognition it deserves.

References

ACIPA. *Institutional Development: Improving Management in Developing Countries.* Washington, D.C.: The American Consortium for International Public Administration, 1986.

Almond, Gabriel A., and Verba, Sidney. *The Civic Culture.* Princeton, N.J.: Princeton University Press, 1963.

Bjur, Wesley E., and Zomorrodian, Asghar. "Toward Indigenous Theories of Administration: An International Perspective." *International Review of Administrative Sciences* 52, no. 4 (1986):397–420.

Frost, Peter J.; Moore, Larry F.; Louis, Meryl Reis; Lundberg, Craig C.; and Martin, Joanne. *Organizational Culture.* Beverly Hills: Sage, 1985.

Heady, Ferrel. "The Globalization of Public Administration Education and Research." Paper prepared for 10th General Assembly, Eastern Regional Organization for Public Administration (EROPA), Seoul, Korea, 1983.

———. *Public Administration: A Comparative Perspective.* 3d ed. New York: Marcel Dekker, 1984.

Moe, Ronald D. "Privatization: An Overview from the Perspective of Public Administration." Washington, D.C.: Congressional Research Service, The Library of Congress, Report No. 86-134 GOV.

Nachmias, David, and Rosenbloom, David H. *Bureaucratic Culture.* London: Croom Helm, 1978.

Pinto, Rogerio F. "Institutional Development, Organizational Socialization and Group Dynamics: Cross-Cultural Technical Assistance in Management Development." Ph.D. dissertation, School of Public Administration, University of Southern California, 1981.

2

State of the Art: Comparative Public Administration and Development Administration

O. P. DWIVEDI and KEITH M. HENDERSON

FOLLOWING WORLD WAR II a new field came into being—comparative public administration as a subdiscipline of public administration. Scholars and practitioners in the comparative administration field set out to achieve greater understanding of the administrative style, structures and functions of the other countries with whom their countries became suddenly involved. Their primary concern at first was to concentrate on countries of Europe. This concern originated from the valuable exposure gained by contact with different administrative structures abroad during wartime, postwar occupation, and during the period in which technical assistance programs were being put in place (Heady 1979, p. 10). Interaction with Europeans enabled these scholars to compare not only their own domestic systems, but it also encouraged them to broaden their horizons to include countries of Asia, Latin America and Africa when the programs for foreign aid got started. By the early 1960s, when several Asian and African nations gained independence, North American (and later West European) scholars were impelled by curiosity, need for consultants, and aid management to shift their attention from established nations to the emerging Third World, and in the process they created a new field: development administration. Further, spurred on by the Ford Foundation's desire to develop new paradigms and easy funding, scholarly emphasis increased on administration for developing countries with a great fervor and missionary zeal to transplant Western administrative technologies. While the number of Western academics researching and consulting in developing countries increased by

9

leaps and bounds (resulting in a rich variety of studies, theories, paradigms and models), comparative studies of public administration between the countries of the West also continued. By the 1970s, two separate fields became distinct: comparative public administration (with emphasis on similarities and differences), and development administration (concerned with change processes in the Third World). Essays contributed to this book as separate chapters, thus, reflect these two trends as we scan the world through studies of selected countries from all continents. In this introductory chapter, we will examine these trends, and briefly discuss the field and its protégé, development administration. We will examine the dilemmas faced in the discipline of comparative administration, as well as explain the book's construction.

Comparative Public Administration

In the pre–World War II period, the focus of comparative public administration was largely on comparing the civil services (and their reforms) of selected European countries with the U.S. With Leonard D. White's book, *Civil Service Abroad* (1935) and a few books on British, French and German bureaucracies, an interest emerged in some American universities to understand and compare the administrative style and operations of other civil services. Meanwhile, British scholars such as Herman Finer and William MacKenzie had already started showing sustained interest not only in nations across the English Channel but also in the U.S. Of course, students coming from dominions and colonies to British universities were encouraged to research on their homeland.

World War II, the emergence of UNO, and the postwar era of reconstruction in Europe suddenly propelled a great amount of interest on comparative public administration. In the U.S., scholars such as Dwight Waldo, Lynton K. Caldwell, Fred Riggs, Ferrel Heady, W. J. Siffin, and F. M. Marx, to name a few, started teaching and writing about comparative administration beyond what L. D. White had initiated in the 1930s. But the main spurt of scholarly activity came in the late 1950s and early 1960s when the Ford, Carnegie and Rockefeller foundations gave generous grants to American universities to support research on the problems of administration – not only in the industrialized West, but also among the newly independent developing nations. Side by side, the International Institute of Administrative Sciences at Brussels was taking the lead in Europe to encourage research and publications in comparative administrative science. However, the field was able to take the quantum leap in 1962 when a Ford Foundation grant to the American Society for Public Administration enabled its Comparative Administration Group (CAG) to organize regular seminars and conferences, and to encourage research and publications. A flood of scholarly activities engulfed the field (Caldwell 1965; Heady 1962; Henderson 1971; Raphaeli 1967; Riggs 1961; Siffin 1957; Waldo 1964). This was further supplemented by the contributions made by scholars from across the Atlantic and in interaction with the developing countries' researchers. Among scholars, it was the innovative leadership by Fred Riggs that provided the necessary theoretical underpinnings to the discipline.

Riggs discerned three trends in comparative administration: (1) a movement from normative to more empirical approaches, (2) a movement from idiographic to nomothetic approaches, and (3) a shift from a nonecological to an ecological form of study (Heady 1962). These trends stressed the need for empirical description and explanation, a distinction between unique case studies as opposed to those aimed to test general propositions, and a shift from the isolated study of administrative institutions to placing them in a larger context or societal framework. From this, Riggs suggested that, ideally, the work of CAG should be generally empirical, nomothetic, and ecological. Although, such a paradigm was more appropriate in the context of the West where empiricism and theory-testing was considered a routine matter rather than a concerted effort or anthropological venture; nevertheless, Western public administration experts continued work on developing nations trying to make sense out of the unfathomable and unpredictable situation in those countries. Undaunted, the "experts in public administration, not only from the United States but from several European countries as well, were scattered around the world, engaged in similar projects to export administrative technology, largely drawn from American experience, to a multitude of developing countries" (Heady 1979, p. 17). They all were enthused with translating the dream of the American way into a reality by changing, transplanting and replicating the administrative system that they knew best.

The fifties and sixties were, actually, the days of great visions and hopes that the whole world might eventually speak the same administrative language. But, within a decade, and certainly by the early 1970s, a serious crisis emerged in the field partly due to the decline in funding by American foundations, which constrained research, and partly to the failure of the American dream materializing in the transfer of administrative technology to the developing nations. Not only did CAG go out of existence in 1973, even its flagship, the *Journal of Comparative Administration,* ceased publication in 1974, after only five years of existence (Heady 1979, p. 23). Keith Henderson, writing for the "new public administration" (the Minnowbrook Conference), predicted in 1971 that the future of comparative public administration might be relegated to insignificance partly because of the funding shift to research on the problems of cities and local government, and partly due to rejection of CAG thinking by the public administration establishment (Henderson 1971). From then on to the mid-1980s, the field suffered a period of disillusionment, confusion, identity crisis, and retrospection. Only by the late 1980s, did interest in comparative public administration slowly start to resurface due to the assertion by some scholars in developed as well as developing nations, who came to recognize the usefulness of multicultural and multidimensional approaches to administration; thus a new emphasis emerged, generally involving globalization of paradigms.

Development Administration

At the end of World War II, a program of reconstruction for Western Europe was begun with the help of the Marshall Plan; this plan was aimed at providing a massive infusion of foreign aid to rebuild the devastated economies of Europe. Later, the Marshall Plan became the prevailing model of development for the new independent colonies. Thus, when the age of imperialism came to an end and the rapid process of decolonization began, it was thought that with sufficient foreign aid and a revamped administrative system, these colonies would closely follow, if not altogether achieve, the industrial progress of the West (Dwivedi 1987). Aid and administration for development became mechanisms to fight the war on underdevelopment (Dwivedi and Nef 1982).

With the exception of Latin America, the Third World was a legacy from the prewar colonial order dominated by European powers. As the process of decolonization began, the efforts of the leadership in the new nations transformed formal diplomatic sovereignty into conflict with the West. A new breed of essentially anticolonial and anti-laissez-faire nationalists emerged in what were formerly colonial territories (Nef and Dwivedi 1981).

In China, Malaysia, the Middle East, Indonesia, Southeast Asia, India, West and East Africa, a new wave of expectant peoples strained the emerging neoclassical order while tearing down the remnants of the imperial system. Development had become the dominant issue in the Third World. In the 1960s, the West responded to the development challenge in a number of ways. The first was to conceptualize the notion of development administration by blending all necessary elements of human endeavor with financial and material resources in order to achieve developmental goals that were generally recommended by the Western experts. Such characterization of development administration emphasized the formal and technical aspects of government machinery. Developmental goals were assumed to be agreed upon by the local- and Western-educated elites. These goals were usually referred to as "nation-building and socio-economic development" (Esman 1966). Swerdlow has identified two interrelated tasks in development administration: institution building and planning (1975). Also, development administration was seen as concerned with the will to develop the mobilization of existing and new resources, and the cultivation of appropriate capabilities to achieve the developmental goals. Thus development administration became an essentially action-oriented, goal-oriented, administrative system geared to realize definite programmatic values. In fact, development administration was seen as a mutation to colonial administration by injecting development goals and structures into the old core of civil servants. The task of the developed countries was perceived as the creation of external inducements to change (Braibanti 1966) through technical assistance and transfers of technology and institutions. Such strategy of westernization was directed to both the administrative machinery and to the whole national community.

But, it was not realized by the Third World that the most fundamental ingredient in the process of induced development was going to be inputs of foreign expertise and capital, either in the form of aid or investment. A number of techniques popularized during this era, such as program planning, community development and personnel management, reflected the aforementioned bent for external inducement towards modernization and westernization (Schaffer 1973). A related perception was that institutional imitation was bound to produce similar results to those obtained in the developed world: efficiency, increased rationality and the like at a very general level. The more "developed" (i.e., bureaucratic and westernlike) an administration system became, the greater the likelihood that it would have developmental effects.

Development administration was supposed to be based on professionally oriented, technically competent, politically and ideologically neutral bureaucratic machinery. It was to retool the foreign aid (both in the form of funds received and ideas suggested) and also to act as a main instrument for nation building by transforming the inputs received into development outputs. The ostensible output was modernization — induced and predictable social change following Western perceptions — preceded by institution-building and modernization of the indigenous bureaucratic machinery to undertake developmental tasks. Thus, the developmental bureaucracy, as a spearhead of modernization was seen more as an adapter than as an innovator.

But what was missing from the expected picture-perfect imitation in the Third World was the necessary set of conditions for bringing about a number of social, economic, cultural and political changes. These included an expanding economic base, a tax base, professionally trained manpower, political legitimacy, cultural secularization, universalism, a relatively open society, and a strong political superstructure capable of governing. The absence of these qualities, in turn, presented another paradox: governing and managerial capabilities were most scarce where they were most needed—in the underdeveloped regions.

What happened in many cases is that in spite of much rhetoric, the emergent administrative systems tended to be imitative and ritualistic. Generally practices, styles and structures of administration unrelated to local traditions, needs and realities succeeded in reproducing the symbolism, but not the substance of a British, French or American bureaucracy. Administrative reforms, when and if attempted, tended to have the long-run consequence of strengthening the old framework. Moreover, given the acute shortage of qualified human resources to manage the public service, innovations often originated with expatriates and foreign experts, or were simply cosmetic structural changes that brought no real alteration in the status quo. Also, over-planning and over-administration tended to have the same nefarious results (or lack of results) as lack of planning and under-administration. Confronted with an ineffectual developmental bureaucracy, the Western solution was more administrative development. Technical solutions about means were more palatable than much-needed substantive political decisions to bring about real socioeconomic change.

As mentioned earlier, one of the basic assumptions of development administration has been the belief in a scientific, technical, and value-neutral administration. The Western myth that value-laden decisions are actually in the domain of politicians while public servants purportedly work in a fact-filled environment with no room to influence policy choices and decisions was transplanted to Third World societies. While this may have been possible in the public bureaucracies of the Western countries with a tradition of separating the domains of policy decisions from regular administration, developmental administrators were in reality, from the day of independence, never free from value-laden decisions. With the concentration of authority and discretionary power in the hands of a few administrators, and because of the absence of social and political accountability for the use of such enormous state power, they found themselves playing an almighty role in the allocation of scarce resources. Thus, among the various misapplications of the Weberian concept of bureaucracy in the Third World, the value-free administrative system appears to be one of the most counterproductive myths that has been transplanted. This has created an environment in which administrators hesitate to express their views on policy issues openly on the pretext of civil service neutrality. In fact, what is needed is a cadre of administrators who are willing to state their opinions and values on programs and projects. Expressing individual values does not mean that public servants ought necessarily to become committed party functionaries. As a matter of fact, and based on the record of success of some Third World countries, it appears that the attainment of developmental goals is strengthened where the administrative machinery has freedom to express its values and beliefs without fear or favor. Actually the developing nations require a band of competent people for complex and highly specialized tasks of socioeconomic development. These range from fact-finding and analysis of resources to financial management, construction of multipurpose projects, industrial development, administration of housing and social welfare programs, and management of health, agriculture and educational projects.

The role of bureaucracy in national development cannot be overemphasized. The programs of community development and the implementation of economic growth objectives presuppose deep administrative insight and a keen evaluation perspective on the part of officials. All development programs require considerable direct involvement and participation by the bureaucracy at all stages of their formulation and implementation. In the context of these new responsibilities, the bureaucracies in the developing countries are confronted with a series of problems. In its new setting, the bureaucracy cannot maintain its earlier colonial image of power, nor can it continue to exist as a high-prestige class enjoying exceptional privileges. It needs a closer identification with the masses and a shedding of its former paternalistic and authoritarian tone of administration. Actually, it will not be inappropriate to suggest that officials brought up in the colonial administrative culture and wedded to the Weberian model of bureaucracy are totally unfit for the responsibilities of development administration. Development administrators have to be flexible in their approach, amiable in nature, outgoing, people-oriented and should be willing to take risks and make on-the-spot decisions, rules and regulations notwithstanding. For this, the developmental bureaucracy needs a framework that: (1) is flexible in its operation; (2) is pragmatic, i.e., able to take into consideration the exigencies of the circumstances from a practical point of view; (3) encourages open decision-making processes based on dissent and discussions among colleagues; (4) is centered around client-oriented philosophy; and (5) is laden with human values of service and sympathy for all, especially for the weaker sections of the community.

The above discussion, although primarily concerned with the role of developmental bureaucracy and the status of development administration, leads us back to its lineage, the field of comparative public administration. In the next section, we present dilemmas confronting the entire field.

Dilemmas of the Art

If the state of the art is as described above, and if it relates to the comments of Ferrel Heady in the Introduction and the interpretation of the Caidens (see Chapter 17), then the field is faced with certain dilemmas, all of which follow from its current circumstances as an academic exercise. Several of these dilemmas are discussed below.

1. How does one encourage globalization?
2. How can the myriad of discrete studies be aggregated and related?
3. How can comparative public administration come to terms with overlapping academic enterprises, specifically, comparative public policy and its implicit "gap analysis?"
4. How much of the experience of comparative public administration can be useful in development administration?

Encouraging Globalization

Both editors of this volume have logged many thousands of miles through numerous countries around the globe in the last several years. From the thousands of "street-level bureaucrats" to a handful of top-level decision-makers, their encounters have confirmed the impression that public officials and their organizations deserve greater study. The behavior of the Turkish Hava Polis, German Burgomaster and India's district collector will remain a mystery until they are systematically studied (and, perhaps, restudied). Similarly, the enormous number of other officials, programs, agencies, and policies that have not been examined provide a continuing challenge to the comparative public administration specialist. Strictly legal/formal accounts, official government statements, or self-serving promotional materials will not suffice (although even these are sometimes impossible to find or nonexistent). What is required is a dedicated cadre of academic specialists around the world who undertake careful analyses of the myriad subjects available. Logic dictates that those researching a given country's administrative system be familiar with that country (fresh viewpoints from outsiders notwithstanding) and particularly its culture; and it is reasonable to expect that the best expertise will come from the country itself. Quality studies of all kinds, including, most importantly, quantitative empirical analyses, are called for. Globalization suggests that the studies rendered are capable of being understood in other countries and that they meet certain standards of excellence. The difficulty of avoiding the stigma of Western research techniques along with other vestiges of "neocolonialism" is alluded to in the essay by Henderson (see Chapter 14, "Rethinking the Comparative Experience").

Aggregating and Relating Studies

Mere proliferation of academic studies for its own sake is not a desirable goal. The exponential growth of academic efforts in some fields and countries has already resulted in information overload.

The problem in comparative public administration as well as in development administration is the separateness and uniqueness of the case documentation. This lack of common framework or even agreed basic concepts makes the student's task enormous, and the difficulty of drawing conclusions or utilizing studies in practice well nigh impossible. Recognizing the need for some commonality, the editors of this volume provided a framework to contributors which does bring focus to the various country studies.

Comparative Public Policy

In the United States today and in other Western countries that share essentially the same scholarly pursuit, comparative public policy (or equivalent terms) has become a dominant theme. The concept "policy" raises numerous issues for students of public administration since it tends to subordinate administrative concerns to broader policy matters and relegates administration to an implementive role. The basic difficulty is with the exclusivity of the approach and, when applied to developing countries, its implicit reliance on "gap analysis." Policies are official government designs that are carried out by administrators, usually in ways that are dysfunctional. In this thinking, attention is given to the gap between design and execution and reasons ascribed for "failure." Nazih Ayubi, in Chapter 3, quotes Bernard Schaffer and others to develop the point that making lists of what went wrong in carrying out plans or documents implies a distinction between implementation and planning which is not operationally valid. "This may very well suggest that much of the failure in implementation in the Third World is probably due to the irrelevance of the policies or the plans themselves, and not simply to some casual operational difficulties." Ayubi goes on to encourage a stress upon existing patterns that may be conducive to good performance and useful for development, and accentuating and building upon those. The assumed or idealized model is rejected in favor of a proximate real one.

Comparative public policy and the analysis of "policies" does not force the analyst to utilize gap analysis, but it strongly encourages him or her to do so. It directs thinking towards the carrying out of established designs, usually those deriving from top-level political leadership, and is process oriented. There is little concern with institutions as such.

Application of Knowledge

Ultimately, the test of comparative public administration is its usefulness in development administration. The latter may be thought of in terms of change programs intended to solve pressing national problems. Several of the chapters in this volume allude to the role of the civil service in development and the importance of understanding the workings of the public service in attempting change. Many of the suggestions are controversial. Would higher salaries for officials be beneficial as Quah recommends? Is administrative reform the precursor of effective service delivery as is assumed in many Commonwealth countries? What is the secret of Japanese economic success?

As most countries of the world grapple with the same needs to improve the living conditions of their members (Who can argue with better health and welfare, better nutrition, and protection against the bad elements as worthy goals?), the importance of useful knowledge increases. Greater complexity, heightened interdependency, and the rapid pace of change require intelligent responses. Whether top down or bottom up strategies are employed, governments must take numerous corrective actions. That many of the actions are counterproductive does not argue for inaction. (It may, however, argue for private-sector initiatives and downsizing of government.) Comparative public administration as an academic study can assist the practicing administrator and change agent by providing information and insights not otherwise available. Objective knowledge, uncensored and uncontrolled, is the best hope for conscientious administrators embarking on change strategies.

About the Book

Lynton Caldwell said in 1965 that the "ultimate test of the value of comparative studies of administration in and beyond the comparative public administration movement will be their effect upon administrative practice. . . . The ultimate value of comparative public administration will therefore be in stimulating some development which had nowhere before existed in precisely the same form or manner" (Caldwell 1966, p. 244). Essays contained in this book reflect on the above-mentioned test by providing a stimulating comparison about administrative practices that are vastly different yet share common problems and visions among the nations: how to serve the multitude effectively and responsibly, and what steps to take in order to restore or enhance public trust and confidence in the administration's ability. This central concern permeates the country or regional studies, which focus on policy developments and administrative changes in their respective countries or regions. All major regions of the world are covered by these essays except socialist countries where the editors faced an unsurmountable task of securing essays about their administrative practices. Time constraint did impel us not to wait too long for such an essay. Hopefully, this omission can be rectified in the next edition.

The collection of essays is based on the view that readers ought to know not only what are the general trends in the field of comparative public administration, but also what to look for in surveying the unfamiliar terrain. Thus, we have assembled a world-wide cast of specialists who are eminently qualified to answer questions about their areas. Our main purpose in assembling such a competent team has been to let our readers see the situation on a first-hand basis without being constrained by blinkers, be they American, European, or the Third World.

The book is divided into three parts: Part I provides an introduction to the field of comparative public administration, with a lead article by Ferrel Heady who is a doyen of the discipline. Part II consists of original essays on Africa (both east and west regions), Arab countries, Asian countries (India, Japan, and Southeast Asia), Australia, Latin America, European nations (France and the United Kingdom), and North America (Canada and the United States). These country/regional studies constitute the major part of the book. Each author was asked to address some general concerns such as major policy developments and administrative changes during the past two or three decades, and to highlight some specific administrative issues facing their areas/regions. Thus, a commonality exists among these essays; yet one can discern cultural and socioeconomic differences in their administrative practices and styles. Part III, then, provides an overview of the field through three pieces, concluding with a perceptive essay by the Caidens, who are trailblazing comparative public administrationists. This volume, itself, is a true example of international cooperation in scholarly pursuit as evident by the joint work of its editors and contributions by a host of authors.

References

Braibanti, Ralph. "Transnational Inducement of Administrative Reform: A Survey of Scope and Critiques of Issues." In *Approaches to Development: Politics,*

Administration and Change. Edited by John D. Montgomery and W. J. Siffin. New York: McGraw-Hill, 1966.

Caldwell, Lynton K. "Conjectures on Comparative Public Administration." In *Public Administration and Democracy: Essays in Honor of Paul H. Appleby.* Edited by Roscoe Martin. Syracuse, N.Y.: Syracuse University Press, 1965.

Dwivedi, O. P., ed. *Perspectives on Technology and Development.* New Delhi: Gitanjali, 1987.

Dwivedi, O. P., and Nef, J. "Crises and Continuities in Development Theory and Administration: First and Third World Perspectives." *Public Administration and Development* (U.K.) 2 (1982):59–77.

Esman, Milton D. "The Politics of Development Administration." In *Approaches to Development: Politics, Administration and Change.* Edited by John D. Montgomery and W. J. Siffin. New York: McGraw-Hill, 1966.

Heady, Ferrel. *Public Administration: A Comparative Perspective.* Englewood Cliffs, N.J.: Prentice Hall, 1979, 1984.

Heady, Ferrel, and Stokes, Sybil L. *Papers in Comparative Public Administration.* Ann Arbor, Mich.: Institute of Public Administration, 1962.

Henderson, Keith M. "A New Comparative Public Administration." In *Towards a New Public Administration.* Edited by Frank Marini. Scranton, N.J.: Chandler Publishing, 1971.

Nef, J., and Dwivedi, O. P. "Development Theory and Administration: A Fence Around an Empty Lot?" *Indian Journal of Public Administration* 27, no. 1 (Jan.–Mar. 1981):42–66.

Raphaeli, Nimrod, ed. *Readings in Comparative Public Administration.* Boston: Allyn and Bacon, 1967.

Riggs, Fred W. *The Ecology of Public Administration.* New Delhi: Asia Publishing House, 1961.

Schaffer, Bernard. *The Administrative Factor.* London: Frank Cass, 1973.

Siffin, W. J., ed. *Towards the Comparative Study of Public Administration.* Bloomington: Indiana University Press, 1957.

Swerdlow, Irving. *The Public Administration of Economic Development.* New York: Praeger, 1975.

Waldo, Dwight. *Comparative Public Administration: Prologue, Problems and Promise.* Chicago: American Society for Public Administration, 1964.

White, L. D. *Civil Service Abroad.* New York: McGraw-Hill, 1935.

2

Country/Regional Studies

3

Policy Developments and Administrative Changes in the Arab World

NAZIH N. AYUBI

THE ARAB WORLD should provide the comparativist with an unrivalled laboratory situation. In spite of the generally arid-zone environment, the common cultural background, and the shared Third World status, the twenty-odd independent Arab countries of today manifest a remarkable set of dichotomies: the old versus the new states, the large versus the small states, the rich versus the poor states, and the radical versus the conservative states.

It is remarkable, however, how practically all Arab countries — regardless of the differences just noted — have tended both to expand their bureaucracies quite fast and to regard this expansion almost as equivalent to development itself, or at least as development's main vehicle. It is our suggestion in this study that the policies adopted by the Arab states in the area of administrative change and reform were in no way radical or innovative enough for grooming the bureaucracy for the crucial role that it was expected to play.

The Arab states did indeed declare the 1980s as "the decade of Arab administrative development" (Zoubi 1982, p. 7), and while there can be little doubt about the awareness in various Arab states of the crucial role of the "administrative factor," it is by no means certain that the actual efforts at capacity improvement have been correctly oriented. The purpose of this chapter is to attempt a critical review of efforts in the field of development administration in the Middle East — especially its Arab "core" — during the last three decades. An alternative approach is suggested that combines an

23

ecological approach with a contingency approach. Our main hypothesis is that too much bureaucratization has limited the effectiveness of many of the efforts in both the development administration and administrative development fields, and that there is a definite need for resorting to a new strategy.

Bureaucratization in the Arab World

The term bureaucratization here is meant to indicate two things: (1) bureaucratic growth, i.e., expansion in public bodies of the sort that can be measured by increases in the numbers of personnel and administrative units as well as the rise in public expenditure, including in particular wages and salaries; and (2) an orientation whereby the administrative and technical dominate over the social. Generally it is a tendency that goes very much in the direction of centralization, hierarchy and control.

Bureaucratization in both aspects has grown substantially in the Middle East in the last 30 years. The remarkable thing is that this has happened in all states and regardless of the various differences; in the big and the small, the old and the new, and in the radical and the conservative. Thus we find heading in the same direction a country like Egypt, Weber's "historical example" of a large developed bureaucracy, a country like Algeria that started its statehood only twenty years ago with no bureaucracy worth mentioning and with what appeared to be a revolutionary distaste for things bureaucratic, and a country like Saudi Arabia, which is always speaking about "free enterprise" even while possessing one of the largest public sectors in the region, complaining nevertheless at the same time of "bureaucratic inflation" (Othman 1979, p. 34–41).

Some Cases of Bureaucratic Growth

Let us now describe the dynamics of bureaucratic growth in a number of quite varied Arab countries (in terms of size, age, resources and politics) before we investigate some of the possible reasons for the expansion. (Parts of the following analysis have appeared in *Beyond Coercion: Durability of the Arab State,* Zartman and Dawisha 1988, 14–34).

Egypt

The disproportionate growth of Egypt's public establishment is not a new phenomenon. However, with the 1952 revolution, the public bureaucracy grew more rapidly and extensively, under the impact of the regime's policies for expanding industrial activities, welfare services, and free education (Ayubi 1980, Chap. 3). This growth was particularly striking after the "socialist measures" of the early sixties, which involved wide nationalizations of industry, trade and finance, worker participation in management and profits, and also an extensive program for social services and insurance.

Between 1952 and 1970, as statistics show, the public bureaucracy grew steadily in size when measured by the number of administrative units, the size of employment, the development of wages and salaries, and of current expenditure. The most notable changes followed the socialist measures of the early sixties and can be summarized thus: From 1962–63 Egypt's national income increased by 68 percent, resting on an increase in the labor force of no more than 20 percent. Yet at the same time, posts in the public bureaucracy had increased by 70 percent and salaries by 123 percent. Thus far, the rate of bureaucratic growth had quite exceeded the rate of growth in population, employment and production.

The main irony, however, is that in the seventies, and indeed following the adoption of the "open door" economic policy (*infitah*) in 1974, the impetus of institutional growth continued under its own momentum even though the role of the government and the scope of the public sector were starting to diminish in importance. For example, the 1975 budget indicated that current expenditure and costs had risen to the tune of £E4,747.6 million, of which £E652.8 million went to wages and salaries. Current expenditure accounted for 66.2 percent of the total financial outlay of the budget, while wages and salaries accounted for 10.5 percent (Ministry of Finance 1975). The budget proposed for 1978 offers another example of this rise. It included some £E5,470 million for current outlay and expenditure, £E1,097 million of which was allocated for wages and salaries. If current outlays in the period from 1973 to 1978 are considered as a whole, one finds that salaries had more than doubled while current expenditure had trebled during this time (Ministry of Finance 1979).

The only thing that might have decreased somewhat in the seventies is probably the number of some types of administrative units. In 1975 it was decided, with few exceptions, to do away with public organizations (*mu'assasat*). In 1978 the government was also considering the liquidation or transformation into companies of around 95 public authorities (*hai'at*) throughout the country, although in reality this did not materialize. In the eighties there has been talk about bringing back some of the *mu'assasat,* practice having proved the difficulty of coordinating the activities of private enterprises in their absence. Apart from this, however, and in spite of the changing role of the government, Egypt's public bureaucracy remains distinctly, and curiously, large in size.

In terms of manpower, the public bureaucracy—that is, the civil service and the public sector excluding enterprise workers—employed in 1978 over 1.9 million persons. If state companies are added, the public establishment at the beginning of 1978 was employing about 3.2 million officials and workers (Central Agency for Organization and Administration (CAOA) and Ministry of Finance 1978 and 1979). The most detailed study of employment in the public sector indicates that in 1975 the Egyptian public sector employed over 868,000 people, of whom about 573,000 worked in 170 industrial companies, about 266,000 in 160 service companies, and about 29,000 in agricultural companies (INP 1975, p. 13).

At the beginning of the eighties, the still expanding Egyptian bureaucracy looked even bigger. It employed 2,876,000 individuals in the central and local government as well as in the public sector. This represented about 6.6 percent of the population and some 25 percent of the labor force. The bureaucracy spent £E1,343,915 on salaries (excluding public companies), and £E5,394,699 on public expenditure (excluding companies).

One of the main problems about bureaucratic inflation that has occurred since the adoption of *infitah* is that it has been happening at a time in which the public economy as a whole and state industry in particular are not expanding fast enough, given the reorientation of policy and the changing role of the government, to make these increases in personnel and in expenditure a rewarding exercise. It is therefore probable that bureaucratic inflation will represent increasingly more of a strain on the national resources. One of the unhealthy aspects that accompanied this inflation in public expenditure was the decline in the percentage of such expenditure on economic activities from 35 percent in 1962 to only 22 percent of the total outlay in 1976. Other problems also emanate from bureaucratic growth, such as excessively slow action, very low remuneration, and of course, as a result, extremely poor performance.

The Gulf Countries

Compared to Egypt, the origin of whose bureaucracy goes back thousands of years and whose formation in a modern form dates back for over a century, the bureaucracies of the Gulf are both new and created from scratch. Their main expansion has been an outcome of oil wealth, which urged the state towards large-scale social welfare programs and into very ambitious economic development plans.

The Saudi Arabian bureaucracy was initiated in the fifties and its growth has been remarkable in the three decades of its life so far. The number of ministries has grown from four to twenty; thus, for example, the Council of Ministers formed in 1975 included sixteen "operational" ministers and three ministers of state without portfolio (Al-Farsi 1982, p. 98–

99). Over forty public authorities and corporations have been established, compared to none before 1950 (Othman 1979, 234 ff). These include the General Petroleum and Mineral Organization (Petromin), the Silos and Mills Organization, the Hassa Irrigation and Drainage Authority, the Saline Water Conversion Corporation, the Saudi Basic Industries Corporation (SABIC), the Saudi Consulting House, and many others.

Civil service employees who numbered no more than a few hundred in 1950 increased to about 37,000 in 1962–63, to 85,000 in 1970–71, and to over 245,000 in 1979–80. The ratio of public employees to the total population in the early eighties was approximately 3.5 to 4 percent, which is not in fact excessively high, but government civil servants represented 10 percent of the total labor force and 13 percent if one counted non-career personnel.

The oil boom manifested itself in a massive increase in revenues, which jumped most dramatically from $2,744.6 million in 1972 to $22,573.5 million in 1974. This was immediately followed by large increases in expenditure. Salaries and benefits grew remarkably, from SR 3,122.8 million in 1972–73 to SR 41,127.6 million in 1981–82. Current expenditures (Section Two) grew during the same period from SR 1,365.1 million to SR 18,656.5 million. In estimating bureaucratic outlays and expenditures in the Saudi case, one has also to look at some unusual categories such as those relating to local subsidies, municipal facilities, and human resources/manpower development.

Even if growth in public employment in Saudi Arabia has not been particularly exaggerated so far, the expansion in public expenditure has definitely been most impressive.

In Kuwait, a handful of administrations and directorates that existed in the early fifties were developed into ten departments in 1959. These were turned into ministries in 1962 and three more were added, making a total of thirteen ministries. By 1976, the number of operating ministries had reached sixteen in addition to two ministers of state (Marouf 1982, 32–39). In addition, a number of higher councils have been created (for Petroleum Affairs, for Housing Affairs, etc.), and over 25 public authorities and corporations have been brought into being, such as the Social Security Organization, the Public Ports Organization, the Public Investment Authority, the Petro-Chemical Corporation, and the Flour Mills Corporation.

The numbers of government employees grew remarkably. In 1963 they were 22,073; in 1965–66 they were 69,520; in 1970–71, 70,922; in 1975–76, 113,274; and in 1979–80 they had risen to 145,451 (Central Statistical Office 1982). By official accounts, government employees represented 12.5 percent of the population and about 34 percent of the total labor force of Kuwait in 1975. The Kuwaiti bureaucracy is overstaffed, by all accounts. In 1979 the Amir of Kuwait expressed the view that some 64,000 civil servants in Kuwait were redundant, and a World Bank report on Kuwaiti public administration suggested a total freeze on all new appointments.

Government expenditures have also grown most remarkably. They increased from KD 154.1 million in 1964–65 to KD 271.6 million in 1967–68 to KD 256.7 million in 1970–71 although they dropped slightly in 1968–69 and 1969–70. Wages and salaries followed suit, increasing from KD 6.9 million in 1964–65, to KD 98.6 million in 1967–68, and to KD 119.8 million in 1970–71. As is to be expected the most dramatic increases took place after the oil boom, thus raising current domestic expenditures from KD 227 million in 1972–73 to KD 658.4 million in 1975–76 to KD 881.4 million in 1978–79, and to a budgeted KD 1196.4 million for 1979–80. Of these expenditures, the following amounts were spent on wages and salaries: KD 188.9 million in 1972–73; KD 353.5 million in 1975–76; KD 456.6 million in 1978–79; and a budgeted KD 645.4 million in 1979–80. Wages and salaries do indeed swallow up a large amount of public expenditure: in the 1978–79 budget, for example, they totalled KD 485.8 million out of KD 1,969.4 million, and ranked as the main item in the budget (Central Bank of Kuwait, 1978 and 1979).

It is estimated by some that nearly 39 percent of all government expenditures can be classified as being of an organizational nature. This includes items such as the "head of state" and the "Amiri Diwan" (The Princely Court), with their huge allocations, as well as more standard things such as expenses of the Employees' Bureau and of "supplementary allocations."

In the United Arab Emirates (UAE), the first federal government was formed immediately after the Union was declared in 1971, with Abu Dhabi being the main sponsor. In 1968 Abu Dhabi had some 20 government directorates, which, by 1970, had increased to 25 in number. The first council of ministers of Abu Dhabi was formed in 1971, including 15 ministers, but this was abolished in 1973, with a federal cabinet being created instead that contained 28 ministers, and with Abu Dhabi establishing an executive council to run its own affairs. A number of public authorities and corporations have also been created in the UAE in recent years, such as the Abu Dhabi Steel Works, the General Industry Corporation, and the Abu Dhabi Investment Authority.

The number of government employees has grown most substantially. In 1968 the Abu Dhabi administration employed about 2,000 officials. By 1970 their number had already doubled, and by 1974 had reached 5,352, of which 37 percent were UAE citizens, 42 percent were other Arabs, and 21 percent were foreign nationals (Rashid 1975). In just eight years after this (by 1982), the number of public employees in Abu Dhabi had jumped to 24,078 (AIPK 1983, p. 35ff.).

Public employment on the federal level has also grown at an impressive rate; it had indeed quadrupled in size in just one decade, from 10,500 in 1972 to over 40,000 in 1982 (Arabian Government 1983, p. 231). The explosion in public employee numbers is, in fact, the most dramatic among the three Gulf countries studied, given the country's minute population base, its extremely recent state of independence, and the fact that the oil boom more or less immediately followed its formation. The UAE is representative, but in an extreme way, of what happened in other desert states where the local human base could not support the required expansion, leading therefore to heavy reliance on expatriate labor. In the Abu Dhabi bureaucracy, which is the largest and most established within the UAE, a ludicrous 83.6 percent of all officials are foreign nationals.

There are several indications that the state bureaucracy may have stretched itself far beyond its capabilities. In 1983, this country, which ranks among the highest in the world in terms of its per capita income, suffered a budgetary deficit of DH 5,461 million, and had, among other things, to delay the payment of salaries to its public employees for a number of months. As the budgetary deficit was expected to reach the even larger amount of DH 6,635 million in 1984, the Ministry of Finance and Industry issued various ministries with memoranda forbidding the creation of any new public post for noncitizens during the following financial year (*Al-Watan,* 7 May 1984).

A huge expansion in public finances has been taking place in the UAE, especially since the oil boom. Thus the federal budget (mainly financed by Abu Dhabi) had grown from BD 21 million in 1971 to BD 81 million in 1974, and to DH 1.69 million in 1975 (BD 1 = DH 10). The various states continued to maintain separate budgets and accounts, however. The state accounts for Abu Dhabi, for example, show most clearly how the revenues doubled and expenditures more than doubled in just one year (from 1973 to 1974) as a result of the oil boom. Of these expenditures, outlays for Abu Dhabi and federal ministries accounted for nearly 40 percent of the total (Aziz 1979, p. 55–70). In the Abu Dhabi budget for 1976, current expenditures both for the Emirate itself and for the federation as a whole had grown even further. In this year, Abu Dhabi contributed DH 4 million to the federal budget of DH 4.152 million (or about 96.3 percent of the total). A high percentage of the federal budget also went to current expenditures: In the 1977 federal budget it was DH 9,833 million out of DH 13,150 million, or 74.8 percent of the total.

In 1982, budgetary outlays in the federation were estimated at DH 22,559.5 million, of which only DH 3,539.5 million went to investments while DH 19,019.6 million represented current expenditures. Among the latter, Section I (mainly salaries and benefits) was responsible for DH 3,893 million.

Since 1984, the oil boom has given way to an oil glut with consequent drops in price and losses of income for the oil-exporting states. Even so, bureaucracies remain bloated, although the trend toward rapid expansion has slowed down somewhat with the loss of revenues.

Syria and Jordan

Most "intermediate cases" convey similar features in terms of bureaucratic growth. The number of ministries often increased from fewer than 10 at the time of independence to more than 20 by the eighties (e.g., 22 in Jordan; 24 in Syria). Public sector organizations also emerged and increased in number, with noticeable speed. Thus in Syria in the early eighties there were some 60 public organizations (*mu'assasat*) and some 25 public corporations, while in Jordan there were around 38 public organizations of various descriptions (Abu Shikha 1983).

In terms of employment in Syria, there were in 1982 some 440,000 public officials working in the civil service and the public sector, excluding the armed forces, police and security. Compared to total population for the same year (of 10,788,000) the ratio is one to 25, or 4 percent (Minister of State 1984). Related to a total labor force of 2,174,000 in 1979, this means that civilian public employment represented 20 percent of total employment (Syria, Central Statistical Office, 1981). In Jordan, according to the 1979 census, the population amounted to 2,152,000; the labor force was estimated at 398,000, or 18 percent, of this figure. In 1982, 59,000 people worked for the government, excluding daily and project workers (Public Statistics Department 1982; Al-Khidma al-Madaniyya, June 1983). Thus government officials represented 2.75 percent of the population and 14.9 percent of the labor force.

Looked at in terms of expenditure, one finds that in the Jordan state budget of 1981, current expenditures amounted to JD 363 million (out of total outlays of JD 638 million). Current expenditures of the civilian sectors amounted to JD 141 million, out of which figure wages and salaries accounted for JD 77 million (State Budget Department 1981). In Syria, current expenditures amounted to 57 percent of the total outlays in 1984. Of the current expenditure, about 18 percent went to salaries and wages (Statistical Yearbook for 1984).

The reasons for this tremendous bureaucratic growth are multiple: the traditional prestige of public office (for a long time associated with the powerful foreigner), the strong belief in the developmental role of the bureaucracy, the importance of public office for building the contacts deemed necessary for pursuing private business, and possibly the impact of the Egyptian model both as an exemplar and also through the role of the large number of Egyptian officials working in many other Arab countries. This applies in particular to Kuwait, North Yemen, Bahrain, Qatar, the United Arab Emirates, Oman and Libya (Nurallah 1978, p. 108–9).

In the early eighties, a million to a million and a half Egyptians were working in other Arab countries (Ayubi 1983). Many of these worked in administrative and technical jobs in general, and a significant proportion worked in the government administration in particular. For example, in the Kuwaiti government administration, Egyptians in 1976 represented 28 percent of all officials, second only in importance as an expatriate group to the Palestinians (30 percent) who constitute a special case in that country. Egyptians represented nearly a third (31.7 percent) of all non-Kuwaiti Arab employees (Kuwait Ministry of Planning 1978, p. 70–71). There are also signs that Egyptians figure very highly among those engaged in public administration education and training in other Arab countries: There are indications in Saudi Arabia, for example, that they represent the top group among all administrative educators and trainers (Jreisat 1982, p. 56). Most important probably is the fact that the majority of all varieties of teachers in most oil-exporting countries are Egyptians. Through such channels the Egyptians have for a long time acted, among other things, as an intermediary in the dissemination of knowledge and in the transfer of technology between the industrial countries and the rest of the Arab world.

Some of the reasons for bureaucratic growth were entrenched in the social and political conditions of the society. Most important is the phenomenon of huge expansion in formal higher education that is in no way related to the economic needs and manpower requirements of the society. Under pressure from people aspiring to higher social prestige, and under the unproved belief that expanded "qualification" produces economic development, the Middle East has witnessed a strong case of what one expert has called "the diploma disease" (Dore 1976).

This tendency, which reached alarming proportions in a country like Egypt, has also caught up even with the small city-states of the Gulf, where everybody is racing to build yet another new university, regardless not only of the market needs for graduates but even of the availability of students. In a country such as Egypt where there exist three times the number of engineers that are required by the country's industrial base, and where only 20 percent of agronomists work in agriculture, where can the remaining graduates go but to the public bureaucracy, where they do very little in return for receiving a fair proportion of public expenditure. Indeed, the share of wages and salaries in Egypt's total public expenditure has risen steadily in the past 20 years or so.

Excessive attention has been given to formal higher education in comparison with technical education and vocational training in all Arab countries. In most industrialized countries, educational expansion has in fact followed, not preceded, industrial development, with only the possible exception of Japan where the two went more or less hand in hand. The Muhammad Ali's experiment in 19th century Egypt of expansion in higher education without a similar proportion of on-the-job training being developed for the various crafts, resulted in virtually no real industrial development, and the country had to start more or less from scratch in the inter-war period. All Middle Eastern countries are currently repeating the same mistake, with very high ratios of university graduates and relatively low levels of solid industrial development. One important outcome is an inflated public bureaucracy, with too many controllers, inspectors and supervisors, but with very few functioning personnel to control, inspect or supervise!

Several writers have explained how bureaucracy survives by projecting the image of serving the general interest. In the Middle East, the bureaucracy does the same, but it also projects the image of being the main vehicle for development. Middle Eastern leaders called upon the bureaucracy not only to fulfil the conventional "law and order" functions but also to involve itself in industry, trade, education, culture, and so forth. The literature of the fifties and sixties was also replete with praise for the developmental potential of the public bureaucracy—to many people it represented an orderly alternative to the agonies of a social or a cultural revolution. Following the oil boom of the seventies, the bureaucracy has become for the "petro-bedoucracies" of the Gulf their main instrument for circulating the oil money while maintaining the political control of the ruling princely elites (Ayubi in Zartman and Dawisha 1988). Such uses of the bureaucracy must also have contributed to its fast expansion, especially in the period 1974–1984.

Administrative Development and Reform

The direction of development administration in the Middle East was clear: expand and consolidate departmental-type administration, involve your bureaucracy in national comprehensive planning, in extensive industrialization programs, in urban construction and in a rapidly expanding system of conventional higher education. (Parts of the following analysis have appeared in *International Review of Administrative Sciences,* Vol. 52, 1986, pp. 201–22.)

Discovering—usually halfway along—that the bureaucracy is probably ill-equipped to deal with this heavy load, the authorities declare that in order to have successful development administration there must first be effective administrative development. Since administration is regarded as a science that has reached its maturity in the West, administrative development was to a large extent considered as an exercise in the transfer of technology, and modernization of the administration was seen as the solution to most of its problems. (For a historical review on this subject, see Wickwar 1963). The fifties and sixties were also a heyday of technical assistance, both national and international, concentrating, in the Middle East, first on Turkey, Egypt and Iran, and then proceeding to the rest of the Arab World.

American technical assistance involvement in Iran was by far the largest and costliest. One of the earlier projects lasted from the mid-fifties to the early sixties, cost over $2.3 billion, and placed several advisers in each of the Iranian ministries except foreign affairs and war. The majority of such advisers, some of whom remained in the country until 1978, had very little knowledge of the local environment or culture, and they expended most of their energy in trying to change local practices without even understanding why they existed. It is hardly surprising therefore, that, with the only exception of the police department, these advisers were not on the whole successful in transferring their techniques across cultural boundaries (Seitz 1980, p. 407–12).

A combination of the ideas of such people as Fayol, Taylor and Weber, with their underlying concepts of economy, efficiency and rationality, were presented—sometimes in the simplified form of POSDCORB and "principles"—as the passe-partout "science of administration." One does not need to go out of one's way to illustrate the hold that the ideas of such authors, and particularly those of Max Weber, had and still have on experts on administration in the Arab World. All one has to do is to pick up any piece of writing by any reputable Arab expert on administration and there they will be. Of course, there is nothing wrong with referring to these writers; the problem is that the exercise very often not only begins with them but also ends up with them, making no reference at all to the relevance of their ideas to an Arab society.

With this science of administration in mind, efforts for administrative reform in the Arab countries have adopted a variety of approaches, including the following: (1) issuing new legislation or amending and supplementing the existing laws and regulations; (2) organizing and reorganizing: whenever a problem is found, create or rearrange an organization to deal with it; (3) personnel management: especially things like position description and classification, merit systems, and central personnel agencies; (4) in the area of public finance and management of the economy: performance or program budgeting, cost accounting techniques, management by objectives, etc.; and (5) training, especially institutionalized training, was very popular, but without adequate adaptation of the content or the methodology.

In attempting the various methods of administrative reform, the Arab countries tend to follow a set of distinct phases:

1. In an early phase, the emphasis will usually be on new legislation, especially in the area of legalizing, rationalizing, and coordinating personnel laws and regulations in all sectors all over the country.

2. In a following phase, a Civil Service bureau or commission will be formed and an institute for the training of public servants will be established. There is hardly an Arab country that has not followed this Academy model, so that nearly every one of them by now has its own institute(s) for administrative training (see Table 3.1).

3. In a subsequent phase, calls for work simplification will inevitably lead to many attempts at reorganization, Organization and Methods units will be installed in various public organizations, and a central agency for organization and administrative reform will sometimes be created. There are very few Arab countries that do not by now have at least one central commission or agency that is in general charge of its public service (see Table 3.2).

4. In a later stage, it will be found that although the legal standardization of personnel systems has had some undeniable benefits, it has not been particularly conducive to raising efficiency. Calls are therefore heard for relating pay to the nature and requirements of every post rather than to the person occupying the post or to the diploma that he carries. Attempts are then made in the area of job description and job classification. These efforts, however, remain painfully slow, as they seem to stumble over so many problems of implementation, and to encounter such a considerable amount of social, and sometimes political, resistance. In no Arab country do there exist systematic performance and productivity standards in the public service to which a system for individual *and* organizational incentives can be related (Jreisat 1985, p. 6).

Let us now look more closely at the role and activities of some of the agencies and institutions for administrative development that have proliferated in the Arab World in the last two or three decades (Ayubi 1985, p. 17–30). We observe first that public service commissions and agencies vary in terms of their organizational status and affiliation, ranging from an administration within a certain ministry (as in Qatar where the Personnel Affairs Administration comes under the jurisdiction of the Minister of Finance and Oil), to a board affiliated directly to the prime minister (as with the Civil Service Board in Kuwait), or attached to a Minister for Administrative Affairs (as with the Central Agency for Organization and Administration in Egypt). Sometimes there is a minister for administrative affairs

TABLE 3.1. National Institutes of Administration in Arab Countries

State	Institute	Date Established	Comments
Algeria	National School of Administration, Algiers	1964	
Bahrain	Training and Administrative Department, Bahrain	n.a.	
Egypt	Administrative Sciences Academy, Cairo	1981	Succeeded the National Institute for Management Development (1970), which followed the Institute of Public Administration (1953), the National Institute of Management Development (1961) and the Institute of Local Administration (1967)
Iraq	National Centre for Administrative Consultancies and Development, Baghdad	1970	Succeeded the Centre for Industrial Management Development (1961)
Jordan	Institute of Public Administration, Amman	1968	
Kuwait	Training Department of the Civil Service Commission, Kuwait	1960	
Lebanon	National Institute of Administration and Development, Beirut	1959	
Libya	National Institute of Administration, Tripoli	1953	
Mauritania	National School of Administration, Nouakchott	1968	
Morocco	National School of Public Administration, Rabat	1948	Succeeded the Centre for Rapid Administrative Formation (1966) Called the Moroccan Administrative School until 1972
Oman	Institute of Public Administration, Muscat	1976	
Saudi Arabia	Institute of Public Administration, Riyadh	1961	
Somalia	Institute of Administrative Development, Mogadishiu	1965	
Sudan	Administrative Sciences Academy, Khartoum	1981	Succeeded the Institute of Public Administration (1960)
Syria	Centre for Administrative Development and Productivity, Damascus	1967	
United Arab Emirates	Training Department of the Civil Service Council, Abu Dhabi	1973	
Yemen (North)	National Institute for Public Administration, Sanaa	1963	

Sources: Arab Organization for Administrative Sciences (AOAS), *Questionnaires on Institutes and Agencies of Administrative Development in the Arab States* (Amman 1982); Hassan Abashar Al-Tayyib, *Arab Administrative Development Institutions* [in Arabic] (Amman: AOAS, 1984).

without an affiliated central agency (as with the State Scribe [Minister] for Administrative Affairs in Morocco).

Furthermore, while some Arab countries—such as Egypt—have adopted the principle of a unified agency in charge of all activities of administrative development, most other countries have gone for a multiplicity of agencies, possibly under the influence of the French or the American model (e.g., Lebanon and Tunisia, Saudi Arabia and Kuwait). The jurisdiction of such agencies also ranges from a narrow brief related to

TABLE 3.2.   Central Agencies for the Civil Service and Administrative Reform in the Arab Countries

Country	Agencies (date established in parentheses)
Algeria	National Directorate for Administrative Reform and Innovation (1984)
Bahrain	Civil Service Commission (1975); Civil Service Council (1980)
Egypt	Central Agency for Organization and Administration (1964; incorporating the Civil Service Commission established 1951)
Iraq	National Centre for Consultancies and Administrative Development (the Public Service Board was abolished in 1979, its functions distributed among ministries)
Jordan	Civil Service Commission (1955); Royal Commission for Administrative Development (1984)
Kuwait	Civil Service Commission (1960); Civil Service Council (1979); Higher Committee for the Development and Modernization of the Administrative Apparatus (1984)
Lebanon	Civil Service Council (1959); Research and Guidance Administration of the Central Inspection Department (1959); Public Personnel Disciplinary Board (1965)
Libya	General Popular Committee for Public Service (1979)
Mauritania	Ministry of the Public Service, Labour and Youth (1986)
Morocco	Ministry of State for Administrative Affairs; Public Service Department (1958)
Oman	Civil Service Commission (1975); Civil Service Council (1980)
Qatar	Civil Servants' Administration (1964)
Saudi Arabia	Civil Service Commission (1978); Civil Service Council (1978); Higher Committee for Administrative Reform (1963)
Sudan	Department of Administrative Organization and Reform; Ministry of State for Administrative Affairs (1974)
Syria	Organization and Administration Directorate of the Cabinet Affairs' Bureau (1967); State Personnel Registry (1985)
Tunisia	Ministry of State for the Public Service; Central Administration of the Public Service (1953)
United Arab Emirates	Civil Service Bureau (1972) Civil Service Council (1973)
Yemen (North)	Ministry of the Civil Service and Administrative Reform (1980)
Yemen (South)	Ministry of Labour and Civil Service (n.a.)

Sources: ʿAbd al-Muʿti ʿAssaf, *An Integrated Model for the Study of Public Administration* [in Arabic] (Al-Zarqaa: Fahum, 1982); Fawzi Hubaish, *Public Service and Personnel Administration* [in Arabic] (Amman: AOAS, 1982); Nadir Abu-Shaikha, *Administrative Organization in Thirteen Arab States* [in Arabic] (Amman: AOAS, 1983); Arab Organization for Administrative Sciences (AOAS), *Third General Arab Conference: State Reports* [in Arabic] (Amman & Rabat, 1984); AOAS, *Public Administration and Administrative Reform in the Arab World* [in Arabic] (Amman, 1986).

conventional personnel matters, to a much broader one (as for instance in Egypt) where most matters of administration and organization within the state are involved.

Then, in addition to personnel bureaus and civil service commissions, some countries also create "higher committees" whose titles imply that particular emphasis is attached to development and reform, such as in the higher committees of Saudi Arabia and Kuwait. The latter case is particularly interesting as the term "modernization" is actually included in its title, while the title of the Algerian equivalent is equally fascinating since it speaks of "administrative innovation."

This variance in titles and affiliations reflects, among other things, diversity among the Arab countries in terms of how comprehensive their strategies of reform are: Most countries have opted for an incremental, piecemeal approach, experimenting with various methods at different stages. The rational-comprehensive approach has received a great deal of academic and rhetorical support but has not been adopted by anyone other than the Egyptians, and only partially by them.

As for administrative development institutes (Al-Tayyib 1984), the scope of their educational training and research activities also varies, especially between the *Maghrib* (North African) countries that favor the French-inspired "formation" approach and the *Mashriq* (Arab East), where conventional "in-service" and "refresher course" methods are preferred in professional training. In organizational terms, however, most countries (15 in number) have opted for what has been termed "The Academy Model." Examples are the Academy of Administrative Sciences in Egypt, the National Centre for Administrative Development and Consultancies in Iraq, the National School of Administration in Algeria, the Centre for Administrative Development and Productivity in Syria, the Institute of Public Administration in Saudi Arabia, the National Institute of Administration and Development in Lebanon. In fact, the national institutes for administrative sciences in Egypt, Sudan and Yemen have turned themselves into degree-giving, educational establishments (in addition to offering conventional training programs). Research and consultancy, however, have not received as much emphasis. In a few of the smaller countries, the training center or institute of public administration is affiliated to the personnel bureau or the civil service commission (e.g., in Bahrain, the United Arab Emirates, and Kuwait). In a few cases, ministerial rank is given to the chairman/director of the institute to indicate the political support attached to its activities (e.g., in Saudi Arabia, Yemen, Syria, and Sudan).

All such public service agencies and administrative development institutes have been very active in all kinds of programs, as we have indicated briefly, yet one cannot help getting the impression that far less coordination than is actually required has been taking place between the activities of the public service agencies on the one hand and the training institutes on the other. Even less coordination has been taking place with other organizations in the state that are also involved in planning, organization and manpower affairs. South Yemen is an interesting exception in this respect; here the civil service actually falls within the jurisdiction of the Ministry of Labour.

On the whole, we feel that while the State in the Arab World plays a functional and economic role similar to that known in socialist or "corporatist" systems (note the huge "public sector" even in the conservative Gulf countries), its administrative machinery remains structurally fragmented, and continues to function according to models borrowed from the Western capitalist countries, where the private sector is expected to carry the main burden of economic development (Ayubi 1985, p. 17–30).

Even in the countries that have recently declared their intention of launching "privatization" policies, the economic role of the State remains dominant and would still warrant the existence of a dynamic public bureaucracy, if only to lay a sound infrastructure and encourage the private sector to invest (Ayubi 1989, p. 62–78).

Implementation as the "Achilles' Heel"

By the seventies, and particularly in the eighties, it was becoming clear that neither the strategy of development administration nor the policy of administrative development that usually followed was capable of solving the problems it had been hoped they would solve. First, concerning development administration, there was a decline in agriculture and the countryside; urban crowding, decay and a growing and frustrated lumpenproletariat; acute balance-of-payments problems, dependence on the outside world for finance and for technology; unemployment of the educated and lopsided cultural development; domination by a bureau-technocratic elite . . . and so forth. A relative growth in Gross National Product (GNP) in the fifties and sixties was soon to decline from the early part of the seventies in most of the non-oil-exporting countries while many basic needs remained unsatisfied. The "oil boom" itself has shown that abundance in finance does not automatically solve the problems of underdevelopment and dependency. Second, in the area of administrative reform, the changes introduced were never fully satisfactory, either to the clientele or to the political leadership, so that they always had to be repeated, each time with more vigorous rhetoric but less effective performance.

A proposed explanation and a solution appeared here: the concepts were good but the application was bad (e.g., socialism was noble but its application — *tatbiq* — went wrong); the "planning" was perfect but the "implementation" was defective. But this merely reflected a fallacy that confused the process of planning with the act of writing a plan. Bernard Schaffer describes this approach succinctly:

> This new version of an old fallacy seems to be arguing thus. Administrative reform (or urban policy, etc.) is the writing of reform plans and documents. Examples are the reports of reform committees. Then little enough seems to happen quickly or directly. The explanation, as quoted is: there are two phases, writing and implementing, again. There is a weakness, (an Achilles heel) but only in the second, separate phase (implementation). Why? Because in the second phase the 'reforms' encounter 'obstacles', including 'a lack of political will'. What can the reformers do about that? They can list these obstacles! (Someone else can then presumably remove them). . . . the longer and tidier the list, the more advanced the literature and method: the more powerful an instrument of reform! So the lists quoted are now very long indeed. (Will they soon summarise the whole of life? After all, that is what they mean) (Schaffer 1980, 194).

Such "lists" of obstacles abound in Arabic organizational literature. A relatively recent book enlists no fewer than 20 groups of major "obstacles in the way of developing civil service systems and agencies in the Arab countries." These range from the "underdevelopment of means of production," through "predominance of lowly habits," to "frequency of political changes" (Al-Shaikhali 1982).

It is our view that implementation cannot be separated from planning as a possible cause of failure. Implementation requires political support from the leadership, dedication from the lower administrative echelons, cooperation from the clientele or the public, and coordination at all levels. If mechanisms for ensuring these requirements cannot be incorporated into the planning process, there may very well be a case for considering this particular type of planning an "inappropriate technology" for this type of society at this stage of its development (Weinstein 1981, 116–18).

Although the problem of implementation is not confined to the developing countries (indeed there has been much on the subject published in the United States since the seventies), many observers believe that it is more of a complex "problematique" in Third World countries (M. Grindle, "Introduction," and P. Cleaves, "Conclusion," in Grindle 1980). This may very well suggest that much of the failure in implementation in the Third World is probably due to the irrelevance of the policies or the plans themselves, and not simply to some casual operational difficulties. An analysis that would confine itself only to "obstacles to implementation" will not be sufficient in this case, and one's whole approach to policy and administration will have to be reconsidered if effectiveness is to be achieved.

"Traditionalism" as an Explanation

This fallacy of "obstacles to implementation" can be likened to the once dominant, and still influential, school of writing about "obstacles to modernization," whereby any local differences from a presumed or North American model were so described (Schaffer 1980, p. 192–93). This same approach also characterized many attempts at administrative reform and practically all the ones where an element of "technical assistance" was involved. The United Nations public administration teams of experts in the fifties and sixties are illustrative of this approach. One of their reports on administrative reform in Turkey tells the whole story. As Bernard Schaffer describes it: "[T]he United Nations report was typical. The dominant features of the Turkish public service were seen as 'problems'. It followed that 'Turkey is ripe for reform of its administration'" (Schaffer 1974, p. 285–86). This trend has always been part of modernization theory. Very often, aspects of the Egyptian, Syrian or Saudi society are *described,* then they are presented as the *cause* of the underdevelopment of these countries or the inefficiency of their people. Middle Easterners are not advanced, or not efficient, because they grow moustaches, because they do not eat pork, or — as Atatürk put it — because they wear the fez!

A slightly more articulate school, inspired by Orientalism and promoted by Weber, would maintain that Middle Easterners are not advanced, or not efficient, because most of them are Muslims (Turner 1974). A variety of latent Orientalism has characterized much technical assistance to the Middle East and has reflected itself in the thinking of most Western-educated elites in the Middle East itself. The following passage by an Arab (Jordanian) expert on administration is typical of the "obstacles" approach expressed in behaviorist terminology:

> [T]he value dimension is most important. There are some values in our societies that sometimes obstruct the effective offering of service to the citizen. . . . Of these values it is obsequiousness and "going along" in Arab society which leads to waste of time and avoidance of the effective confrontation of problems. Other values include concern over appearance and formalities . . . and the values of domination and authoritarianism . . . and the scorning of manual labour which leads to inflation in the number of desk-type positions. Then there is the belittling of women which deprives the administration of half the society, and there is also the careless attitude to time (Ribhi al-Hasan in ʿUlwan 1977, p. 142–43).

A more elaborate treatment of such behavioral obstacles to development in the Arab World is to be found in the writings of an Egyptian psychiatrist and expert on administration (Girgis 1974, 1975).

Such analyses that simply attribute underdevelopment and inefficiency to cultural traits are interesting; but they are often misguided, and are rarely useful. Most concepts and principles of organization and management are derived from Western concepts and norms. If that which is in reality no more than the organizational manifestation of Western norms and attitudes is taken to be "*the* science of management," then it is no wonder that any departure from this stereotype was considered an expression of a prescientific stage of development.

But this approach is faulty on at least two accounts. First, there are very few universal scientific principles about a great deal of administration and management as they are presented in the standard American textbooks. As Isaac Deutscher commented, was Weber really doing much more than paraphrasing the Prussian code of good official conduct? (Deutscher 1969). Most so-called "principles" of management are little more than "proverbs" and are therefore inherently culture-bound and often difficult to transfer to a different sociocultural environment. Second, on a prescriptive level, this approach is futile (not to mention ethnocentric) since it seems to suggest that if the Middle Easterners want to improve, to develop, and to become more technologically advanced, they have to cease to be Egyptians, Tunisians, Syrians, and so forth. As William Siffin put it: "This 'culture vs. technology' view can be pushed to the level of chauvinistic absurdity (just as the 'traditional vs. modern' dichotomy can be elevated into an absurd oversimplification). As an explanation of why technologies won't work, 'culture' is sometimes the refuge of the very pragmatic negativist" (Siffin 1977, p. 57).

The cultural and ecological school of public administration initiated by Gaus, enriched by Crozier, and brought to its full flowering by Riggs, has been useful in reminding people that administration is a social, and therefore a culturally bound, activity. It is fortunate that this school has acquired a reasonable following in the Arab World (Al-Kubaisy 1974). For example, the *bedoucracy* and the *shaikhocracy* concepts, developed to describe certain organizational attitudes in the Gulf countries are both interesting and insightful (Ayubi 1988).

But the achievements of the cultural school can be easily negated if its findings are used merely to prove that certain people will continue to have certain insurmountable problems simply because of the specific features of their culture. Among other things, the question should be asked: Is the "sala model" or the "bazaar approach" something more related to a stage of socioeconomic development, or is it more related to a particular cultural sphere regardless of its stage of development? It would be useful here to bring in the historical discussion as to whether the "Islamic city," the "Islamic guild," and so on, were so specifically *Islamic,* or whether they were medieval cities and medieval guilds but located in Muslim lands (Hourani 1981). Authors who write about Islam as an obstacle to development will also have to explain to us how the same Muslim societies could be so scientifically and organizationally advanced in medieval times, and why the whole of the Third World — and not only its Muslim component — is now underdeveloped (Rodinson 1978).

The Benefits of a "Contingency" Approach

An analysis that would combine the ecological approach with the contingency view of organization may prove more effective in dealing with the problems of administration and development in the Middle East. While the ecological approach has achieved a fair degree of currency among administration experts in the Arab world, the contingency approach has very few followers. Among the few available exceptions are the study by Ayoubi on Jordan and the study on Egypt by Badran and Hinings (Hickson and McMillan, eds. 1981, p. 95–132). Such analysis would have to start by evaluating the achievements of the last three decades. As in most of the Third World, various improvements were introduced in the functions of personnel, budgeting, planning, organization and training, usually at the central secretariat level and in the capital city. However, the line agencies, functional departments, sectoral units and operating levels of organizations — the real carriers of development — did not benefit as much from administrative development efforts (Islam and Henault 1979, p. 259).

The cost, inefficiency and authoritarianism of the omnipotent bureaucracy is indeed a current dilemma that most Middle Eastern countries have to cope with. As in many other countries of the Third World, the dependence upon the national bureaucracy as a vehicle for economic development has given rise to an ironic situation, whereby societies that are lacking good administration establish the *most* comprehensive and complex array of administrative controls over every aspect of investment, production and trade (Weinstein 1981, p. 120). Egypt under the "open door" economic policy — as explained elsewhere — is a very good case in point (Ayubi 1982).

Middle Eastern bureaucracies have not, on the whole, succeeded in solving most of the developmental problems of their societies that they had been called upon to solve. Poverty persists, although it has often been modernized (Haq 1976; Amin 1980). Technology-intensive industrialization failed to create a sufficient number of jobs to absorb a rapidly expanding labor force, and the so-called "trickle-down effect" from the modern industrial sector to the poor in general and to the countryside in particular remained negligible. In short, the quality of life for the majority of the population continued to be abysmally low, with many of the basic needs for food, water, shelter, health and education still unsatisfied. Nor has the administration managed to reform itself and to improve upon its own performance as an instrument of service. Quite the contrary: in many Middle Eastern societies the bureaucracy has actually become a major instrument for political domination and the bureaucrats have turned into an exploitative new class (Ayubi 1988).

Why has the record of development administration in the Arab states been so poor? A study by Palmer and Nakib enumerates an impressive array of "administrative problems besetting the Arab world." They have been classified into four main categories: structure and organization; bureaucratic attitudes and behavior; client attitudes and behavior; and political inputs into the bureaucracy (Palmer and Nakib 1978).

Problems related to structure and organization are the most technical in nature and also the most closely related to the bureaucrat's immediate training and experience. Dealing with these sorts of problems has therefore proved to be relatively more manageable than it has been with others.

Political problems are certainly more tricky. No one can deny that there is a whole host of problems that relate to "political inputs" into the bureaucracy. When the role of the politicians is not welcome, there is a tendency to speak of political intrusions in the work of the bureaucracy; when their intervention is desired but not obtained, there is a tendency to speak of the "lack of political will." The truth of the matter, however, is that no public bureaucracy is politically neutral, that in no situation is there a lack of political will but rather a conflict between various political wills. Quite often the complaint by the official of political interference is little more than yet another enlisting of a further "obstacle" in an attempt to exempt himself from some of the blame for the poor performance of the administration. In practice, there are in the Third World many poor performers among development programs, which apparently have significant political support and commitment programs behind them (Paul 1982, p. 5–6).

The most interesting part of the essay by Palmer and Nakib (1978) is the section that deals with "behavioral and attitudinal" problems associated both with the officials and with the clientele, in which they quote delightful passages from Arab authors to illustrate all such problems. There is nothing more tempting than to make fun of the bureaucrats, and the temptation to blend their poor performance with aspects of their environment and habitat, or to attribute their bureaucratic behavior to the general culture of the society to which they belong, is always strong. It is one way of releasing our impatience with the irritations of bureaucracy and with the slow rate of change in the society at large; a practice of which the present writer is himself not altogether innocent (Ayubi 1980; 1982). But what use can this be? The point here is not that culture is unimportant, nor are we denying that certain cultural traits may be unfavorable to certain aspects of development. It is that little is known about the exact impact of culture on efficiency and effectiveness, and that therefore there is always a risk of too easily offering culture as the explanation for every drawback or failure. This has its dangerous practical outcomes as it tends to lead to passivity and inaction.

Palmer and Nakib are not unique in maintaining that quite a few problems of administration in the Arab world "find their roots in Arab culture" (p. 11). Typically, they also emphasize that "many of the structural problems discussed are merely overt manifestations of deeper cultural, behavioral and political problems endemic to the area" (p. 20). These two distinguished writers then arrive at the tempting, but rather disconcerting conclusion that:

> The Arab bureaucracies, after all, are a sub-set of the population as a whole. They originate from the general population and, by and large, they mirror the values and behavior of the population at large. As the Arab public generally manifests low regard for civic responsibility, it is hard to expect bureaucrats to do otherwise. In much the same manner, the low skill and education levels which are characteristic of many Arab bureaucracies are also true of the population in general. A poorly educated population deeply endowed with traditional values and behavior patterns is less able to understand, appreciate and support the modernization projects which the bureaucracy is entrusted with implementing than are the populations of educated, technically skilled and modern oriented societies such as one is likely to find in the United States or Western Europe (Palmer and Nakib 1978, p. 15).

This passage is reminiscent of a favorite theme in much of modernization theory that laments the lack of understanding on the part of the ignorant, traditional, fatalist public of the brilliant ideas of the political or administrative modernizer—e.g., the modernization programs of Muhammad Reza Shah were too sophisticated to be understood, and occurred too rapidly to be assimilated by his people. This variety of modernization theory, like its equivalent in administrative studies, is often lacking in explanatory power and is almost always lacking in prescriptive value. It is lacking in explanatory power because it would fail to explain to us how a country like Japan had managed to industrialize and raise productivity while maintaining some of the norms that modernization theory does not regard as particularly favorable to development (e.g., reverence for age and seniority, consensus-building rather than democratic voting, near-life tenure, etc.). More importantly, even when such studies are factually accurate they tend to be of little prescriptive value. Since they hinge all their expectations on the hope that the whole society will have to change its values and attitudes so that the bureaucracy can function properly, it is no wonder that they usually end up with a pessimistic and rather helpless note.

Let us consider, for instance, a good recent study on the Saudi Arabian bureaucracy (Al-Nimir and Palmer 1982). The authors eloquently elaborate the familiar theme that Saudi bureaucratic behavior differs little from Saudi social behavior in general, this being characterized by the lack of innovation and achievement motivation, by unwillingness to relocate away from the extended family, by disdain for rural or manual labor, and so on. Not only this, but one cannot be optimistic about the future of the Saudi bureaucracy because "the bureaucratic behaviour of the younger and more educated members of the bureaucracy does not differ significantly from that of their older, less educated colleagues" (p. 94). The difficulty with this kind of analysis is not that it is lacking in accuracy—I do indeed believe that it is alarmingly true—but with the fact that it is not very helpful in policy terms. What shall we, experts in and practitioners of administration, do after attributing everything to culture? Should we simply sit and wait until the values and attitudes of the Saudi society are somehow changed before we can do something about Saudi administration?

It is my contention in this paper that a more effective approach toward administrative development may be to reverse the present order, and rather than attempt to test the efficiency and effectiveness of Middle Eastern organizations by measuring their proximity to an idealized version of organization (or social relations) developed elsewhere, to start instead from the existing situation and to try—in light of the needs of the clientele and characteristics of the environment—to develop the best possible ways of improving the capacity of the administration to deal with the challenge.

In other words, one should start from the last page of the report by Palmer and Nakib (1978), where they speak of the possible "strengths" of the various Arab bureaucracies as well as their weaknesses. As they rightly suggest, "a thorough survey of existing data would enable us to study in detail those facets of Arab public administration that have worked well, so that other Arab states might benefit from their experience." This also, they hope, "would suggest possible patterns for working within the cultural and political environment of the Arab world" (p. 23).

Learning from Failure and Success

Cases of managerial, organizational and developmental success *do* occur in the Arab world, and the beginning of wisdom should partly revolve around a stocktaking of such cases. In Egypt, the same bureaucracy that failed in promoting the agrarian reform is the one that succeeded in managing the Suez Canal and in building the Aswan High Dam (Ayubi 1980). The same Egyptian people had managed, contrary to all expectations, to plan and implement the impressive crossing of the Suez Canal in the October War of 1973, and managed — in a society notorious for its inability to keep a secret — to keep the war as a total surprise (where was the culture "hiding" then, one would wonder?). In Algeria and in Iraq, the bureaucracy seems to be managing the oil industry quite effectively. The Lebanese banking system has actually been expanding and improving during the difficult years of the country's instability and torment.

Even the cases that have not been a glowing success can be useful as a source of learning. Why did the Gezira project in the Sudan start as a successful endeavor in *agricultural* development, though it ended up being a less than impressive experiment in *rural* development? What was probably the largest project in the world for the sedentarization of nomads, in Somalia, ended up with little overall success, but why was it *relatively* more successful in the case of turning the nomads into fishermen than turning them into farmers? Careful analysis of such experiments with their failures and their achievements can provide a good basis from which to proceed. This can be supplemented by comparative studies of other endeavors that did work in similar contexts and environments in other Third World countries. In this respect, the study of exceptional performers will quite possibly prove to be more useful than analysis of averages, since the need is to identify the characteristics of the high performers in order to duplicate or adapt them. As one expert who has done such a comparative study confirms: "The insights and understanding to be gained from high performers will be far more valuable than the incremental gains to be derived from further investigations of low performers, about whom we already know a great deal" (Paul 1982, p. 4–5).

Also, rather than singling out the normative and behavioral differences between an abstracted Middle Eastern society and an abstracted Western society as problems or obstacles, why not start the other way round by considering the existing Middle Eastern values and practices that may be *conducive to* good performance and *useful for* development, and then try to accentuate and improve upon them? Through success, the Middle Eastern administrator or expert is also likely to gain a sense of self-confidence that is, in our view, an integral part of any enduring development (one knows of no civilization that developed and prospered as a result of a process of self-denigration and of belittling its potential for improvement).

It may be worth pondering that the only non-Western societies that managed to break the vicious circle of underdevelopment and to start on the path of development are those that did not believe that they had to cease to be themselves in order to develop; by these I mean China and Japan, where, in spite of two opposing ideologies, "authenticity" seems to have been an important characteristic of their respective developmental strategies. Compare their case, for example, to that of Turkey or the Philippines, both of which, in their own ways, represent a case of the "Westernization of poverty."

The Arab countries have to examine what they can possibly do well, and then have to make the best of it — and this should be the starting point, rather than a start to be made from an assumed or idealized model. This does not imply that there is nothing in the outside world for the Middle Easterner to learn from, for indeed there is a great deal. It will only mean a reversal in the order of affairs (again reminiscent of Japan and China) where things will be adopted and adapted according to their suitability for meeting a real need and fulfilling a required function, not the other way round (i.e., wanting to conform to the model for its own sake). For example, drinking coffee at a special time in a special place in the middle of the working day is a European habit; drinking coffee at various times and by the desk of the official is a Middle Eastern habit: both are simply customs and neither of them is necessarily responsible for the high or the low performance of employees. It is therefore futile for Middle Eastern leaders to try to fight this habit (as sometimes happens) in the mistaken belief that this will automatically raise efficiency.

The guidelines that would therefore be useful in trying to learn from one's errors and achievements would be as follows: (1) to see how certain arrangements fared in practice in the same socio-organizational environment or in one that was similar; and (2) to consider the possibility of broadening and generalizing these arrangements and to determine the degree of their "transferability."

The main point to keep in mind is that there is no single best way of getting things done, that "it all depends," as contingency proponents put it. Rather than speak resignedly of an idealized end result, and then leave the whole exercise at that (perhaps hoping that by some miracle the situation will change by itself in the desired direction), the emphasis should be on how to proceed, on describing the process of change itself, and how to "get there."

A contingency approach need not be identified with an evolutionary rather than developmental model (Bendor 1977, p. 481–514). It is true that the developmental model prevalent in American political science in the sixties did not stress the concepts of adaptation, capacity and problem-solving, and that it assumed a single common and irreversible route to progress. But this should call for sharpening our definition of development, not for discarding the concept entirely. Bendor rightly observes the confusion in American political science usage of the term evolution with the term development. We believe that the idea of *purposeful* change is crucial in defining the concept of development. Fortunately, the Arabic language distinguishes between two terms both derived from the same root: *numuw* — i.e., spontaneous or unintended growth — and *tanmiya* — i.e., induced growth, therefore indicating alteration at least in the proportions if not in the whole direction. We agree with Bendor and others that the mere fact that change is planned and that a policy is the product of desire or intent, is no guarantee that it will prove to be successful (adaptive) in reality. However, this should not automatically lead to jettisoning the whole concept of development, but should lead to redefining it in a way that takes account of the element of adaptability: that is, one should not only elaborate on describing the end result, but also on giving detailed operational analysis of the process of "getting there." An analogy can be taken from the applied natural sciences: through design and selection agronomists have *purposefully* succeeded in "developing" superior breeds of animals and plants.

The variety of contingency approach that would prove most helpful in this respect is the one that emphasizes the need for innovation and not simply for survival. To a reasonable extent, the leadership of an organization does define the constraints and uncertainties, and therefore the environment, under which their organization functions, and review of a number of development projects in various Third World countries suggests that projects responded *selectively* to different forces in their environment (Bryant and White 1982, p. 65–68; 163–65).

In other words, a contingency approach should not be taken to mean a status quo approach, but a change-process approach. The "dialectic" of a contingency approach should be based on understanding the present situation in order to deal with it and eventually to change it. As Honadle and Klauss put it: "Although a 'contingency' focus contains a bias towards adapting to entrenched present conditions, the purpose of development is to transform existing situations. This must be kept in mind, so that anticipation of 'unalterable' factors will not lead to their reinforcement" (Honadle and Klauss 1979, p. 211–12).

Prospects for the Future

In considering the record of failure and achievement in the Arab world in recent decades, it would obviously be ridiculous to continue with something

that experience had proved to be faulty. Bureaucratization policies as practiced in the fifties and sixties did not deliver, so why not experiment in the
new directions of local and rural development; labor-intensive production;
participative-interactive planning; appropriate or intermediate technology;
integrated rather than parallel or sectorial development; basic needs rather
than GNP-oriented development; and so on (Islam and Henault 1979, p.
261). The important thing is that these new directions should be regarded as
areas for experimentation and not as new developmental dogmas to replace
the older ones of "centralization," "industrialization," "technocratization,"
and so on.

For example, in some Middle Eastern countries where political integration is still limited, excessive decentralization may have its high costs. Recent experience has also shown that overcentralization may lead to such
malfunctions as misallocation of funds and resources by the local community, and abuse of power by the local leaders, and the case of popular
committees in Libya illustrates that the temptation is often strong on the
local level to be more concerned with distributional rather than productive
policies. Excessive delegation to agencies with no adequate funds, resources
or personnel is quite meaningless, as has recently been the case with Sudan's
new local government system.

In any case, decentralized and participative rural development will
almost always require the promotion of dynamic interactions between organizations at different levels (vertically) as well as between organizations
performing different functions at the same level. There are already, internationally and within the Middle East (for example, Egypt and Syria), quite a
few interesting experiments in organization for rural development, and
there are cases where agricultural or rural development went wrong (e.g.,
the Gezira Project in the Sudan). A careful examination of the former and
the latter should help to promote the number of cases that can succeed.

It is sometimes argued, for example, that techniques such as linear
programming, network analysis and cost benefit analysis are more easily
transferable to the developing countries because they represent more
management "technology" than management "ideology." While such techniques are undoubtedly less social and "cultural" in nature than, say,
POSDCORB and other management "proverbs," most of them are by no
means politically, socially or culturally neutral (Schaffer and Lamb 1981, p.
70–79; Meier 1982, p. 143–62).

At the same time, some techniques developed in the West may be
relatively more transferable than others, and can therefore be more successfully made use of in Third World countries, including those of the Middle
East. For example, various techniques associated with program budgeting
(PPBS) have been successfully adopted in the Middle East. The problem,

however, is that by themselves these tools have little to do with enhancing the quality of the allocative choices that make up the core of the budget (Najjar 1978, p. 498–511). A technology transfer should not therefore be expected to solve the problem of public choice by itself.

Many of the conventional methods that are already in use may become more effective if utilized in the right way and in the right context. Administrative training, for example, which is a great favorite in the Middle East because of its relative ease, tends to be at its worst when it centers around midcareer programs with generalized, weakly career-linked recruitment, when it is staffed by professional career trainers, and when it claims to be introducing behavioral and attitudinal changes (Schaffer 1974, p. 441–42). Many training programs in the Arab countries are of these varieties. Institutionalized administrative training can, however, be quite successful for cadre induction and policy conferences, for subsidizing educational inadequacy and for imparting technical skills. In the Arab world, a number of induction programs and executive conferences have certainly proved their worth, and the experience of Egypt undoubtedly stands out in this respect (Ayubi 1980, p. 313–38).

But many training efforts are still caught up between the requirements of academic respectability and the need for career (and social) relevance (Roy 1975, p. 135–48), while some training agencies have—in the words of an insider—simply "taken to tourism in the guise of training" (Nurallah 1978, p. 113). Very few institutes of administration went into research, and although some have taken to consultancy, this was mainly motivated by a desire to follow fashion and therefore remained quite formalistic and irrelevant, or by the obsessive desire to make money and therefore often slipped into downright "sorcery." Any attempt at improving the relevance and effectiveness of training will therefore have to start with an assessment of when and why training was more useful, and when and why it was less so.

In a word, one can suggest that it is only through careful evaluation of the outcomes of various activities in specific and actual situations that Middle Easterners can hope to acquire the capability to improve their performance. And it is such evaluation mechanisms, properly linked to action-oriented research, that the Arab world is lacking most. Without evaluation, neither the performance of administration in general, nor the effectiveness of administrative reform in particular, can be assessed. It is about time that the Arab public bureaucrat and the Arab administration expert were restrained from getting away with the argument that the application of programs for administrative reform *must* have been effective in practice simply because there was a perception that a problem had actually existed and that some solution was indeed required.

References

Abu Shikha, Nadir. *Al-Tanzim al-idari* . . . [Administrative Organization in Thirteen Arab States]. Amman, Jordan: Arab Organization for Administrative Sciences, 1983.

Amin, Galal. *The Modernization of Poverty: A Study in the Political Economy of Growth in Nine Arab Countries, 1945–1970.* Leiden: Brill, 1980.

Arabian Government and Public Services. Directory. London: Beacon, 1983.

Arab Institute of Planning in Kuwait (AIPK) and Centre for Arab Unity Studies. *Al-ʿamala al-ajnabiyya fi aqtar al-khalij al-ʿarabi* [Foreign Employment in Countries of the Arabian Gulf]. Beirut: CAUS, 1983.

Arab Organization for Administrative Sciences. *Administrative Reform in the Arab World: Readings.* Amman, Jordan: Arab Organization for Administrative Sciences, 1986.

Ayubi, N. *Bureaucracy and Politics in Contemporary Egypt.* London: Ithaca Press, 1980.

_____. "Organization for Development: The Politico-Administrative Framework of Economic Activity in Egypt Under Sadat." *Public Administration and Development* 2, no. 4 (Feb. 1982).

_____. "Bureaucratic Inflation and Administrative Inefficiency: The Deadlock in Egyptian Administration." *Middle Eastern Studies* 18, no. 3 (July 1982).

_____. "The Egyptian Brain Drain: A Multi-dimensional Problem." *International Journal of Middle Eastern Studies* 15(1983).

_____. "Local Government and Rural Development in Egypt in the 1970's." *Cahiers Africains d'Administration Publique* 23 (1984).

_____. "Ajhizat al-tanmiya al-idariyya wa mu'assasatuha fi al-aqtar al-ʿarabiyya" [Public Service Agencies and Institutions in the Arab Countries: Their Status and Role]. *Arab Journal of Administration* 9, no. 4 (Fall 1985).

_____. "Bureaucratization as Development: Administrative Development and Development Administration in the Arab World." *International Review of Administrative Sciences* 52 (1986).

_____. "Arab Bureaucracies: Expanding Size, Changing Roles." In *Beyond Coercion: Durability of the Arab State.* Edited by W. Zartman and A. Dawisha. London: Croom Helm, 1988.

_____. "Bureaucracy and Development in Egypt Today." *Journal of Asian and African Studies* 24, no. 1–2 (1989).

Aziz, Muhammad. *Anmat al-ifaq w'al-istithmar fi aqtar al-khalij al-ʿarabi* [Expenditure and Investment Patterns in Countries of the Arabian Gulf]. Cairo: Institute of Arab Research and Studies, 1979.

Bendor, Jonathan. "A Theoretical Problem in Comparative Administration." *Administration and Society* 8, no. 4 (Feb. 1977).

Bryant, Coralie, and White, Louise. *Managing Development in the Third World.* Boulder, Colo.: Westview Press, 1982.

Central Bank of Kuwait. *Economic Reports,* 1978 and 1979.

Deutscher, Isaac. "Roots of Bureaucracy." *The Socialist Register.* London: Merlin, 1969.

Dore, Ronald. *The Diploma Disease: Education, Qualification and Development.* Berkeley: University of California Press, 1976.

Egypt, Ministry of Finance. *The State Budget,* 1975, 1979.

Al-Farsi, Fouad. *Saudi Arabia: A Case Study in Development.* London and Boston: Kegan Paul International, 1982.

Girgis, Malak. *Saykulujiyyat al-shakhsiyya al-misriyya . . .* [Psychology of the Egyptian Character and Obstacles to Development]. Cairo: Rose al-Yusuf Press, 1974.

_____. "Some Cultural and Behavioural Obstacles to Socio-Economic Development in the Arab Gulf" (in Arabic). *Al-Mudir al-ᶜArabi* 52 (July 1975).

Grindle, Merilee S., ed. *Politics and Policy Implementation in the Third World.* Princeton, N.J.: Princeton University Press, 1980.

Haq, Mahbub ul. *The Poverty Curtain: Choices for the Third World.* New York: Columbia University Press, 1976.

Hickson, D. J., and McMillan, C. J., eds. *Organization and Nation.* Westmead, Hampshire: Gower, 1981.

Honadle, George, and Klauss, Rudi, eds. *International Development Administration.* New York: Praeger, 1979.

Hourani, Albert. *The Emergence of the Modern Middle East.* Berkeley: University of California Press, 1981.

Institute of National Planning. *Bahth hasr wa taqdir al-ihtiyajat min al-ᶜamala bi al-qitaᶜ al-ᶜam* [Employment in the Public Sector . . .]. Edited by Md. ᶜAbd al-Fattah Munji. Cairo: INP, 1975.

Islam, Nasir, and Henault, Georges. "From GNP to Basic Needs: A Critical Review of Development and Development Administration." *International Review of Administrative Sciences* 45, no. 3 (1979).

Jreisat, Jamil. "Public Administration Education and Training: Cases from Jordan and Saudi Arabia." *Arab Journal of Administration,* April 1982.

_____. "Building Administrative Capacity for Action: The Arab States." SICA *Occasional Papers,* second series, no. 8. Austin: University of Texas Press, 1985.

Al-Kubaisy, Amer K. *Administrative Development in New Nations, with Reference to the Case of Iraq.* Baghdad: Al-Jumhuriyah Press, 1974.

Kuwait, Central Statistical Office. *Annual Statistical Abstract,* 1982.

Kuwait, Ministry of Planning. *Employment in the Government Administration,* July 1978.

Marouf, Nawal. "Administrative Development in Kuwait." *Arab Journal of Administration,* April 1982.

Meier, Kenneth. "Political Economy and Cost-Benefit Analysis: Problems of Bias." In *The Political Economy of Public Policy.* Edited by Alan Stone and Edward Harpham. Beverly Hills: Sage, 1982.

Najjar, George K. "Social Systems Delineation and Allocative Mechanisms: Perspectives on Budgeting for Development." *Administration and Society* 9, no. 4 (Feb. 1978).

Al Nimir, Saud, and Palmer, Monte. "Bureaucracy and Development in Saudi Arabia: A Behavioral Analysis." *Public Administration and Development* 2, no. 2 (1982).

Nurallah, Kamal. "Administrative Development and Socio-Economic Development in the Arab World" (in Arabic). *Al-Mustaqbal al- ʿArabi* 1, no. 4 (Nov. 1978).

Othman, Osama A. "Saudi Arabia: An Unprecedented Growth of Wealth with an Unparalleled Growth of Bureaucracy." *International Review of Administrative Sciences* 45, no. 3 (1979).

Palmer, Monte, and Nakib, Khalil. "Bureaucracy and Development in the Arab World: An Outline for Future Research." In *Strategies of Development in the Arab World*. International Conference, Louvain, Belgium, 11–14 Dec. 1978.

Paul, Samuel. *Managing Development Programs: The Lessons of Success.* Boulder, Colo.: Westview Press, 1982.

Rashid, Ahmad. "Government and Administration in the UAE." *Bulletin of Arab Research and Studies.* Reprint, vol. 6, 1975.

Rodinson, Maxime. *Islam and Capitalism,* trans. Austin: University of Texas Press, 1978.

Roy, Delwin A. "Development Administration in the Arab Middle East." *International Review of Administrative Sciences* 41, no. 2 (1975).

Schaffer, Bernard B., ed. *Administrative Training and Development: A Comparative Study.* New York: Praeger, 1974.

———. "Insiders and Outsiders." *Development and Change,* 11, no. 2 (1980).

Schaffer, Bernard B., and Lamb, Geoff. *Can Equity be Organized?* Paris and Farnborough: UNESCO and Gower Publishing Co., 1981.

Seitz, John. "The Failure of U.S. Technical Assistance in Public Administration: The Iranian Case." *Public Administration Review* 40, no. 5 (Sept.–Oct. 1980).

Al-Shaikhali, ʿAbd al-Qadir. *Muʿawiqat tatwir . . .* [Obstacles in the Way of Developing Civil Service Systems and Agencies in the Arab Countries]. Amman, Jordan: Dar al-Fikr, 1982.

Siffin, William J. "Two Decades of Public Administration in Developing Countries." In *Education and Training for Public Sector Management in Developing Countries.* Edited by Lawrence W. Stifel et al. New York: Rockefeller Foundation, 1977.

Al-Tayyib, Hasan A. *Muʾassasat al-tanmiya al-idariyya al- ʿarabiyya* [Arab Institutions of Administrative Development]. Amman, Jordan: Arab Organization for Administrative Development, 1984.

Turner, Bryan S. *Weber and Islam: A Critical Study.* London: Routledge and Kegan Paul, 1974.

ʿUlwan, Muhammad Yusuf et al. "A Dialogue on Theory and Practice in Administration and Bureaucracy" (in Arabic). *Majallat al- ʿUlum al-Ijtimaʿiyya* 4, no. 4 (Jan. 1977).

Weinstein, John M. "A Structural Analysis of the Modernizer's Dilemma." *Comparative International Development* 16, nos. 3, 4 (1981).

Wickwar, W. Hardy. *The Modernization of Administration in the Near East.* Beirut: Khayat, 1963.

Zartman, W., and Dawisha, A., eds. *Beyond Coercion: Durability of the Arab State.* London: Croom and Helm, 1988.

Zoubi, Abdulla R. "Towards a Decade of Administrative Development in the Arab World." *Arab Journal of Administration,* April 1982.

4

Civil Bureaucracy in East Africa: A Critical Analysis of Role Performance Since Independence

W. OYUGI

Introduction

East Africa is defined broadly to encompass what is sometimes distinguished as Central (Middle) and Southern Africa as well as Kenya, Tanzania, and Uganda. There are many similarities to the 16 countries in the West African subregion and even to the Arab magrib countries. In one sense, because of the divergence, there is no "East African administration" or "West African administration;" in another sense there is a common sub-Saharan black Africa, which was subjugated by the colonial powers, sought and found independence, and is now struggling—politically, socially, and economically—for self-sufficiency.

Whether in civilian or military-ruled regimes, in English or non-English-speaking East Africa, the civil bureaucracy has emerged as a major actor in society. Any analysis of societal dynamics is at once also an analysis of at least some aspects of the behavior of the bureaucracy. In analyzing role performance by the bureaucracy (i.e., by the civil service), two functions are inherent and critical, namely, system maintenance and system change—sometimes known as governance and development, respectively. These are the two major conventional functions any government in an orderly society has to carry out. The classical theory of administration in the modern state used to stress the instrumental role of the civil service as an agent of the executive. Our experiences in the 20th century have cast doubts on that belief much more so in Africa, where, since the emergence of the colonial state in the 19th century, the civil service has remained a major actor in the maintenance and change of the society; indeed, colonial government was governance by bureaucrats.

Decades after the collapse of the old colonialism, one still finds in many African countries structures, orientations, and behavior that are reminiscent of the colonial past. The survival of relatively powerful civil bureaucracies in Africa is a phenomenon whose consequences are just beginning to be felt. I say "relatively" because the experience shows that the degree of such power appears to vary from country to country, depending on each country's unique circumstances or milieu. Riggs once lumped all the factors influencing administrative behavior under one term: ecology. The ecology of bureaucracy in Africa, as indeed elsewhere in the world, has acted as a major influence on the structure and behavior of administrators. I will detail in this chapter the relationship between ecological factors (politics, economy, history, and sociocultural configuration) and the behavior of civil bureaucracies in East Africa.

The analysis covers the experiences of both the English- and the non-English-speaking countries in black East Africa. Although some space is devoted to the analysis of traditional and colonial roots of the present system, the major accent is on the postindependence experiences. I must say, however, that the scope of the study is rather too ambitious to be treated in as detailed a manner as some readers might wish. The main purpose of this chapter is to outline in a rather broad manner the factors largely responsible for the orientations and behaviors that appear to be common among East African civil bureaucracies.

Historical Roots

In the precolonial state in Africa, the role and weight of the bureaucracy was felt more in those societies with an elaborate form of government. In such states, the so-called centralized states, the traditional ruler maintained a network of organizations, that was manned at various levels by a cadre of trusted lieutenants. This cadre was the direct representative of the ruler in a particular territory, and consulted with him or his senior representatives regularly.

Away from the center of power, the state bureaucrats wielded a lot of power. They were both makers and executors of policies, but they operated according to the norms established by the center, to which they were loyal and responsible. The ruler depended on them to maintain the system; they in turn depended on the ruler for the legitimate exercise of such powers. In many centralized African states, the ruler-King was the institutional embodiment of every legitimate act.

On the other hand, there were other precolonial states that lacked centralized authority, administrative machinery, and constituted judicial institutions. Accordingly, they lacked an elaborate form of government. Political anthropologists have told us that in such states there were no sharp divisions in rank, status or wealth (Fortes and Evans-Pritchard 1940; Mair 1977). In the context of today, one can say that these societies lacked bureaucracies. Writing of the Nuer of Southern Sudan, E. E. Evans-Pritchard observed:

> The Nuer constitution is highly individualistic and libertarian. It is an acephalous state, lacking legislative, judicial and executive organs. Nevertheless it is far from being chaotic. It has a persistent and coherent form which might be called 'ordered anarchy'. The absence of a centralized government and of bureaucracy in the nation, in the tribe, and in tribal segments—for even in the village, authority is not vested in anyone—is less remarkable than the absence of any persons who represent the unity and exclusiveness of these groups (Evans-Pritchard 1940).

In such states, therefore, the emergence of an elaborate government and its attendant bureaucracy must be regarded as consequences of colonial penetration.

The introduction of modern bureaucracy in the colonial states occurred at a time when in Europe itself the ills of such a system were beginning to be felt. The increasing powers of growing administrative organizations accompanied by the decreasing power of the rest of society to resist its further growth and control was already under attack in England. The great English civil service reformer, Sir Stafford Northcote, who himself had influenced the introduction of more bureaucratic tendencies (e.g., meritocracy) into English civil service would fourteen years after the 1870 civil service reforms speak of the dangers of a bureaucratic despotism in which "the permanent officials will take the management of affairs into their hands and Parliament will have little to do" (Albrow 1970).

Regardless both of the European power that occupied an area and the political arrangements obtained in the individual area, in colonial East Africa civil administration was government by bureaucrats.

Two approaches to colonial administration had been adopted—direct and indirect rule. Largely because of their policies of assimilation, the Portuguese (as with the French, who were largely absent from East Africa) adopted a strategy (direct rule), which at once enabled them to regard colonial states as mere appendages and, therefore, extensions of the metropolitan authority. The policy of direct rule was accordingly applied regardless of the form of political arrangements that had existed in the colonized state. (An excellent account of French colonial administration in Africa is found in Suret-Canale 1971.) The British on the other hand applied both the direct and the indirect approaches depending on the situation prevailing in the individual territories. But the substance of administration remained essentially the same.

As a result of colonialism, East African political systems were disorganized and fundamentally undermined through the introduction of new forms of organization and relationships. In the process, these systems lost both their characteristics and authority. The superimposition of new organizations on the old ones sooner or later relegated the old organizations to subordinate positions. That was the meaning and essence of colonialism. The new organizations were to be manned by men of knowledge, trained in the art of governing. Their recruitment would emphasize their formal qualifications as well as their personal characteristics. They were to work within a framework set by the home government. In this sense, colonial administration was a bureaucratic extension of the imperial authority. It can be demonstrated that the structures and orientations of the East African bureaucracies today have their roots in colonial administration (Oyugi 1980). The notion of a legal, rational bureaucracy, servicing the established order was itself a colonial import. The establishment of a national bureaucracy meant also the differentiation of roles. Role differentiation in the early phase of colonialism meant the separation of man from office. This differentiation was felt more in the so-called centralized political systems. The differentiation involved the establishment of organizations, popularly referred to as departments, to take charge of specific functions. Soon a sense of departmentalism (i.e., excessive concern with departmental independence) began to develop. Departmentalism remained a major bureaucratic problem on the eve of independence.

The colonial powers also established highly stratified civil service systems. This was true not only of the British colonies, where separation of the races was an official policy, but also of the Portuguese territories, where assimilation and integration were the official doctrines.

The Europeans occupied all the administrative and professional positions. The other migrant communities, notably the Asians, filled most of the executive and technical positions. The Africans were mainly to be found in the clerical and subordinate positions (Adu 1969). The policy of Africanization, introduced on the eve of independence, merely involved the replacement of expatriates with Africans. It left the structure itself fundamentally undisturbed. The beneficiaries of the Africanization policy saw no shame in arguing for the retention of the privileges associated with the old structure. Commenting on the experience of Kenya, one observer writes: "The structure predisposed educated Africans confined in subordinate roles prior to independence, to perceive themselves as presumptive elite, as the rightful beneficiaries of the system of inequality" (Okumu 1970). The class structure of the bureaucracy was thus inherited at independence. It would later become a major factor influencing role performance by the bureaucracy.

To control the colonies effectively, the colonial powers introduced within the individual colonies a kind of deconcentration, which involved the establishment of a generalist political administration in the field. Known as the provincial or regional administration (in the British colonies), this branch of the administration was the one charged with the maintenance of law and order. Perhaps it is this branch of the service that Dube had in mind when he observed:

> Within the framework of the overall policy laid down by the imperial power in day to day administration the bureaucratic machine enjoyed considerable freedom from interference. Thus there were few hindrances to its exercise of power, which was often authoritarian in tone and content. Bureaucracy had in general a paternalistic attitude to the masses. The masses on their part accepted the position and looked to Administration for a wide variety of small favours (Dube 1967).

The colonial Governors depended on field administration for the day-to-day governance of the colonies. And, as Stanley Dryden correctly observes in the case of Tanzania, it occupied a central position as a link between the central governing authority and the governed (1968). This structure was retained throughout the continent, and has been largely responsible for the so-called law and order orientation of field administration in Africa.

The departing colonial powers also established structures for purposes of recruitment into the civil bureaucracy on merit. The civil service commissions were established with the objective of "removing the civil service from possible political intrigue and influence" (Wamalwa 1975). Thus, on the eve of independence, the apolitical nature of the civil service was being emphasized more than at any time in colonial history. This myth of an apolitical bureaucracy was inherited at independence.

The inherited structures carried with them a number of behavioral orientations: (1) class orientation of the bureaucracy culminating in the tendency on the part of bureaucrats to regard themselves as a special (privileged) group in society; (2) departmental-professional loyalties that make coordination of interdependent roles and functions difficult to achieve; (3) acceptance of rational values of the Weberian type in the face of lingering ascriptive norms, which then lead to paying of lip service to formal rules; (4) tendency to adhere to formal procedures and to routines regardless of the situation in hand; (5) law and order orientation, especially among political administrators, which impedes their effectiveness as development coordinators; and (6) love for exercise of power, which makes decentralization difficult to achieve.

We shall now analyze how these structures and orientations have affected the performance of roles by the bureaucracy.

The Governing Role of the Bureaucracy

The political history of East Africa since independence tends to suggest that the power exercised by the civil service during the colonial period has remained, by and large, undisturbed. In many East African countries today, civil servants are the effective governors. The experience spares no regime, whether dominant single party or military. The liberal theory of government that portrays the civil service as a passive agent of the political authority in the exercise of governmental functions thus appears to be a myth in relation to East Africa.

Factors Influencing the Emergence of a Powerful Bureaucracy

The problem has to be seen in its historical setting. During the colonial period, bureaucracy was the dominant institution in the society. It was allowed a steady growth and development where other institutions — notably the political institutions — were openly discouraged as a matter of imperial policy. In British colonies where quasi-political associations emerged a little earlier, such associations were never allowed to transform themselves into modern political parties until after World War II. But even then, manifestly political activities were tightly controlled and the impression was created by the attitude and behavior of the colonial governments that it was not a safe thing to openly associate with a political party. The tribal associations such as Kikuyu Central Association, Kavirondo Taxpayers and Welfare Association (both in Kenya), and the Tanganyika Africa Territorial Association all started in the 1920s.

The British believed that political development in the colonies could come about only through the introduction of and/or the strengthening of local authorities. This policy was already in use in the areas (such as parts of Uganda) that were being administered indirectly, when it was extended in the 1920s to other areas through the establishment of the so-called local authority councils. The policy was in part responsible for promoting parochial and inward-looking political orientations in many countries. When national political formations were finally allowed, this policy made it difficult later for parties to mobilize national local support. Consequently, the centralizing characteristics of the bureaucracy in a political milieu characterized by centrifugalism gave the bureaucracy a growth advantage.

The advantages of the bureaucracy were further reinforced at independence with the decline of agitational politics. Upon the attainment of independence, the mass following that the political parties tended to command before began to wane. Most of the parties had operated like political movements of some sort, and were quick to lose support as soon as independence was won. Contributing to this quick decline was the inability of the ruling parties to provide patronage to the mass of the people that had given the independence movement their support. This decline began to occur at a time when the implementation of the policy of Africanization was afoot. It would contribute to the steady growth of the civil service as party cadres opted to move out of the party to the civil service.

Apart from colonial heritage, a number of other factors have combined to strengthen the ruling hands of the bureaucracy since Independence. These factors are political and economic as well as social. We discuss them below.

Political Influences

During the colonial period, the relationship between the nationalist leaders and the colonial bureaucracy had been marked by mutual hostility and suspicion. With the achievement of independence, there were attempts by the new political leaders to create some goodwill within the bureaucracy. In some countries (e.g., Tanzania) an attempt was made to politicize the bureaucracy as a means of neutralizing its potential hostility. The bureaucracy was expected to become an agent of the dominant party in nation-building efforts. In the process, however, it emerged as a partner. This was largely because the politicians, most of whom lacked experience in governance, began to depend increasingly on civil servants in the formulation of policies. Having aroused the expectation of the masses over the import of independence, they were now prepared to collaborate with the men of knowledge to ensure successful implementation of policies in order to sustain the spirit of independence. Over time, the bureaucracy managed to regain its old glory with the decline of meaningful competitive politics soon after independence. Even in countries characterized by competitive political parties, the experience was similar after the achievement of independence. Concerned with the destruction of opposition parties, the ruling parties turned to the state bureaucracy for support. At once the civil service began to frustrate the activities of the opposition parties. It had no choice, for not to do so would have led to the accusation of being disloyal to the government and the ruling party. In many countries (e.g., Kenya, Uganda,

Zambia) the government resorted to the use of the political administrators (i.e., field commissioners) to control political activities in the field. Their law and order powers were restored. They could issue or refuse to issue licenses for political rallies. In this position they could frustrate not only the opposition politicians but also the dissidents within the ruling party (Gertzel 1966, 1970). At the center, sympathizers of the opposition could be frustrated by senior civil servants through a myriad of options, such as denial of business licenses and of appointment to strategic positions. Increasingly, the important and strategic place being occupied by the bureaucracy began to be felt and the politicians began to turn to them for favors instead of the other way round.

As a result of being scared of opposition parties, in most parts of East Africa legislation for one-party states has been enacted. Intense intraparty contests have been reported in the initial stages. Conflicts within the party have tended to push decision-making away from the party in favor of the executive. As a result, most of the one-party regimes are today dominated not by the party but by the executive. The right hand of the executive is of course the bureaucracy. This trend seems to have developed in both relatively stable one-party regimes like Tanzania as well as in faction-ridden one-party regimes like Zambia (Scott 1980). In fact, the emergence of a dominant executive in East African politics appears to be an *import* of the one-party phenomenon. By removing real decision-making from party organs, the executive has either by design or default strengthened the ruling hands of the bureaucrats. Referring to presidential domination in policy-making in Zambia, Ian Scott writes: "When outside opinions on policy matters were sought reference was made, not to the central committee (of the ruling party) but to the relevant civil servants in ministries. . . . The civil servants' powers actually grew as they became more involved in policy-making and as decisions were increasingly taken at state House" (Scott 1980). In other states, the civil servants actually took policy initiative and only involved the chief executive at the last stage. The defacto one-party state in Kenya under the late Mzee Kenyatta functioned along these lines.

The requirement of the one-party state that civil servants should freely participate in the affairs of the party without similar opportunities being extended to the politicians has given civil servants undue advantage over the politicians (e.g., in Tanzania and Zambia). In Tanzania, for example, the head of the civil service, who is still a civil servant, sits in all key policy-making organs of the party. Civil servants also freely get leave to run for elective offices, and many get elected and even become cabinet ministers. In many countries, ties between such cabinet ministers and their former colleagues in the civil service have added a new dimension to the special power of the bureaucracy in a one-party state.

Currently, several of the countries under review in this chapter are under military rule; the question arises whether the situations there are any different. Available evidence tends to show that any difference is more apparent than real. In Zaire, which I would still want to regard as a military regime, the president and the bureaucratic elites (both civilian and military) run the show and not the ruling *Mouvement Populaire de la Revolution.*

Even in the erratic military regimes, such as existed in Uganda under Idi Amin, the bureaucracy though scared and demoralized still provided the only hope for the continued existence of the state.

In short then, one can say that the decline of competitive politics, both inter- and intra-party, in East Africa has led to the emergence of powerful bureaucracies, which have consequently displaced political parties as key actors (if they ever were) in the governance process.

Economic Influences

A major source of a bureaucracy's powers is its expert knowledge. In nation building, economic development is a major preoccupation of the ruling elite, both political and bureaucratic. But most East African countries depend on foreign aid for national development, and aid has to be negotiated for before it can be realized. Since a certain amount of technical expertise is required in effective negotiations, politicians usually rely on the senior bureaucrats to carry out the detailed negotiations. This has enabled senior civil servants to establish very close relationships with donor agencies as well as with technical-assistance personnel operating within the country. A combined force of expatriate-local bureaucrats has been the most important source of major development policies in many East African countries. More often than not the two groups share the same values.

Again, the bureaucracy has emerged as the most privileged economic group in society. It has been the beneficiary of Africanization both in commerce and industry. The "open door" policy of allowing civil servants to engage in business in many East African countries (Kenya, Zaire, Malawi) has led to a situation in which business partnership between civil servants and politicians has become a common phenomenon. This has resulted in civil servants using their positions to get access to state resources and to deny them to others. It has also enabled civil servants to flout rules of access openly without expecting any criticism from political leaders.

In the course of time, a situation has arisen in which the bureaucracy has to a large extent virtually monopolized patronage, both in commerce and industry. This, together with their patronage in civil service recruitment, has given them a dominant role in the management of the economic affairs of the state.

In short, the point made above is that East African countries are economically underdeveloped, and the quest for development has led to heavy reliance on the men of expertise—the bureaucrats—in economic management. The bureaucracy has in turn taken advantage of the situation and used it to its own material and political advantage in gaining power-leverage over other institutions in society.

Social Influences

There is an ongoing debate as to whether the bureaucracy in East Africa constitutes a socioeconomic class and, therefore, wields the power based on it (Barkan and Okumu 1979). Discussing this assumption with respect to Kenya, Goran Hyden takes the view that the civil service today is a mirror of the Kenyan Society at large; the individualistic ambitions, the social obligations to the extended family and the tribal inclinations are characteristics of civil servants as of any other category of the population. From here he concludes that the government bureaucracy lacks social cohesiveness, and that it is the political groups based on tribal affiliations or any other parochial interests that seem to be the most influential pressure groups (Hyden 1972; Barkan and Okumu 1979). In fact, in his later comparative analysis of public policy making in Kenya and Tanzania, he reiterated his rejection of the notion that the bureaucracy constitutes the major scene of policy making as implied by Riggs and others with reference to developing countries (Barkan and Okumu 1979).

My own contention here is that Dr. Hyden may be right in the sense that bureaucracy in East Africa does not constitute a class in the classical Marxian sense. Beyond that, however, bureaucracy is the only inclusive social category in African society today that has a staying influence. Both in civilian- and military-ruled regimes, the bureaucracy is looked upon as a refiner and implementor of policies and programs. It is a group with an institutionalized influence in society. It may have internal cleavages, but still, in comparison to other social groups in society, it has the capacity to defend group interest nonetheless.

The success with which civil services in East Africa have resisted internal reforms is a case in point. In many countries, for instance, civil servants have resisted any attempt to remove them from participation in business. Political groups based on tribal or any other parochial interests may be influential, but that influence is built around the connections that the group in question has in the government. When that government is no more, the group gets into disarray. The dismantling of giant tribal associations in Kenya under the regime of Moi and, notably, the dismantling of the once very powerful Kikuyu–Embu–Meru Association is a case in point.

Bureaucratic power on the other hand tends to survive such political changes. Expounding on this theme, Donboos has observed that regardless of ideology and of the regime in power, bureaucracy in East Africa remains a dominant institution that initiates and implements policies and programs (Donboos 1982).

Assessment of Governance Role

There is no doubt that the civil service in East Africa has had a major role to play in the governance process. The service areas where the success or failure of the Civil Service may be assessed include: maintenance of law and order, management of public resources (finance, machinery, personnel), establishment of service ethics, promoting democratic values, defense, and promotion of public interest. The actual performance has varied from one country to another. Overall, however, the picture that emerges is one of dismally poor performance.

There is no underrating the role that civil servants have played in maintaining law and order in those countries where the administrators are still charged with these tasks. The enthusiasm with which these tasks have been carried out has, however, tended to interfere with the rights of innocent individuals.

The District Commissioners and their assistants (the district officers and chiefs) have been known for their inclination to harass and arrest individuals who disagree with them in principle or over the manner in which certain things are being done. The paternalistic attitude of the colonial days appears to have left an indelible imprint in the service. The administrators usually expect the people to be seen and not heard. Since field administration is the link in many countries between the government and the governed, such attitudes and behavior can only alienate the people from the government. Experience has shown that even in countries where some of the senior field administrators are politicians (e.g., Zambia, Tanzania, Malawi) the practice has been the same (Tordoff 1974; Finucane 1974).

In the management of public resources the bureaucracy has not fared well either. One needs only to read the reports of the Auditor General in order to appreciate the magnitude of the problem. There have been cases of outright embezzlement of public funds without any reprimand or punishment of the culprits. Tenders have been awarded to the lowest bidders and later revised upward simply because the "winner" of the tender is a business partner, a friend, or a relative. Year in and year out such malpractices are detected and reported in the local papers and parliamentary committees, but rarely are correctional measures taken.

Furthermore, there have been cases of ministries spending funds on items never approved in the budget. In many ministries, overexpenditure appears to have become a budgetary strategy used in getting what was originally asked for but not approved by the Treasury. It has in many countries led to lack of discipline in financial management.

Wastage has not been confined to financial management alone. In those countries where civil servants have been allowed to participate in business, the use of government resources in the furtherance of the interest of the individual civil servants has been a common occurrence. Those with businesses in other cities use government office telephones to reach their business partners or employees, and vehicles are used for private services here and there.

Many bureaucracies in Africa lack service ethics. At its Third Round-table Conference in 1979, the African Association of Public Administration and Management (AAPAM) felt sufficiently concerned about the matter to pass a resolution urging member states of the association to consider doing something about the problem (AAPAM 1979).

A major manifestation of lack of service ethics is corruption. The problem is widespread in East Africa, and a lot has been said and written about it. In Zaire for instance, it is a cancer that has eaten up the body politic (*Africa Now* 1982). The bureaucracy is accordingly very corrupt (Gould 1978). A magazine article quoted Mobutu as having admitted:

> Our country risks asphyxiation. . . . Everything is for sale; everything is bought in our country. . . . The use by an individual of his most legitimate right is subjected to an *invisible tax,* openly pocketed by individuals. Thus an audience with an official enrolling children in school, obtaining school certificates, access to medical care, a seat on the plane, an import licence, a diploma among other things is subjected to *this tax* which is invisible, yet known to the whole world (*New African* 1980).

Similar sentiments have been expressed about many other African countries. I need not repeat them here since they have been appropriately cited elsewhere (Oyugi 1980).

I wish to emphasize that the degree of corruption appears to be greater in countries (such as Zambia, Kenya, Malawi, Zaire) where the civil servants have been allowed to operate private businesses. In such countries, the laissez-faire attitude to management of societal affairs has provided corruption with a breeding ground and a fertile soil for germination. If good governance implies, among other things, the eradication of social vices such as corruption, then one must come to the sad conclusion that, in Africa, the ruling bureaucracies have fared rather poorly.

One other area where the performance of the bureaucracy has been disappointing is the establishment of democratic structures and behavior in the government system. I refer specifically to the attempts in many countries to introduce governmental structures through which popular views can be expressed. Decentralization of government administration has been frustrated in many countries largely because of the prevailing attitude of senior bureaucrats. Many senior civil servants view their organizations as "monocratic" structures that must be held together at any cost. Victor Thompson observes that in such organizations there is only one point or source of legitimacy. Such structures are bad in that they inhibit innovation. On the other hand, he believes that innovative organizations must be characterized by structural looseness, with less emphasis on narrow, nonduplicating, nonoverlapping definition of duties and responsibilities. In such organizations, he says, communication will be freer and legitimate in all directions. Assignments and resources decisions will be much more decentralized. . . . Departmentalization arranged so as to keep parochialism to a minimum (Thompson 1966). Senior bureaucrats in Africa have been reluctant to allow such organizations to emerge. The reluctance has been experienced especially in the effort to establish local development committees through which popular participation in decision making for development could take place. In countries where the establishment of such committees has been tried, their (the committees') weaknesses have been attributed, in part, to the centralizing attitude of the civil servants (Chambers 1974; Finucane 1974; Tordoff 1974, 1968; Hirschmann 1981; Oyugi 1981). Writing about East Africa in general, Donboos observes that the dominant trend in the three East African countries of Uganda, Kenya, and Tanzania has been one of bureaucratization and centralization; the logic of an organizing state whose centrality is vital to its own existence ultimately appears to leave very little room for participation (Donboos 1982).

Role in Socioeconomic Development

The role of the bureaucracy in national development both generally and with respect to individual countries has been the subject matter of many books and journal articles. In this section, I do not, therefore, intend detailed coverage and analysis. I will merely summarize the experiences in this area since independence.

To start with, we should accept Dudley Seers's contention that "development" is a normative concept, and that to pretend otherwise is to hide one's value judgments (Seers 1972). Seers goes on to state that the concept is usually treated as a synonym for improvement. On that point he concurs with J. D. Montgomery who conceives of it as an aspect of change that is desirable (1966). But, unlike Montgomery, Seers goes a little further and puts his cards on the table. He states:

> The questions to ask about a country's development are therefore: What has been happening to poverty? What has been happening to unemployment? What has been happening to inequality? If all of these have declined from high levels, then beyond doubt this has been a period of development for the country concerned. If one or two of these central problems have been growing worse, especially if all three have, it would be strange to call the result "development", even if per capita income doubled. This applies of course to the future too. A "plan" which conveys no targets for reducing poverty, unemployment and inequality can hardly be considered a "development plan" (Seers 1972).

He does not accept national income as an indicator of development, but he does not reject it as totally irrelevant either. He contends that a rise in per capita income with corresponding stagnation, say in employment, tends to suggest that the country has achieved development *potential* for the future because, as he puts it, the fiscal system could bring about development more rapidly, because of the income available for transfer to the poor (Seers 1972).

I find Seers's position useful as a point of departure in assessing the development role of the bureaucracy in East Africa. An attempt is accordingly made below to assess the performance of the bureaucracy along the suggested lines. A historical approach is adopted here.

A lot of literature on colonial administration tends to suggest that a major preoccupation of colonial administration was with the maintenance of law and order and the collection of revenue. While I do not totally reject the contention, I want to say for the record that these concerns were the preoccupation of only the political administrators—the ones who, in the context of today, head the various regions, provinces and districts in many African countries as district governors or commissioners. The few technical staff as might have existed were primarily concerned with improvement-orientated programs. But they worked under very strict guidelines, usually centrally determined, and they lacked discretionary powers. This was true of both central and field level agencies.

The experience varied from country to country though. In "settlement" colonies like Kenya and Rhodesia, for example, the colonial bureaucracy pursued "development" policies that tended to build and accentuate the material and social differences among the races. Very substantial building of potential, say in agriculture, occurred in the white settled areas. The result was regional disparities in addition. In nonsettlement territories such as Tanganyika, although racial discrimination was not institutionalized in development policies, the commitment to development on the part of the colonial bureaucracy was rather half-hearted. The result was that on the eve of independence very little was visible on the ground in the way of tangible change.

The concern of the East African governments in the immediate postindependence period, as in other colonized countries, was to correct the imbalances and problems created by colonialism. Institution building became a major preoccupation. New departments had to be created and staffed. Old attitudes and practices were to be done away with by retraining and resocialization; new institutions for staff training were quickly established. The Africanization policy initiated on the eve of independence was given added impetus. That was the formal outlook. In practice, however, there were problems.

Accelerated Africanization resulted in the short run in the creation of bureaucracies that were predominantly inexperienced in many ways. The need for on-the-job training was felt and implemented. In the process, however, this yielded an "unintended consequence" in that instead of being concerned with administration of development programs the bureaucracy became more concerned with its own development. To strengthen local manpower needs, a program of technical assistance was instituted. At once technical assistance personnel began to assume major roles in decision making for change. It can be submitted that whatever failures or successes the East African bureaucracies have had in the field of development since independence, technical assistance personnel share a big portion of the responsibility. Major decisions in the field of development in many East African countries have been influenced by expatriates. There is no major "ideological" position paper on development in East Africa created entirely without the aid of expatriates. Accordingly, they have been quite influential in determining the general direction in which change should occur. What we have today in many East African countries are mounting problems of poverty, inequalities and unemployment. Students of political economy of East Africa would be quick to submit that the expatriates have been partly responsible for underdeveloping the continent. Even the conventional students of politics and administration in East Africa have been very critical of the contribution of technical-assistance personnel to the administration of development (Tandon 1973).

One area where technical assistance was intended to play a critical role is the field of manpower development. Since independence, in many East African countries, the number of expatriate personnel seems to be increasing instead of declining. This itself is evidence that they have not been successful in developing local skills so that their presence may be considered redundant. We hear a lot about the so-called lack of administrative capabilities in Africa! What, then, have technical-assistance programs been tackling in more than two decades of independence?

Even in more operational areas the story has been similar. In the area of planning, for instance, very little has been achieved. At independence, planning was assumed to be a panacea for all development problems. Several years later we have seen very little relationship between planning and development (Waterson 1965; Seers and Fable 1972). The administrative infrastructures that have been made to service planning have been rendered ineffective by bureaucratic tendencies in the services. The requirement of development administration is that organizations involved in development should be loosely structured. The experience as we pointed out earlier is that, in many countries, bureaucrats tend to enjoy a concentration of power. As a result, they have opted for the retention of V. Thompson's "monocratic" structures, which by their very nature are antidevelopmental.

Indeed, the failure of many administrative reform programs intended to strengthen the "development front" in East Africa and elsewhere can be largely attributed to bureaucratic orientations. The many administrative reforms introduced in the first decade of independence were frustrated by the bureaucracy itself. New planning machinery was created to decentralize decision making through the use of local development committees. But the center never took the exercise seriously. No powers were delegated and the committees sooner or later ceased to have any meaning in the planning system. Creating new departments involved increased coordination; but the love for departmental autonomy and independence would not allow for that. Consequently, the structures of government bureaucracies in many East African countries have remained as "monocratic" as they had been before independence.

The attitudes and orientations (i.e., values) of the bureaucrats in East Africa have been the most inhibitive factors in development. The "class" orientation of the bureaucracy by which they regard themselves as a special (privileged) group in society stands in the way of any change effort that is not in their interest.

The pattern was as follows: A commission would be set up (e.g., The Ndegwa and Waruhiu Commissions in Kenya; Whelan, O'Riodarn, and Mwanakatwe reports in Zambia) that would recommend structural changes in the government aimed at rationalizing work procedures and considering salary increases. Invariably, the bureaucracy would ignore everything but the salary increases! And there have been many such commissions since independence. The result has been steady increase in wages in the modern sector, which has contributed to mounting inequalities in East African countries.

Value orientation has also been responsible for neocolonial relations between local bureaucrats and donor agencies. The quest for the good life has led to a symbiosis between the two groups. They have come to see their interests as being intricately intertwined. This has often resulted in business partnerships and other close liaisons. The consequences for development have been quite negative. The local agents have been used to facilitate the external control of the domestic economies, thus enabling the process of peripheralization to take root. Indeed, the emergence of classes that students of political economy are so much concerned with today originates in part from the said relationship.

In summary, then, one is tempted to conclude that what has taken place in East Africa since independence does not deserve being characterized as development. Like Seers, we cannot underrate the achievement in infrastructure building which has led to the high growth rates in some countries and therefore to the growth in per capita income. We agree with Seers further that what has been achieved in many countries is the building of potential, which could be exploited for development purposes at some future time. However, the current situation may be described as the "development of underdevelopment."

The underdevelopment "theory" of administration is a recent "invention" by mainly "Africanists" working in the field of public administration. It has emerged in part as an effort on the part of the said scholars to "catch up" with their counterparts in the field of political economy.

According to underdevelopment-dependency theorists such as Samir Amin, John Saul, and Colin T. Leys, the economies of Africa are dependent economies dominated by international capital and as such are not serving the interest of the local people. Such economies are characterized by, among other things, heavy reliance on foreign capital and technology, unequal distribution, abject poverty, and rising unemployment. They have accordingly argued that what is taking place in most African countries cannot be characterized as development. It is instead development of underdevelopment.

Conclusion

The material presented in this chapter suggests that the bureaucracy in East Africa (indeed in black Africa generally) has performed rather poorly in its twin tasks of system maintenance and system transformation. Instead of becoming an instrument of development, it has instead emerged as an instrument of antidevelopment.

Any discussion of development or lack of development in Africa must, therefore, critically examine the factors that have conditioned the structure and orientation of the bureaucracy in a historical perspective. A historical analysis similar to the one that has been attempted in this chapter would enable us to establish how the problem unfolded and developed.

There is a need now for more country-specific studies similar to the one Gould has done for Zaire (1978) to illuminate our understanding of underdevelopment-dependency perspective of public administration. As of now, we may not accept that such a "theory" or movement exists; but the notion of *underdevelopment administration* is one we shall be hearing a lot about before the close of the decade. I would be surprised if it failed to emerge as a distinct movement similar to the development administration that it attempts to discredit.

References

Adu, A. L. *The Civil Service in Commonwealth Africa.* London: George Allen and Unwin, 1969, p. 21.

African Association of Public Administration and Management. *Proceedings of AAPAM Round Table Three,* Nairobi, August 1979. Addis Ababa, Ethiopia.

Africa Now. "Mobutu's Empire of Graft." Mar. 1982.

Albrow, Martin. *Bureaucracy.* London: Pall Mall Press Ltd., Chap. 1.

Amin, Samir. "Underdevelopment and Dependence in Black Africa: Origin and Contemporary Forms." *Journal of Modern African Studies* 10, no. 4 (1972).

Berg, R., and Whitaker, J.S., eds. *Strategies for African Development.* Berkeley: University of California Press, 1986.

Chambers, R. *Managing Rural Development.* Uppsala: Scandinavian Institute of African Studies, 1974.

Donboos, M. R. *Bureaucracy and Rural Development in East Africa: Recurring Penetration Strategies.* Paper tabled at the First International Conference on the Comparative Historical and Critical Analysis of the Bureaucracy, held at Gottlieb Duttweiler Institute fur Wirtschaftliche und Soziale Studien, Ruschli-kon/Zurich, Switzerland, 4–8 Oct. 1982.

Dryden, Stanley. *Local Administration in Tanzania.* East African Publishing House, 1968, p. 12.

Dube, S. C. "Bureaucracy and Nation Building in Transitional Societies." In *Readings in Comparative Public Administration.* Edited by Nimrod Raphaeli. Boston: Allyn and Bacon Inc., 1967, p. 214.

Finucane, James. *Rural Development and Bureaucracy in Tanzania.* Uppsala: Scandinavian Institute of African Studies, 1974.

Fortes, M., and Evans-Pritchard, E. E., eds. *African Political Systems.* Oxford University Press, 1940.

Gertzel, C. "The Provincial Administration in Kenya." *Journal of Commonwealth Political Studies,* Nov. 1966.

_____. *The Politics of Independent Kenya.* Heinemann and East African Publishing House, 1970.

Gould, David J. "From Development Administration to Underdevelopment Administration: A Study of Zairian Administration in the Light of the Present Crisis." In *Les Cahiers du Cadaf* 6 (1978).

Hirschmann, D. *Administration of Planning in Lesotho*. Manchester Papers on Development 2, Nov. 1981.

Hyden, Goran. "Social Structure Bureaucracy and Development Administration in Kenya." *The African Review* 1, no. 3 (1972):118–29.

_____. "Administration and Public Policy." In *Politics and Public Policy in Kenya and Tanzania*. Edited by Joel Barkan and John Okumu. New York: Praeger, 1979.

Leys, Colin T. *Underdevelopment in Kenya: The Political Economy of Neo-Colonialism*. London: Heinemann, 1975.

Mair, L. P. *Primitive Government*. London: Scholar Press, 1977.

Montgomery, J. D. "A Royal Invitation: Variation on Three Classic Themes." In *Approaches to Developments: Politics Administration and Change*. Edited by J. D. Montgomery and W. Siffin. New York: McGraw-Hill, 1966, p. 259.

New African Magazine. London, Aug. 1980:4.

Okumu, John J. "The Socio-Political Setting." In *Development Administration: The Kenyan Experience*. Edited by C. Hyden et al. Nairobi: Oxford University Press, 1970, p. 37–38.

Oyugi, W. "The African Public Services: Challenges and Prospects." In *Indian Journal of Public Administration* 26, no. 3 (July–Sept. 1980):792–813.

_____. *Rural Administration in Kenya*. New Delhi: Vikas Publishing House, 1981.

Saul, John S., and Arrighi, Giovanni. *The Political Economy of Africa*. New York: Monthly Review Press, 1973.

Scott, Ian. "Party and Administration under One Party State." In *Administration in Zambia*. Edited by W. Tordoff. Manchester: Manchester University Press, 1980.

Seers, Dudley. *The Meaning of Development*. Communication Series No. 44, Institute of Development Studies at the University of Sussex, 1972.

Seers, Dudley, and Fable, M. *Crisis in Planning,* vols. I and II. London: Chatto and Windus, 1972.

Suret-Canale, Jean. *French Colonialism in Tropical Africa*. London: Hurst, 1971.

Tandon, Y., ed. *Technical Assistance Administration in East Africa*. Uppsala: Dag Hammarskjold Foundation, 1973.

Thompson, Victor. "Bureaucracy and Innovation." *Administrative Science Quarterly* 10 (1966):1–20.

Tordoff, W. *Journal of Administration Overseas* 7, nos. 3, 4 (July–Oct. 1968).

_____. *Politics in Zambia*. Manchester: Manchester University Press, 1974.

Wamalwa, W. N. "The Role of Public Service Commissions in New African States." In *A Decade of Public Administration in Africa*. East African Literature Bureau, 1975.

Waterson, A. *Development Planning: Lessons of Experience*. Baltimore: Johns Hopkins University Press, 1965.

5

Policy Developments and Administrative Changes in West Africa

DELE OLOWU

Introduction

The sixteen countries comprising the West African subregion have a total population of 163 million, almost a third (30.3 percent) of the African population. However, more than half of this West African population is to be found in only one country, Nigeria, which has more than 15 percent of the total African population. (For a concise introduction to the West Africa subregion, see Dunn 1978.)

There are many ecological, historical, economic, and political differences among West African countries (see Table 5.1). Much of the coastal regions belong to the forest zone whereas the more northerly portions are in the Sahel. Hence, countries such as Senegal, Mali, Mauritania, and Niger have experienced the drought scourge while others have scarcely been touched by it. The most outstanding difference, and one that is important for our consideration, is the difference between French and British colonial policy in West Africa. Ten of the countries in the subregion were former French colonies and actually belonged to a federation of French West Africa, the capital of which was Dakar. On the other hand, although Britain had only four colonies in West Africa, its influence was equally substantial in that it controlled about two-thirds of the total population of the region. Guinea-Bissau and Cape Verde are the only former Portuguese colonies in West Africa while Liberia, settled by American missionaries and freed slaves, although English-speaking, can hardly be regarded as an ex-colony.

TABLE 5.1. Basic Data on West African Countries

Country	1984 Population (millions)	Area (thousand)	GNP per capita (U.S. $ 1983)	Year of Independence	Life Expectancy 1983	1980
Benin	3.89	113	290	1960	48	42.5
Cape Verde	0.32	4	320	1975	64	57.0
Gambia	0.63	11	290	1965	36	34.8
Ghana	13.04	239	310	1957	59	52.0
Guinea	5.30	246	300	1958	37	40.3
Guinea-Bissau	0.88	36	180	1974	38	43.0
Ivory Coast	9.47	322	710	1960	52	47.1
Liberia	2.12	111	480	1847	49	49.1
Mali	7.83	1,240	160	1960	45	42.0
Mauritania	1.83	1,031	480	1960	48	44.0
Niger	5.94	1,267	240	1960	45	42.5
Nigeria	92.04	924	770	1960	49	48.6
Senegal	6.35	196	440	1960	46	43.3
Sierra Leone	3.54	72	330	1961	38	34.0
Togo	2.84	57	280	1960	49	48.8
Upper Volta	6.79	274	180	1960	44	42.0
Totals/averages	162.79	6,143	360		46.9	46.5

Sources: United Nations Fund for Population Activities (1984); World Bank's *World Development Report 1985* (Washington, D.C.).

A lot has been written about the implications of French and British colonial policies on the administrative systems of their respective excolonies. Even where, as in the case of Guinea, independence involved discord between the metropolitan government and the newly independent state, the basic framework and philosophy of the colonial administration has been maintained. The contrast is usually made in the literature between the centralist thrust of French colonial (and postcolonial policy) as distinct from the more decentralized British philosophy of colonial administration based on the concept of separate development of the races. This is reflected in the French policy of assimilation as distinct from the Dual Mandate policy of the British (Mazrui 1983). To a large extent, colonial tutelage (more in former French colonies than in others) has survived the transition to independence. This has had important implications not only for the philosophy, structure of policy making, and the administrative apparatus but also for national political ideology. The French-speaking countries are generally more dependent on France—politically, economically, and militarily—than their British counterparts. Moreover, as will be shown later, the principles of administrative reform and policy changes are usually initiated or inspired by developments in the respective mother countries. Even within these broad "blocks," however, a few countries have tried to adopt different ideological postures. Guinea-Bissau, Guinea, Ghana, Mali, and Benin have tried different brands of socialism while the remaining countries have followed a mixed economy strategy that allows greater participation by the private sector and inevitably by foreigners in the management of the economy (Young 1982).

In spite of all these differences, however, there are also remarkable similarities among West African countries. They are all generally economically underdeveloped, a large percentage of their population is still in agriculture, and there have been few industrial successes. All their economies are still export-oriented and are therefore subject to the vagaries of the international market. All of them have adopted European administrative standards and procedures. All of them, including the most conservative, have adopted a strategy of reliance on the state bureaucracy for managing the development process. As shown in Table 5.1, most of these countries are very poor by world standards. The average per capita gross national product (GNP) is just $360, yet only five of the sixteen countries exceeded this average. Even in the seemingly most successful economically—Nigeria and Ivory Coast—their life expectancy levels, regarded as a key indicator for measuring general quality of life among a country's population, are low absolutely and in comparison to other countries in the world with similar GNP levels (Stewart 1985).

The sum total of all these observations is that West Africa remains generally an underdeveloped part of the world, and one in which the state has formally designed a role for itself of leading and managing the development process. This common socioeconomic condition forms the background to the similarities of the response of West African governments as reflected in their programs of policy and administrative change. In the next section, we shall discuss the major elements of such efforts aimed at administrative change.

Nature of Policy and Administrative Change in West Africa

These are and have been four major themes of administrative change in West Africa:

1. How to transform the public service from an institution created primarily for maintaining law and order to one for promoting socioeconomic development.
2. How to replace European expatriates with West African indigenes without loss of professional standards.
3. How to maintain a productive relationship between politicians and administrators.
4. How to debureaucratize the public service in an age of overall economic decline.

We shall examine each of these issues in turn.

The Public Service as an Instrument of Socioeconomic Development

If there was one concept generally accepted in West Africa regarding the role of the public service after independence it was that it should be transformed from an institution for ensuring control to one for stimulating rapid socioeconomic change. This is understandable given the high expectation that the inheritors of colonial power had of political independence. Kwame Nkrumah, whose country was the first to be independent in 1957, had proclaimed to his people: "Seek ye first political independence and every other thing (material improvement) shall be added unto you."

How was this to be achieved? There have been four policy preferences used in different combinations in the West African region. The first was *development planning*. Even though West African governments, like their counterparts elsewhere, lacked the wherewithal to undertake comprehensive development plans such as the ones undertaken in the USSR, they are fascinated by them. Hence, in spite of the controversy surrounding the utility of development plans, all West African countries have continued with their respective versions of planning. The state assesses resources and makes short-range plans for about five years in which it sets investment targets for both the public and private sectors. Given the vagaries of external resources and externally determined prices of products, the two bases on which plan financing rests together with a host of other problems (executive capacity, planning disciplines, reliable statistics, etc.), development planning has generally been a disappointment in West Africa. Nevertheless, the implication of its continued use is that the public service must expand and develop its capacity to make and manage development plans.

This brings us to the second strategy being utilized, the *adoption of management techniques and technologies,* which has proved especially profitable in private sector institutions in the West, in the public services of West African countries. These new techniques are regarded as the key to enabling public servants to perform as efficiently as their counterparts in the private sector. Nigeria is the one country that has gone furthest in these attempts as we shall discuss below, but there have been similar experiments in Ghana and the Ivory Coast. There is still substantial controversy, however, as to the applicability of private sector management concepts in the public services of West African countries (of any public service for that matter). These techniques include budgeting systems, management by objectives, manpower review, and job classification.

A third strategy has been an attempt to *decentralize the public service* in two directions. The first is in the direction of parastatals (government corporations, companies, etc.). Parastatals were regarded as necessary to enable the public service to perform essential services in the most efficient manner possible without the encumbrances of the rigid civil service rules. There are parastatals for air, postal, telecommunication, banking, hotels, city management, industries, agricultural marketing, and financing. Parastatals are perceived as the convenient strategy for government involvement in the area of socioeconomic activity. Hence, parastatals have increased everywhere all over the continent. There were over 200 parastatals at the federal level in Nigeria in 1981 and many state governments have about a dozen (the range is from 4 to 50). Ivory Coast had over 50 in 1984.

Unfortunately, however, the record of these parastatal agencies has been dismal. The reasons are manifold but two are outstanding. First, the institutions never enjoyed the autonomy that their status was supposed to confer on them. They were run as civil service agencies and in many cases (except in Francophone Africa, especially Ivory Coast until recent times), their staffing conditions were a step or two lower than in the public service itself. Second, politicians often packed these corporate institutions with their partisan supporters (rather than with competent managers), making accountability difficult and leading to considerable losses through venality and corruption. None of the several administrative/judicial enquiries into their operations have been able to change matters substantially.

Nevertheless, it might be useful to note that parastatals have not failed completely in West Africa. Guinean enterprises responsible for infrastructural service activities, such as railways, roads, air transport, electricity, mining, and banking, were reported as "relatively successful," in the 1970s although the commercial agencies performed poorly. Also, two of Ghana's 15 state manufacturing enterprises made a profit under Kwame Nkrumah. Another important trend worthy of note is that the governments of these countries have not given up on attempts to improve parastatals' effectiveness. For instance, the 1981 World Bank Report on Africa (the Berg Report), which was generally critical of public management practices in the continent, noted the highly successful Senegalese experiment of negotiating contract agreements with its parastatals (World Bank 1981).

Local governments have also been involved in the move toward decentralization. Local governments for a long time have not generally been regarded as relevant to the administration of socioeconomic development plans beyond maintaining elementary school buildings, small rural clinics, and law and order. Attempts to involve them more vigorously have led to significant efforts to transfer resources and specific responsibilities to them and involve them in the planning process. Gambia, Sierra Leone, and Nigeria have gone furthest, but even in these countries progress has been halting and unsure. The most successful cases of local government involvement in development activities continue to be mainly in the major cities of West Africa (Adamolekun, Olowu, and Laleye 1984).

Finally, there have been attempts to *restructure the civil service* so as to permit greater mobility on the one hand within the service itself (laterally between generalists and professionals and vertically between the rigid classes), and on the other hand between the civil service and other institutions (such as the universities and the organized private sector). The process has gone furthest in Ghana and Nigeria. One other dimension of restructuring the service is the attempt to bridge the wide gaps between the lowest and highest income classes within the civil service without destroying incentives for performance. Ghana is currently doing its best in this regard following hard after Nigeria, which attempted a similar exercise some ten years earlier.

As we shall discuss in greater detail below, most of the reform efforts are not entirely generated from endogenous influences. In many instances, the impetus for reform is exogenously generated — usually from the former metropolitan countries.

Indigenization and Professionalization

One of the challenges that faced almost all West African countries was the need to recruit indigenes for senior service jobs that had hitherto been held by colonial expatriates. Indeed this was one of the most important benefits conferred by independence. Senior positions in the civil service were reserved exclusively for the white races until the dying years of colonial rule in (West) Africa. Hence, in almost all countries—more so, however, in Anglophone than in Francophone West Africa—there has been a rapid pace of indigenization. In Western Nigeria this was achieved before independence, but in countries or areas where skilled human resources were lacking, there has been more hesitancy and a slower pace of indigenization.

The problem is, however, not only one of finding indigenous replacements. Though this was not always the case, the fear is real that indigenes who are rapidly promoted to positions of authority because of vigorous indigenization policies may not be able to function effectively—in terms of skills and ethics—compared to expatriates. On the other hand, besides the security implications of expatriates occupying sensitive government positions, there is also the economic burden that expatriates constitute to their host country. French expatriates in the Ivory Coast (whose numbers have increased since independence) are known to earn about three times the salaries they would earn in France. This is besides home-leave passages and the regular repatriation of foreign exchange. Such policies have prompted questions about the real beneficiaries of development, even when it does take place. Ivory Coast's "Ivorianisation" policy, although initiated and articulated much later than other West African countries, has become one of the major policies for economic and political reform.

In order to meet this dual-headed challenge (indigenization and competence) described above, a combination of two policies is followed. First, an expatriate recruitment policy is pursued—in areas of highly specialized skills, on a contract basis. For instance, even in Nigeria, there is still a high expatriate presence in a wider range of highly specialized skills—engineers, scientists, technicians, and university professorships. The Federal Civil Service reported 17,000 unfilled senior posts as of June 1985. Second, very elaborate training programs have been designed for public servants. In French-speaking countries, these are normally carried out by ENAPs (public administration programs modeled on the French Ecole Nationale). Anglophone countries have created similar institutions while at the same time using a number of other colleges and higher educational institutions as training outposts. Furthermore, the whole educational system is geared in this direction—the rapid production of indigenous graduates, either locally or overseas. Whereas the immediate needs of setting skilled hands to man positions are increasingly being realized, there are doubts as to the ethical competence of some of these late recruits into the service.

One other dimension of indigenization needs to be mentioned: the attempts by West African governments to indigenize the organized private sector (commerce and light manufacturing). Again, the greatest strides in this direction were made in Nigeria through her two indigenization decrees of 1974 and 1977. The new Ivorization policy referred to above also contains provisions of a similar nature (*West Africa* 1985). This policy, however, raises a dilemma for the public sector. First, competition with the private sector for scarce indigenous skilled personnel will most probably lead to a drain of such high calibre staff from the public service, at a time when they are most needed. Second, such policy measures could act as a disincentive to much-needed foreign investment.

Political and Administrative Leadership

There was a strong tradition in the early comparative public administration literature that underscored the necessity for political roles for an overdeveloped bureaucracy in the Third World. Administrators made and executed policy during colonial rule in West Africa as in other parts of Africa (Burke 1969; Ferkis 1962). Independence was expected to change that situation. To a large extent, the control of the public service was secured after independence either by one-party or military political leaders. But over the years, there has also been a tendency for these groups of political leaders to rely more on the civil service than on their political parties or the military for the prosecution of their political and economic development programs. The explanation for such a turn of events is understandable under military rule. The civil service represents the most immediate link between military leaders and their civilian populations. The primacy of order and discipline within the two institutions also provides opportunities for the development of close affinities between the military and civil bureaucracies (Riggs 1977). In one-party controlled states, the increasing weakness of the party in favor of its leader has also meant there is a need for greater reliance on the state rather than on the party bureaucracy (Zolberg 1966).

This brings us then to the second problem confronted by the civil service in this respect in West Africa: the increasing adoption of a political rather than professional role by the civil service. Increasing reliance by politicians on the civil service has meant an increasing pressure on civil servants for the demonstration of loyalty to the party, person or group in power. In a situation in which power changes hands regularly or where the party interests of the ruling elites diverge substantially from what state officials consider to be the national interest, officials are placed in a dilemma. The trend, therefore, has been in the direction of politicizing the bureaucracy, such that top career officials increasingly see their role as political rather than professional. Indeed, it has been suggested that the notion of career service, with its concept of civil service neutrality, should be dispensed with in favor of recruitment to top position on the basis of demonstrated loyalty. This issue became a major controversy in Nigeria since the mid-1970s. It was aggravated by the various interpretations of the 1979 constitution on the issue during the second Republic and it cannot be said to have been resolved by now. As the proceedings of several conferences of African civil servants showed in the 1960s, this problem was not peculiar to Nigeria (Rweyemamu and Hyden 1975).

One other effect of the increasing centralization of power and reliance on the state bureaucracy has been the intense pressure for a representative bureaucracy. This was inevitable in a situation in which representative institutions were in varying levels of rupture and effective policy making was carried out by senior civil servants. So a major problem has been to work out rules, formally or informally, for balancing merit with proportional representation in recruiting persons into the government bureaucracy. Informal procedures that had been in use since independence were formalized in the 1979 Nigerian Constitution, which stipulated that recruitment for jobs at all levels of government (federal, state, and local) must reflect ethnic or regional diversity rather than merit considerations alone. Formal rules of this nature have also been worked out for admission into higher educational institutions and for scholarships. There are similar arrangements in the Ivory Coast, Ghana, and Guinea under Sekou Toure (Rothchild 1985).

Privatization and Decentralization

Global economic troubles, combined with environmental disasters and unproductive economic domestic policies pursued by governments in Africa, have resulted in a grinding African crisis, of which West Africa has had its lot.

One major policy response that has been highly orchestrated by the International Monetary Fund, the World Bank, and a number of other Western analysts has been privatization of the public sector or debureaucratization. Although very close concepts, the two are not the same. One calls for the greater involvement of the market mechanism in economic management, whereas the other is more concerned with decentralization in the political sense to subnational units, including the market.

Whereas this was at first resisted by African governments, it is now generally accepted that the centralization of power in most African countries, especially in the national state bureaucracy, has not helped the development process in African countries, leading as it does to three lopsided priorities: urban instead of rural, industry instead of agriculture, and central rather than local.

This has become a major policy shift in Africa from the immediate postindependence years that prompted the expansion of the central government bureaucracy. It is not surprising that this policy shift has happened within such a short time, as the two institutions mentioned above have adopted this as part of their aid-giving conditions. Hence, in Abidjan, Ivory Coast, services such as garbage collection, water supply, bus transport, and sewage processing have been passed on to the private sector, and other countries are attempting similar experiments. Almost all West African governments have embarked on policies aimed at rationalizing their bureaucracies. By December 1985, 27,000 out of an estimated 38,000 employees of the Ghanaian public service had been retrenched and a recent announcement from Nigeria put the number of those retrenched from the federal civil service alone, excluding parastatals, at 15,000 between December 1984 and June 1985.

In order to demonstrate more clearly the patterns of administrative and policy change, we discuss in greater detail below the public service reform effort in Nigeria that got underway in 1975.

Policy and Administrative Change in Nigeria: From the Udoji Reforms to the Present

The distinguishing mark of Nigeria's socioeconomic and political history within the last two decades, besides her size, political complexity, and civil war, has been the commercial exploitation of oil in large quantities since the late 1960s. With the oil crisis of 1973, Nigeria's oil started to bring in windfall gains in revenues and foreign exchange earnings. This made possible the very rapid expansion of the Nigerian public sector, far beyond its traditional confines. The manpower strength of the public service rose from 658,000 in 1974 to 3.7 million in 1981. This latter figure constituted 65 percent of the workers estimated to be in the employ of the modern sector of the country's economy (see Table 5.2). Another 7 percent is employed in jointly owned government and private interests, leaving only 28 percent in the organized private sector. The public sector's 65 percent is shared almost evenly between the federal and state governments in a ratio of 28 percent:27 percent, with the local government employing the remaining 10 percent. A rationalization for changes in the public sector, particularly pay increases,

TABLE 5.2. The Composition of Nigeria's Modern Sector Manpower 1981

Sectoral Shares	Number (thousands)	%	Makeup of Public Sector Component (%)	
Public sector	3,705	65	Federal government	28
Private sector	1,596	28	State government	27
Joint ventures (public/private)	399	7	Local government	10
Totals	5,700	100		65

Source: National Manpower Board, *Nigeria's Manpower Requirements: Implications for Education and Training* (Lagos: Mimeo, 1983).
Note: Estimates based on sample survey.

was provided by the Udoji Commission recommendations—a classic statement of Western-influenced public administration thinking.

The federal military government of Colonel Gowon inaugurated in September 1972 a Public Service Review Commission of eight under the chairmanship of Chief Jerome O. Udoji, a former head of the civil service of the eastern region of Nigeria. Its task was to examine the organization, structure, and management of public services (federal, state, and local, and their agencies) and recommend reforms where desirable. It was also to undertake a regrading of all posts in the public services as well as review legislation regarding pensions and superannuation schemes in the public services. This was the first commission to be given wide-ranging powers to review all aspects of the whole public service.

The commission was expected by the government to tackle its terms of reference, "having regard to the need to secure adequate development and optimum utilization of manpower and to increase the efficiency and effectiveness of the public services in meeting the challenge of a development-oriented society." The preoccupation of the military regime at this time was how the windfall oil gains could be transformed into rapid economic growth. The commission proceeded to appoint a large number of foreign consultants, mainly from Western countries (especially from Canada and the United Kingdom), and also traveled to Ottawa and London to collect evidence on how to proceed with its assignment. There was an attempt to involve a cross-section of Nigerian elites, especially those in government (both military and civil bureaucrats), university professionals, and leaders of trade unions. Nevertheless, 51 foreign consultants were involved in the work of the eight task forces that contributed to the final report and they dominated the three most critical task forces: those on the civil service (British), parastatals (British), and the most important of them all, salaries and grading (Canadian). It was therefore not coincidental that the commission's report (in 1975) drew considerable inspiration from the report on the

British civil service of 1968 chaired by Lord Fulton. This was evident in its major recommendations:

1. The adoption of a results-oriented public service which has new tasks (those of promoting socioeconomic development rather than simply keeping law and order) and therefore required new men with new (more business-like) orientations and new skills.

2. These new skills involve, most especially, the adoption of management techniques that have proved useful in the private sector, namely plans, programs, and budgeting systems; management by objectives; and performance evaluation.

3. The acquisition of these new skills through a more elaborate, systematic, and continuous training program.

4. Abolition of the rigid class divisions between departments and work cadres, the creation of a senior management group to integrate the dual hierarchies between specialists and generalists in the public service.

5. The adoption of a unified grading and salary structure throughout the public service.

6. The use of merit as the sole criterion for recruitment and promotion within the public service.

7. Proposed salary increases that will make public sector salaries closer to those in the private sector.

Most of these recommendations received the blessing of the government of the day but after 11 years of the "reform"—and three changes of government—an appraisal of the reform by a conference of senior government officials from federal and state governments and representatives of training institutions and the universities convened by the office of the head of the civil service of the federation was unanimous that the reform had not achieved its objectives. The salary increases proposed in two stages by the commission were implemented in one fell swoop for purely political reasons, thereby stimulating inflationary trends from which the economy is yet to recover.

As for the techniques, very little success has been achieved and even though states in the southwestern parts of the country have tried to sustain progress made in their budgetary innovations, which they started before the commission was established, the progress has been modest. The federal government recently adopted a common budget policy that set all the states back to line-item budgeting. The management by objectives (MBO) has been a nonstarter. As for the role of merit in personnel administration, what has dominated the discussion—especially in the late 1970s to date—has not been merit, but the extent to which the demands for a representative bureaucracy should determine recruitment and promotion prospects within the public services.

There is, however, a greater awareness of the role of training in the development of civil servants. The federal government had previously benefited from the report of a study it commissioned in 1967 and after the publication of the government's White Paper on the Udoji Report it went ahead to streamline the training institute, Administrative Staff College of Nigeria (ASCON), which it established in 1973 some 60 kilometers from Lagos. Most state governments that did not have their own training policies also commissioned reports on their training needs and developed modest institutions (civil service training schools) for the training of their junior-level officers who are not covered by programs for high- and middle-level cadres in the universities and polytechnics. Even here, however, severe problems remain. There is as yet no clearly articulated training policy; wide gaps exist among groups and classes, and financial commitment to training has not been consistent. Training is still regarded as either punishment or reward rather than a necessary part of career development. Hence, as of January 1985, 2,000 management-level senior civil servants had not participated in the induction course that should have taken place within three months of joining the service. Intermediate and junior-level officers are also poorly covered.

During the last two to three years, the preoccupation of policy makers with respect to the public service has been on devising the best way for trimming down the size of the public sector. As a result, a large number of public officials have been forcibly retired or laid off. About two-thirds of the 1986 budget was wiped out by the sharp drop in oil prices.

The task of evolving an effective Nigerian public service seems to have defied all the bold attempts made to improve governmental efficiency. These included higher remunerations, liberal pensions, lavish provision of training facilities especially after the Udoji reforms of 1975, and the creation of a number of control institutions to ensure that the Nigerian public service performed creditably and honorably. But the reverse was the case. As to efficiency, Nigerian public administration researchers submit that efficiency was higher during the colonial period in a number of governmental organizations—agriculture, railways, the police, road construction and electricity generation—compared to the post-independence years (Balogun 1983). Higher perks and salaries seem to have quickened the decline of public morality and the rise of corruption. Institutions created to assist in ensuring efficiency and public-spirited public services themselves became corrupt or otherwise obsolete, and not even systematic training and retraining of officials whose case was so eloquently made by the Udoji Commission have either been effectively organized when resources were made available or had significant impact on public sector performance.

Apologists of the public service point to the declining resources made available to the public sector to renew itself while others maintain the fundamental inability of the public service of a young state to serve the great ideals of development administration.

Retrenchment has thus gone hand-in-hand with a reappraisal of the role of the private sector in the development process. This process has been assisted by Nigeria's creditors and borrowers who insist on certain conditions as well as Nigeria's policy makers who see "privatization" as the only means of reviving the Nigerian economy. Domestically, the strongest argument in favor of privatization has been the horrendous inefficiency and corruption of public service institutions, especially in those commanding heights of the economy—dominated by government (see Table 5.3). Today, many of Nigeria's parastatals, both at the federal and state levels are being either wholly or partially sold out to the private sector or completely confiscated.

TABLE 5.3. The Share of Public and Private Sectors in the Nigerian Economy, 1957–1985

	Planned Expenditure		
Period	Public Sector (%)	Private Sector (%)	Total (millions)
Gross fixed capital formation, 1957–1963	42.3	57.7	254.8
1st National Development Plan, 1962–68	56.4	43.6	2,366.6
2nd National Development Plan, 1970–74	54.8	45.2	3,608.0
3rd National Development Plan, 1975–80	71.9	28.1	45,730.0
4th National Development Plan, 1981–85	86.0	14.0	82,000.0

Sources: *Economic Indicators* Vol. 2, No. 11 (Lagos: Federal Office of Statistics, 1965); Government Plan Documents (1962–1985). Extracted from Dele Olowu, "State-Level Governments and the Development Process." In E. L. Inanga, (ed.) *Managing Nigeria's Economic System* (Ibadan: Heinemann, 1985), p. 49.

We may thus state the causes of the overall failure of the public service reforms in Nigeria generally. The competition between the political and administrative class for relative power advantage is an intense one. Under military rule or unstable leadership, the power of the administrative class increases. In such a situation, it is only natural that in seeking the national interest public servants also seek their own interest as well (Adebayo 1986; Olowu 1987).

Conclusion

What emerges from our discussion of the trends and dynamics of administrative change in West Africa can be summarized. In spite of its wide diversity, the West African subregion is relatively poor, both in terms of economic growth and the quality of life of its people. There has also been a
growing convergence in terms of administrative practices, innovations, and
changes. The response of all the governments in the region initially, especially in the years following independence, was to expand and attempt to
reinvigorate the bureaucracy so that it might be transformed from a negative to a positive and catalytic institution as far as the development process.
The extent to which any government could attempt this depended heavily
on the resources available to it.

In more recent years, especially given the very dismal performance of
African economies (due not only to domestic factors), governments have
started to reconsider the appropriateness of this basically bureaucratic approach to development. Aided by multilateral aid-giving organizations,
such as the World Bank and the International Monetary Fund, and other
international interests, several West African governments (like their other
counterparts in Africa) have already started to experiment with a policy
exactly the opposite of the one they started with—one of debureaucratization and privatization.

The Nigerian case study gave further insight in support of the fact that
internal factors alone did not determine the range and nature of policy
changes. There are also important inputs from the international arena,
especially from the mother country. Yet this is not peculiar to Nigeria.
Michael Cohen also notes that in Francophone Africa (which is mainly in
West Africa), governments have started to adopt privatization innovations
partly at the urging of French firms, and that some of the urban innovations such as regional/spatial planning authorities, creation of population
districts, and use of interministerial commissions to coordinate urban development efforts are patterned after the French model (Adebayo 1986;
Olowu 1987). Similarly, it was the American consulting company of Mc-
Kinsey Incorporated that designed the decentralization reform for socialist
Tanzania.

But administrative reform is about power redistribution. There is thus
a need to be more keenly aware of the political nature of the public service,
both in terms of its own internal structure and its relationship to other
social subsystems. The idea that the public service should play a significant,
if not a dominant, role in the political economy of a new state would seem
an inevitable though not an ideal measure. But the Nigerian example dram-
atizes the unforeseen and unfortunate effects of bureaucratic expansionism

without a generally accepted supporting public service morality amongst public officials who are clothed with power.

West African public administration, like others that evolved out of a colonial past, is still basically despotic and authoritarian in its character and relationship with the people it is supposed to serve. Any attempt to improve the public service by making more resources available to it (including the power of control) only strengthens this despotic character. What is required in thinking of public sector reform, therefore, would seem to transcend the public service per se to the stimulation and creation of a range of organizations, public and private, through which the public service could be made to effectively serve its public.

The real thrust of future reform efforts should be to integrate the efforts of the central government with locally organized activities, especially in the rural areas far away from the cities where central government activities are concentrated. For this to occur, however, major political reforms might be necessary that will enable the rural local people to make more effective demands on the central government bureaucracy than they do at present.

References

Adamolekun; Olowu, Dele; and Laleye, O. M., eds. *Local Government in West Africa: Developments Since Independence.* Lagos: Lagos University Press, 1984.

Adebayo, A. *Principles and Practice of Public Administration in Nigeria.* Chichester: John Wiley, 1986.

Balogun, M. V. *Public Administration: A Developmental Approach.* London: Macmillan, 1983.

Burke, F. G. "Public Administration in Africa: The Legacy of Inherited Colonial Institutions." *Journal of Comparative Administration* 1, no. 3 (Nov. 1969):345–78.

Dunn, John. *West African States.* Cambridge: Cambridge University Press, 1978.

Ferkis, Victor. "The Role of the Public Services in Nigeria and Ghana." In *Papers in Comparative Administration.* Edited by F. Heady and S. L. Stokes. Ann Arbor: University of Michigan, 1962, p. 173–81.

Mazrui, Ali A. "Francophone Nations and English-Speaking States: Imperial Ethnicity and African Political Formations." In *State Versus Ethnic Claims: African Policy Dilemmas.* Edited by Donald Rothchild and Victor Olorunsola. Boulder, Colo.: Westview Press, 1983, p. 25–43.

Olowu, Dele. *The Nigerian Federal System.* Ibadan: Evans Press, 1987.

Riggs, Fred. *Bureaucracy and Development Administration.* Occasional Paper. Washington, D.C.: American Society for Public Administration, 1977.

Rothchild, Donald. "State-Ethnic Relations in Middle Africa." In *African Independence: The First Twenty-Five Years.* Edited by G. Carter and P. O'Meara. Bloomington: Indiana University Press, 1985.

Rweyemamu, A. H., and Hyden, Goran. *A Decade of Public Administration in Africa.* Nairobi: East African Literature Bureau, 1975, part 1.

Stewart, Frances. *Basic Needs in Developing Countries.* Baltimore: Johns Hopkins University Press, 1985.

West Africa. "Ivory Coast: Coping with the Crisis." 7 Jan. 1985.

World Bank. *Accelerated Development in Subsaharan Africa: An Agenda for Action.* Washington, D.C.: World Bank, 1981, p. 39.

Young, Crawford. *Ideology and Development in Africa.* New Haven: Yale University Press, 1982.

Zolberg, A. *Creating Political Order: The Party States of West Africa.* Chicago: Rand McNally, 1966.

6

Adaptation and Innovation in Australian Public Administration

ROSS CURNOW and **ROGER WETTENHALL**

Introduction

Isolating the unique features of Australian public administration is difficult. Given the ubiquity of the bureaucratic form of administration, there is a certain sameness about the craft of government and the conduct of public affairs whether the location be the continent of Europe, North America or Australia. Yet there are also differences between Munich, Minnesota and Melbourne in the style or "culture" of administration – differences that often owe their origins as much to folklore as to rigorous analysis.

Australian institutions reflect their historical origins. The various colonies which federated in 1901 – New South Wales, Victoria, Queensland, South Australia, Western Australia and Tasmania – all had been founded by Britain and from the 1850s onwards were bequeathed the basic pattern of responsible parliamentary government. This Westminster model is still recognizable, despite indigenous modifications. Yet when the various colonies joined together to transfer certain of their functions, such as defense, customs, immigration and communications, and sections of their public services to the new Commonwealth government, these arrangements were enshrined in a written constitution that borrowed from the U.S., Canada and Switzerland. Thus emerged the crude and somewhat misleading summation of Australian government as an amalgam of the British and American systems along with one of the clichés of Australian political and administrative culture, namely that our structures and processes are derivative; that we lack the capacity to innovate and rely heavily on imitation and adaptation.

Unfortunately, clichés — like proverbs — often come in contradictory pairs. There is at least one area where some originality and initiative are implied, namely the peculiar role of the state. This pervasive thread in our tapestry of administrative culture is interwoven in various forms: our talent for bureaucracy (Davies 1958, p. 1), the state as a vast public utility (Hancock 1930, p. 61), our penchant for creating "organs of syndical satisfaction" (Miller 1954, p. 110–18), the historical importance of government from the very foundation of the colony (Connell and Irving 1980, p. 31–32), our search for equality (Encel 1970, p. 58–79) and so on. It is certainly true that government has played a key role from the earliest days; indeed Australia was established and initially administered by the British as a penal settlement, with commercial, strategic or religious considerations playing a less overt role than was the case in most other colonial ventures. Gradually, with the abolition of transportation, the establishment of representative and responsible institutions, the discovery of gold and the growth of agriculture and commercial interests, the relative size of the public sector declined. But that did not prevent a robust enthusiasm in the second half of the nineteenth century for the state taking a key developmental role. "Colonial socialism" or "le socialisme sans doctrines" (Butlin 1959, p. 26–78; Metin 1901) paid less attention to ideological fervor than to pragmatism; if the state alone had the resources to provide the necessary infrastructure, then so be it. The public corporation became the favorite administrative device for operating public enterprise; industrial disputes were settled by quasi-judicial commissions, not by collective bargaining; and, even if bureaucracy by its nature is authoritarian, its universal standards go some way in providing equality of treatment.

The problem when discussing the past 15–20 years, which is the main object of this chapter, is that the supposed unique features of Australian public administration may not be as unique as they once were. On some counts the size of the public sector in Australia is relatively small. For instance, recent Organization for Economic Co-operation and Development (OECD) figures showed Australia ranking 18th out of 22 countries in terms of general government spending as a percentage of gross domestic product (Saunders and Klau 1985).

Similarly, notwithstanding media claims, the size of the government work force in Australia is no more inflated than in comparable countries (approximately one-quarter of the work force). Even when one looks at the functions or activities undertaken by the government the matter is far from clear; with the complex and convoluted arrangements that now exist in most countries between the "public" and "private" sectors, disentangling what is and is not a governmental activity is not an easy task. However, a detailed treatment of these and other aspects of Australian administrative culture — particularly those involving the social and personal relationships of a society that allegedly places little emphasis on class—is well beyond the scope of this chapter. The imitation/initiation theme will be restricted to a consideration of general administrative reforms, the "new administrative law," the public enterprise—statutory authority sector, and decentralizing arrangements during the past two decades.

Administrative Reform

Public Service Inquiries

Administrative reform in Australia from colonial times has been characterized by waves of general inquiries that periodically sweep the public sector. The 1970s and early 1980s saw one such wave with only the state of Queensland seemingly unaffected by the swell.[1] A number of inter-related features were responsible for the establishment of these inquiries, including the election of reformist governments, most of which felt that the public bureaucracy was either unwilling or unable to implement new programs. Also of importance were the "mood of the times" and what might be called the "measles theory" of change, which is the likelihood of any development in one state spreading across its borders to others.

The scope and methods of these inquiries varied, as did the recommendations and their implementation. Table 6.1 gives a simplified summary of the format of the inquiries, but the remainder of this section will center on the themes that emerged from the recommendations and their implementation, before moving to the next set of inquiries that led to dramatic changes—at least in the Australian context—in administrative law.

The attention paid to these more formal methods of administrative reform is not to suggest that the contributions of individual politicians and administrators have been negligible; indeed, in some cases they have been substantial for the reason that their executive actions have not been subject to the same degree of public debate and challenge as the recommendations of a commission.

None of the inquiries has abandoned the "old-fashioned" theories of economy or efficiency in its report, but the preferred methods have differed. Some have centered on structural/functional questions such as the number, size and activities of departments and statutory corporations and have engaged in what is pejoratively called "bureau-shuffling." More pretentiously, much the same activity has been dubbed "managerial corporate-

---

1. This chapter was written in 1987 before the appointment of the Fitzgerald Inquiry into political and administrative corruption in Queensland.

planning type reforms." Others have stressed equal employment opportunity, affirmative action, industrial democracy and participative management as the route to efficiency, while some have embraced a range of plausible techniques, irrespective of whether or not they form a consistent package.

Most reports have been concerned with bureaucratic power, and particularly with making public bodies more responsible and responsive to the government of the day. The means for so doing have centered on accountable management, program budgeting, cost-benefit analysis and other such "rational" techniques as well as on bolstering the minister's position with the appointment of advisers and consultants.

In addition to these broad-ranging reviews, there have also been a number of single-issue inquiries. The most common have been of the "razor-gang" variety, established to reduce government expenditure, generally by eliminating activities or functions. Others have dealt with promotion appeals and related personnel matters.

Taken together, what has been the impact of these inquiries? Disentangling their effects on administrative reform from the contributions of other factors is not possible; they were both partial causes and partial consequences of the mood of the times. At least it can be said that they reinforced or gave an extra push to contemplated changes, particularly in the fields of accountability and administrative scrutiny, and equal employment opportunity and affirmative action.

Accountability and Scrutiny

The public services at all levels — federal, state and local — are now much more "managerialist." The language of corporate and strategic planning, priorities, program evaluation, efficiency audits and performance review is common currency. There are, however, many variations on this theme. Thus, for example, in the state of Victoria, "policy formulation and direction, firm overall control and accountability now rest with the ministry, with operating functions hived off to agencies" (Holmes 1984, p. 106–7) and ministers are seen as executive directors, not chairmen of boards. In the Commonwealth public service heavy emphasis is placed upon management training, while in New South Wales there were, for a time, at least four different bodies carrying out similar reviews of administrative performance.

Many of these developments in the area of accountability and review are tied to budgets and expenditure. The current orthodoxy was epitomized by a recent Commonwealth discussion paper on budget reform, which emphasized a ministerial "strategy review" of politics and priorities to set the

TABLE 6.1. Inquiries

	Committee of Inquiry into the Public Service of South Australia (Chairman: Professor D. C. Corbett)	Board of Inquiry into the Victorian Public Service (Chairman: Sir Henry Bland)	Royal Commission on Australian Government Administration (Chairman: Dr. H. C. Coombs)	New South Wales Machinery of Government Review (Chairman: Hon. T. J. Lewis; Hon. F. M. Hewitt)	Review of New South Wales Government Administration (Professor P. S. Wilenski)	Review of Tasmanian Government Administration (Stage I: Task Forces; Stage II: Chairman: Sir George Cartland)
	May 1973–April 1975	October 1973–October 1975	June 1974–July 1976	July 1974–April 1976	February 1977–February 1982	May 1978–December 1981
Characteristics						
Composition	Committee	Single member	Committee	Committees	Single member	Stage I: Committees Stage II: Single member
Background	Academic; public servant; businessman	Public servant	5 members combining academe, public service, and industrial relations	Various committees, mainly ministers but some public servants and businessmen	Academic (formerly public servant)	Stage I: Public Servants Stage II: Academic (formerly colonial administrator)
Terms of Reference General/specific	General	4 inquiries: 1 general, 3 specific	General	Specific	General	Stage I: Specific Stage II: General
Recommendations (Major thrusts)						
Efficiency	X	X	X	X	X	X
Effectiveness	X	X	X		X	X
Accountability to						
Ministers	X	X	X	X	X	X
Public		X	X		X	X
Central authorities		X				

TABLE 6.1. Inquiries (Continued)

	Committee of Inquiry into the Public Service of South Australia (Chairman: Professor D. C. Corbett)	Board of Inquiry into the Victorian Public Service (Chairman: Sir Henry Bland)	Royal Commission on Australian Government Administration (Chairman: Dr. H. C. Coombs)	New South Wales Machinery of Government Review (Chairman: Hon. T. J. Lewis; Hon. F. M. Hewitt)	Review of New South Wales Government Administration (Professor P. S. Wilenski)	Review of Tasmanian Government Administration (Stage I: Task Forces; Stage II: Chairman: Sir George Cartland)
	May 1973–April 1975	October 1973–October 1975	June 1974–July 1976	July 1974–April 1976	February 1977–February 1982	May 1978–December 1981
Access/participation						
Public	X		X			
Public servants (industrial democracy)	X				X	
Equity						
EEO	X		X		X	
Representative bureaucracy			X		X	
Restructuring						
Machinery of government	X	X	X		X	X
Internal organizational	X	X	X	X	X	X
Career service		X				X
Administrative Reform Dimensions[a]						
Time perspective	Medium-term	Short-term	Medium-term	Short-term	Medium-term	Short-term
Risk acceptability	Low	Low	Low	Low	Medium	Medium
Incrementalism vs. innovation	Incremental	Innovative (in Victorian context)	Incremental	Incremental	Innovative (in New South Wales context)	Innovative (in Tasmanian context)
Balance vs. shock-oriented	Balance	Shock	Balance	Balance	Shock	Shock
Comprehensiveness vs. narrowness	Comprehensive	Narrow	Comprehensive	Narrow	Comprehensive	Narrow
Implementation	High	Medium	Medium	High	Medium	Medium

[a]Based mainly on Dror in Leemans, 1976: p. 126–41.

"broad framework" for the budget, integration of human resource and financial budgeting, and "an improved information base for parliamentary and public scrutiny of the budget and expenditure programs" (Minister for Finance 1984).

A number of moves in the accountability area have been designed to integrate ministers and public servants in the policy-making process, or at least strengthen the hand of ministers. Cabinet subcommittees covering various policy areas have public servants in attendance or acting as influential secretaries to the subcommittees. The role of premier's departments in some states has been upgraded from that of "post office" to provision of policy advice and coordination, as was the Commonwealth Department of Prime Minister and Cabinet under the Fraser Governments of 1975–1983. But policy advice is also provided by ministerial advisers, now a feature of Australian public administration accepted by the major political parties. As James Walter's recent study of federal political "minders" concluded:

> Personal advisers are a third force alongside the politicians and bureaucrats. They are part of the collective process of decision-making, and to understand that process all of its participants must be understood. The ministerial staff structure is now an institutional fact of Australian politics. But political executives everywhere will continue to need such assistance: it is a consequence of the complex demands on political leadership of modern society (Walter 1986, p. 187–88).

We return to this "third force" in subsequent sections.

Nor has Parliament left accountability entirely to the executive. With scant regard for the traditional wisdom that the strong party discipline prevailing in Australia was incompatible with an effective committee system, the Senate (upper house) in the Commonwealth Parliament reasserted its identity partly by the establishment of committees that were concerned with both policy and scrutiny of the administration. Other parliaments, including their lower houses, have taken note of this development and ambitious back-benchers have seen chairmanship of a high-profile committee as a precursor to ministerial office.

At the time of writing, public sector management and accountability for the use of resources are being given even greater emphasis. A downturn in the economy has concentrated political and administrative minds on cuts, "streamlining" and leaner public services.

The concern with accountability and scrutiny has had its impact on the machinery of government. Committees of inquiry have been important here, as all have recommended or implied varying degrees of restructuring, but they alone do not explain the increased rate of reorganization evident during the past two decades. To quote one writer who has studied the proliferation of portfolios:

The 1970s witnessed an intensified period of portfolio multiplication, reflecting a new wave of policy initiatives, recognition of new groups in the community to be cultivated, new pressures affecting the machinery of public administration, new interactions between Commonwealth and State governments and— perhaps—a new concern with the display of attractive labels (Hughes 1984, p. 270–71).

When combined with the new administrative review bodies and the resilience of nondepartmental forms, the overall impression is one of increasing institutional complexity. While this may be the case if the relative stability of the 1950s is taken as the benchmark, it should be remembered that other periods in the history of Australian public administration have also experienced equivalent "revolutions" (as this phenomenon has been dubbed in England). No doubt during the period following responsible government Australian colonists felt that their governments were becoming more complex, but whether today's changes are relatively more so than those of the mid-nineteenth century is problematic. "Complexity" is no easier to define and measure than other common administrative terms such as hierarchy and specialization.

The Career Service Revisited

Some of the developments already discussed have questioned traditional notions of the Australian "career service," but none more so than in the areas of equity and access. In some public services reality fell little short of the ideal-typical career service, cogently summed up as follows:

In a career service, you start at the bottom; but once you're in, you're there for life. Your prospects aren't menaced by outsiders coming in later on. As you get older, you get more senior, and so you expect better jobs. Your first appointment is based on relevant qualifications and practical tests of your ability; your promotion is based on seniority, past performance and future promise in the work; both are outside the control of politicians. But you are in the service only to do what elected politicians want. When you are senior enough you can also advise the politicians. Because they can't control your job, you can give them advice that might be good for them—and the country—even though they mightn't like it. For example, you can suggest some things that they ought to want; or suggest that some of the things they do want are unwise, or could be better tackled in a different way, or are too hard altogether. The experience of your long career and the security of your job give you unmatched skill and detachment for advising politicians in all these ways. But the politician remains on top; the career service is simply the linchpin that holds firm the wheels of government, whatever speed or direction the politician chooses (Parker 1989, p. 382).

While these career public services may have been characterized by a high degree of probity, they were said to fall short on many other counts. In particular the political role of the career service caused concern. Ministers were no match for the professionalism and expertise of public servants whose position was bolstered by security of tenure. Perhaps this would not have mattered so much if their role in policy formulation and implementation had been "impartial," but as a self-perpetuating enclave of middle-class, white, Anglo-Saxon, protestant males, the predominant values of the upper echelons were essentially conservative. The "merit principle," claimed the critics, had been perverted to the detriment of women, ethnic groups and other minorities.

"In many ways the validity of competing claims about the career service mattered less than political perceptions of the situation" (Curnow 1989, p. 16); the career service was seen by reformers as neither responsible nor responsive. The solutions to these shortcomings were a dash of politicization and a large dose of equity and access.

Politicization can mean a number of things, but in the recent Australian context it is the appointment of ministerial advisers and partisan public service appointments that have been of major concern. The role of ministerial advisers has already been touched upon; it is worth noting here that at the federal level those who had assisted with policy development in opposition are now assisting with its implementation in government, thus suggesting a "ministerial bureaucracy." Further, contemporary advisers share with their predecessors, those who worked for the Whitlam and Fraser governments: "the characteristics of being mostly male, relatively young, highly educated and disproportionately from non-government schools. About half are from inside and half from outside the public service" (Walter 1984, p. 203). This is hardly a representative group. After some initial adjustments on both the part of the public service and the advisers, a modus vivendi has now been established and the institution of advisers and in some cases, consultants, is an accepted part of the machinery of government in the Commonwealth and a number of states.

The issue of partisan appointments to the public service proper is more contentious. Here the question centers on whether party affiliation is a necessary if not sufficient condition of appointment or promotion to the senior ranks. It is an area beset by innuendo and gossip, not amenable to rigorous analysis. In some public services it is uncertainty about the "rules of the game" that causes unease; while it is now generally accepted that the government has the right to appoint departmental heads rather than a central personnel agency, does the minister have the right to determine or even influence middle-management appointments? One view of the prevailing situation has been encapsulated by a political journalist as follows:

> In the old days you never asked a Public Servant about his politics and he wouldn't tell you if you did. These days have gone. The best way of advancement today for a young Public Servant is to publicly declare his or her politics and join a Party branch that will prove as vital to top level promotion as working well and hard.
>
> One of the most important career decisions that young Public Servants in the future will have to make, is which political party do they side with at what stage.
>
> Some of the Public Servants I've known I guess would be prudent enough to leave that decision until later in their careers, before jumping one way or the other, but the difficulty of that will be that you might miss out when the time comes. So it's a new complexity (Farmer 1986, p. 8).

As against this line there are certain structural changes to the public services either in train or in place, which should go some way in resolving the uncertainty surrounding senior appointments. A "Senior Executive Service" is now a reality in the Commonwealth and the State of Victoria, both having been influenced by the North American experience, although Victoria is closer to the U.S. model with its annual merit payments. The similarity in terminology, however, does not imply slavish imitation; the debate about the desirability of a separate category of senior officers has a long history, and the "Second Division" of the Commonwealth Public Service had for some time been a de facto senior executive service.

The politicization issue is not confined to the public service. The boards and commissions of statutory corporations and other "fringe bodies," as we shall see later, form the bulk of the public sector in terms of staff numbers, and have always offered wide scope for political patronage. A rewarding study could be undertaken of the "pluralists" and "spiralists" who cumulate such offices (Mackenzie 1981).

While politicization is seen by many as weakening the career service, other reforms are said to be strengthening it. Australia was no less affected by debates about the position of women, ethnics, aboriginals and homosexuals than other countries, and the public sector has been the pacesetter in granting access to such groups in the way that it has been used as a vehicle for social reform at other times in its history. Thus efforts have been made to achieve a more "representative" bureaucracy, especially at the senior levels, and equal employment opportunity and affirmative action programs are widespread. Such efforts have had some success and there is evidence to show that disadvantaged groups are in fact moving into senior positions. But again the process has not been without its critics. Most of the debate centers on whether or not reverse discrimination is occurring: are "targets" actually de facto "quotas"?; has merit now been redefined to favor the disadvantaged?; and so on. There is no more likelihood of resolving this issue in a scholarly fashion than in settling the politicization question "scientifically."

Once more we are on safer ground talking about the institutionalization of the mechanisms to achieve equity and social justice in the public sector. To take the State of New South Wales as an example, the field is embraced by bodies such as an Equal Opportunity Tribunal, an Anti-Discrimination Board, a Director of Equal Opportunity in Public Employment, Equal Employment Opportunity Coordinators who have been appointed to many organizations, as well as groups that have specific interests such as the Ethnic Affairs Commission, Women's Coordination Unit, Ministry of Aboriginal Affairs, and so on. The area has become a specialized field of personnel administration, within which a career is possible. "In terms of administrative reform, this 'bureaucratisation' should go a long way to ensuring its success if the cliches about self-interest and the difficulty of dismantling public bodies are correct. Further, commitment to equal employment opportunity is now a factor in appointment to or promotion in many public services" (Curnow 1989, p. 25).

However, there are signs that social and equity considerations may be yielding their place on the reform agenda to the creed of managerialism. Public Service Boards have been abolished in the Commonwealth and in all states except Victoria.

One general conclusion that can be drawn from the career service reforms is that a career in the public sector no longer implies a lifetime in the one organization, or indeed a lifetime within the public sector itself. "Lateral recruitment" has seen movement mainly among Commonwealth and state governments and academe and between departments and statutory corporations. Relatively little has occurred between the public and private sectors. One reason for this may be because of the public sector's negative image, a stereotype occasioned as much by the cost of government in difficult economic times as by rational perception. This may not bring much comfort to those who have argued that the public service should import managerial skills from the private sector, but it will please those who believe that management in the public sector is different, and that private sector values are as likely to corrupt as to improve.

The "New Administrative Law"

Administrative Review and the New Administrative Law

In terms of implementation, the "new administrative law" is the success story of the past decade. This package of reforms, described as "bold and imaginative" (Griffiths 1985, p. 445) has greatly widened the scope of administrative review.

Until the 1970s, any external review of administrative decisions was essentially limited to the minister or to a handful of administrative tribunals in fields such as taxation or veterans' affairs. Redress through the courts could be costly and risky, and coming to grips with the legal niceties of natural justice or the prerogative writs was a daunting task even for the cognoscenti.

Thus the Ombudsman, that most successful of administrative transplants, was welcomed as a cheap and humane way of obtaining redress of administrative wrongs. Encouraged by New Zealand's promising experiment with the Scandinavian institution in the Westminster setting in the 1960s, Western Australia was the first of the Australian states to do likewise in 1971. Since then the remaining states and the Commonwealth have all followed suit. Although the institution is no longer regarded as novel, there are still lively disputes about the extent of the Ombudsman's powers. Often these center on what constitutes the "political" (and hence ministerial) sphere as against the "administrative," accepted as the legitimate concern of the Ombudsman.

Similarly, freedom of information legislation owes its existence partly to Swedish and American precedents. As part of its commitment to open government, the Whitlam government in the early 1970s foreshadowed a Freedom of Information Act, but it was not until December 1982 that legislation was passed. Proponents of freedom of information were critical of its limited scope, but it has proved useful in particular to those seeking access to their personal files. Such access is generally granted without charge (although fees are levied for "business" applications) but at an average cost of $900 per request, this sum is now being weighed against its benefits. Two other states have also passed freedom of information acts; others are hastening slowly.

Continental and United Kingdom practice in administrative law had some influence on the most radical of developments in the Australian context, namely the creation of the Commonwealth Administrative Appeals Tribunal. This general appeals body has the power to set aside an administrative decision and to substitute its own decision in areas such as social security, customs, immigration, air navigation, postal bylaws and freedom of information. Such review on the merits is sometimes on appeal from other, more-specialized tribunals. Although the Administrative Appeals Tribunal is "flexible" in its procedures, and is supposed to function with a minimum of formality and technicality, its full-time members are all drawn from the legal profession— either federal court judges or lawyers—while its part-time members, who sit as required, are "technical" experts in particular fields. On questions of law, a further appeal from a decision of the

Tribunal may be made to the Federal Court of Australia.

This whole question of the legality of administrative action is covered by the Administrative Decisions (Judicial Review) Act of 1980. In addition to simplifying the procedure for obtaining judicial review and conferring jurisdiction on the Federal Court of Australia, it also provides that any individual adversely affected by an administrative decision should be given reasons for that decision; thus it has been described as lowering "a narrow bridge over the moat of executive silence" (*Minister for Immigration and Ethnic Affairs v Pochi* [1980] 31 ALR 666, 686). While the area of greatest use has been promotion and disciplinary decisions within the public service, customs, income tax and migration matters have also been prominent.

Finally, some mention should be made of the Administrative Review Council, an independent advisory body, which has general oversight of the processes of administrative review and which is the government's main source of external advice in the field. One of its major tasks is to ensure that the system develops on a rational basis: for example, whether all specialized review tribunals should be embraced within a uniform hierarchical system headed by the Administrative Appeals Tribunal or whether flexibility and independence are more appropriate.

The new administrative law has been seen as a revolution by the standards of Australian administrative reform, but it has been a bloodless revolution. Committees of inquiry that examined the public services as a whole caught the imagination of reformers during the 1970s, rather than the low-key committees that examined the field of administrative law, the nature and extent of administrative discretions and the prerogative writ procedures. But during the past five years, criticisms have emerged. In particular, the question of review on the merits has caused concern. Thus, for example, one eminent lawyer has argued that:

> in Australia, in recent years, great steps have been taken in the reform of administrative law and procedures. The aim is to give easier and more effective redress to citizens aggrieved by the acts (and omissions) of a vast and pervasive bureaucracy. It may be that some of the new powers assigned to review bodies in this area are too large, that the pendulum has swung too far in prescribing what is for the decision of the government and what for a reviewing body, be it a court or a special tribunal (Cowen 1983, p. 29).

By way of contrast, the Administrative Review Council has defended the Administrative Appeals Tribunal's power to substitute its decisions for certain of those of the minister and statutory bodies by quoting the Chief Justice of the High Court of Australia. When commenting on the Tribunal he observed that: "This is truly a fertile new province for the law and it is one to which the citizen can gain entry cheaply and easily. There are some who criticise this statute as going too far for the good of speedy and efficient administration, but it represents a bold experiment which has given general satisfaction" (Administrative Review Council, 1984–85, p. 43).

There are many other areas of contention, not least of which are the costs involved, especially when considered in relation to the benefits the new system provides. To its credit, the Administrative Review Council has sponsored research on this topic, which is no easier to quantify than many other areas of public policy. For example, consider the following statistics from the annual reports of the Administrative Review Council, which relate to the Administrative Appeals Tribunal for the past three years: number of cases now finalized each year, 2,000 (approximately); percentage of decisions affirmed, 12–17; percentage of decisions set aside and decisions substituted, 9–12; percentage of decisions varied by decision-maker, 33–40; and percentage of cases withdrawn by applicant, 22–26. Are these data evidence of the need for such a body; the "correctness" of the majority of administrative decisions; a substantial "gray" area in administrative decision making; or all three?

Other areas in dispute include whether or not primary decision-makers are now prone to take the "soft option," that is, a decision favorable to an applicant in order to avoid what can be a lengthy and enervating process of review. As against this line of argument, some claim that the quality of decision making has been enhanced dramatically within the public service, now that reasons for decisions may be required. It should also be added that the prospect of freedom of information legislation forced departments to systematize their procedural manuals, policy directives and other such documents and thus improve their records management. A more general issue is whether or not institutionalizing the new methods of administrative review and scrutiny has led to the creation of a parallel bureaucracy with overtones of a Byzantine form of administration. We shall return to this question in the conclusion.

Overseas Influences

Excluding developments in administrative law, it is difficult to pinpoint any of the recent reforms that do not have their counterparts overseas. Whether parallel developments indicate causality is another matter, although there is a fashionable line of argument that administrative (and other) developments in Australia follow from five to ten years after their appearance overseas. The cynical corollary adds that they are adopted in Australia at the same time as disenchantment is setting in elsewhere. Even in the second half of the nineteenth century, when Australia's isolation was exacerbated by primitive communications, some of the committees of inquiry went out of their way to obtain information about the public services of other countries, not merely Great Britain. Many of the contemporary inquiries have continued this tradition, and with both Australian and overseas politicians, public servants and academics attending conferences or embarking on study tours, and Australian high commissions and embassies reporting on administrative developments elsewhere, there is at least an awareness of numerous overseas systems. Some dismiss such systems as inappropriate to the Australian administrative milieu; others embrace particular developments with enthusiasm. During the 1970s, for example, the grass in Canada and Sweden seemed particularly green.

Only a detailed examination of workings of each of the committees and the implementation or otherwise of their recommendations would enable some sort of conclusion to be drawn about overseas influence, which can range from "inspiration" through local adaptation to slavish imitation. Nor should it be forgotten that the exchange is mutual; Australian developments, particularly in the field of administrative law and to a lesser extent ministerial staff, are of interest at least to other Commonwealth countries.

Even in the case of administrative law reforms the inspiration can be traced to an overseas investigation. In reviewing the Franks Committee, which traversed the ground in the United Kingdom, Mr. Justice Else-Mitchell called for the reform of administrative review procedures in Australia (Else-Mitchell 1965). But had not his suggestion been taken up by strategically placed individuals and had not a series of fortuitous circumstances prevailed, then the new administrative law may have been limited to the Ombudsman and freedom of information.

Public Enterprise and Statutory Authorities

Public enterprise is one area in which, in the development of its administrative culture, Australia can claim to have done much that is distinctive and innovative. It is here that the debate about the role of the state has played itself out most fully. The seeds of this particular development were sown way back in the beginnings of European settlement: the convict origins of most of the Australian colonies meant that, at the beginning, their major resource was government-supplied labor — the convicts themselves and their official "supervisors," both civil and military — and this resource was applied abundantly to the construction of the early public works, communications and agricultural infrastructure. After the transportation of convicts had ended, the new colonial/state governments discovered, against their laissez faire political and economic inclinations, that it was still the case that only government could marshall financial and manpower resources on the scale necessary to ensure development. So they borrowed money and recruited labor lavishly to push settlement out from the coastal towns and generally to extend all the infrastructure services.

These colonies thus began their journey towards statehood with much larger public enterprise networks than conventional Anglo-Saxon wisdom allowed for, and for half a century or more British observers were scandalized by this socialism at the periphery of the empire. Australians were, however, simply responding pragmatically to the demands of a harsh physical environment. Indeed, after 30 years or so of experience with rapidly enlarging public enterprises, particularly the state railway systems, they concluded that operation of such enterprises by ministerial/public service forms left much to be desired, and so turned in a distinctly managerialist direction. They innovated once again, producing an administrative revolution nearly as significant as the democratizing Westminster revolution. In this early post-Westminster stage, the emphasis would be on managerial authority and competence. For government-in-business, expert commissions would be placed in charge of the various enterprises, and instructed by their enabling statutes to run them mostly free of constraining civil service rules, and with ministerial control reduced to a small number of matters strictly defined in the statutes.

This transformation was radical when it occurred, and the Australian states were then following no overseas models. Administrative history reveals that spontaneous experimentation elsewhere soon demonstrated the need for similar solutions to the problem of government-in-business. There is evidence both that some Australian lessons were influential overseas (as in the creation of the Pacific Cable Board by the British parliament in 1901) and that later Australian legislation borrowed from overseas design (as in the modeling of the Australian Broadcasting Commission and Tasmania's Hydro-Electric Commission in part on the British Broadcasting Corporation and the Ontario Hydro-Electric Power Commission, respectively, as well as in the use of TVA-based argument in the creation of the Snowy Mountains Hydro-Electric Authority in 1949). All the Australian states and the Commonwealth have made great use of the statutory corporation device, and in the design of newer corporations there was borrowing both from early Australian examples and from overseas examples. Thus the themes of innovation and adaptation are closely interwoven in the public enterprise experience.

The statutory authority/corporation device has proved so popular with Australia's legislators that its use over the years has extended into areas outside the original public enterprise field. Many appellate and regulatory bodies have been accorded this form, as have bodies vested with the management of cultural, research and higher education activities (for example, all the nation's universities). With this proliferation, it has proved difficult to keep count of all the authorities in existence. One of the more comical features of Australian public administration over the past ten or fifteen years has been the attempt to establish a precise map of this authority sector. A Victorian parliamentary committee recently located more than 9,000 "public bodies" in that state, after early press estimates that it would find about 1,000 (PBRC 1981, p. vii); no other Australian government has made such extensive use of authorities as the Victorian, and yet we know that there are at least several hundred of them in each of the other six major jurisdictions.

Proliferation has had another important consequence. As the authority sector has become the major area of public employment (it employs about three-quarters of the nation's government officials) and a vast earner, investor, borrower and spender of funds, it has become harder and harder for governments to allow its constituent members — the individual corporations and authorities — the managerial autonomy that was originally the principal hallmark of their form of organization.

Looking over the whole sector, there are some authorities that perform well by commercial standards. It is one of the myths of Australian public enterprise that government enterprises never make profits: some do this consistently and handsomely. On the other hand, some are not managed well and there have been over the years a few dramatic public authority collapses. Some authority managements have simply shown insufficient recognition that they have to operate within a public sector environment; and without any doubt at all, others have been weakened or even ruined by hostile political, sometimes governmental, actions, both accidental and deliberate. The sector was so large, so diverse and so little understood that it was ripe for serious study when the (Coombs) Royal Commission on Australian (i.e., Commonwealth) Government Administration began its work in the mid-1970s.

This Royal Commission reported that there was need for caution in the creation of statutory authorities. However there was no doubt that they were justified in some areas and, when created, politicians and administrators needed to respect their separateness from the generality of government and treat them differently from departments. In particular, all ministerial directions to them should be in writing and reported to parliament in authority annual reports. There was also emphasis on these annual reports as a primary means of ensuring that authorities did account to the elected representatives of the people in parliament. The Royal Commission urged that firm guidelines should be drawn up to govern the use of authorities, but it did not attempt that task itself (RCAGA 1976, p. 81–95).

In the decade since the Royal Commission reported, this last recommendation has been taken seriously within the Australian administrative system. Study teams of one kind or another have been at work within government, within political parties and within parliaments. Particularly significant statements have emerged from the (Commonwealth) Senate's Standing Committee on Finance and Government Operations (SSCFGO 1979–82) and comparable committees of state legislatures (notably PAC/NSW 1983; PBRC 1980–81), and some reformative action has been taken. Most recently initiatives within the Commonwealth government have led to the production of sets of "proposed policy guidelines" for statutory authorities and government business enterprises generally and for commodity marketing boards in particular. Novelties in these papers include the new emphasis on corporate planning and on accountability to industry as well as to parliament and ministers—recognition of a notion of "dual accountability" given expression, in the Australian context, in reforms to the group of commodity marketing boards over the past few years (Department of Finance 1986; Department of Primary Industry 1986).

It is arguably no longer the case that the Australian public enterprise network is particularly large by comparison with other mixed-enterprise countries. As already indicated, recent OECD figures have ranked us 18th out of 22 countries in terms of general government spending as a percentage of gross domestic product. There has not, however, been any serious Australian mapping to show how that statistic relates to the actual number and size of government-owned businesses in the countries being compared. What is certain is that there has been contraction as well as expansion over the years in the list of specific Australian enterprises and their activities. Government shipping lines and bus lines have been sold as well as bought. Governments have disposed of their interests in mixed public-private enterprises in fields such as oil refining, wireless development and aluminum production. Government whaling and flax industries and coal mines have been sold. Branch railway lines have been closed, being replaced sometimes by publicly owned, sometimes by privately owned buses. The public-private mix has varied over time in metropolitan transit systems. Sometimes organizations themselves have undergone status-shifts, as when the private kindergarten union of South Australia won for itself statutory authority status (and therefore inclusion within the public sector) as a way of protecting and improving the service it offered. So the frontier between the public and private sectors is ever-shifting, even though Australia has scarcely experienced any successful acts of "nationalization" in the British or French fashion.

Of course such nationalization was long a plank of the Australian Labor Party's political platform, and a succession of leaders of the major non-Labor parties made electoral capital out of its very existence. It must surely be one of the great achievements of Gough Whitlam as Labor Prime Minister from 1972 to 1975 that he succeeded in emancipating his party from that millstone around its neck. Labor was thus assisted to move to the middle-of-the-road electorally, and in the 1980s we have observed its political opponents developing a hard-line attachment to an extreme policy of "privatization." To this end they have made much use of the word "quango," in its pejorative rather than literal sense: "beware—the quangoes are taking over," railed one conservative politician (Rae 1979). It is too early to judge whether this new policy will succeed electorally: the judgment that can be drawn at this point is that this shift is heavily influenced by overseas developments. Australian liberalism has hitherto shown considerable sympathy for state enterprise whenever it can be seen to be aiding development or contributing to general community wealth; indeed, the non-Labor parties have created most Australian public enterprises. That earlier stance has been characteristically and sometimes quite distinctively Australian. Now, to counter Labor's new middle-ground approach, the Liberals and their political allies veer hard-right and promise to withdraw the state from much public sector activity. Their gurus have become Margaret Thatcher, the Adam Smith Institute of London, and others of like mind from Britain and North America. They have moved to a borrowed rather than distinctively Australian position. The question remains: will the Australian electorate buy that shift? (What is most surprising in the later 1980s is that, at least at the federal level, Labor's right-wing leadership also has become infected with thoughts of privatization.)

Decentralization

In comparing the Australian government with that of other nation-states, it is customary to focus on institutions of the Commonwealth (or federal) government, and this chapter has mostly followed suit. From what has already been said, however, it will be apparent that *in this federation* the state governments had historical priority. All six of them were, in the late nineteenth century, embryo nations in their own right, and in that time (and sometimes even later) they adopted the adjective "national" for some of their own institutions. When eventually they decided to federate, it was as though they were delegating some of their powers, for mutual benefit, to a new common government, but one strictly delimited in its own powers. The six state constitutions remained in force. The new constitution fashioned for the Commonwealth government carefully specified the functions that were being transferred: all residual, or unspecified, functions remained with the states. This federal constitution provided for its own amendment by referendum process, and to this day few amendments proposing expansion of Commonwealth government powers have gained the necessary majorities.

That the Commonwealth government has grown substantially in the number of its functions and institutions cannot be denied. This has happened mostly, however, because it has moved to a position of financial dominance in the federation: it gained an effective monopoly of income taxes as a war measure in the 1940s, and that shift has not since been reversed. From time to time High Court decisions on jurisdictional disputes have been favorable to the expansion of Commonwealth powers. The states now acquire most of their revenue by transfer from the Commonwealth, and the price the Commonwealth has exacted is often one of supervision of spending and checking of administration. So increasingly the Commonwealth has established institutions in areas constitutionally reserved for the states. And, needing the revenues, the states have rarely resisted.

The Australian Labor Party was long theoretically committed to the abolition of the states and the introduction of a unitary system of government. But all the political parties are themselves federal structures, and they too generally support maintenance of a system of strong states as managers of the major regions and defenders of their interests. The Labor Party itself has moved away from its early position, and the states remain powerful actors in the Australian political system. There have been occasional movements for the creation of new states by splitting off parts of original states, or for the establishment by federal action of a tier of regional governments within states, but they have come to nothing. The prevailing state system appears robust, so that such radical challenges to the status quo appear to have little chance of success.

The states have of course decentralized within their own boundaries. Before federation, each of them had established its own local government system, and as these systems filled out in the early years of the twentieth century the number of local governments across the six states (variously styled cities, towns, boroughs, municipalities, districts and shires) grew to almost 1,000. There were also, in New South Wales, county councils administering some services over the territories of several base-level authorities. As the outcomes of state legislative action, these local authorities were always comparatively weak, and some state governments have intervened frequently in their affairs. Mid-nineteenth century efforts to introduce the English pattern of local government had failed: the systems that emerged certainly borrowed something from English municipal practice, but there was much that was distinctively Australian about them. Until the early 1970s, the Commonwealth government had never taken much interest in local government, but all that changed with the election of the Whitlam Labor government at the end of 1972.

When the government was dismissed three years later, federal funds were flowing directly to local government, the Commonwealth was actively involved in improving the quality of local government personnel, local government had gained representation in constitutional conventions, it was participating in federally sponsored "regional organizations of councils," and so on. While the incoming Fraser Liberal-National Coalition government did not share all the reforming impulses of its predecessor, some of the changes endured. Intergovernmental relations (IGR) in Australia had been transformed from a two-point (Commonwealth-state and state-local) to a three-point (Commonwealth-state, state-local, Commonwealth-local) process.

In many service-delivery areas, moreover, Commonwealth and state departments and authorities were establishing their own networks of field offices throughout the nation, scarcely connecting with each other, and connecting even less with the established network of local governments. The governmental map had become a representation of conflicting areas and ill-coordinated institutions. Advocates of regional-level solutions sought to remedy this situation but, as already noted, they had little success. There have also been several state-initiated efforts to reduce the number of separate local governments by amalgamation, but until recently—except for a few notable cases such as the creation by amalgamation of the City of Greater Brisbane in 1925—they also have had little success. More recently many New South Wales towns have been united with their rural hinterlands, previously administered by separate shire councils. The number of local governments has thus been reduced to 835 in the mid-1980s.

Since early in the federal period, two parts of the Australian mainland have stood apart from the prevailing pattern of state and local government. These are the internal federal territories, the Northern Territory and the Australian Capital Territory, transferred to the Commonwealth in 1911 from South Australia and New South Wales, respectively. Both came to be administered by departments of the Commonwealth public service, subject to retention of state servicing in a few areas (notably education). In 1978, however, the Northern Territory was advanced to self-government by legislation of the Commonwealth parliament, and it now exercises most of the powers of the original states. Among other things, it is in the process of creating its own local government system. There has been agitation to confer a similar measure of self-government on the Australian Capital Territory (ACT), and the Hawke Government introduced legislation to create a governing ACT Council in 1986. That was, however, opposed in the parliament both because it involved an electoral system likely to favor the Labor Party and because the "government" envisaged would have been a very weak one. At the time of writing, the bill has been withdrawn. The ACT's situation is often likened to that of federal capitals situated in separate national territories (like Washington, D.C.), and contrasted with that of others located within the territories of constituent federal states (like Ottawa and Bonn). Whether the national interest should deprive residents of the first group of federal capitals, but not the second, of normal political and administrative rights and obligations is a moot point indeed.

Would-be reformers in Australia often join observers from unitary systems in lamenting the complexities of Australian government. Whether those complexities are more apparent than real, it is, however, a nice debating point. Once more, those OECD figures do not suggest that we are overgoverned in comparison with other OECD members. Our outlying states have some powerful defenses against the center. Our system allows, one way or another, a variety of political parties to participate in government; it also allows a degree of policy innovation and experimentation that might not be achieved under a unitary constitution. As supporters of federal systems argue, one of the great advantages of these systems is the hindrances they place in the way of aspiring central despots: pluralist values, diversity and regional interests alike do better under such systems.

Moreover federalism has provided administrative challenges to which Australia has responded in inventive fashion: if the political map has scarcely changed since federation, that cannot be said of the apparatus of administrative institutions involved in governing the federal nation. There has been rich experimentation in this area, and a lush growth of "lubricating" institutions (Wettenhall 1985), ranging from the Commonwealth Grants Commission, established in 1933, whose current task is to give equalizing grants to the smaller and financially weaker state and local governments, through two score ministerial councils bringing together ministers with similar portfolio interests (but often different political colors) and their supporting committees of officials, to intergovernmental agencies representative of two or more concerned governments and administering on a collective basis a wide range of services such as river valley development, hydro-electric power generation, border-straddling urban development, coal mining regulation, crime statistics and rail and road research. Capping them all for several years was the special body established to monitor the whole IGR process, the Advisory Council on Inter-Government Relations, on which Australian local governments were represented as well as the Commonwealth and state governments. (That it had been abandoned during 1986 after inquiry by a closed committee of cost-conscious bureaucrats does Australian public administration no credit.) Other federations necessarily demonstrate a similar interest in this IGR process, and again there has been much exchanging of ideas. Manifestly, however, this is another area in which Australian public administration has innovated.

Conclusion

During the past two decades in Australia the concerns with accountability, equality and access have coexisted uneasily with the push for economy and the careful husbandry of resources. Institutionalizing the processes by which administrative decisions are reviewed and by which the public sector has been "opened up" to disadvantaged groups has been costly, worthy though these concerns are. At the time of writing, this tension between cost and desirability has been exacerbated by a marked downturn in the economy, which has given new urgency to the rhetoric of "streamlining," "slashbacks," "privatization" and the like.

The increasing complexity of the government machine – or at least the increasing number of institutions – is due not merely to the "quality of life" functions now undertaken by governments, but also to the growth of these specialized scrutinizing bodies. The Weberian point about escaping from one bureaucracy only by creating another holds true in the contemporary Australian context, and with various bureaucracies checking on one another it is difficult not to draw on the analogy of Byzantine administration to analyze recent developments.

It will also be interesting to see whether lawyers continue to play an increasing role in Australian public administration. More and more decisions are seen as "justiciable" – an attitude encapsulated in the comment of a university administrator that the greatest change during the past 20 years has been the shift from "what do I need to do to be eligible?" to "to whom do I appeal?". To date, no one professional group has dominated the upper echelons of Australian public administration and it may be that the legal profession will feature most prominently only in the areas of scrutiny and review.

Judicial administration has recently gained prominence for reasons other than the new administrative law. Allegations of corruption in this area have increased, and convictions of police and certain judicial officers have come as a sharp reminder that probity in public affairs cannot be taken for granted. Other areas of public policy have also produced instances of official behavior falling below the accepted norms, although by international standards Australian public administration stands high in terms of integrity.

In so many ways debates about corruption, patronage, politicization, an "overstaffed" and inefficient public sector and the like are reminiscent of the concerns of 100–150 years ago. While there is a sense of the wheel turning full circle, the context of the debates has differed. Political patronage in the nineteenth century setting of factional politics, for instance, differed in various ways from patronage in the current two (or two and a half) Australian party system. Similarly, indigenous and expatriate influences are still in evidence, but are now even more difficult to disentangle, especially as the expatriate elements are more cosmopolitan. To conclude with a gastronomic analogy, we may think of this as the "modified Cornish pasty" theory of administrative transplants. For the Cornish miners of the nineteenth century the cold, half-moon pasty with essentially potato filling provided a meal to be eaten underground. In Australia, the shape remained, but the filling included meat and various vegetables, generally served hot. Nowadays, more exotic fillings reflect influences other than British, and the term "Cornish" is problematic. Alongside such local adaptations of British institutions are the "all-Australian" meat pie and American hamburger. Critics of our federal administrative system find this an indigestible repast; others savor the diversity of tastes.

References

Administrative Review Council. *Eighth Annual Report.* Canberra: Australian Government Publishing Service, 1983–1984.

Butlin, N. G. "Colonial Socialism in Australia." In *The State and Economic Growth.* Edited by H. G. J. Aitken. New York: Social Science Research Council, 1959.

Connell, R. W., and Irving, T. H. *Class Structure in Australian History.* Melbourne: Longman Cheshire, 1980.

Cowen, Z. *The Virginia Lectures.* Canberra: Sir Robert Menzies Memorial Trust, 1983.

Curnow, G. R. "The Career Service Debate." In *Politicization and the Career Service.* Edited by G. R. Curnow and B. Page. Canberra: University of Canberra and Royal Australian Institute of Public Administration, 1989.

Davies, A. F. *Australian Democracy.* Melbourne: Longman Green, 1958.

Department of Finance. *Statutory Authorities and Government Business Enterprises.* Canberra: Australian Government Publishing Service, 1986.

Department of Primary Industry. *Reform of Commonwealth Primary Industry Marketing Authorities.* Canberra: Australian Government Publishing Service, 1986.

Dror, Y. "Strategies for Administrative Reform." In *The Management of Change in Government.* Edited by A. F. Leemans. The Hague: Martinus Nijhoff, 1976.

Else-Mitchell, R. "The Place of the Administrative Tribunal in 1965." Paper delivered to the Commonwealth and Empire Law Conference, Sydney, 1965.

Encel, S. *Equality and Authority.* Melbourne: Cheshire, 1970.

Farmer, R. "The Media and the Public Sector." *Australian Administration* 1 (Winter 1986):7–10.

Griffiths, J. "Australian Administrative Law: Institutions, Reforms and Impact." *Public Administration* 63 (Winter 1985):445–63.

Hancock, W. K. *Australia.* London: Benn, 1930.

Holmes, J. "Victorian Statutory Corporations in the 1980s." *Australian Journal of Public Administration* 43 (June 1984):103–11.

Hughes, C. A. "The Proliferation of Portfolios." *Australian Journal of Public Administration* 43 (Sept. 1984):257–74.

Mackenzie, W. J. M. "Quangos, Networks, Pluralists, Spiralists, Commentators." In *Understanding Public Administration.* Edited by G. R. Curnow and R. L. Wettenhall. Sydney: George Allen and Unwin, 1981.

Metin, A. *Le Socialisme sans Doctrines.* Paris: Felix Alcan, 1901.

Miller, J. D. B. *Australian Government and Politics.* London: Duckworth, 1954.

Minister for Finance. *Budget Reform.* Canberra: Australian Government Publishing Service, 1984.

PAC/NSW (Public Accounts Committee of New South Wales). *Report on the Accounting and Reporting Requirements of Statutory Authorities.* Sydney: Government Printing Office, 1983.

Parker, R. S. "The Politics of Bureaucracy." In *Politicization and the Career Service.* Edited by G. R. Curnow and B. Page. Canberra: University of Canberra and Royal Australian Institute of Public Administration, 1989.

PBRC (Public Bodies Review Committee, Victoria). *Third Report to the Parliament: Auditing and Reporting of Public Bodies.* Melbourne: Government Printer, 1981.

Rae, Senator P. "Beware—the Quangoes are Taking Over." *Australian,* 7 June 1979.

RCAGA (Royal Commission on Australian Government Administration). *Report.* Canberra: Australian Government Publishing Service, 1976.

Saunders, P., and Klau, F. "The Role of the Public Sector: Causes and Consequences of the Growth of Government." *OECD Economic Studies* 4 (Spring 1985):10–37.

SSCFGO (Senate Standing Committee on Finance and Government Operations). *Statutory Authorities of the Commonwealth: First-Sixth Reports.* Canberra: Australian Government Publishing Service, 1979–1982.

Walter, J. "Ministerial Staff under Hawke." *Australian Journal of Public Administration* 43 (Sept. 1984):203–19.

_____. *The Minister's Minders.* Sydney: Oxford University Press, 1986.

Wettenhall, R. L. "Intergovernmental Agencies: Lubricating a Federal System." *Current Affairs Bulletin* 61 (Apr. 1985):65–72.

7

Political Management in Canada

O. P. DWIVEDI and **RICHARD W. PHIDD**

Introduction

This chapter examines the interrelationship between political and bureaucratic actors within the Canadian political system, and develops the position that two institutions, among others, have had important influence on
the formulation and management of public policy in Canada: political parties and the public service. The relationship between these institutions has
been subject to change. The study suggests that these two institutions
should be carefully examined in terms of the effects of their reciprocal
evolution on the functioning of the democratic system. The position is
taken that some tensions have always existed between the two institutions.
Because political parties seek the support of the electorate, they perceive
the public interest from a different perspective than the public service,
which consists of those who possess professional skills and, as a result, are
influenced by professional norms.

In the early study of public administration the spheres of the two
institutions were defined in terms of the politics-administration dichotomy
in which the politicians were to be concerned with the making of good laws
and the public service was concerned with the efficient execution of the
public will as expressed by politicians. Elected officials were perceived as
the guardian of the public interest. It is argued later that this concern with
expressing the public will led to the establishment of machinery by the
political party officials, especially those who gained elected office, to
engage in effective political management (Henderson 1966).

In the early years of the Canadian state, concern with patronage and
spoils led to the establishment of a Civil Service Commission to institution-
alize the practice of hiring public officials on the basis of merit. The subse-

quent evolution of the Civil Service Commission has demonstrated that its operation may, at times, conflict with the objectives of political management, one dimension of which includes the staffing of higher positions within the public service—essentially the concern with effective personnel management (Hodgetts 1973; Mallory 1971).

Important insights into the tensions that have occurred in managing the public sector may be gained through a review of selected developments of the roles of the Civil Service Commission (CSC), the Treasury Board of Canada and the Privy Council Office to the formulation of political priorities, the staffing of the public service, and with issues such as expenditure management. Earlier studies in this area referred to them as the central agencies (Campbell and Szablowski 1979; d'Aquino 1974; Hay 1982; Hockin 1977; Hodgetts 1972; Lalonde 1971; Robertson 1971). However, while some attention has been given to the central agencies, very limited analysis has been done on their interrelationships. Even greater complexities emerge if we focus on the contemporary operations of the Prime Minister's Office, the Privy Council Office and the Public Service Commission.

This chapter is concerned with the performance of political and technical roles within the executive branch of the government of Canada. We will critically examine political management roles as they relate to senior appointments because the effective conduct of such roles has not been the subject of serious scrutiny (Wilson 1985; Yates 1982). Moreover, there are major difficulties associated with the manner in which these roles have been, and should be, performed. Analyses of European systems have demonstrated that the tensions currently existing between political and bureaucratic role-players have been longstanding. By way of illustration, Professor Brian Chapman identified "an unhealthy turnover at the top of the administrative structure of major European systems in the late 1800s because of the widely held view that a government needed to have confidence in the support and sympathy of the senior administrators" (Chapman 1963, p. 30–32).

The growth in the Canadian public sector briefly described below and the need to staff it have led to further tensions in the interrelationship between political and bureaucratic actors. The election of political parties with different ideologies, the personal orientation of various prime ministers and the frequent reorganization of governments accompanying the changes have presented new political and managerial challenges for the system (Canada 1979a).

Concerning the concept of political management, this chapter shows that the most recent attempts to restructure governments have alerted us to the importance and critical nature of political management roles, among others (Phidd 1984; Wilson 1985). It is further argued that effective distinctions should be made between political, public sector and economic management roles. These concepts can assist in the development of greater appreciation of distinct aspects of the operation of the public sector. The Glassco and Lambert Commissions were partially helpful in this regard. The concept of political management relates more to the activities of the political party in power and is likely to be reflected in the operations of the Prime Minister's Office and the Privy Council Office (PCO); the public sector management concept relates more to the operation of the Treasury Board (TB); the concept of personnel management is identified with the operations of the Public Service Commission in concert with the TB and PCO; and the economic management concept relates more to the activities of the Department of Finance in concert with the economic management departments.

Evolution of the Public Sector Management System

In the study of public administration and public policy, the relationship between political parties, the cabinet and the public bureaucracy is increasingly being recognized as an area that requires careful scrutiny. There are historical as well as contemporary reasons for the renewed interest in the interrelationship just specified. Significant changes have occurred in our system of government, suggesting a reexamination of some of the ideas that influenced the operation of the Canadian political system. Our political institutions are under severe pressure and there are frequent debates concerning the prospects for reforms. In such debates, the view is sometimes expressed that some of our institutions are in need of reform.

The rise of modern political parties and the public service was in response to systemic needs toward the end of the previous century. It is interesting to note that as we approach the 21st century a new debate is brewing concerning these institutions.

In a previous publication, *The Administrative State in Canada,* we critically examined this concept, its rise and the limitations of the growth of the modern state (Dwivedi 1982). We pointed then to some of the tensions posed by the ever-expanding Leviathan.

The modern development, particularly the economic growth, of Canada is a consequence of the intervention of the state. This intervention was necessary, and it was so seen by the political leaders given the pioneer nature of the country, the physical structure of the nation spanning half of the continent and the absence of entrepreneurs who could risk their investments without guarantee from the state. The state intervention, then, needed as an infrastructure a growing bureaucracy to provide the necessary administrative support, to regulate the economy so supported, and to ensure that the society received its due return on the investment. It is not surprising then to find that the federal public service grew in relation to increasing governmental intervention in the economy, and also to manage the many social welfare programs that were undertaken. Thus, we see that the federal public service grew from 25,000 at the beginning of World War I to 120,557 at the end of World War II, and then on to 214,930 by 1987 (Hodgetts and Dwivedi 1974; Canada 1988). However, if one adds to the above data the number of employees who are beyond the jurisdiction of the federal central personnel agency, the growth will be truly exponential. (One example of such a growth, even in a relatively short period of time, can be seen where the federal governmental manpower increased from 337,981 in 1959 to 572,493 in 1987). This expanded bureaucracy had to be managed.

The establishment of the first central personnel agency in Canada preceded various demands for elimination of the patronage and spoils system in the federal bureaucracy. The impetus also came from two other, yet related sources. In 1881 President Garfield was assassinated by a disappointed postal clerk who was dismissed from his job by the newly elected political party. The assassination resulted in the passage of the Civil Service Act, 1883. Also, another influence, this time coming from across the Atlantic, was the major civil service reforms in Britain due to the establishment of the merit system of examination for India service, and recommendations resulting from the Northcote-Trevelyan Report, 1853. So in Canada, as narrated by Hodgetts and Dwivedi, the first movements of reform focused on the federal level, sponsored by indigenous moral and social reform movements of a scattered and not highly organized nature but nourished by the British example and later much influenced by the importation of American scientific management precepts (Hodgetts and Dwivedi 1974, p. 3–15). The Royal Commission on the Civil Service, reporting in 1908, stressed the need to establish a central personnel agency so that patronage appointments could be controlled and civil servants could be forced to abandon their political involvement with the party in power. The royal commission also reported how protégés of influential politicians secured a greater share of federal government vacancies, while other suitable candidates, often more competent than those appointed, were rejected; how civil service salaries were not only inadequate, but had not been increased over the past several decades despite constant increases in the cost of living; how the rudimentary classification system produced an inequitable compensation system; and how the promotion procedure favored mostly those who were expert in office politics. In fact, civil service reformers thought that the efficiency and morale of the civil service had generally deteriorated.

These findings, though limited to the federal level, shocked the nation as a whole and triggered efforts to examine the provincial situation (Hodgetts and Dwivedi 1974, p. 16).

The federal government established an independent central personnel agency in 1908. No doubt the federal liberal administration was pressed to take action in 1908 largely because the opposition was raising the matter on the election hustings. Having been reelected, the liberals were duty-bound to administer the first moderate dose of civil service reform by creating the new commission, but they limited the commission's jurisdiction to the inside (headquarters) civil service.

The comparative significance of the design and functioning of the modern state is manifested in publications such as Richard Scase, ed. *The State in Western Europe* (1980). One contributor to the volume pointed to the manner in which the growth in state intervention and its changing forms are associated with significant changes in cabinet organization as well as other respects of the state apparatus. The author pointed to a series of changes in the postwar period. As mentioned above, such a massive transformation of the state has led to new tensions among several institutions (Scase 1978, p. 23–93).

The present study deals specifically with the interrelationships among political parties, the cabinet and the public service as major actors in the Canadian political system. We will look at the manner in which these institutions, among others, have shaped the formulation of public policy in Canada. The evolution of these institutions in Canada is explored. By way of illustration, J. R. Mallory has described the emergence of the modern public service against an almost Continental system of patronage. The emergence of the modern cabinet presented problems between politicians and officials. First, there were the political officials who were required to have seats in Parliament and who were responsible for making major decisions. Second, there were the appointed officials who were to restrain from politics. Another consideration was the manner in which the officials were to be appointed. Thus, a royal commission was established in the early years of the Canadian state and its recommendations subsequently led to the establishment of the Civil Service Commission in 1908 (Mallory 1971, p. 110–79).

The necessity to establish effective public personnel policies to cope with the demands of an ever-expanding state led to conflicts between the Treasury Board, the Civil Service Commission and the Privy Council Office. The tensions are revealed through longitudinal studies of the changing roles of departments and agencies just mentioned. The conflicts are due in part to the legislative mandates of the respective agencies. In the Canadian setting these tensions are evident in the works of J. E. Hodgetts and J. R.

Mallory, among others (Hodgetts 1973; Mallory 1971).

Between 1908 and 1960 (when the Glassco Commission was established to examine the various aspects of the federal administrative machine), three major events influenced the management of public personnel at the federal level. Although the 1908 Civil Service Act introduced competitive examination for entrance in the Dominion civil service, the scope of such competition was limited to the "inside" service at Ottawa. The limitation of such legislation was first tested in 1911 when some 11,000 civil servants were removed from their posts by the newly elected Borden Government after the defeat of the Laurier Government (Hodgetts 1972, p. 14). Such an intrusion by political parties could not last long, given that by World War I, further demands for the extension of the jurisdiction of the Civil Service Commission were being made, not only by politicians but also by war returnees. Consequently, the 1918 amendment to the Civil Service Act ushered in a new era in which merit was emphasized in the management of the entire federal civil service.

While there were no major changes in the managerial philosophy of personnel administration between 1918 and 1946, it should be noted that the interference of political parties in the civil service continued due to the fact that a major portion of the federal jobs were removed from the jurisdiction of the Civil Service Commission. For example, revenue postmasters comprising a force of about 12,000 persons continued to be appointed by political parties in power on the patronage basis (Hodgetts 1972, 1973).

While the prestige of the federal Civil Service Commission was fading during the interwar years, the advent of World War II, and the demand for cleaning-up the federal system of appointment, promotion and job-classification forced the King Government to appoint a Royal Commission on Administration Classification, which reported in 1946. World War II had forced the government to look for better qualified and more professional public servants. The Commission was appalled to find that there were not enough men of high calibre in the middle and senior levels; and also there was "overlapping of duties and responsibilities between the Civil Service Commission and the Treasury Board." However, most of the Gordon Commission recommendations were not accepted by the King Government.

The third major event was the appointment of A. D. P. Heeney as Chairman of CSC by Prime Minister St. Laurent in late 1956. However, in June 1957, John G. Diefenbaker received an upset victory thereby ending a 22-year rule of the liberals in Ottawa. Although Heeney reported in 1958, his recommendations were not fully appreciated by a political party that was suspicious of senior federal bureaucrats. It was not surprising, therefore, to see Prime Minister Diefenbaker appointing a Royal Commission with a very broad mandate in July 1960 to examine all aspects of federal civil service management.

As the above survey indicates, the major reforms adopted between 1908 and 1961 were in response to competing philosophies with respect to improved management of an expanded public service. At the same time some changes were in response to shifts in governments. The election of the Progressive Conservative Government in June 1957 led to perhaps the most significant reform in the system of management of the public service by the appointment of the Glassco Commission. However, before the Royal Commission could complete its report, an amendment to the old Civil Service Act was effected in 1961. These changes demonstrate that while some reforms were due to efforts directed at improving efficiency and productivity, others were motivated by partisan considerations.

New Perspectives on Public Sector Management

The most recent attempts to restructure governments have alerted us to the performance of political management roles among others. Thus in a recent paper we have made distinctions between *political management, public sector management* and *economic management* (Phidd 1984). The first concept relates to the role of the political party in power, the Prime Minister's Office and the Privy Council Office. The second relates more exclusively to the role of the President of the Treasury Board in the overall management of the public service. The third relates to the role of the Department of Finance and related agencies in the formulation of economic policy. The performance of these roles suggests that we examine more carefully the criteria governing public sector organizational behavior and the systemic concerns with efficiency and effectiveness. A prerequisite for doing this is a clarification of the meaning of the concepts "political," "public sector" and "economic management."

H. T. Wilson associates the term *political management* with "an attempt to merge representative and democratic processes with effective government in the public interest. It assumes the priority of politics over economics, and refuses to equate politics with the state and government" (Wilson 1985). The author went on to assert that management is understood to be an approach to problems soluble only provisionally and only by citizens and publics along with their politically elected representatives and those in appointed or tenured positions of public trust. Political management is the collective self-care for public things coupled with the continuous requirement of determining just what these things are at any given time. It is becoming indispensable with the rise of the public sphere and the increasing role of government in society and in the international economic and political arena.

Public sector management is inevitably concerned with the interplay between responsiveness and effectiveness associated with political manage-ment and the efficiency concerns associated with other market behavior or with the administrative and managerial state. These conflicting norms and values further compound the interrelationships between political and bu-reaucratic actors within the public sector (Keeling 1972; Self 1979).

The foregoing suggests that in the study of public sector management we focus more directly on issues such as the formulation of political priori-ties, the appointment of senior officials in government and on the complex relationships which have developed between political and administrative actors in the execution of such tasks. In this regard, the paper explores the contributions of the Privy Council Office, the Prime Minister's Office and the Public Service Commission to the performance of the above-mentioned roles. It was indicated elsewhere that the performance of these roles has been influenced by changes in political leadership, which, in turn, has led to the appointment of new-style administrative leaders. In many ways, the relationship that had existed between political and administrative leaders from the 1930s to the 1960s underwent changes between the 1960s and the 1980s. In an earlier paper, we looked at the evolution of the relationship between political and bureaucratic leadership in Canada by focusing on the roles of the central agencies, especially the Prime Minister's Office, the Privy Council Office, the Treasury Board of Canada, the Department of Finance and the Public Service Commission (Phidd and Dwivedi 1976). In a preliminary way, we attempted then to relate the activities of these central agencies to prime ministerial power. Consistent with the approach, the rela-tionship between the senior public service and a number of Prime Ministers (Pearson, Trudeau, Clark and Mulroney) can be critically reviewed. In another paper, "Public Sector Organizational Reforms: The 1960's to the 1980's," we looked at the restructuring of government that occurred in the Pearson/Trudeau years.

The two decades between the 1960s and the 1980s have witnessed ma-jor changes and periodic governmental reorganizations in Canada. These changes have pointed to a variety of uses of systems methodology and to varied application of the concept "management in government" such as *financial, public sector* and *economic management* (Self 1979; Phidd and Doern 1978).

First, there were the changes in the mid-1960s occurring in response to the reform proposals of the *Royal Commission on the Organization of the Government of Canada* (Glassco). One of the major reform proposals dealt with the need to separate the Treasury Board, the secretariat that supports the cabinet committee on financial and personnel management, from the Department of Finance. In effect, it made a distinction between "management in government" in which the Treasury Board was expected to perform the lead role and "management of the economy" for which the Department of Finance was expected to perform the lead role. The reforms of the early 1960s led to the necessity of distinguishing "public sector management" from the combined operations of both the public and private sectors. Accordingly, economic management refers to the interactions between the private and the public sectors; hence the need to develop appropriate mechanisms to facilitate complementary performance between the public and the private sectors. Some analysts have characterized this relationship as the challenge of modern capitalism (Shonfield 1965).

The separation of the Treasury Board from the Department of Finance gave formal recognition of the significance of the central managerial coordinating role, which was traditionally embraced within the Department of Finance. The change created a separate ministerial portfolio, the President of the Treasury Board. While the decision was made in 1963, it was statutorily confirmed in 1966. As indicated above, it amounted to the creation of a small department concerned with management. The evolution of the Privy Council Office (the Cabinet Office) from its traditional menial role as a central record-keeper when its permanent head was made Secretary to the Cabinet to a central strategic department should be listed in this realm of change. The expanded role of the Privy Council is reflected in the altered status of its ministerial head, the President of the Privy Council. Simultaneously, a Prime Minister's Office was established to assist the incumbent in the capacity of leader of the political party in power. The separation of the board from finance and its evolution is really a subject in itself. The creation of the board as a separate department was followed by major civil service reforms, one dimension of which included the introduction of collective bargaining. There was also the introduction of a bilingualism policy. Therefore, a more realistic presentation of the effects of the 1966 reorganization would involve the examination of the organization charts for the Privy Council Office, the Treasury Board and the Department of Finance (Hay 1982; Hicks 1973; Johnson 1971a, 1971b; Lalonde 1971; d'Aquino 1974; Robertson 1971).

Second, there was the series of reforms designed to provide the general coordination function as well as common services. Several governmental functions may be identified in this regard; central recording and registering of government decisions, through special coordinating and planning tasks, to financial provisioning and other special services for all departments. The desire to improve common service and the criticisms made of the Office of the Comptroller of the Treasury led, ultimately, to steps to create a ministerial position called the Minister of Supply and Services and the Receiver General for Canada. The foregoing demonstrates that as the size and complexity of the Government of Canada increased the coordination function was dispersed to a number of departments. The various changes and the concomitant rationale for them revealed signs of the emergence of a polycentric system of coordination in the Government of Canada (Self 1979).

Third, a series of organizational initiatives was taken shortly after the Right Hon. Pierre Elliott Trudeau became Prime Minister of Canada in 1968. They represented efforts to modernize certain areas of government as well as to provide for more flexible and innovative structures. Some were in the economic and social policy areas and will be discussed later. In this regard, a number of new or expanded departments were established and a novel use of ministers emerged with the establishment of Ministries of State. The Government Organization Act of 1969 established a Department of Regional Economic Expansion (DREE) to be concerned with economic development in the depressed regions of Canada. In effect, the establishment of the department depicted the centralization of a multiplicity of regional programs some of which had existed since the 1930s. It transferred several regional responsibilities from sector departments and created an integrated department concerned with regional development. The same Act integrated the Department of Industry created in 1963 with the old Trade and Commerce Department that had been in existence since the 1890s. In effect, it created a comprehensive department of industry, trade and commerce. The Act made provision for other departments of communications, supply and services, and fisheries and forestry. The Department of Regional Economic Expansion was partially designed to improve Canadian unity by reducing regional disparities.

The Government Organization Act 1970 established a Department of the Environment (Dwivedi 1980) and made amendments to the Department of Energy, Mines and Resources. A most innovative measure was introduced whereby the Prime Minister may appoint Ministers of State and create Ministries of State "for formulating and developing new and comprehensive policies which warrants the establishment for the time being of a special portion of the public service presided over by a Minister of State." This new measure was designed to provide more flexible structures within the federal public service. In retrospect, some of the Trudeau initiatives focused more on social policies initiated earlier by Pearson than on economic development; an issue with which he became concerned very late in his prime ministerial term. Perhaps the most significant use of the ministries of state device, initially, was in the areas of urban affairs and science and technology. In 1978 a Board of Economic Development Ministers

(BEDM) was established, which later became the Ministry of State for Economic Development. In 1983 it became the Ministry of State for Economic and Regional Development (MSERD). The 1983 changes reversed the approach which had established a single department concerned with regional development. One rationale for the establishment of BEDM and MSERD was the need to emphasize microeconomic concerns in contrast to the macroeconomic orientation of the Department of Finance.

The initial effect of the Glassco Commission recommendations was to emphasize a distinction between management in government and management of the economy. Yet the creation of the Economic Council of Canada in 1963 led to a series of recommendations for the differentiation of more precise areas of economic management.

Distinguishing Public Sector Management from Economic Management

The Government Organization Acts for 1966, 1969, 1976 and 1983 emphasized the necessity for clarifying more precisely a number of economic management roles. Thus another series of organizational reforms emanated from the economic policy sphere, which led to changes in the delegation of authority to the economic management departments within the Government of Canada. The establishment of the Economic Council of Canada as a representative, externally located advisory body in 1963 led to a number of highly specific reform proposals which, in part, influenced the establishment of a number of new departments of which the following are illustrative: a Department of Consumer and Corporate Affairs, which has made major recommendations designed to improve Canadian competition policies; a Department of Manpower and Immigration in 1966 concerned with labor market policies, which was further reorganized in 1976; a combining of the Departments of Industry and Trade and Commerce in 1969 concerned with industrial and trade policies; a Department of Regional Economic Expansion in 1969 concerned with the formulation of regional policies; the Ministry of State Act in 1971, which led to the establishment of a number of innovative ministries, for example, science and technology and small business; the Government Organization Act of 1976, which established a Commission and Department of Employment and Immigration; and the Government Organization Act 1983, which established a separate Department of Regional Industrial Expansion, an enlarged Department of External Affairs concerned with foreign and trade policies and an enlarged Ministry of State for Economic and Regional Development concerned with industrial development and regional policies. A new cabinet committee concerned with economic and regional development policies was established at this time through the Prime Minister's Statement *Reorganiza-*

tion for Economic Development issued on January 12, 1982. The foregoing suggests that a series of initiatives were adopted during the Pearson-Trudeau years that significantly impinged on the activities of the former economic policy-making departments such as finance.

Economic management examines the establishment of goals, the delegation of authority to specific departments and agencies and the utilization of selected instruments to achieve the chosen goals. The managerial approach emphasizes that departments are organized to achieve certain goals, which lead ultimately to the development of "agency philosophies." The agency philosophy influences the use of the instruments for which they are responsible. The foregoing suggests that the organization behavior approach can be effectively applied to the study of the formulation of economic policy. It is most important to note that one of the fundamental flaws in the operation of the Canadian system of public sector management identified by the Lambert Commission was the diminution in the roles of the Department of Finance and the Treasury Board. Recent studies of the Government of Canada suggest the formulation of at least three distinct concepts and approaches to the study of Canadian public administration: political management depicted by the operations of the Privy Council Office; public sector management depicted by the operations of the Treasury Board of Canada; and economic management depicted by the operations of the Department of Finance in interaction with the various economic management departments (Phidd 1984).

Emanating from the initial separation of the Treasury from the Department of Finance the analysis went on to enumerate a series of governmental reorganizations specifically designed to influence the formulation of economic policy. It was suggested that contemporary economic management problems may be usefully examined through careful analysis of the delegation of authority to the various departments and their concomitant relationships with the Department of Finance and the Cabinet. The creation of the Board of Economic Development Ministers (BEDM), the Ministry of State for Social Development (MSSD), and the Ministry of State for Economic and Regional Development (MSERD) represented new approaches improving political, public sector and economic management (Phidd and Doern 1978; Phidd 1984). The report of the Lambert Commission on Financial Management and Accountability and the subsequent responses by the Privy Council Office and the Treasury Board point to further innovation along lines suggested above.

It is asserted therefore that significant innovations have occurred in the design of the Government of Canada. In particular, during the 1960s and the 1970s a series of political and organizational changes led to the strengthening of the cabinet committee system, all designed to give politicians greater control over policy decisions. In some respects, these changes led to conflicts between political, economic and managerial criteria in governmental management and to the necessity for clarifying the role of previously powerful departments such as finance. Those changes should be reviewed because they were partially responsible for a debate over the effective organization of government and, in addition, to what constituted the appropriate responsibilities of selected ministers and departments in the broad area of public sector management in Canada.

The various changes made in the Prime Ministers Office (PMO) and in the Privy Council Office (PCO) can be best explained as attempts to improve political management. In an age of elected representative governments, Parliament and the cabinet have struggled to gain and retain supremacy over the professional bureaucracy. Since Parliament cannot effectively manage the Government of Canada, the Cabinet has been delegated this responsibility. This suggests that ministers are more than elected representatives and are, in effect, managers of the public interest; a requirement which has led to a constant search for methods to improve the delegation of authority to various ministers as managers of the specific sphere of governmental activity delegated to them. From this perspective, political parties establish objectives and endeavor to achieve them during the life of the government. The style of political management followed is partially reflected in the design and operation of the PMO and the PCO. The type of decisions made by the PCO are reflected in the Cabinet Committee system and in its mode of operation. The Cabinet Committees are as follows: (1) Cabinet Committee on Priorities and Planning (chaired by the Prime Minister); (2) Treasury Board, the Cabinet Committee on Personnel, Expenditure and Management Practices (chaired by the President of the Treasury Board); (3) Cabinet Committee on Economic and Regional Development (chaired by the Minister of State for Economic and Regional Development); (4) Cabinet Committee on Social Development (chaired by the Minister of State for Social Development); (5) The Cabinet Committee on Foreign and Defense Policy (chaired by the Secretary of State for External Affairs); (6) Cabinet Committee on Government Operations (chaired by the President of the Privy Council); (7) Cabinet Committee for Legislation and House Planning; (8) Cabinet Committee for Communications; (9) Cabinet Committee for Security and Intelligence; (10) Cabinet Committee for Labor Relations; (11) Cabinet Committee for Public Service; and (12) Cabinet Committee for Western Affairs. The first six committees manage expenditures.

Governmental reforms in the 1980s in Canada can be linked to the establishment of a Machinery of Government Branch within the PCO, a group which monitors governmental structure and periodically recommends changes. The group was extremely active during the 1970s and the early 1980s.

The cabinet committee system adopted by the Right Hon. Brian Mulroney consists of the following eleven committees: Priorities and Planning; Communications; Economic and Regional Development; Federal-Provincial Relations; Legislation and House Planning; Foreign and Defense Policy; Security and Intelligence; Social Development; Special Committee of Council; Treasury Board; and Privatization, Regulatory Affairs and Operations.

Organizational Change, Innovation and Administrative Reforms

The management concept is increasingly used to refer to the capacity of organizations or segments thereof to adapt their internal functions to forces operating in their environment (Phidd 1985). Consequently, political, economic and public sector management concepts all relate to ways in which the political system may respond to forces of change. They are extremely useful in assisting with our understanding of issues related to change and adaptation. Consequently, the various changes mentioned above point to the necessity to review public sector reforms from the perspective of the academic interest placed recently on theories and concepts such as administrative change, innovation and governmental reforms. There are several dimensions to the organizational change literature. First, there is the influence from open system theories and models that have been applied to organizational and policy analysis. This approach has also emphasized the relationship between organizations and their environments; an approach linked to the political economy perspective discussed elsewhere. Second, the more general systems approach has been applied increasingly to the study of public sector organizations. In this regard, the work of Desmond Keeling in Britain and Ira Sharkansky in the United States may be mentioned (Keeling 1972; Sharkansky 1982). Third, at a more operational level, the work of Professor J. E. Hodgetts in Canada and Herbert Kaufman in the United States may be mentioned (Hodgetts 1973; Kaufman 1976, 1985). Fourth, the theoretical framework is increasingly being used in the realm of public sector administrative reforms. The analysis of Gerald E. Caiden and Szanton should be mentioned—they attempted to identify strategies for administrative reforms (Caiden and Siedentopf 1982; Szanton 1981). In this chapter, only implicit references are made to the theoretical frameworks outlined by the authors mentioned. As such, major emphasis is given to cataloguing a number of public sector reforms in Canada and to discussing them from the perspective of the system's adaptation to environmental pressures.

The Machinery of Government Branch, PCO

The various governmental reforms were facilitated by the establishment of a Machinery of Government Branch within the Privy Council Office. In the Trudeau years (essentially 1968–1984) the Machinery of Government Branch performed an important role in engineering major governmental reorganizations. The various reorganizations, coupled with the fact that the Prime Minister is responsible for the appointment of Deputy Ministers and for the operation of the public service in general, has meant that the PCO has had a significant influence on the planning and formulation of Canadian public policy. Perhaps the role of the Machinery of Government Branch is most vividly illustrated in the rather revolutionary governmental reorganizations made in 1978 and in 1983, which are discussed below.

The Decline of the Mandarins

The various decisions to improve political management led to a number of significant changes in the Government of Canada. As pointed out by Granastein in *The Ottawa Men* the Canadian public service, especially during the period between the 1930s and the 1950s, was extremely powerful (Granastein 1982).

One of Canada's most significant prime ministers, the Right Hon. W. L. Mackenzie King had been a public servant before becoming Prime Minister. In fact, he was the first Deputy Minister of the Department of Labour. The Right Hon. Lester B. Pearson followed that precedent. During and after the war years several public servants had performed major roles in the formulation of several strategic policy decisions. As a result, a close working relationship had developed between the top echelons of the public service, which lasted well into the 1960s. In many respects, therefore, a study of governmental reorganizations in Canada since the 1960s becomes, in fact, a study of the decline of the postwar mandarins.

The Trudeau initiatives of the late 1960s and the 1970s led to the early departure of the last of the mandarins. The appointment of the relatively young Michael Pitfield to the prestigious and most senior position of Clerk of the Privy Council expedited the departure of the senior mandarins. It also represents a change from a highly informal system of decision making to a highly structured one. In fact, the reforms have been a subject of debate during the 1980s (McCall-Newman 1982).

The new appointments to the senior positions in the public service were perceived as the introduction of the new Harvard Business School style of management to the Canadian public service. Prior to this period, the key deputy ministers were appointed after years of experience under highly respected seniors. In addition, because of the continuity in office of the liberal party, deputy ministers held their positions for very long periods of time. The Trudeau-Pitfield era brought that to an end. One of the most visible characteristics of this period was the rapid turnover of deputy ministers, which was perceived by some observers as an attempt to break the power of the previously powerful mandarins. Selected case studies of governmental departments vividly demonstrate the rapid turnover of deputy ministers (Phidd 1984, 1985).

The Critics of the New System: The Economic Council, the Auditor General and the Lambert Commission Toward Improving Economic and Financial Management

The new approach to public sector management was criticized from at least three sources in the late 1960s and early 1970s. First, the Economic Council of Canada, influenced in part by its functional representative structure, pointed to the necessity for external groups to participate in the process by which priorities and goals were formulated and put into the legislative process. It also criticized the top-down system of rationality by which priorities were formulated in the Government of Canada (ECC, Sixth Annual Review). The Economic Council criticisms are well supported by academic analysis such as Ida Hoos, *Systems Analysis in Public Policy* (1972), which suggests that systems methodology emphasize a top-down approach to public policy-making.

Second, the Auditor General of Canada, Maxwell Henderson, periodically identified waste in government which he characterized as "unproductive spending." His criticisms were made when the Government of Canada had partially implemented PPBS. As a result, the president of the Treasury Board entered into open controversy with the Auditor General for exceeding his mandate. Serious criticisms of the system of financial management within the Government of Canada in the mid-1970s by the Auditor General of Canada led to the establishment of a *Royal Commission on Financial Management and Accountability,* which identified a number of flaws in the system as it had evolved and, consequently, advocated "a mutually compatible management system" designed to clarify the roles of key actors in the policy-making system. In Vickers' approach it outlined a different "appreciative system" (Vickers 1968).

Third, the Lambert Commission report clearly indicated that it saw the cabinet as a system in which different ministers imposed constraints on others. It articulated a system of collective management in which selected ministers perform lead roles. It suggested that "the establishment of a mutually compatible management system appropriate to the requirements of government begins at the centre." The mutually compatible system outlined was as follows: (1) the Cabinet Committee on Priorities and Planning chaired by the Prime Minister was at the center; (2) the Department of Finance, as the central agency with responsibility for economic management, should be assigned the lead role for developing the fiscal plan; (3) the Treasury Board for overseeing the management of government including personnel and financial management; and (4) the five year fiscal plan should be submitted annually to Parliament to a new standing committee on government finance and the economy.

The Government of Canada responded with a new *Policy and Expenditure Management System* (1981a) designed to integrate the formulation of policy and expenditure decisions. In another publication, *Accountable Management* (1981b) a more comprehensive system of responsibility and accountability was outlined. The *Policy and Expenditure Management System* (1981) responded to the charge of fundamental flaws identified by the Lambert Commission by integrating policy and expenditure decisions which, after the Glassco Commission, were separated. The control of expenditure was decentralized to a group of Cabinet Committees that manage resource envelopes. Basically, the system operates under the principle that committees cannot generate new expenditures unless they make savings from the resources made available to them. It should also be emphasized that the system emerged because no money was available; it was the poor performance of the economy that generated the new system. This suggests that organizational change should not be examined without due consideration to environmental forces. The various criticisms, mentioned earlier, led to a number of major financial management reforms. First, the Auditor General's Act was amended in 1977 giving him the power to conduct comprehensive audits. His independence and salary were placed beyond the reach of the political executive. He is, in fact, an officer of the Parliament of Canada. Second, the Treasury Board was given the position of another Deputy Minister. The post of Comptroller General of the Treasury was established. In effect, the system of financial and managerial practices has been significantly strengthened (Canada 1981a).

The Board of Economic Development Ministers (BEDM), Later MSED

Between the late 1970s and the early 1980s a series of steps were taken to improve the methods by which economic development decisions were made in the Government of Canada. First, a Board of Economic Development Ministers (BEDM) was established in 1978 with the objective of improving the formulation of policies with respect to economic development.

It subsequently became the Ministry of State for Economic Development. In addition, a Ministry of State for Social Development was subsequently established to deal with this rather large segment of public expenditures. The creation of BEDM represented the first phase of a series of decisions in the economic development area. This initiative was followed by others in 1982, which culminated in the reorganization of the economic development departments. The decision to create a Board of Economic Development Ministers can be attributed to the poor performance of the Canadian economy between 1973 and 1978. The Minister of Finance, John Turner, in his 1975 budget had sent signals to the provinces that the Government of Canada was committed to reducing public expenditures, the largest portion of which was in the form of transfer payments to the provinces – essentially, in the social policy area. The introduction of wage and price controls was regarded as an emergency measure. Accordingly, prior to the removal of wage and price controls the Government of Canada published a discussion paper entitled *The Way Ahead for Canada* in which it discussed post-controls options (Canada 1976).

It was generally accepted that in a relatively no-growth situation resources had to be shifted to the economic development from the social development area, which was emphasized during the 1960s. There was general agreement at the Economic Summit in Bonn that government expenditures should be reduced and that resources should be directed at achieving growth; hence the shift to a microeconomics orientation.

Prime Minister Trudeau, following his return from the Bonn Summit, announced a very sudden reduction in public expenditures without even consulting the Finance Minister. At the same time, new initiatives were announced to establish a Board of Economic Development Ministers (BEDM). It was dissatisfaction with this drastic change that led to a search for a more effective method of making expenditure decisions (a search for an improved system of political management).

A committee of ministers was established to effect new economic development expenditure decisions. The committee was to be supported by a Ministry of State, i.e., a secretariat to service the committee of approximately 18 ministers. This new structure was retained by the conservative government of the Right Hon. Joseph Clark but it was renamed the Ministry of State for Economic Development. A Ministry of State for Social Development was also established at that time. In effect, it was the Clark government that initially established the system of expenditure envelopes.

With the return of Prime Minister Trudeau in 1980, the Ministry of State for Economic Development outlined a functional framework for promoting economic development in Canada. In addition, the Minister of State for Economic Development started a series of consultations with the provinces and with selected sectors of the economy in an endeavor to formulate an economic development strategy for Canada. In the MacEachen budget of 1981 such a document was tabled entitled *Economic Development for Canada in the 1980's*. While this paper followed the National Energy Program it presented a much broader strategy for influencing economic change in Canada.

Reorganization for Economic Development
and the Government Organization Act, 1983

On January 12, 1982, Prime Minister Trudeau culminated the changes made in 1978 designed to improve the method by which economic development decisions are made when he announced *Reorganization for Economic Development,* which subsequently led to the passage of the Government Organization Act, 1983. It provided for the establishment of a new Department of Regional Industrial Expansion concerned with industrial development and for an augmented Ministry of State for Economic and Regional Development (regional industrial development policies). This reorganization returned the formulation of regional policy to the various sector departments and, accordingly, depicted a change in the criteria for coordinating regional development policies in Canada.

The Government Organization Act also provided for an expanded Department of External Affairs (DEA) led by a Troika: three Ministers—the Secretary of State for External Affairs, a Minister of State for International Affairs and a Minister for Trade. This is a rather revolutionary change that cannot be assessed here. It should be emphasized, however, that the reorganization elevated the role of DEA in the cabinet committee system and established a secretariat for making foreign and defense expenditure decisions. The change certainly impinges on the role of the Department of Finance discussed elsewhere. The making of economic development decisions was placed under a Cabinet Committee of Economic and Regional Development for which the secretariat is provided by the Ministry of State for Economic and Regional Development (MSERD). The approach makes provision for locating senior public officials in the regions of the country.

The new Department of Regional Industrial Expansion (DRIE) was established through the merger of the sectoral approach to industrial policies of the old (DITC) and the regional approach of the former (DREE). Accordingly, the new department (DRIE) is concerned with the formulation of both industrial and regional development policies. There are other elements that should really be the subject of more detailed analysis.

The various reorganizations provide different illustrations of the use and application of systems theory and management principles in the Government of Canada. Thus, by the use of systems theory, as outlined by analysts such as Sir Geoffrey Vickers, *Value System and Social Process,* the rationale for the reorganizations and the implications of the changes for the effective functioning of the system can be examined (Vickers 1968). It demonstrates that major emphasis was placed on reforming internal governmental machinery rather than on public-private sector relationships; the latter poses a challenge for the 1980s. In fact, the early reforms of the 1980s have been concerned with the development and modernization of both public and private sector organizations in Canada. Significant progress has been made in improving the structures of the Government of Canada. However, as the Pearson-Trudeau years ended, major initiatives were required for improving federal-provincial and public-private sector relations.

New Challenges to the System: Personnel and Financial Management

The analysis conducted to this point suggests a number of challenges to Canadian public sector management emanating from different system criteria. A number of gray areas appear with respect to the need to reconcile *political, personnel, financial* and *economic management* roles in the Government of Canada. It is interesting to note that a number of conflicts have emerged from the different perspectives presented by political parties, the Glassco and Lambert Commissions, the D'Avignon Task Force, the Auditor General and the Economic Council of Canada. Other approaches are emanating from sources such as the Neilsen Task Force. The system is also affected by certain entrenched institutional norms governing prime ministerial appointments, the operation of a professional public service and the necessity for political control of the government apparatus. The ensuing discussion addresses issues relating to the interplay between policy, personnel and expenditure management (Dwivedi 1985, p. 1041–58). Let's look at these issues from the perspective of the changes that occurred between the 1960s and the 1980s.

The Glassco Commission and Its Aftermath: 1962–67

Of the various commissions of inquiry appointed by the Canadian federal government to examine and report upon the many facets of public service, none left a more far-reaching imprint on governmental operations than the Royal Commission on Government Organization (Glassco Commission). It was the most extensive review of governmental structures and processes in Canada's history. It preached a new philosophy of management in the public service. It let out a battle cry, "let the managers manage," and recommended a significant shift in the balance of power among institutions. The Glassco Commission advocated a massive devolution of authority from the two central agencies (Treasury Board and Civil Service Commission) out to various departments, agencies and corporations. The Glassco Commission employed a whole battery of management consultants to review various reports prepared by its project officers. First, draft recommendations were examined by advisory committees of private and public corporation presidents, and then by the commissioners themselves. Consequently, the imprint of the business world approach to problem solving is clearly evident in its recommendations.

PERSONNEL MANAGEMENT. The Glassco Commission was sharply critical of the state of civil service management. It clearly stated (Canada 1962, p. 255):

> There is a waste of human resources, because of the failure to give orderly consideration to the best methods of providing and utilizing people and the consequent frustration of many individual careers; the procedures are costly and time consuming; personnel management in departments is generally misdirected, mainly because accountability for the effective use of personnel is fragmented or virtually non-existent.

The commission thought that central direction on all aspects of management was to come from a central agency which was also to be responsible for expenditure management. For Glassco, all the three resources — human, finance and material — had to be directed and managed by only one central agency which had a direct responsibility to the Cabinet; and certainly it was not to be the Civil Service Commission, which already was acting as an arm of Parliament and was thereby independent of management concern. Consequently, the Commission recommended that the development and coordination of personnel policy should rest with the Treasury Board while the departments and agencies would have more freedom in staffing, employee mobility, and other personnel functions. The CSC was to become a staffing agency to certify all initial appointments in the public service — to ensure fairness, to provide service-wide training and development programs under the guidelines developed by the Treasury Board and to act as an appeal board on grievances relating to disciplinary matters. By doing this, the Glassco Commission took the control mechanism of managing human resources from the independent central personnel agency and gave it to the Treasury Board and partially to the departments and agencies. From the Glassco viewpoint, the existing system resulted in confusion and resentment mainly because "efficient performance cannot be secured where intervention in the supervisory process by a nonmanagerial body displaces the exercise of necessary authority by departmental management" (Canada 1962, p. 256). Thus, the Glassco Commission concluded that once all departments and agencies were empowered to exercise that responsibility and authority for management of human resources essential to good management itself, any anomaly relating to effective performance of the public service "would be removed at a stroke." These recommendations were accepted by the Pearson Government, and immediate actions were taken to implement the major changes in the personnel administration system.

FINANCIAL MANAGEMENT. While the CSC was undergoing major organizational changes, preparatory to the forthcoming legislation that would put a formal seal of reduction in its authority, the Treasury Board Secretariat was growing, both in size and influence, to undertake the major tasks and responsibilities recommended to it by the Glassco Commission. The major propositions were: collective responsibility for the managerial decisions (both for the financial and personnel sectors) would rest with the board; and it will have its own minister and a separate identity as a full-fledged department of government. In essence, the Treasury Board emerged as "general manager" of the public service. However, complicated administrative maneuvers had to be undertaken to place with the board necessary powers required for its new role as the management arm of the cabinet (Hodgetts 1973, p. 257–62).

Between 1963 and 1966, when an internal realignment of powers and responsibilities in the bureaucracy was being effected, the Pearson Government appointed a Preparatory Committee on Collective Bargaining, which recommended in 1965 in favor of collective bargaining in the public service and suggested that the Treasury Board was to be the locus of managerial responsibility for negotiating with employees' associations and unions (Dwivedi 1965, p. 359–67). Thus, the board not only became an overseer of public service programs but also started acting as an employer on behalf of the Government of Canada.

The Treasury Board was proclaimed a separate department on October 1, 1966, under the Government Organization Act, 1966. The secretariat of the Treasury Board was transferred to the new portfolio. The newly established, but powerful department, was to be responsible for ensuring effective expenditure management, personnel management and the development of management improvement practices throughout the public service. Out of these three mandates, it was the expenditure management (done under the program branch) that became the focal point of the Treasury Board's relation with all departments and agencies on matters of program priority, content, manpower allocation and allocation of budget to programs. Effectiveness and efficiency of particular programs were to be judged through expenditure management and control.

Along with the Financial Administration Act, also passed was the Public Service Employment Act, 1967, which spelled out clearly the extent of the jurisdiction to be enjoyed by the Public Service Commission. Anything not expressly mentioned under the enabling legislation had to be assumed to be reserved for the Treasury Board. The legislation confirmed the independence of the commission, and it empowered the commission to make appointments based on merit. However, while prescribing selection standards as to education, knowledge, experience, language, age, residence or other matters, the commission's requirements would not be inconsistent with the classification standards prescribed by the Treasury Board (Canada 1967).

From Glassco to Lambert/D'Avignon: 1967–79

Between the release of the Glassco Commission report in 1962 and the retirement of Pearson as Prime Minister in early 1968, four critical decisions taken by the federal government predated extensive changes brought about by Pierre Elliott Trudeau during his administration from 1968 to 1984 (with a short interlude in 1979). In a short span of time, 1963–1967, the Pearson Government: enthusiastically implemented major recommendations of the Glassco Commission by appointing a President of Treasury Board, a new ministerial portfolio; introduced collective bargaining in the public sector; initiated major streamlining of the Cabinet committee system including the establishment of a (Cabinet) Committee on Priorities and Planning under the chairmanship of the prime minister; and began the implementation process of the recommendations of the Royal Commission on Bilingualism and Biculturalism, which ushered the era of representative bureaucracy (as far as the French-Canadian population was concerned) in the federal government.

But it was Trudeau who became the Prime Minister in April 1968, and who after receiving a clear mandate in the July 1968 general election, ushered in an era of political, financial and administrative reforms unprecedented in the history of Canada. The previous system of informal decision making where mandarins played a significant role was replaced by the appointment of new executive-type managers who brought the Harvard Business School style of management in government. A Planning Programming Budgeting System (PPBS) was introduced in 1968; it required departments to define their broad objectives, assign appropriate programs to individual objectives, and then determine what activities had to be performed in order to achieve such stated objectives. This was naturally a major improvement over the former system where departmental expenditures were divided among its branches and units without any concern for program objectives, productivity and results achieved. Also, a system of five-year expenditure-planning was introduced to force departments into considering long-term impacts of their programs and policies rather than staying with the incremental expenditure-planning process. But the PPBS was unable to produce a system of measuring the performance of departmental activities, although it did succeed in identifying resource input against specific program activities. Consequently, a new system, Operational Performance Measurement System (OPMS) was introduced in the mid-1970s as a means to evaluate the efficiency of a multitude of diversified government operations. The basic philosophy of OPMS was that if an operation was not measurable, it (the activity) did not exist. In addition to PPBS and OPMS, some government departments seriously considered utilizing the Management by Objective (MBO) System; whereas PPBS was a top-down objective setting, the MBO, on the contrary, was a bottom-up system. These reforms in the expenditure management system were one side of the story, as other changes in the creation of new departments and agencies were also happening during the first phase of the Trudeau era, 1968–1976. But these efforts were shadowed by events that led to the appointment of a Royal Commission on Financial Management and Accountability in 1976 and a Special Committee appointed to review personnel management in February 1977.

THE LAMBERT COMMISSION: 1976–79. While the Glassco recommendations and other such principles of management as PPBS and MBO were being implemented, the country was shocked by the annual report of the auditor general who indicted the federal government with a devastating attack on the quality of financial management, and warning that the government and indeed parliament might have lost, or was in the process of losing control over the public purse. This claim by the public watchdog generated an immediate public demand that the Trudeau Government do something. And the government almost immediately did announce the appointment of a Royal Commission on Financial Management and Accountability, chaired by Allen Lambert.

The Lambert Commission was appointed on November 26, 1976, with a mandate to examine and report on the management system required in the interrelated areas of: financial management and control; accountability of deputy ministers and heads of crown agencies relative to the administration of their operations; evaluation of the administrative performance of deputy ministers and heads of crown agencies, and the interdepartmental structure, organization and process applicable thereto (Canada 1979a, p. vi).

The commission emphasized that any proposal for reform must respect the dictates of responsible government operating within the framework of the parliamentary system. The government must be held responsible to parliament and the government in turn must necessarily exact an accounting from the public service. As the commission explained (Canada 1979a, p. 31):

> Such a system of management must unequivocally reinforce the capacity of Parliament to fulfil its historic and crucial role of calling Ministers collectively and individually to account for the conduct of the nation's affairs. This must be matched by an increased capacity on the part of Ministers collectively and individually to hold departments and agencies fully accountable for the efficient and effective discharge of their responsibilities.

The commission did not advocate a return to centralization but urged the delegation of authority with attendant accountability. A return to the pre-Glassco period would not work since, in the judgment of the commission, the size, diversity and complexity of government had long since passed the point where any highly centralized organization could possibly implement the great number of policies and programs that had been developed to achieve the multiple objectives of the governmental system. Accordingly, individual departments and agencies must be delegated authority with responsibility to achieve specific objectives and be provided with the necessary human and financial resources. On the other side of this model are the functions of central control agencies, which include working with ministers in clarifying the roles and goals of operating departments and agencies, "providing strong leadership and direction" with respect to how objectives should be achieved, and assuming overall jurisdiction related to administrative policy and sound management practices.

The style of management proposed by the Lambert Commission does not differ in kind from that of the Glassco Commission. Both commissions propose that the government should set priorities, undertake financial planning, and allocate resources, but that program execution should be left to managers subject only to general guidelines. Lambert does not so much disagree with the substance of the Glassco recommendations as argue that they were not successfully implemented. Decentralization was introduced without concomitant accountability. The Lambert Commission recommended a style of management and a system of accountability that can be aptly summed up from one paragraph of the report (Canada 1979a, p. 34):

> Having determined its priorities, established a fiscal plan and allocated resources for carrying out the policies and programs formulated to give effect to

its priorities, the Ministry (Cabinet) must assign to departments and agencies responsibility for implementing its plans. While it may establish certain guidelines and controls and reserve certain rights as to direction, it should be up to the individual departments and agencies to manage their affairs in a way that will best achieve the objectives assigned to them with the resources available. What is crucial to this system of management is that the centre should hold the constituent parts to account fully for the manner in which they have discharged the responsibilities assigned to them. Parliament, in turn, should hold the Government equally accountable for the management of the nation's affairs.

THE D'AVIGNON COMMITTEE ON PERSONNEL MANAGEMENT: 1977–79. Immediately after the establishment of the Lambert Commission, the federal government decided to appoint a special committee on the review of personnel management and the merit principle in the public service. The committee, chaired by Guy R. D'Avignon, submitted its report in October 1979. During its tenure, the committee met with the Lambert Commission and both decided to restrict their jurisdictions. Thus, the commission's examination of the details of personnel management is negligible. However, the committee, taking the lead from the Lambert Commission, declared that the present state of personnel management is a result of the failure of successive governments to provide an effective corporate management structure and system. It recognized the authority vested in the Treasury Board to function more fully as the corporate manager. It listed the following basic problems in personnel management (Canada 1979b, p. 5): (1) absence of a corporate management, hence of leadership and absence of any philosophy of management, a public service organization without a head; (2) excessive and inflexible regulation and slavish adherence to universally applied regulation in the name of merit at the expense of efficiency and effectiveness; (3) arising from the first item, managers and supervisors who are poorly equipped to manage, no requirement that they undergo even minimally essential training, and low priority accorded to training; and (4) no accountability for effective personnel management.

The committee made 179 recommendations compared to 165 made by the Lambert Commission. The major elements of the committee's extensive list of recommendations are: (1) the essence of effective management is the commitment of management, starting at the top, and a clear line of accountability from the junior management level through to the top level; (2) while the merit principle remains the cornerstone of staffing, the system itself has brought the principle into disrepute; therefore, certain supplementary principles should be enshrined in law, such as sensitivity and responsiveness, equality of opportunity, efficiency, effectiveness and equity; (3) in order to provide a bold, unified corporate policy direction of the personnel function the board of management (as recommended by the Lambert Commission) should have a vice-president as well as a secretary for personnel management. Consequently, the role of the public service commission would be restricted to mostly audit and appeal functions; and (4) public servants should be given greater freedom to participate actively in the political process with the exception of the senior management group.

It is clear that the D'Avignon Committee fully shared the basic belief of the Lambert Commission that the managerial wisdom of the private sector would solve public sector problems.

MANAGEMENT CATEGORY FOR SENIOR PUBLIC SERVANTS. Another major reform introduced in 1981 was to establish a management category in the public service with the view to improve the effectiveness of the talents of senior officers. The main objective is to increase managers' sense of identity, providing a common and unified approach to their salary structure, and maximizing the optimal use and deployment of managerial resources in departments and elsewhere. This approach ushered in a new era in personnel policy at the federal level because, so far, the entire position-classification system has been based on a job-oriented (appointment to a position) system rather than on the British system of rank-oriented (appointment to a level/class/career) classification (Hodgetts and Dwivedi 1974, p. 121–25). The major defect of the job-oriented system is that a person cannot be moved between similar positions, which are at the same salary and responsibility levels, without creating a fresh vacancy and going through the normal process of recruitment and appointment approved by the Public Service Commission. Previously, this resulted in such difficulties as: departmental heads being unable to transfer able officers within their department from one position to another; delays in filling positions because each such move had been considered a fresh appointment; and inability of central agencies to move persons from one department to another. These difficulties were also recognized by the United States federal government when, in 1978, it created a senior executive service (Rosen 1981, p. 203–7). The Coombs Commission of Australia had already made a similar recommendation in 1976 for establishment of a senior executive category (Australia 1976, p. 272). The Canadian plan introduced in 1981, aims to minimize the barriers to flexible deployment of senior personnel, such as interposition transfer within departments, and so to maximize program efficiency and effectiveness. The concept offers more managerial authority and flexibility to act in return for greater accountability for results achieved.

By the end of 1984, there were 4,281 members appointed to this category by the Public Service Commission. The category is divided into two occupational groups: Executive (EX), and Senior Management (SM). A head of department, now, has the flexibility in the use of his senior executive officers by deploying them between positions, so long as such a transfer does not affect salary level of an individual; previously, such transfers within a department were not feasible. Interdepartmental transfers are also possible. It seems that a career-concept is emerging in the senior public service due to the establishment of a management category.

The above listed four major reforms have produced a new era of scientific management in the federal public service. These reforms have created great expectations on the part of the governed. These sentiments were also shared by the President of the Treasury Board when he introduced these reforms in 1981 (Canada 1981b, p. 4). "We must continue, with discipline and dedication, to improve management and reduce waste, never losing sight of the fact that government is only the trustee of public funds and that the public must receive value for money."

Each Prime Minister has placed his own mark on the Canadian system. Mulroney's stress on streamlining and expenditure control has resulted in numerous structural and procedural changes. Overall, he has relied more on the PMO than the PCO and, in January 1989, announced a new cabinet committee system which altered the decision-making process. Drastically reduced public spending is foretold (Savoie 1990, pp. 348–56).

Conclusion

In a paper entitled *Bureaucracy, Politics and Public Policy* (1976) we made some preliminary comments concerning the changes in political and bureaucratic relations in the Government of Canada. We pointed then to the organizational reforms instituted by the Diefenbaker, Pearson and Trudeau governments. The present study represents an attempt to expand on those observations. The period between the 1960s and the 1980s has demonstrated even more significant changes than those referred to in the mid-1970s. The Canadian political system is confronted with major managerial challenges from a highly volatile international and domestic environment. The environmental forces suggest improved system capabilities. While it has become fashionable to endorse the concept of management there are several facets that should be critically examined.

This chapter suggests that we examine these challenges from the perspective of a number of related concepts: political, public sector, personnel, financial, public-private sector and economic management. We should review these concepts especially with respect to problems of efficiency and effectiveness, staffing, and issues related to responsibility and accountability. The recent focus on management science suggests that we attempt to clearly define the tasks and responsibilities just alluded to.

It was indicated at the outset that a major objective was to explore distinguishing features of political and administrative roles, especially with respect to the effective functioning of a number of key institutions. Significant demands are being made on political parties and the public service; i.e., on political and administrative elites, among others. The paper suggests that we carefully examine the roles and functions of the Prime Minister's Office, the Privy Council Office, the Treasury Board, the Public Service Commission and the Department of Finance with respect to effective public sector management.

The utilization of concepts such as political and public sector management, among others, requires that we identify the distinguishing features of the key central agencies referred to earlier.

Key institutions perform important roles in the setting of political priorities and are important in developing improved appreciation of how such priorities should be established. The performance of political and bureaucratic leadership roles are essential to the effective functioning of a democratic system of government.

The recent debate over the need for more efficient government has also raised questions concerning the relationship between the public and private sectors. In this regard, we are concerned with the effective functioning of both private and public sector organizations. Such concerns lead to reexamination of the design of both private and public sector organizations and the criteria used for holding them accountable.

A recent article by Ian Clark of the Privy Council Office attempted to explain the ever-evolving division of responsibilities between the central agencies (Clark 1985). The rise and demise of the Ministries of State for Social Development and Economic and Regional Development point to some difficulties inherent in contemporary public sector management. Our earlier review and analysis suggests that the performance of political management roles poses serious challenges for political parties upon assuming office. It raises questions concerning the parties' preparation for assuming the roles. Similar developments in the United Kingdom had led Sir Richard Clarke to address the issues of *New Trends in Government* (1971). Some of these issues were evident in the Clark and Mulroney transitions in Canada.

A number of issues are worth exploring. There is the issue of the design of the central agencies, the PMO and the PCO, for purposes of dealing with political priorities. Then there is the related issue of the relationship between the Prime Minister, the Cabinet and the senior public service: What precisely is the Canadian tradition? How should deputy ministers be appointed? What type of turnover should exist in relation to ministers and deputy ministers? In this regard, it may be noted that between Confederation and 1963 there were six Deputy Ministers of Finance and between 1969 and 1984 there were six. Further, there is the issue of how many central agencies and how should they relate to each other?

Improved understanding of various aspects of public sector management and economic management can be gained through more careful scrutiny of the Treasury Board and the Department of Finance. Both central agencies were seriously challenged during the last two decades, and both are under reform.

Apart from the issue of the higher public service there is the problem of the public personnel policy planning versus the merit system. This issue raises the question of the relationship between the Public Service Commission, the Treasury Board and the Privy Council Office. This issue is touched on in a preliminary way because further research needs to be conducted. However, it does not appear that there is a clear perception among the practitioners in government regarding which are appropriate institutional relationships. The institutional tensions are further affected by the phenomenon of limited or declining resources.

Our research in this area suggests that we should take a retrospective look at how the various institutions have evolved. In addition, we should critically assess current challenges and attempt to set realistic courses of action for the various institutions involved. A prerequisite for doing this is to better understand why and how selected institutions were designed. The frequent reorganizations of governments, in recent years, have made it extremely difficult to comprehend the present system. At the same time, there are further pressures for new reforms, for which we must carefully examine the relationship between political and bureaucratic actors with a view to making constructive reform proposals. Should we be addressing the issue of political party reforms at the same time as we ponder reforms of the public service and Parliament? The concept political management may prove useful in such an endeavor. Is political management the same as business management? What are some of the long-term implications of the Glassco, Lambert and Auditor General reform proposals? Obviously, there is a significant need to reexamine the managerial and administrative components of public sector management in Canada.

References

Australia. Royal Commission on Government Administration. *Report.* Canberra: Australian Government Printing Service, 1976.

Caiden, Gerald E., and Siedentopf, Heinrich, eds. *Strategies for Administrative Reforms.* Lexington, Mass.: Lexington Books, 1982.

Campbell, C., and Szablowski, George J. *The Super Bureaucrats.* Toronto: Macmillan, 1979.

Canada. *Royal Commission on Government Organization.* Vol. 1: *Management of the Public Service.* Ottawa: Queen's Printer, 1962.

_____. *Public Service Employment Act,* 1967, Section 12(1).

_____. *The Way Ahead: A Framework for Discussion.* Ottawa: Supply and Services, 1976.

_____. *Royal Commission on Financial Management and Accountability.* Ottawa: Supply and Services, 1979a.

_____. *Economic Development for Canada in the 1980's.* Ottawa: Supply and Services, 1981.

_____. *Reorganization for Economic Development.* Ottawa: Supply and Services, 1982.

Canada. Privy Council Office. *The Policy and Expenditure Management System.* Ottawa: Supply and Services, 1981a.

Canada. Public Service Commission. *Annual Report,* 1987. Ottawa: Supply and Services, 1988.

Canada. Special Committee on the Review of Personnel Management and the Merit Principle. *Report.* Ottawa: Queen's Printer, 1979b.

Canada. Treasury Board. *Accountable Management.* Ottawa: Supply and Services, March 1981b.

_____. *Role of the Treasury Board Secretariat and the Office of the Comptroller General.* Ottawa: Treasury Board, 1983.

Chapman, B. *The Profession of Government.* London: George Allen and Unwin, 1963.

Clark, Ian D. "Recent Changes in the Cabinet Decision-Making System in Ottawa." *Canadian Public Administration* 28, no. 2 (1985):185–201.

Clarke, Sir Richard. *New Trends in Government.* London: Her Majesty's Stationery Office, 1971.

d'Aquino, T. "The Prime Minister's Office: Catalyst or Cabal? Aspects of the Development of the Office in Canada and Some Thoughts about Its Future." *Canadian Public Administration* 17, no. 1 (1974):55–79.

Dwivedi, O. P. "Recent Developments in Staff Relationships in the Public Service of Canada." *Public Administration* (Sydney) 24 (1965):359–67.

_____. "Administrative Reforms in Canada." *Indian Journal of Public Administration* 31, no. 3 (1985):1041–58.

_____, ed. *Resources and the Environment: Policy Perspectives for Canada.* Toronto: McClelland and Stewart, 1980.

_____. ed. *The Administrative State in Canada.* Toronto: Toronto University Press, 1982.

Granastein, J. L. *The Ottawa Men: The Civil Service Mandarins, 1935–1957.* Toronto: Oxford University Press, 1982.

Hay, M. A. "Understanding the PCO–The Ultimate Facilitator." *Optimum* 13–1 (1982):5–21.

Henderson, Keith M. *Emerging Synthesis in American Public Administration.* London: Asia Publishing House, 1966.

Hicks, Michael. "The Treasury Board of Canada and Its Clients: Five Years of Change and Administrative Reforms, 1966–71." *Canadian Public Administration* 16 (1973):182–205.

Hockin, T. A., ed. *Apex of Power: The Prime Minister and Political Leadership in Canada.* Scarborough: Prentice Hall, 1977.

Hodgetts, J. E. *The Canadian Public Service: A Physiology of Government, 1867–1970.* Toronto: University of Toronto Press, 1973.

Hodgetts, J. E., and Dwivedi, O. P. *Provincial Governments as Employers.* Montreal: McGill-Queen's Press, 1974.

Hodgetts, J. E. et al. *The Biography of an Institution: The Civil Service Commission of Canada, 1908–1967.* Montreal: McGill-Queen's Press, 1972.

Hoos, Ida R. *Systems Analysis in Public Policy: A Critique.* Berkeley: University of California Press, 1972.

Johnson, A. W. "Management Theory and Cabinet Government." *Canadian Public Administration* 14 (1971a):73–81.

_____. "The Treasury Board of Canada and the Machinery of Government of the 1970's." *Canadian Journal of Political Science* 4 (1971b):346–66.

Kaufman, H. *Are Government Organizations Immortal?* Washington, D.C.: The Brookings Institution, 1976.

_____. *Time, Chance and Organizations.* New Jersey: Chatham House, 1985.

Keeling, Desmond. *Management in Government.* London: George Allen and Unwin, 1972.

Kernaghan, K., and Siegel. D. *Public Administration in Canada.* Toronto: Methuen, 1987.

Lalonde, M. "The Changing Role of the Prime Minister's Office." *Canadian Public Administration* 14, no. 4 (1971):509–37.

McCall-Newman, C. *Grits: An Intimate Portrait of the Liberal Party.* Toronto: Macmillan, 1982.

Mallory, J. R. *The Structure of Canadian Government.* Toronto: Macmillan, 1971.

Phidd, R. W. "Public Sector Organizational Reforms in Canada: The 1960's to the 1980's." In *Organizational Policy and Development.* Edited by L. R. Moise. University of Louisville Interdisciplinary Conference, 1984, 191–208.

_____. "Toward a Framework for Analyzing Canadian Public Administration and Public Policy Issues." *Public Policy and Administrative Studies* 2 (1985):1–19.

Phidd, R. W., and Doern, G. B. *The Politics and Management of Canadian Economic Policy.* Toronto: Macmillan, 1978.

Phidd, R. W., and Dwivedi, O. P. "Bureaucracy, Politics and Public Policy: An Appraisal." Paper prepared for the Annual Conference of Canadian Political Science Association, Laval University, Quebec City, June 1976.

Robertson, G. "The Changing Role of the Privy Council Office." *Canadian Public Administration* 14, no. 4 (1971):487–508.

Rosen, Bernard. "Uncertainty in the Senior Executive Service." *Public Administration Review* 41, no. 2 (1981):203–7.

Savoie, D. J. *The Politics of Public Spending in Canada.* Toronto: University of Toronto Press, 1990.

Scase, Richard. *The State in Western Europe.* London: Croom Helm, 1978.

Self, Peter. *Administrative Theories and Politics.* London: George Allen and Unwin, 1979.

Sharkansky, Ira. *Public Administration.* San Francisco: W. H. Freeman, 1982.

Shonfield, Andrew. *Modern Capitalism: The Changing Balance of Public and Private Power.* London: Oxford University Press, 1965.

Szanton, Peter. *Federal Reorganization: What Have We Learned?* Chatham, N.J.: Chatham House, 1981.

Vickers, Sir Geoffrey. *Value Systems and Social Process.* London: Tavistock, 1968.

Wilson, H. T. *Political Management.* Berlin: W. DeGruyter, 1985.

Yates, Douglas. *Bureaucratic Democracy: The Search for Democracy and Efficiency in American Government.* Cambridge: Harvard University Press, 1982.

8

The Administrative System and the State in France: Interpreting Policy Developments and Administrative Changes

GÉRARD TIMSIT

TODAY IN FRANCE, some analysts interpret certain signs as indicating the demise of the state. And, simultaneously, others denounce an excess of state ("le trop d'Etat"). A mystery or a double error? Or perhaps two truths?

An excess of state? It was in fact what was already believed—polemics and partisan differences aside—by all those who, since the end of World War II, had exercised political responsibility, regardless of the political party to which they belonged. Michel Debré manifested his concern as early as 1947: "Our State, because of centralization, has become a virtual skeleton. . . . Our State no longer has anything but skin covering its bones." Valéry Giscard d'Estaing was to affirm 30 years later that, "Centuries of centralization weigh on us." At the same time, the political platform of the Socialist Party proclaimed that "France still lives under Napoleon." And the Communist Party itself denounced "the influence of the State over the totality of social relations" and "administrative totalitarianism"—a denunciation that echoed the description of former RPR Minister Alain Peyrefitte of the reign of "Statist unreason." An excess of state, to be sure. At the same time, however, it is the end of the state that seems to be revealing itself and that others announce. The penetration of private interests into the state

Translated by Suzanne L. Pucci, Associate Professor, Modern Language and Literature, State University of New York at Buffalo.

structure in recent years, the increased power of corporate structures, the development of self-governing mechanisms, are not simply reactions to the influence of the state over society. They are above all new forms of the administrative phenomenon, new forms of the state, of a state "dedifferentiated," whose democratic procedures, the market and special interests prepare the ground for dissolution and deinstitutionalization (Birnbaum 1985).

So, that is the dilemma, at least theoretically. Because the two things must come down to one. Of the two phenomena described — the excess of state or its decline — either one corresponds effectively to the reality and the other is only an intellectual view. Or the two in fact describe accurately the reality, and what is necessary therefore is to successfully translate that reality into terms and concepts that permit us to account for the apparent contradiction. The reality of the state and its administration in France is such that one cannot content oneself with traditional analyses in order to express it. Some analysts have proposed moreover the concept of integration (Timsit 1985–1986) as designating a mode of internal structuring of administrative systems, and the notion of a relative model of integration to designate the specific manner in which the French administrative system is structured. I would like to show here how the French administration, in the evolution it has undergone and the contradictions that run through it, responds effectively to the characteristics of this model: a model of *integration* and a model of *relative integration*.

A Model of Integration

The *integration,* of which it is a question here, is that of the administrative system itself. And not — as the word is customarily applied — that of the social group in which the system is immersed or that it administers. Integration is thus a mode of *internal* structuring of the administrative system, a type of articulation of the actions that constitute it.

In this regard, an observation must be made. It concerns the very nature of the actions that constitute the administrative system. We cannot reduce it simply to the actions that one traditionally calls administrative. We cannot limit the term "administration" to an ensemble of parts perfectly defined, clearly circumscribed and totally isolated from its environment. The sociology of organizations — and Michel Crozier in particular, with his notion of a system of action (Crozier and Friedberg 1977) — has pointed out the integration of systems and their environment, the absence of a boundary between organizations and the milieu with which they are integrated. Administrative, political, economic and societal affairs are in constant interaction and one can legitimately and scientifically situate administration only at the intersection of the total network of relations thus constituted. Now this network, at the center, at the intersection of which administration is found, presents in France a character that is very strongly integrated.

Integration, first of all, of the political and administrative, results from the principle of subordination of the administration to the government set forth by article 20 of the 1958 Constitution: "The Government determines and directs the policy of the Nation. It controls the administration and the armed forces." It could not be clearer. This constitutional principle would be of no importance, or of little importance, were it not supported by institutional mechanisms and favored by political factors permitting the power in charge to base its authority on the administration.

Institutional mechanisms? The existence of two types of structures — transfer and diffusion — characterized by their dual political and administrative character and situated on the fringe of the two powers guarantees that subordination of the administration to political power. Structures of transfer first: these are structures destined to assure the transmission and flow of political decisions in the direction of the administration. They are essentially composed of the "political officials" of whom Weber speaks. The most important among them is constituted by the staff of the President of the Republic — the General Secretariat, the Cabinet, the Special Advisor to the President — who form an essential liaison between the president and the administrative apparatus of the state. General de Gaulle wanted the duties to be shared between the Cabinet and the General Secretariat of the President in line with the principle that the Cabinet was charged with organizing the contacts of the president with the nation — political, union, cultural representatives, etc. — while the General Secretariat assured his contacts with the state, the ministerial staff and administrative units. Today, that division of duties most certainly no longer prevails, but one can nonetheless be sure that the General Secretariat of the President of the Republic plays an essential role in the liaison established between the president and the ministries, although that liaison greatly slackened between March 16, 1986, and the 1988 election with the emergence of what has commonly been termed in France "cohabitation," that is, the coexistence of a president elected by a leftist majority and a Prime Minister and Parliament that represent a rightist majority. The important characteristic of these channels of relay for presidential political power is that the proportion of civil servants, and particularly of the senior officials who are members of the upper echelon (Grands Corps) of the state (State Council, the Bureau of Audits, Inspector of Finance, the Diplomatic Corps) has significantly increased.

The ministerial posts — and above all that of the Prime Minister — present from this point of view the same characteristics. They also constitute channels of relay between the Prime Minister and the ministers along-side whom they are placed as well as the staff over which these political figures exercise their authority. Assistants to the head and to the members of the government, these cabinets are made up of teams of personnel who in principle remain in service as long as the members of the government for whom they work. There again, the composition of these cabinets is quite characteristic and the proportion of cabinet members of civil servant standing is very large, while their recruitment is in principle subordinated to political considerations—a demonstration of allegiance to the man or to the political parties in power or at least a demonstrated lack of hostility to the political makeup of the government—90 to 93 percent of the members of the ministerial cabinets under the Fifth Republic are affected.

One of the most efficient institutions of transfer in the French administrative system is constituted by what are called "public offices at the discretion of the government." It is enough to recall the debates—bitter and fierce—that occur concerning these offices each time there is a change in the majority in order to measure their importance in the functioning of the state. Fixed most recently by a Decree of July 24, 1985, the list of these offices, not restrictive, includes all the highest posts in the administrative hierarchy—general secretaries, director generals and directors of central administrations, ambassadors, prefects, etc. The persons occupying these posts can be named and can be recalled at will. The freedom enjoyed by government in the appointment and the dismissal of these persons implies that—without every change in majority or in government necessarily resulting in a complete turnover of personnel occupying these posts—these personnel generally fulfill the conditions of political allegiance or of nonhostility, conditions similar to those set forth regarding members of ministerial cabinets. In this respect, it seems that the idea has spread in the most recent years of the Fifth Republic that the best guarantee of the subordination of the administration to political power is found in the placement in these posts at the upper level of the administrative hierarchy of officials whose political opinion conforms to that of the politicians holding positions of ministerial responsibility.

Structures of diffusion make it possible, moreover, in the French administration, to assure the consolidation of the ensemble of the administrative organization under the authority of the political power in office. These horizontal structures make the apparatus coherent and homogenous and assure the dissemination of information and the diffusion of political will at the heart of every administrative system.

The *Grands Corps* constitute the essential part of these structures. One is aware that public function in France is divided entirely into classes of civil servants, that is, into groups of officials observing the same particular regulations, trained for the same career and fulfilling the same sort of functions. The *Grands Corps* customarily include the Ministry of Finance, the State Council, the Bureau of Audits, certain Engineer Corps recruited by the technical institutions of higher learning (the *Grandes Ecoles:* Polytechnic, Central, Public Works, Mines), as well as, depending on the particular case and the time, the Diplomatic Corps and the Prefectoral Corps. *Grands Corps* officials belong to the upper levels of the administrative hierarchy and hold positions of control or authority. One of the characteristics of the *Grands Corps* is that their members are present in large numbers at all strategic points in the French administrative system: on the staff of the President of the Republic where, at least up to the presidency of François Mitterrand, they represented more than half the strength of the staffs, in the ministerial cabinets where—taking into account solely the three *Grands Corps:* Finance, State Council, Bureau of Audits—they furnished, before 1981, significantly more than 10 percent of the cabinet members in the executive posts of the central administrations and public corporations. Such a situation results in a very strong homogenization of the administrative milieu: "The Corps is a homogeneous milieu at the heart of which information may be disseminated in full secrecy. . . . The second characteristic of the *Corps* is its institutional transversality that allows it to bypass bureaucratic divisions. But, above all, it is able to pass beyond institutional segmentation to achieve organizational integration" (Gremion 1976, p. 392). That says enough about the role of the *Corps* in the phenomenon of the diffusion of political will at the heart of the administration.

The ad hoc administrative commissions (administrations de mission) that have multiplied in France since the 1960s have contributed to the reenforcement of this phenomenon of diffusion. As we know, it is Edgard Pisani to whom we owe the notion of an "administration de mission." It is he who, at the end of the 1950s, proposed to distinguish more clearly between the traditional bureaucratic administrations, encumbered by their procedures, by their unwieldiness and rigidity—the classic ministries with their vertical operation—and the autonomous, specialized administrative bodies, temporary and dynamic in character, founded on the action of a single individual or a team driven by the spirit of enterprise, whose jurisdiction and power operate in a horizontal manner that redistributes the field of action of various traditional ministries. Since World War II, we have witnessed in France the appearance of structures of this type: the Planning Commission, the Delegation for Land Development (D.A.T.A.R.), the Interministerial Commission for the Development of the Languedoc-Roussillon Coastal Region. In all these cases, it was a case of a streamlined administration (composed of a reduced number of civil servants—on the order of a few dozen officials, as opposed to the work force of the French ministries that currently operate with more than 20,000 or 30,000 officials in the central administration).

The civil servants who belong to these ad hoc administrative commissions are officials belonging to the upper echelons. The commission they are charged with crosses over several vertical administrations: land development, conservation, regional industrialization, development of tourism in a particular area, etc. Sometimes these ad hoc administrative commissions are limited in function to the conception or elaboration of a project whose execution is ultimately carried out by administrative bodies belonging to traditional management. Since 1970, these ad hoc administrative bodies have made great strides and we have seen a proliferation of these types of horizontal structures headed by an individual official who is identified by the media with the particular mission confided to him. Thus, we have seen the appearance, for example, of "Mr. Highway Safety" (M. Gerondeau, appointed in 1972 as the director of a group charged with studying the means to improve and strengthen safety on the nation's highways and superhighways), "Mr. Public Morals" (M. Pinot, appointed in 1975 to control prostitution), "Madame Drug Prevention" (Mme Pelletier in 1975), etc. And the tendency has not slowed down in the eighties: a national jobs administration (Decree of October 6, 1981), a commission for the study and prevention of natural disasters (Decree of November 12, 1981), a delegation for the social economy (Decree of December 15, 1981), a standing committee for the study and restructuring of government agencies (Order of March 3, 1982), etc. The State Council has called attention in one of its reports (1982–1983, p. 106) to the fact that these horizontal structures, by reason of the quality and youth of those involved in and directing them, and by reason also of the closer unity of the teams forming them, "have managed to facilitate the task of coordination, to permit the introduction into traditional administration of fresh viewpoints and experience, to facilitate innovation." These are in effect structures of diffusion. What the State Council does not spell out is that this diffusion comes about perhaps at the price of a certain form of politicization of the administration: the personality named to head an ad hoc administrative commission is often a politician in the guise of a technocrat, or a technocrat biding his time for a political appointment, and sometimes appointment to such a post—one of those posts to which he can be appointed only by an order from the Council of Ministers: a post above "the dictates of the government"—serves only as a springboard for a political career to be undertaken. And in actual fact undertaken, and often successfully.

One can legitimately question the factors that favor in France such an integration of the political and administrative realms. Several factors have to be singled out.

The first has to do undoubtedly with the statute of public liberties set forth for civil servants. We know the fundamental distinction made in French law between freedom of opinion and freedom to express that opinion. The freedom of opinion enjoyed by the French civil servant is total. No reference can be made in the dossier of a civil servant to his political, philosophic or religious opinions. That is to say, any measure that would impact on the rights of a civil servant by reason of his opinions would be inadmissable according to law. The civil servant has a total freedom of thought. His freedom to express his thought is, on the other hand, more restricted. The expression of thought can take the most varied forms: declarations, writings, attitudes, behavior, participation in a demonstration, in an electoral campaign, membership in a political party, candidacy in an election, etc. The law customarily observes a distinction between the expression of one's opinion in one's capacity as a public servant, which is forbidden—to prevent doubt being thrown on the neutrality of the state and of the civil servant in the service of the collective body of the state—and the expression of personal opinion, which is permitted with the sole condition that one respect a so-called obligation of discretion, that is, the obligation of the civil servant to express his opinions, whatever they may be, favorable or hostile to the political party in power, with moderation, with prudence, without giving them a provocative, injurious or gross character. According to that single condition, whose observance is assured under the control of administrative jurisdiction, the civil servant is totally free to express his opinions, even those most radically hostile to the government, to obtain leave to participate in an electoral campaign under the banner of an opposition party, to be reassigned elsewhere in order to carry forth the trade-union or political mandate conferred on him, to reassume his original assignment in the administration at the completion of his mandate if his party has not been ousted by the electoral body. One can see that this particularly favorable situation of the French civil servant with respect to the exercise of his public liberties has not discouraged him from participating in political activities. On the contrary. The fact of a civil servant participating in such activities constitutes no risk at all for him in his career. At the worst—if he loses—he takes up his previous post in the administration. At best—if he succeeds—he enters into a public career as deputy or senator. And in the event that he does not succeed in such a career, as long as his party is in power, ministerial cabinets or management would be able to offer him possibilities of a post or an attractive promotion.

If the marked liberality of the political statute governing civil servants were the only factor of administrative drift, we could scarcely satisfy ourselves with the explanation that that drift has been particularly pronounced since the advent of the Fifth Republic. This statute dates, in fact, in its liberality, from 1946, while the tendency of the growing integration of political and administrative actions that we observe in France has grown to the scope we know at present only after 1958. The fact remains that a second factor of drift has arisen, which, paradoxically, has resulted from the political stability of the administration put in place by General de Gaulle. Under the Fourth Republic, the political instability that reigned made the administration the sole guarantor of the continuity of the action of the state. Undoubtedly, political appointments occurred in the administration, but the rapid accession of different majorities and governments to power prevented the administration from remaining in the hands of a single party, political faction or tendency. In the worst of cases—and they were rare—if there was a politicization of appointments, contrary or different politicizations effected by succeeding governments put things in balance and in the long run cancelled each other out. Under the Fifth Republic, the stability of a quasi-presidential government fundamentally changes things. Such a government enjoys the longevity and continuity necessary for the progressive politicization of the administration. The very nature of the government, in the process of presidentialization, requires such a politicization of the administration.

There is a third factor of administrative change or drift: a tendency, of recent origin it appears, arises that consists in invoking, in order to assure a greater efficiency in public service, the necessity of politicizing appointments to it. The argument on which that thesis is founded is that a government, if it wishes its political aims to be realized, if it wishes its programs to be followed, must be able to call upon, in the command positions and in all the strategic places in the administration, personnel who are dedicated to it:

> People have spoken about the administration's resistance to change. And they think too readily that that resistance is passive, that conservatism manifests itself in the form of a redoubtable official opposing inertia to change coming from outside. I am convinced of the contrary: if resistance exists, it is strongly active. The consequence of these multiple movements of the different parties of the whole—anyone in this case can see that various configurations of the body politic prevail through their persistence over all the political changes occurring—is that the administration appears to possess its own legislative and political force (Delarue 1983, p. 60).

And the tendency has been to justify by such an argument the politicization of high public office after 1981. To which responds, as if in echo, between March 16, 1986, with the defeat of the Left in the legislature and the 1988 election, the appointments to high offices in the administration of persons close to the Right majority, designed to break the grip of the former majority over administrative apparatus—"the ebbing of the pink wave." Thus occurs integration.

The integration of the economy and the administration is scarcely less pronounced. "A governed economy" is what the French economy has been called. And to be sure, the role of the state in the functioning of economic mechanisms cannot be ignored. It reveals itself at once in the constant expansion that, up to the present time, the public sector has known, and in the type of economic policy that dominates in this country.

The frontiers of the public sector have been constantly rolled back since the end of World War I. The business sector in France before 1981 was essentially developed through the two waves of nationalization occurring in 1936 and in 1945–1946. In 1936, two principal economic sectors were affected by nationalization: production of war materiel (the Act of August 11, 1936) and the railroads (the Decree of August 31, 1937, creating the SNCF—the National Organization of Railways, a limited company based on a mixed economy). The second great wave of nationalization in France came with the Liberation at the end of World War II: it offered a double innovation in comparison to that of 1936. First, its extent: entire sectors of the economy were nationalized—coal, natural gas, electricity, that is, basic industries; deposit banks and insurance companies. Second, its methods: practically no place was left in the national corporations thus created for private capital, and nationalization gave rise to either the establishment of state corporations (Renault, SNECMA) that replaced purely and simply the limited companies that existed previously, the state thus becoming the sole holder of capital or of stock of the new nationalized firm, or to the restructuring of the economic sector that has just been nationalized and to the absorption of the commercial and industrial firms that constituted this sector, such as the electric, natural gas and coal firms of Electricité de France (E.D.F.), Gaz de France (G.D.F.) and Charbonnages de France.

The public corporate sector thus constituted before 1981 has two sorts of tendencies. First, a tendency towards the multiplication of subsidiaries created or acquired by businesses already in existence—subsidiaries of firms the greatest part of whose capital belongs to a corporation in the public sector associated or not with other public corporations or conglomerates. This movement towards the creation of subsidiaries has been one of the most noticeable phenomena in the evolution of the sector of public corporations in France. The movement towards the creation of subsidiaries, which accompanied a strong concentration in the number of parent companies, produced prior to the beginning of the 1970s the constitution of large public conglomerates—thanks to what has been termed "a sort of second-degree sector" (Jeanneau 1984, p. 41)—that has led the public sector to intervene in areas that had remained up to then totally outside its sphere of action and has justified reference to that activity—even if the term is more polemical than juridical—as "silent nationalizations."

The second tendency that has affected the public corporate sector in France has been analyzed, in certain areas of opinion, as a movement towards privatization. The Left already pointed out that the multiplication on the part of the public corporations of minority shareholders resulted in the flight of an important part of the capital and activities of a great number of these firms from the control of public power, and, to that degree, we observed a virtual partial denationalization. But over and above that, and at the same time, from the 1970s on we saw the governments of the Fifth Republic take a certain number of measures destined to favor private-share offerings in public corporations: a certain number of public corporations (Renault management, national banks, insurance companies, the air industry) found themselves offered the possibility, within limits strictly fixed by legislation, of proceeding to free distribution or sale of a certain percentage of their shares either for the benefit of employees or even for the benefit of stock buyers totally unrelated to the firms (the result of the Laws of January 2, 1979, and January 4, 1973).

The Nationalization Law of February 11, 1982—taking into account the fact that "the public sector in France has been a decisive element in economic development" and that the State "must affirm itself as one of the principal agents of change" (report on the motives behind the project for the law of nationalization, Doc. AN no. 384, 1980, 1981)—steered a course opposite to the tendency mentioned. On the one hand as a minor measure, the law decided to renationalize the shares of the national banks that had been transferred or had belonged to the private sector by virtue of legislation prior to the coming of the Left to power; on the other hand and above all, the law decided to nationalize a considerable part of the industrial and banking sector as well as two financial firms. It is in this way that the nationalization effected in France in 1982 brought the public corporations in the national economy to levels that other Western European countries are

TABLE 8.1. Valuation of Public Corporations

	Increased Valuation	Present Valuation	Investments
France			
After the 1982 nationalization	20.0	11.0	35.0[a]
Before the 1982 nationalization	11.0	8.0	30.5
Austria	14.0	13.0	35.0
Sweden	14.0	12.0	30.0
Italy	12.0	11.5	30.0
United Kingdom	10.0	12.0	29.0

Source: J. Blanc & Charles Brulé. Les nationalisations françaises en 1982. Notes et Etudes Documentaires (French Nationalization in 1982. Notes and Documentary Studies) no. 4721, 4722 (20 June 1983).

[a]PTT (postal savings) excluded.

for the most part far from attaining: France underwent spectacular progress in its public sector and reversed the movement towards privatization
that appeared to be taking shape before 1981.

The boundaries of the public sector have been pushed back very far,
since henceforth there are more than 6 million personnel who work in the
public sector, or 34.1 percent of salaried employees. The number of civil
service employees of the state had risen from 494,000 personnel in 1914 to
2,210,000 in 1979. To which figures must be added the complement of
personnel of regional organizations and the 700,000 supplementary public
personnel coming from the 1982 nationalization to arrive at the 6 million
total.

Thus, more than one salaried employee out of three was working in
France in the public sector on the eve of the defeat of the Left in the
legislative elections of 1986 and of the adoption of the Law of Privatization
of 1986, which undoubtedly brings about a noticeable decline in the public
sector.

But even if this decline were to come about perceptibly, France is most
certainly not on the verge of witnessing the end of a "planned economy."

This type of economy is not only the fact of the existence of an important public sector; it is also the result of a certain type of economic policy.
Now, whatever might be the approach that we take to French economic
policy, we note the significant role the administration plays in it and its
primary function of integration. Already, in the 1970s, Erhard Friedberg
had noted, in regard to the French economy, that: "The modes of economic
intervention of the State are not the product solely of the administrative
apparatus, of its internal structures and operation. They can be understood
only in connection with the structuring, the organizing principles and the
practices of the business world, at the same time the partner and the target
of the action of the State" (1974, p. 103). Two systems, two organized
groups are interacting: the administrative "system" and the industrial "system." A relational model has existed since the end of the nineteenth century
to the beginning of the 1960s, according to Friedberg, that was discernible
in the coexistence of two systems of relations of unequal importance: one
system (system A) largely of the majority, resting "on the intense interaction
of the two 'specialized peripheries' in contact in the two groups — on the one
hand the sectorial support services, on the other the professional (trade)
associations instituted by the industrial milieux" (1974, p. 115); another
system (system B), of much less importance, resting "on direct contacts
between firms and the different administrative segments concerned" (1974,
p. 118). System A, by far the most common, was the essential channel for
intervention between the state and industry, system B operating only on a

temporary basis to fill in for the deficiencies of the first (p. 120).

In the course of that entire period characterized by the juxtaposition of sectorial regulations mediated through the relational systems A and B, the state remained, at least in appearance, external to the power structures of the managerial realm: "Remaining aloof most often from business, that it touched directly only occasionally and sporadically through a series of discrete actions, that intervention (of the State) — from an 'essentially macroeconomic perspective' — related to the business sector, that is, to the industrial sector (indeed to the industrial branch or division) considered as an aggregate of agents equal in rights and duties" (Friedberg 1974, p. 122).

To this model of exteriority another came to be substituted — the model of the entrepreneurial State, a model of integration: "The State henceforth participates directly in the determination and realization of structural changes at the heart of the industrial sector. In so doing, the State enters into the power structures of its sphere of intervention: it becomes an industrial agent entirely distinct" (Friedberg 1974, p. 124).

We witness here a double restructuring of the industrial world, characterized by its hierarchization and unification around oligopolistic, if not monopolistic corporations, which organize it more and more. We witness a restructuring of the administrative system, marked by a weakening of the specialized control structures in contact with the spheres of intervention. Concurrently, owing to the last evolution that deprives it of its "filtering periphery" (p. 133), marked by the growing importance and soon the preponderance of the Ministry of Finance and particularly of its "highminded directorates," of which the Office of the Treasury is the most influential, we witness: "progressive affirmation of a center coordinating most of the decision-making systems in regard to industrial matters and contributing to the unification of their action" (p. 138).

Henceforth, the state is itself engaged in the power structures of the industrial world. It is integrated into the economic apparatus. And this established fact of integration ought not to be different even though one might adopt another approach to the problems of economic policy in France. Thus, Jack Hayward describes the "dual policy style" that characterizes the French economy in recent years (Hayward 1982).

Two styles of economic policy appear to exist: the one, a planned economy, corresponding to a routine, normal and daily relationship between the administration and its economic partners; the other, a regulated economy, corresponding to a crisis situation in which the state attempts to impose its solutions on its partners in the industrial world. Thus, the crisis in the iron and steel industry that arose in France in the seventies witnesses the emergence or reenforcement of the state as principal agent. But as Yves

Meny and Vincent Wright point out, "it is a limited and constrained State; it is omnipresent but not omniscient. It is most certainly not omnipotent" (1985, p. 116). Integration, as we were saying, but relative integration.

A Model of Relative Integration

Despite the high degree of integration that I have just described, of administrative affairs and political and economic affairs, in France we are far from the absolute ascendency of the state and its administration over the totality of society. It is not enough to have inquiries contenting themselves with determining "if the relation of State-society is conceived essentially in terms of the supremacy of the State over Society (following the norm that prevails in France), of the supremacy of society over the State (following the Anglo-Saxon norm) or of the interdependence between society and the State (the norm of West Germany)" (Hayward 1985, p. 123). The supremacy of the state over society that assuredly prevails in France is tempered in two ways. First, the integration of administrative affairs and political and economic affairs is never total. We cannot ignore the principle that continues to govern relations between constitutive actions of the administrative system in a liberal state: a principle of separation, a principle of nonconfusion of actions that gives to relations between actions their particular coloration, even though their integration is very strong. Political and administrative affairs thus remain distinct, because of the rules affirming and guaranteeing the neutrality of the public function regarding political power and because of mechanisms that, while assuring the articulation of the political and the administrative, strictly limit the contacts between the affairs of the two sides to a certain number of obligatory passage points — public offices transcending the dictates of the government and ministerial cabinets — through which pass political will and political information. In the same way, administrative and economic actions remain distinct because: the field of public corporations, though broad in France, remains limited to certain sectors of the economy; the Law of Privatization adopted in 1986 reduced its dimensions; and the system of exteriority (that Friedberg calls System A) of the administration with respect to economic affairs, even if it loses ground, is not eliminated from the economic policy of France. But these are on the whole only dispositions common to every liberal state, to the supremacy of the state over society, the classical translation in French institutions of the principle of the separation of civil society and the state.

There are others who have better characterized the situation and the recent evolution of the French administration as to the relations between *central and local administrative actions* since the early 1980s. The tendency towards decentralization laid out in France by the Law of March 2, 1982, constitutes in that regard the clearest example of the concern to loosen up, to deintegrate the network of constitutive relations making up the administrative apparatus. We know that the French administrative apparatus up to that time was characterized by its overcentralization: a situation underscored by the existence of local collectives, departmental and communal, administered under the strict control of those representatives of the central authority, the prefects, who were at the same time the heads of the deliberative departmental assemblies and directors of the communal collectives. Now the prefects, subject to nomination and dismissal by the government, found themselves totally dependent on the central authority that had at its disposal the most effective institutional means to direct the action of regional organizations. Organizations whose constituency in addition found itself—through the play of those "relational triangles" pointed out by Michel Crozier and Erhard Friedberg (1977)—dispossessed of all power: in the system thus created in fact by the juxtaposition of two political and administrative hierarchies, the regulation of local affairs and the handling of dossiers were executed through agreements between local persons of importance and departmental administrators who, in exchange for concessions to the former with respect to the dossiers that interested them, obtained for their part the implementation of decisions made by the state. Double centralization—jurisdictional, by the domination of the central authority, and sociological, by usurpation of the power of the local constituency.

It is by reason of the desire to end that situation that the Law of March 2, 1982, and the addenda that followed it were adopted. These addenda decided on measures of considerable diversity whose impact it is still difficult to measure at the present time. First of all, the institutions have known a double mutation. The principle of the free administration of local organizations having been brought up, there has been created, besides the traditional regional organizations constituted by the commune and the department, a third level of autonomous administration between the department and the state: the region.

Created as a territorial organization, the region, like the other organizations, has at its disposal bodies elected through universal suffrage. On the other hand, executive power up to then belonging in the departments and the regions to the prefect—representing the state in the collectivity—was transferred to an authority elected by the territorial assembly, the president of the general council (department) or the regional council (region).

All the collectives (communes, departments, regions) had then at their disposal legislative and executive bodies elected (directly or indirectly) by the citizens of each collective. At the same time, the jurisdiction of the communes, departments and regions was enlarged by the transfer, to their benefit, of powers belonging previously to the state. On the whole, homogenous "blocks of power" were transferred to the different sorts of territorial collectives: planning, land use, professional and apprenticeship training transferred to the regions; rural development, social and health programs transferred to the departments; urban development and local facilities transferred to the communes. The other areas (transportation, housing, education, culture, environment) were shared among the three levels of territorial collectives. Prior to 1981 the economic powers of the territorial collectives were rather strictly limited. The new law authorized the territorial collectives to make use of the means and powers necessary for the protection of the social and economic interests of their constituency. In any case, the transfer of state jurisdiction to the territorial collectives was accompanied by the transfer of services and credits and compensated for by the conferral of taxes and allowances in favor of the territorial collectives.

Finally, administrative and financial controls, while not suppressed, are at least considerably eased and replaced by controls of a jurisdictional character exercised by the administrative tribunals and by new jurisdictional bodies created by the Law of March 2, 1982, the regional audit offices. The prefects found their role as guardians of power transformed in important ways. They now carry the title of commissioners of the republic and no longer wield executive power on behalf of the department or the region.

We can measure by such a sign the impact of the transformations brought about by the addenda regulating the relations between central and administrative procedures. They arise undoubtedly out of a concern, which must be translated into reality, to lessen the high degree of integration characteristic of the French administrative apparatus.

This concern is translated also in the very structure of the *central administrations* with the relatively recent multiplication during the years 1973–1978 and again since 1982 of what is called in France the "independent governmental agencies." That notion applies to such bodies as the mediator (the French version of the ombudsman) (1973), the commissions for data processing and civil liberties (CNIL), access to public documents (CADA) (1977–1978), the Audiovisual Regulatory Commission (now replaced by a National Commission for Communications and Freedom of the Media—CNCL), the Film Mediator (1983) and more. All of these agencies exercise their activities in three major sectors—data processing and communications, regulation of the market economy, the regulation of government bureaucracy. They have in common the concern to protect the public against the manipulations of opinion on the part of the state or any other organization, against the abuses of "uncontrolled capitalism," and against the massiveness and excesses of the administrative structure. These agencies are situated at the heart of or in proximity to the central authority, but they remain independent; they do not have the least jurisdiction, but neither are they classic administrative bodies, nor simply consultative organisms, and they are free of all hierarchical subordination, of all control on the part of the central authority. They operate primarily in three ways: by intervention in particular cases (they examine claims, petitions and complaints on which they issue a ruling or an opinion, or provide authorization and, sometimes, prescribe injunctions or sanctions); by participating in the drawing up of rulings (they offer recommendations or propose modifications in existing laws, and even have at their disposal a true regulatory power expressed in the elaboration of norms imposed directly on administrative bodies and private parties); and by the dissemination of information and the sensitization of public awareness which they address through the media and through annual reports widely disseminated by public agencies. These independent governmental agencies are never integrated into ministerial structures. They are directly attached to the Prime Minister if their functions are of broad scope or, if their jurisdiction is specialized, to a particular ministry (Finance, Justice, Culture, Communications, etc.). Having appeared unobtrusively in the French administration, these agencies have attached themselves to it in a remarkable fashion and henceforth play in their respective sectors a role that—if not always precisely as decisive as one might wish for the protection of the public—is nonetheless a growing and extremely important role.

On several occasions, we have seen these independent governmental agencies (the Mediator, CADA, CNIL, the Audiovisual Regulatory Commission) succeed in daunting administrative or corporate bodies that have threatened to abuse their power and make them retreat. CADA, the Commission for Access to Public Documents, for example, although a nonjurisdictional body, has elaborated a veritable system of regulations that ensures the coherence of its own doctrine and provides guidelines for the administration in the decisions it takes to provide access or not to government documents that are demanded by the public. On the basis of that system of regulations, governmental bodies now know the limits of their prerogatives and, preferring to avoid being "called on the carpet" by CADA, defer to the requests for access to government documents that are addressed to them, insofar as these requests accord with the principles laid down in the commission guidelines.

Finally, these independent governmental agencies, which have been described as operating "like a form of autolimitation of the central executive power to which the latter has recourse because of its very power" (Gazier and Cannac 1983–1984, p. 27), appear to respond to several preoccupations that have arisen in the French administration in recent years. Besides their independence, which is their mark, both with respect to political power and to private interests, these independent governmental agencies appear to offer important advantages from the point of view of the central administrative structures. They are extremely streamlined agencies: "Services, manpower, physical facilities, budget—everything is reduced to the minimum. No specific moral persuasion, no hierarchy, no outside control. A controlling body, a few operational guidelines and that's all" (Gazier and Cannac 1983–1984, p. 20).

The controlling body is generally a board of 5 to 20 members at the most, but it could be an individual (the mediator, for example). In most cases, it is the government that names the members of these independent agencies, sometimes the Parliament or certain upper echelon bodies (*Grands Corps*) of the state. In all cases, however, mechanisms are designed to guarantee the independence of the members named, whether through the choice being limited to persons who are members of organizations well known for their independence, or through nominations being accorded for a set term and unrenewable. These groups function therefore not only in an independent manner, but also very economically insofar as "one has only to draw on the potential of qualified and independent personnel that is held in reserve, notably in the upper administration, to furnish a minimum of management and . . . the agency is in place" (p. 29).

Finally, and above all, owing to the handpicked quality of the nominations, the streamlined nature of these agencies, the fact that they present themselves as a body of "savants" directly responsible to the public and not as technocratic bodies, they promise to afford "a type of antidote to overregulation, to corporatism and bureaucracy" (p. 29), which are persistent and ignominious marks of our government.

We see therefore that the questions posed earlier were in any case too simple. An excess of state? An end of the state? Isn't the question rather: another state?

References

Birnbaum, P. "La Fin de l'Etat?" ["The End of the State?"] *Revue française de science politique* 35, no. 6 (Dec. 1985):981–98.

Colliard, C. A., and Timsit, G. *Les autorites administrative independantes [Independent Government Agencies]*. Paris: Presses Universitaires de France, 1988.

Crozier, M., and Friedberg, E. *L'Acteur et le système* [*The Actor and the System*]. Paris: Editions du Seuil, 1977.

Delarue, J. M. "Rapport général de la Commission" ["General Report of the Commission"]. In *Revue Française d'Administration Publique. Administration et Société,* (April–June 1983), p. 60–65.

Friedberg, E. "Administration and Entreprises" ["Administration and Corporations"]. In M. Crozier, et al. *Où va l'administration française?* [*Where is the French Administration Headed?*]. Paris: Les Editions d'organization, 1974.

Gazier, F., and Cannac, Y. "Les autorités administratives indépendantes" ["Independent Governmental Agencies"]. *Etudes et Documents du Conseil d'Etat* 35 (1983–1984):13–78.

Gremion, P. *Le Pouvoir péripherique* [*Peripheral Power*]. Paris: Editions du Seuil, 1976.

Hayward, J. "The Dual French Policy Style." In *Policy Styles in Western Europe.* Edited by J. Richardson. London: George Allen and Unwin, 1982.

———. "Les politiques industrielles et économiques" ["Industrial and Economic Policies"]. In M. Grawitz and J. Leca, *Traité de science politique* [*Treatise on Political Science*]. Paris: Presses Universitaires de France, 4 vols., 1985, p. 89–153.

Jeanneau, B. *Droit des services publics et des entreprises nationales* [*Law governing public services and national corporations*]. Paris: Dalloz, 1984.

Meny, Y., and Wright, V., eds. *La Crise de la sidérurgie européenne* [*The Crisis of the European Iron and Steel Industry*]. Paris: Presses Universitaires de France, 1985.

Timsit, G. "L'Administration." In M. Grawitz, and J. Leca, *Traité de science politique* [*Treatise on Political Science*], in 4 vols., vol. 2, p. 446–509. Paris: Presses Universitaires de France, 1985.

———. "Théorie de l'administration" ["The Theory of Administration"]. *Economia,* 1986.

9

Policy Developments and Administrative Changes in India

R. B. JAIN and O. P. DWIVEDI

Historical Perspectives

The present system of government and administration in India is largely a legacy of the British Imperial rule that ended in the year 1947. The years after Independence witnessed various adminstrative problems not only of law and order, but also of adjusting the old bureaucratic machinery of an alien government crippled by the aftermath of partition to serve the needs of a sovereign democratic nation. At Independence, India was faced overnight with movement of millions of refugees, perhaps the largest exodus of people at any one time anywhere on earth. This posed a great problem of relief and rehabilitation: a challenge to weld the various communities of India divided by languages, culture and castes into the working cohesion of a single union. This task was complicated by the confrontation with Pakistan in October 1947 and by the perennial problems of economic disasters, inflation and food shortages. Each one of the problems not only had political and policy overtones, but also an administrative dimension of gigantic proportions.

This indeed was a monumental task for a nascent democracy, the largest but the poorest in the world, which was devoid of any substantial middle class, educational and technical know-how, and economic and human resources. For a time it was feared that the machinery of government would break down under the stresses and strain of the new environment and the developmental ethos of a democratic government. Yet it must be affirmed to the credit of the foundations laid down by the British system that not only has the structure sustained as a whole, but it has also adjusted to its vastly changed role. This, however, did not mean that the system was in any way free from deficiencies, or that new experiences, techniques, methods and administrative vitality were not needed. The problems in reality had just begun to appear.

The Inheritance

At Independence, India inherited from the British a monolithic, strictly hierarchical administrative structure, with the line of command running unimpeded from the Viceroy and Governor-General in Delhi to the farthest village, but with certain well-established traditions. The purpose of such a system was to keep the interest of the British power in India dominant, make sure that the government got the revenue it needed, and from the point of view of peace and security, to maintain law and order.

The system of administration that had evolved in India since the times of Warren Hastings and Lord Cornwallis during the Imperial rule until Independence had five distinguishing features: (1) the district was the basic unit of administration, and the office of the District Collector was a prototype of a "District-Maharajah," "the alter-ego of the vice-regal authority" controlling, directing and coordinating all administrative activity in his district; (2) centralization was the recognized principle of administration both territorially and functionally, and in decision making in almost all policy areas — public finance, legal and judicial system, education, health and even public works; (3) the steel-frame of administration was the strong institution of a single dominating civil service, with the Indian Civil Service (ICS) an elite generalist service, occupying the top position among other allied and subordinate services down the levels of central and provincial hierarchies; (4) a system of elaborate rules and regulations designed by the British was a means of maintaining control over the decision-making power of their large number of Indian subordinates, who had varying levels of training, outlooks and goals, and who were dispersed far from the administrative centers; and (5) a system of secretariat and executive offices was a split system prevailing both at central and provincial levels, ostensibly separating questions of policy from those of administration (Taub 1969, p. 156).

Such a system of administration suited the British. This was a status quo regime. It maintained and preserved the structure of society in India as it then existed, particularly the large proportion of the rural society. It did not concern itself with any radical or specific socioeconomic changes. The impact of the administration on the large proportion of Indian citizens was minimal. Thus, when the time for transfer of power came in 1947, the administrative system was not appropriately prepared to handle the massive developmental and postindependence tasks (Rai 1976, p. 30).

The Impact of Independence

The period since Independence brought most of the changes in the administrative system. As mentioned earlier, the attainment of independence brought in its trail momentous problems, which simultaneously needed a number of multiple revolutions: (1) the transition from a colonial system of government to a full-fledged parliamentary democracy with a federal structure of government and commitment towards a welfare state; (2) the transformation of a semisubsistence economy into a modern industrial community to solve the problems of poverty, unemployment and want; (3) a social revolution changing the caste-ridden stratified society into a progressive community oriented towards social justice; and (4) a technological revolution to let in the light of modern science on the crusted traditional ways of a conservative people.

The broad strategies adopted by the Indian leadership to usher in a new era were: (1) the political integration of the country; (2) the framing of a new republican constitution; (3) the adoption of adult franchise; (4) a system of rule of law and independent judiciary; (5) the policy of mixed-economy and democratic socialism for agro-industrial growth; (6) the policy of equal opportunity and protective discrimination for furthering social justice; and (7) the policy of nonalignment in foreign affairs. All these strategies have led since then to a number of veritable changes in policy process and the administrative system. But some of the old problems still persist in one form or the other while the processes of modernization and socioeconomic changes over the last four decades have given rise to a new set of problems pertaining to policy and administration.

Constitutional Goals and Administrative Development

The patterns of administrative development in India were largely guided by the imperatives of the republican constitution adopted by the people of India on November 26, 1949, and set into operation on January 26, 1950. The structure of administration had to respond not only to the system of parliamentary government and the principle of federalism enshrined in the constitution, but it also was expected to implement the new policy goals inherent in a number of its provisions relating to socioeconomic dispensations. Some of these are discussed below.

Federalism: The Administrative Implications

Indian federalism has retained the earlier principle of centralization of the British era in the structure of administration; it has vested imposing powers and responsibilities to the Union Government. The emergency powers contained in the Indian Constitution enable India, under certain circumstances, to transform itself into a unitary state. Under emergency provisions, the Union Executive and the Parliament can direct a state government in the use of its powers or assume all of its powers, the Union Executive acting for the state executive and the union Parliament enacting legislation as if it were the state legislature.

Apart from the fact that the central government has the constitutional right to modify the distribution of powers between the center and the states under certain circumstances, the central government also has vast powers over the collection and distribution of revenues, which make the state heavily dependent on the central government for financial support. Although the constitution provides for the devolution of revenue to the states under Article 275, the Union Government under Article 282 has the power to make grants to the states for any public purpose, even though the purpose is one for which Parliament cannot normally legislate. Under this provision, the central government allocates vast amounts of development funds to the state as part of Five-Year Plans drawn up by the National Planning Commission, an advisory body of the central government, putting additional responsibility on the administrative structure of the central government. However, despite these centralized trends, each state has a personality of its own, and can no longer be treated by the central government as merely pieces of territory for administrative purposes. The number, territorial size and composition of states have changed many times since independence in response to the demands of the people.

Fundamental Rights and the Directive Principles of State Policy: The Administrative Imperatives

The Indian constitution is committed to provide fundamental changes in the socioeconomic order through its provision on Fundamental Rights and Directive Principles of State Policy. While the fundamental rights guarantee for each citizen provides certain substantive and procedural protection to the citizens against the state, the Directive Principles of State Policy do not enjoy the legal force through the courts. They provide direction to the nation "to promote the welfare of people by securing and promoting as effectively as it may a social order in which justice, social, economic, and political, shall inform all the institutions of national life" (Constitution of India, Article 38). Taken together, these provisions have required a number of mandatory obligations to be observed by the administrative personnel in the discharge of their functions and a large number of different types of administrative institutions at all levels to carry out the purposes and aspirations of a new nation.

The right of equality under Article 16 of the constitution, for example, guarantees equal protection before the law; provides for equal opportunities in public employment; abolishes untouchability; and prohibits discrimination in the use of public places on the grounds of religion, race, caste, sex or place of birth. At the same time it protects the rights of minorities and provides protective discrimination for the downtrodden and the backward class of population, the so-called scheduled castes and scheduled tribes as mentioned in the constitution. The administrative implications of such constitutional provisions are far reaching; for example, it imposes additional administrative costs to implement preferences for members of scheduled castes and scheduled tribes. In recent years, such provisions have led to public controversies. Not only have there been allegations of lowering of administrative standards due to the induction of candidates with questionable capabilities, it has led to public riots in some states in recent years as a result of reverse discrimination (Jain 1981; Weiner 1983).

The Public Services

Perhaps India is the only country whose public services have been accorded constitutional status, and their rights and privileges have been safeguarded. Article 311 of the constitution provides for a safeguard to a public employee's right to be served with a notice to show cause before he could be dismissed from the service on charges of misconduct, inefficiency or corruption.

But the most unique feature of the provisions of the Indian Constitution is Article 312, pertaining to the creation of all-India Services, which retains the same prestige and status once accorded to the old ICS. The special characteristics of these services are that although officers are recruited and trained by the Union Government, they serve both the Union and the state governments, and occupy top policy-making and executive positions both in the center and the state governments. Moreover, they cannot be dismissed, removed or reduced in rank, except for cause and only after an approval by the Union Public Service Commission.

Apart from the all-India Services, the constitution also provides for the central services for the Union Government, and the state services for the state governments. While the all-India and the central services are recruited by the Union Public Service Commission, the state services are recruited by the State Public Service Commission.

Policy of Planned Economy and Administrative Development

A vast and continuous process of decentralization, diversification and even diffusion and disintegration that has taken place in the wake of the imperatives of constitutional goals and values marks the transition from a colonial administration to that of an administration based firmly on a federal system and democratic responsible government. The initial years of the Indian Republic provided a number of committed and devoted leaders who tried to expect the much needed coordination and integration and discover ways and means to direct the administrative effort to common and comprehended goals in an orderly and sustained manner through their influence in the legislatures in the party system of the Indian national congress, and in the making of the five-year developmental plans through the dominating economic authority of the National Planning Commission. As an inside observer put it:

> The political masters engaged in most operations consolidating India as a union of States, defining policy in the social and economic field, establishing a whole service of relationships between the states and the Union, and within each expressing parliamentary forms of procedure, regulation, and control for the governance of India. It was a time of variegated, comprehensive, carefully directed effort to establish and consolidate a popularly directed administrative system, to start institutions for economic and other purposes, and to define and embark on all-round plans of economic development (Rai 1976, p. 4).

In pursuance of the objectives of a welfare state and rapid-economic growth, India had adopted Five-Year Plans as a major instrument of public policy and the principle of "mixed economy" as the guiding ideology for planned developmental efforts. The objectives of planning and its social promises were derived from the Directive Principles of State Policy set out in the constitution. Attempts to formulate and implement development plans have been accompanied by a vast expansion of various administrative planning institutions and agencies and phenomenal growth of public services for developmental purposes. As governments have assumed greater responsibilities and have intervened in many more areas than before, their administrative structures have expanded. In the process, they have become more and more hierarchical, giving rise to problems of coordination at the horizontal levels. Although the various plan documents also provided directions and strategies for developing administrative capabilities and effecting administrative reforms in order to meet the challenges posed by the policy of planned socioeconomic development, efforts to achieve greater administrative decentralization and a large measure of public participation and voluntary action have been frequently frustrated. The administrative changes that have come about as a consequence of planning have not been able to bridge the large and ever-growing gap between planning and implementation.

Planning and Administrative Development

The strategy of planned economic growth and the consequent formulation and implementation of plan policies have put a tremendous strain on the administrative system. The success of developmental plans and policies depends to a significant degree upon the effectiveness and capability of the administrative machinery. The structural and organizational problems of administration posed by planning start with: (1) establishing the planning machinery itself and its location; (2) defining its powers, functions and responsibilities; (3) defining its work vis-à-vis the other administrative departments; (4) establishing effective channels of communications with the political organization; (5) establishing units for supervision and evaluation of execution; and (6) establishing relations with the state and regional level organizations, private sector, interests groups, trade unions and cooperatives. All these pose structural problems. The lack of qualified, efficient personnel with development orientation not only poses problems in human resources, but also encourages certain behaviors, atitudes and the distinct administrative culture for development (Sharma 1968; Maheshwari 1984).

Planners in India have sought to revamp the administrative machinery by establishing new institutions and procedures specifically needed for the requirements and exigencies of plan formulation and implementation, and by periodically suggesting and prescribing packages of administrative reforms as a substantive component of planning designed to increase the capability of the administrative system to withstand the pressures and strains generated by the acceptance of the new responsibilities. Thus, since the era of planning, a number of institutions having specific responsibilities connected with plan formulation and implementation have been established at every level of administration in India. And in many ways the process of planning has also made a deep impact on the character and functioning of the traditional administrative units and institutions. Two specific aspects need to be discussed.

THE INSTITUTIONAL DEVELOPMENT. The new institutions established as a result of the adoption of planning are the National Planning Commission and the National Development Council.

The National Planning Commission, an expert advisory body at the center, which is responsible for: formulating plans; assessing the resources;

providing for all technical and statistical details needed in planning activities; determining the nature of machinery needed for implementation of plans; and appraising from time to time the progress achieved in the execution of each stage of the plan. The National Development Council, a kind of super cabinet, consisting of the chief executives of all the states of the Indian union has emerged as an apex body to promote national cooperation between the center and the states. In almost all the central government ministries and organizations, planning cells have been established to assist in the formulation of plan projects and targets in each substantive area. Similarly planning boards and state planning departments have come into being at the levels of various state governments for preparation of state plans and integrating them with the national plan.

Due to various historical and political factors, the planning system in India continues to be highly centralized, despite the oft repeated demands for decentralization. The unsatisfactory performance of the centralized planning, however, has tilted the arguments in favor of decentralization. The increased scope of plan activities at lower levels, the recent development strategies emphasis on area development, and the adoption of a target group development approach tend to make the argument of decentralization even stronger. The issue is not so much whether to decentralize, but how and what to decentralize (Prasad 1983). However, efforts to establish a planning machinery at substate levels, although underway for sometime, have been halfhearted with the result that no worthwhile organization for plan formulation has emerged at these levels. Deficiencies have been particularly marked with respect to machinery for project planning and establishing linkages between projects. Successful operation of decentralized planning within a framework of multilevel planning requires appropriate planning organizations at these levels, which must be staffed with personnel of requisite technical expertise especially for preparing sound projects and working out linkages between them (Prasad 1984, p. 14).

As a sequel to the Directive Principles of State Policy provided in the constitution and with a view to associate people in the process of plan formulation and implementation a scheme of community development programs, Panchayati Raj institutions, Block Development officers, and a host of village level workers were introduced in the decade of the fifties and sixties in various state governments. But, in a majority of the cases these institutions have been virtually languishing on account of government indifference and in some cases tacit hostility of political leadership at the state level. The so-called experiments in district planning introduced since 1969 were reduced to a mere collection of felt needs or of disaggregated departmental figures. The late attempts to strengthen district and block level planning in the early 1980s, have not been greatly successful. The execution of plans has greatly suffered due to the absence of appropriate and adequate implementing machinery.

IMPACT OF PLANNING ON TRADITIONAL DISTRICT ADMINISTRATION. The expansion of government activities after independence, and the adoption of planned economic development has inevitably led to an increase in bureaucracy particularly at the lower levels of organization. The planning system has placed a heavy burden and responsibilities on the district as a traditional unit of administration and its head, the collector, district officer or the deputy commissioner, the various designations such officers have been known by in India. The question whether the District Collector, who has traditionally been performing the law and order and revenue collection functions should be associated with developmental functions or not is a question that has been continuously debated since independence. The impact of the British legacy as described earlier – the centralization of decision making, the system of rules and the generalist concept of services – has further affected the pattern of behavior of the district officials. This pattern is characterized by inflexible adherence to and dependence upon rules; a focusing of decision making upwards, and its reverse, a lack of delegation of authority and a generalized rigidity that prevents the organization from adapting readily to changing demands upon it. This pattern is complicated by situational elements such as administrative involvement in development programs, in the context of a developing society itself; and by particularly Indian components as well. Notable among the particularly Indian components are: a tendency for any group of people to divide into small groups on the basis of particularistic ties, heightening a lack of trust and reluctance to delegate authority; a tendency encouraged by the ideology of the caste system to think of human reactions in hierarchical terms; and a tradition of deference toward authority (Taub 1969, p. 161).

Administrative Improvement Through Five-Year Plans

The formulators of Five-Year Plans for planned economic development recognized the imperatives of change and improvement in the existing administration system if the goals of planning were to be realized. To this extent, every plan document has contained a specific chapter outlining suggestions for improving the administrative machinery. Thus in the First Five-Year Plan (1951–56), in a separate chapter on "Reform of Public Administration," it was laid down that the principal objectives of administrative changes were to secure integrity, efficiency, economy and public cooperation. Suggestions for changes in the Prevention of Corruption Act 1947 and the machinery for departmental enquiries were made to secure integrity. Similarly, proposals were made for: changes in methods of work and organization through the establishment of an Organization and Methods Division; a system of intensive training in the economic field; grounding in development administration for the IAS; and constitution of an industrial management cadre. A system of adequate participation, systematic evaluation, and a practice of reward and punishment for securing results for large-scale projects was proposed for financial control and economy in developmental projects (India 1953, p. 115–27).

The Second Five-Year Plan also emphasized the importance of integrity, provision of incentives, continuous assessment of personnel – their training in speedy, efficient and economic methods of work; and recommended the establishment of a vigilance officer in every ministry and department. Proposals were also made to establish Organization and Methods Directorates in the state administration. As a result of its recommendation for better control over spending of public money, a Committee on Plan Projects was formed by the National Development Council to conduct investigations, initiate studies and ensure efficiency in implementation of projects. It also urged the organization of cooperatives for helping people of small means, and the creation of an Industrial Management Service for the administration of public sector enterprises (India 1956a, p. 126–47).

The Third Five-Year Plan also contained a chapter on "Administration and Plan Implementation." It reiterated the need for high standards of integrity, efficiency and speed in implementation. It emphasized the importance of reduction in construction costs, improvement in maintenance and simplification of work procedures, and the need for a line of communication between the planning for the country as a whole and for each district, block and village, preserving the broad national priorities while adapting the plans to conditions and needs of each area and each community (India 1961, p. 276–90).

Noting the increasing gap between planning and implementation, the Fourth Five-Year Plan urged for a concerted drive for better implementation of plans. It noted that since many deficiencies in plan-implementation arose from weaknesses in planning, it was essential that detailed administration and operational plans were formulated for the fulfillment of plan targets. It urged the need for constant appraisal of economic trends and performance so that gaps were noted with sufficient precision, integration of plans for production, imports and exports, improvement in the system of reporting and information, introduction of performance budgeting, economy in construction of projects through preplanning, program management, avoidance of short tenures and frequent transfers and emphasis on quality of performance (India, 1970a, p. 154–71).

Although the emphasis on plan-implementation was continued in the subsequent plan documents, particularly in the sixth and seventh plan, as against recommending general changes or improvement in the Indian administrative system, but there is little evidence to suggest that plan implementation has improved in any substantial manner. Thus for example, the sixth plan document pointed out that planning, implementation and evaluation should be looked upon as an integral process, and need to be strengthened particularly at state, district and block levels. It suggested the startup of the antipoverty programs, the strengthening of district administration by appointment of District Development Officers, and strengthening of the national information center for data storage, retrieval and processing (India 1983, p. 88–96).

Similarly the seventh plan in order to achieve the twin objectives of effective implementation of the antipoverty program and to ensure a balanced regional development at least for minimum needs, laid a fresher emphasis on the decentralization of the planning process and monitoring of plan-projects. To this end, it suggested the decentralization of planning from the start to the district and block levels, and a scheme of effective functioning and financial decentralization, establishing appropriate budgeting and reappropriation, making district officers accountable to a district planning body and establishing data and information centers at district levels. It also laid emphasis on reforms in the administration of public enterprises involving questions of autonomy, accountability and coordination between different sectors of government, including ensuring speedy disposal of cases. Planning should increasingly be concerned with the appropriate administrative arrangements and personnel policies, especially in the less developed and remote areas and in the implementation of programs for the weaker actions. The management and administrative systems have to be improved to eliminate inefficiency, cynicism and lack of integrity (India 1985).

Impact of the Development Plans on Administrative System

The compulsion of planned socioeconomic development has no doubt changed the pattern and complexion of the administration system from the British framework of a stable order to that of a system of continuous strain both politically and administratively, "adopting ad hoc and frequently unsuccessful remedies to a procession of deeper, more intricate, and apparently less easily alleviated crises" (Rai 1976, p. 5). The administrative system, to say the least, has been unsteady throughout India, and is at its lowest ebb in efficiency and integrity. Commenting on this change in the temper and values of administration, an expert who has been a part of the administrative machinery both in preindependence and postindependence periods has observed:

> The British administration in India governed too little and did not concern itself enough with changes in the social and the economic order. Perhaps the Indian governments have governed too much. This may well have been inevitable, part of the temper of times, since India gained independence when the idea of a welfare state was the generally accepted norm. India had also a great deal to make up to come abreast with other nations of the world. . . . Where the life of the community, or at least its vital growth and development depends so heavily on the administrative machine, any inefficiency or erosion in standards has a snowballing influence and gathers speed in geometric progression. India has indeed been caught up in the problems of governing less but effectively, or taking on more ineffectively. Each difficulty, whether economic or social, has tended to produce more rather than less government but the country has by no means turned the corner towards ensuring reasonable standards of prolonged good management (Rai 1976, p. 6).

The Administrative State of India

The expansion of government has brought in its trail an inevitable increase in bureaucracy and public employment at all levels of government, particularly at the lower levels of organization. Government employment has expanded not only because of the radical changes taking place in the nature and growth of government functions, but also because in a country that cannot afford unemployment insurance the creation of lower posts has often been used to placate the massive unrest of the educated unemployed youth particularly at the levels of state administrations. All those have added to the cynicism and disenchantment that generally prevails in the public mind about the efficacy of the public management system as a whole.

In India, after independence, a new urge for social security had been born; freedom from want had become more important than freedom of poverty. Universal franchise resulted in the emergence of the welfare state concept that protects citizens in unemployment, sickness and old age. Today the administrative state is concerned with almost all aspects of human life including such areas as social services, education, exploration and conservation of natural resources, scientific and technological developments and space, satellite and communications research, which all contribute to make public services the largest employer in the modern sector of the economy of most countries throughout the world.

Coupled with the change and increase in governmental functions, the most obvious determinant of the growth in government employment is to be found in a nation's demographic components. Even if it is assumed that the functions of government remain unchanged, a growing population necessitates an expansion of public service. If, at the same time, new groups enter the political system in the expanding participation, the capacity of the government to respond effectively builds up more demands and pressures on the administrative apparatus for new services and more personnel. Two specific aspects require our attention.

Population Growth in India

Among the demographic factors affecting the Indian planning system has been a tremendous growth in population despite an aggressive and extensive family planning campaign. From 251 million in 1921, India's population more than doubled by 1971, reaching 540 million. The census of 1981 reported India's population of 685.48 million, which is expected to exceed one billion by the end of the twentieth century at the present annual rate – about 2.2 percent. The annual rate of population growth has increased from 1.1 percent between 1921 and 1931 to 2.2 percent between 1961 and 1971, and to an average of 2.4 percent between 1971 and 1981 (Dwivedi and Jain 1985, p. 14).

In the 1950s, the urban population in India rose from 61.9 million to 77.8 million, an increase of 0.43 percent in the proportion of urban population to total population. By 1981, India's cities had grown by about 100 million persons at an annual rate of 3.8 percent. The census of 1971 placed urban population at about 24 percent of the total. Cities such as New Delhi, Bombay, Calcutta, Madras, Bangalore and Hyderabad have experienced population explosions over the period through 1981. The percentage of urban population has been consistently increasing.

As a result of the dramatic growth in the population and an increase in nationalization, a large segment of population became increasingly dependent upon certain services provided by the government. Urbanization has been related to industrialism, and these combined with population growth have placed heavier demands on transportation, communication, financial utility, education, medical, health and other services.

Government has become more intensively involved in regulating, planning, stimulating and even undertaking directly economic and commercial activities in many significant areas. The government of India's commitment to the abolition of poverty through socialism and a variety of social services for minorities and the economically disadvantaged classes have further accelerated the demands on government apparatus, and has penetrated more and more sectors of the citizen's life. Citizens' increased dependence upon the activities and the initiative of the government in all spheres of life has further increased public employment (Dwivedi and Jain 1985, p. 16–17).

The Dimensions of Growth

Although it is difficult to establish a direct correlation between government employment and spending, it is quite fair to assume that the changing priorities in government spending show that many new programs have been added, and the increasing budgets of departments have necessarily expanded the public service payrolls. Growth of expenditure in one sector of public activity also generates growth in related sectors, which supports Michel Crozier's thesis of the self-generating bureaucracy. Thus the change in the size and the composition of the government's own labor force does not occur in a vacuum, but is affected by several factors (Dwivedi and Jain 1985, p. 17).

Another way of measuring the growth of public employment is to look at the growing structure of administration. As an illustration, the growth of the secretariat at the union level of administration denotes an upward trend in the number of functions and the evolution of departments and ministries in the central government since 1953, which provides some idea of the growth of public employment. Table 9.1 indicates clearly the growth of public employment at the central government level in India. It seems to support the view held by a World Bank Report that public employment in developing countries has grown rapidly in response to the demands for improved public services (IBRD 1983, p. 101).

TABLE 9.1. Growth of Central Government Employment, 1953–1985

Year	Employment[a] (thousands)
1953	1,561
1956	1,792
1961	2,094
1966	2,710
1971	2,921
1976	3,074
1981	3,242
1985	3,342

[a]Includes regular and nonregular employees.
Source: Dwivedi and Jain, *India's Administrative State* New Delhi: Gitanjali Publishing, 1985), p. 19; A.N. Agrawal, et. al. *India: Economic Information Yearbook, 1987–88* (New Delhi: National Publishing, 1987), p. 78.

Although overstaffing the public service imposes a financial burden on the state, undermines morale and presents a major obstacle to efficient management, and expanding regular government employment does not help to solve the shortage of productive employment opportunities in the economy, most developing countries cannot afford unemployment insurance schemes. For short-term unemployment relief temporary public works (or food-for-work) programs are preferable, both in terms of costs and returns, resulting in indiscriminate additions to line agency payrolls that are likely to become permanent (Ozgediz 1983, p. 9).

Another characteristic of public employment in India is reflected in Table 9.2, which shows distribution of central government employees by ministries and departments during the growth decades of 1961 to 1980. During these twenty years, central governmental manpower increased from 1,986,577 (regular staff) in 1961 to 3,321,072 in 1980, a growth of 1,334,495 employees or 67.2 percent. During this period, the most dramatic growth was concentrated in four ministries (communications, which includes post office, telegraph and telephones; civilian defense; home affairs; and railways), which accounted for 85.5 percent of the total increase. These four growth sectors reflect the conscious public policy decisions made by India to enhance services in these areas. Obviously, maintenance of law and order, along with transportation and communications, are priority items for the government.

The expansion of public bureaucracy has been accompanied by a proliferation in the number of regulations, some of which are virtually impossible to administer and make the processing of transactions cumbersome. The expanding sphere of the role of governments has placed the bureaucracy in a monopolistic position and has enhanced the opportunities for greater administrative discretion. For example, during the first two decades of the postindependence period, legislation output increased by more than three times compared to any period preceding the attainment of independence. During this period about 1,600 statutes, including 21 constitutional amendments, more than 100 regulations, 100 president's acts and 150 ordinances were enacted. In addition, an average of about 5,000 rules were being issued every year (Sarkar 1968, p. 1). Executive regulations together with increased bureaucratic discretion provide opportunities and incentives for corruption, since regulations governing access to goods and services can be exploited by civil servants in extracting "rents" (Krueger 1974). Thus in many developing countries, public bureaucracies have become uncontrolled and unaccountable centers of power pursuing their own interests through the institutionalization of systematic extortion and bribery. Under conditions of uncertainty and with a government that acts as the nation's largest employer, producer, regulator and even the consumer, both

Departments/Ministries	31 March 1961	31 March 1971	31 March 1980	Growth 1961–1980 Numerical	%
Agriculture and Irrigation	29,290	20,227	25,445	-3,845	....
Atomic Energy	4,417	14,492	23,292	18,875	422.2
Cabinet Secretariat	2,093	7,271	195[b]	-1,898	90.68
Commerce and Civil Aviation	....	....	8,209	8,209	....
Communications	241,599	385,560	532,524	290,295	120.2
Defense (civilian)	279,177	473,728	515,319	236,142	84.6
Education and Culture	4,830	11,966	8,776	3,946	81.63
Electronics	....	....	682	682	....
Energy	1,561	5,351	6,639	5,078	325.30
External Affairs	3,448	4,023	4,884	1,436	41.64
Finance	86,833	118,956	158,023	71,190	82.00
Health and Family Welfare	8,194	15,437	19,518	11,324	138.20
Home Affairs	29,357	77,759	237,207	207,850	708.00
Audit and Accounts	38,007	51,091	55,772	17,765	46.70
Industry	12,233	13,540	69,849	57,616	471.0
Information and Broadcasting	9,274	15,234	20,204	10,930	117.80
Labour	4,145	10,336	9,664	5,519	133.14
Law, Justice and Company Affairs	2,024	2,784	3,602	1,578	77.36
Petroleum and Chemicals	....	316	502	502	....
Planning	1,519	1,633	5,975	4,458	293.36
Railways	1,146,921	1,373,634	1,553,229	406,308	35.40
Rural Reconstruction	945	....	1,591	646	68.30
Shipping and Transport	10,293	5,536	5,769	-4,757	-46.2
Space	....	....	9,439	9,439	....
Steel Mines and Coal	6,299	10,294	11,911	5,612	89.10
Supply and Rehabilitation	15,874	14,257	144,402	-1,472	-9.30
Science and Technology	9,962	11,542	17,992	8,030	80.60
Tourism and Civil Aviation	10,742	14,684	17,570	6,828	83.60
Works and Housing	25,936	34,395	39,261	13,325	51.40
Social Welfare	....	1,049	578	578	....
Other departments	1,604	3,562	6,049	4,445	277.10
Totals	1,986,577	2,698,657	3,321,072	1,334,495	67.20

Source: Dwivedi and Jain, *India's Administrative State* (New Delhi: Gitanjali Publishing, 1985), p. 28–29.
[a]Only regular employees included.
[b]In 1977, the Department of Personnel and Administrative Reforms was separated from the Cabinet Secretariat and merged with the Ministry of Home Affairs, reducing the number of employees.

the public and civil servants have come to accept government inefficiency and ineffectiveness as part of the natural order of things (Gould and Amaro-Reyes 1983).

Administrative Reforms and Changes Since Independence

The problem of administrative reforms has received continuing attention both at the center and states during the last four decades of independence. Indeed since the British period, there has been a time-honored practice of setting up prestigious committees and commissions to study particular areas of administration and to make recommendations for improvement (Mishra 1963). Since independence, there have been a large number of changes in the structure, work methods and procedures of the administrative organizations. Although these changes have been gradual, at times not too perceptible, taken together they indicate to a certain extent the government's efforts to affect procedural and policy innovation in the administrative machinery and to keep pace with changed situations and growing needs and exigencies. It is a different matter, however, whether the efforts of the government in this direction have resulted in a lack of solutions to the various policy and administrative problems that arose, or have merely been lip service without really coming to the grips of the basic inherent issues. In order to assess the impact of such reform measures on the administrative systems and the consequent changes, it would be appropriate to refer in brief to some important reform measures suggested by the various committees, commissions and experts.

Beginning with the Tottenham Committee's Report immediately after World War II in 1945 (Tottenham 1946), which sharply advocated a proper division between secretarial departments and executive directorate and services, with liberal delegation of powers to the heads of departments, the question of secretariat organization was further debated by the secretariat reorganization committee, headed by Girija Shanker Bajpai, appointed by the government in 1947, which suggested a reorganization of work methods in the secretariat. In 1948, an economy committee headed by a prominent industrialist Kasturbhai Lalbhai, made many suggestions for effecting economy in central administration and tuning up the general efficiency and mold of the civil service (India 1947). Shortly thereafter, the first comprehensive review of the central government was undertaken by the committee headed by N. Gopalaswamy Ayyangar in 1949, which dealt with organizational changes, improvement in calibre of personnel and improvement in methods of transaction of governmental business. One of the recommendations adopted was the strengthening of the cabinet organization through the formation of standing committees such as Defense, Economy, Parliamentary, Legal Committee, etc. (Ayyangar 1949).

However, none of these attempts on administrative improvement received as much public attention as did the three subsequent reports: Gorwala Committee Report of 1951 and Paul Appleby's two reports in 1953 and 1956. Gorwala Committee, headed by a former ICS officer, A. D. Gorwala, was appointed by the Planning Commission in 1951 to examine existing administrative machinery and methods and to assess whether they were adequate to meet the requirements of planned development. Gorwala's report to the Planning Commission served as the basis for the formulation of certain crucial proposals for the reform of administration, which were later included in the First Five-Year Plan (Gorwala 1951a). In the same year Gorwala submitted another report relating to the efficient conduct of state enterprises (Gorwala 1951b). Appleby's two reports (1953 and 1956) made significant impact on the thinking and interest in administrative reforms among the government officials, educated elites and academics, perhaps because it was the first appraisal of the Indian administrative system by a foreign expert who was critical of the administrative machinery yet had complimented the system as being highly advanced. Appleby's first report dealt more with changes in the basic principles and concepts including the structural changes rather than with details of administrative machinery. Appleby's two main recommendations related to the establishment of a national Institute of Public Administration and the creation of Organization and Methods organizations at different levels of administration. These ideas were implemented immediately and helped the nation to develop necessary infrastructure for research, teaching and improving public administration in India. In his second report, Appleby made several proposals: for streamlining the administration, work procedures, recruitment and training; for improving relations between administration and Parliament, the Planning Commission, and the Comptroller and Auditor General; and for the need for delegation of powers.

The Administrative Reforms Commission and Administrative Changes

In the post-Appleby period (1953–66) a number of other committees and commissions made piecemeal recommendations relating to the qualifications for public service, salary structure, district administration, work procedures, corruption, and reorganization of the Foreign Service, but a comprehensive answer by the administrative system was not attempted until the appointment of the Administrative Reforms Commission in 1966 (India 1956b; India 1959; India 1962; India 1964; India 1966a). The attempts at reforms until now had been far too narrow in their scope and their pace was too slow, diffused and uneven to make any appreciable impact on the administrative system as a whole. Because of the widespread deterioration in administrative efficiency and standards, the idea of setting up an independent commission on the pattern of the Hoover Commission in the U.S. gained ground (Jain 1976, p. 398–434).

Accordingly, the Administrative Reforms Commission (ARC) was constituted on January 5, 1966 under the chairmanship of Morarji Desai, who was later replaced by K. Hanumanthaiya, to consider in particular the following areas: the machinery of the Government of India and its procedures of work; the machinery for planning at all levels; center-state relations; financial administration; personnel administration; economic administration; state administration; district administration; agricultural administration; and the redress of citizens' grievances.

The objectives laid down to guide the commission's investigations were: (1) "to give consideration to the need for ensuring the highest standards of efficiency and integrity in the public service"; (2) to take into account the need "for making public administration a fit instrument for carrying out the social and economic policies of the government and achieving social and economic goals of development"; and (3) to make the administration "responsive to the people" (India 1966b). The two additional objectives were implicit in the commission's terms of reference regarding the promotion of national integration and the maintenance of efficient standards of administration throughout the country.

After a comprehensive and painstaking investigation, the commission prepared and forwarded to the government 20 reports on various aspects of public administration. The reports related to problems of redress of citizens' grievances (interim), machinery for planning (interim), public sector undertakings, finance accounts and audit, machinery for planning (final), economic administration, the machinery of the Government of India and its procedures of work, life insurance administration, central direct taxes administration, administration of union territories and North East Frontier Area (NEFA), personnel administration, delegation of financial and administrative powers, center state relationships, state administration, small scale sector, railways, treasuries, Reserve Bank of India, posts and telegraphs, and scientific departments.

The ARC had stressed that in making the above recommendations it was guided by certain basic considerations, such as: "The intensity or magnitude of the administrative deficiency or inadequacy, the requirements of adapting the administrative system or procedure to the demands of developmental functions or tasks; the availability of the proposed reforms in terms of administrative, social and political challenges; the need for improving efficiency, effecting economy and raising administrative standards;

the need for maintaining a balance between administrative innovation/ change and stability; the need for improving the responsiveness of the administration to the people; the urgency for reform; and finally the demands of the present and the needs of the future" (India 1970b, p. 8).

Some of the most significant recommendations made by the ARC pertained to the: (1) appointment of Lok Pal (at the center) and Lokayuktas (in the states) to deal with complaints of corruption and public grievances; (2) formation of interstate councils under Act 263 of the constitution for dealing with center-state relations; (3) establishment of a central personnel agency at the center (Department of Personnel and Administrative Reforms) under the cabinet secretariat and independent personnel departments in each ministry; (4) introduction of the concept and technique of performance budgeting; (5) procedural reforms related to elimination of delays in sanctioning of pensions to retired officials and prompt payment by check and money orders, rational work allocation; (6) formation of a policy advisory committee and, for each department or ministry, policy cells and policy officers; (7) establishment of an internal standing committee on planning and planning cells in each ministry, constitution of state planning boards, and preparation of project manual and a training program for project management; and (8) the constitution of several corporations for management of the public sector, a clear statement of objectives of public sector undertakings, and constitution of consumer consultative committees. Perhaps the two most important areas touched upon by the ARC in its reports were: minister-civil servant relationships, wherein it emphasized the need for the depoliticization of services; and creation of a climate and culture of administration, where the growth of personal relationship between individual civil servants and minister should be arrested.

The most controversial recommendation, which if implemented would have meant a radical departure from the past traditions and structure of the civil services, was to change the character of the Indian Administrative Service (IAS). The ARC had suggested the regrouping of all the present services in the government of India into eight functional categories, so that "the IAS shall no more be a generalist but shall have a purely functional role of revenue administration" (India 1969, p. 24). This recommendation, which could have changed the entire civil service structure and would have ended the primacy of the erstwhile "steel-frame," had evoked sharp and bitter reaction from among the top hierarchy of the civil services (Sivaraman 1971, p. 384). No wonder, therefore, that the proposal was not only shelved, but was perhaps responsible to some extent in the development of an indifferent and apathetic attitude among the top civil services towards the implementation of the recommendations of the ARC.

In retrospect it seems that despite the extensive work done by the ARC extending over a period of four years it failed to make any real impact on the administrative structure and traditions, much less radically alter it to suit the changing needs of the country. There was no attempt to overhaul the original administrative structure and whatever reforms were undertaken were all within that framework. The ARC seemed to have no philosophy of administration and made no attempt to articulate it. Indeed it had no overall core report on public administration as a whole. It did not ask such basic questions as to what constitutes good administration and in reference to those norms of a good administration what could be considered to be the major reforms in Indian administration. In not raising these basic issues of administrative reforms, the ARC lost a major opportunity (Dubhashi 1985a).

Most of the ARC's recommendations had failed to arouse the authorities to take any positive action to implement them. But the real fact, as observed by a political commentator was: the commission never came to tight grips with the day-to-day administrative lacunae, lapses and shortcomings, much less produced a single, coherent report spelling out in precise and concrete terms the steps needed for effecting a complete overhaul or a real breakthrough in civil administration. The eminent individuals who headed the various study teams and their learned colleagues took only an overall view of the issues entrusted to them and dealt with the larger questions of administrative policies and procedures, but lost sight of specific issues affecting the core of administration. As a result, whatever reforms they have recommended and were acted upon by the government have hardly touched the core of administration. It remains as cumbersome, out-of-date and red-tape ridden as it was before the commission was brought into being (Narayanan 1970).

The failure of the ARC was perhaps also due to the fact that it submitted its reports at different intervals on different aspects of administration thus losing totality from its perspective. Even among these segmented sectors of administration, the focus of attention was only on higher levels of administration, and it neglected the lower structure and levels of administrative hierarchy where the ordinary citizen comes into contact with the administration—the very cutting edge of the system. Yet, another reason for the failure of this huge effort to bring about a modicum of administrative development was that many of these reforms were fraught with political implications. Many reform proposals could not be implemented because of their far-reaching political overtones, or their consequences on the political decision-making process. A reform proposal may be accepted because a particular category of administrators see reform either as a means of increasing their power or as neutral vis-à-vis their existing roles, but similarly they may be scuttled if one part of the powerful bureaucracy sees in it the danger of its downgrading. In such a situation it becomes necessary that "reform must be brought from outside the administration as ancillary to major political, social, or economic reform" (Gorvine 1966, p. 186).

Inadequate long-term commitment to the future of the country on the part of administrators and political leaders has been a source of ad hocism in Indian policy-making. The dominance of the civil services is mostly due to the inability of the ruling party to acquire or develop appropriate managerial and administrative talents among themselves and their limitations in dealing with technical personnel directly. In fact the generalist administrator has retained his present pre-eminence mainly because of the politicians' need for such personnel to function as an essential link between the present type of political leadership and the technocrats. Long-term political and administrative reform must aim at the development of such talent among the leadership cadres of the ruling party. There must be a deliberate drive in the party to recruit at its middle and senior levels administrators, entrepreneurs and professionals, as is being done in countries such as Canada and Japan and in the socialist countries.

The Post-ARC Reform Efforts

After the Administrative Reforms Commission, there have been no major committees or commissions on administrative reforms except for three isolated attempts: (1) to improve the pattern of the combined services competitive examination by introducing a preliminary tier of examinations to eliminate a large number of candidates having less potential for success, as a sequel to the Kothari Committee Report (Kothari 1976); (2) to revitalize the Panchayati Raj system at the grass-roots level by converting the three-tier structure into a two-tier structure (Mehta 1979), which has remained unimplemented because of the 1980 change in government; and (3) to change the system of economic administration (Jha 1986). The government had appointed in 1983 a high-powered commission led by Justice Sarkaria to enquire into the entire gamut of center-state relations, which has yet to submit its report. One of the reasons for such a lack of interest had been the domination of administration by politics in the 1970s and the preoccupation of political leaders with buttressing their positions rather than with administrative reforms. There was some toning up of administration during the emergency (1975–77), but that was more due to draconian measures taken to impose discipline rather than any systematic reform of administration. All these improvements were washed away in the backlash after the emergency; administration actually lapsed into a still greater measure of inefficiency. This only reiterates the danger and futility of undertaking ad hoc measures to tone up administration.

Major Policy Issues of 1980s

"March towards the 21st century" has been the oft repeated slogan in the mid-eighties, which has raised high hopes among the masses, the poor and the deprived. Besides the "technological modernization" that is inherent in such a concept, it has given rise to a number of other policy issues that remain major concerns of the government and the bureaucracy.

POVERTY ALLEVIATION. Among the most important policy issues is the alleviation of poverty, particularly in rural areas. According to one estimate, a third of the world's poor live in India, and 37 percent of India's population lives below a minimum poverty line. The policy of the Government of India as incorporated in the Seventh Five-Year Plan is to register a drop of 11 percent and bring the poverty level to 26 percent by the end of the 1990s. Although living standards have improved in India since independence and people no longer die of famine and no longer depend upon the food doles by foreign governments, poverty persists because neither economic growth nor targeted development spending has been big enough to help the truly poor. Also, poverty is mostly concentrated in the countryside and growth is in the cities. Although the green revolution has created patches of rural prosperity, the benefits have gone mainly to a few prosperous farmers and high- and middle-income landlords, and have not trickled down to low- or middle-level farmers. One estimate says that if incomes were to grow at a speeded-up rate of one percent a year, halving the poverty rate would take 35 years (Economist 1987). The government spends a large amount of money to alleviate the poor below the poverty line. The government of India's budget for 1987–88 has allocated a sum equivalent to U.S. $1.5 billion for antipoverty programs, almost 8 percent of the total government spending. Yet these projects, which consist of mass employment schemes and distribution of income-producing assets such as milch cattle, serve only a small fraction of the poor families.

Both official and unofficial studies have found that subsidies of all kinds, not only agricultural inputs but also food, education and medicine, go disproportionately to the better off. Even in the antipoverty programs, some 15.2 percent of the beneficiaries are the nondeserving, not counting the money squandered by the corrupt. One of the reasons for the persistence of this phenomenon is the excessive centralization in the administration of such welfare programs and another is the noninvolvement of people at the grass-roots level in the implementation of such schemes. As the recent experience of the state of Kernataka indicates, it is high time that such developmental schemes are fitted to local needs. Elected villagers can be expected to achieve far better results than the bureaucrats in reducing the incidence of corruption and identifying the deserving poor.

INDUSTRIAL POLICY AND PUBLIC SECTOR ISSUE. A second major policy issue confronting the government today is the issue of "liberalization" for industrial progress and the role of public sectors in India's economy development. The policy of "mixed economy" adopted by the government in the spring of the Indian Republic has led to the establishment of almost 200 public sector projects at the central level and approximately 700 at the state level, each level representing an investment worth approximately U.S. $25,000 million. However, a majority of these enterprises have failed to live up to expectations. Many have incurred heavy and continuing losses and far from contributing to the resources available for development have become a drain on the public exchequer. One reason for such a phenomenon is the growth and persistence of bureaucratic culture rather than commercial culture in the management of these enterprises, back-seat driving by the ministries leading to a lack of autonomy for managers of public sector enterprises, which is so necessary for decision making. Also cited as attributable causes are a lack of manpower planning and executive training and a lack of marketing techniques. Some of these shortcomings were noticed at the very outset. The company form of public enterprise was envisioned precisely to provide management autonomy. But while the "form" was here, the reality of "autonomy" was found missing (Dubhashi 1985b).

The government at present is trying to remove some of the unwarranted advantages that accrue to the public sector undertakings. "The most over fed part of an under nourished economy." About half of the public sector plants are working at 75 percent of capacity and more than a fifth at less than 20 percent of capacity. Although policymakers have not yet openly advocated "privatization" as the possible remedy, public monopolies in such areas as oil refining, power-generation and telecommunications equipment have been opened to private competition.

The policy of industrial controls and licensing was considered necessary in the early stages for fulfilling the objectives of planning and for ensuring that scarce resources were allocated to priority projects. The system that one economist calls "command capitalism" was originally intended to make India self-reliant, egalitarian and labor-intensive. Although some measure of self-reliance was achieved at the cost of the other two objectives, it has led to the emergence of a parallel black market economy and corruption, which far from promoting rational allocation of resources has only led to the growth of the luxury sector. It has been estimated that the black, or "untaxed," money amounts to at least 20 percent of gross domestic product, with perhaps another 15 percent generated by smuggling.

The policy of delicensing has made little headway in bringing out technological developments and qualitative improvement in India's indigenous industrial products, nor has it expanded the export market of locally produced technology—industrial electronic and software products. The missing link in the economic policy has been the marketing of indigenous products abroad. The recent policies of tax cuts and delicensing have only meant relief to the rich without any lowering of price, improvement in quality, or safeguarding of the consumers' interests. No wonder big business has never been as happy as in the present regime, despite recent government efforts that were well-publicized to pursue highly placed tax-evaders. Whether the Consumers Protection Act 1987 would have the necessary teeth to compel big business to think about the interests of poor consumers remains to be seen.

ENVIRONMENTAL PROTECTION. During the period 1980–87 protection of the environment became an important policy issue in India although some efforts were made beginning in 1972 (Dwivedi 1977). Since then several policy pronouncements have been made in Parliament and through the Five-Year Plan documents. While the First Five-Year Plan had emphasized the coordination of short- and long-term goals of development by promoting the protection and improvement of ecological and environmental assets, the Sixth Five-Year Plan (1980–85) was the first serious attempt to appreciate and plan environmental protection. It laid emphasis on protection of land from degradation due to soil erosion, floods, filtration, shifting cultivation; lack of sanitation; avoiding deforestation and exploitation of grasslands; providing clean drinking water; and social forestry and restoration of vegetative covers (Dwivedi and Kishore 1982).

The Seventh Five-Year Plan has especially emphasized the prevention of water and air pollution. As a result a number of schemes have been formulated with respect to cleaning riverbeds, especially of the Ganges, and sewage and industrial waste – water disposal in the cities of India. Policies checking smoke nuisance as a grave health hazard in cities like Calcutta, Kanpur and Bombay have also been undertaken. Emphasis has also been levied on planned urban development. Unplanned illegal and unserviced urban growth has caused various environmental problems because of human greed in converting prime agricultural land into residential or commercial areas to accommodate the staggering exodus of people from the countryside.

The administrative system in India faces a new form of challenge to devise and implement environmental policies. This requires changing legal, administrative and technical institutions, enabling legislative and regulatory instruments harnessing human resources for achieving the goals of eco-development. Although since the 1970s a number of legal measures have been taken to control environmental damage (Dwivedi 1985), there are several legal and policy inadequacies yet to be surmounted. Since India is a federal system, much of the action in this field has to be decentralized and made the responsibility of state governments. The implementation and enforcement of environmental policies would necessarily have to be devolved on the local administration, which is not only weak but ineffective. The state machinery for protection of the environment, despite the strengthening of their positions through the enactment of the Environment (Protection) Act of 1986, lacks the necessary technical expertise and human resources, as well as adequate support funds, to seriously carry out the enforcement; the result is that environmental crimes are on the rise. However, despite the administrative handicaps, voluntary organizations and judicial activism in India has in recent times raised some hopes by successfully crusading for protection of the environment and creating awareness both among the public and in government authorities about the kind of catastrophes and the nature of various kinds of environmental degradation facing the nation. This, however, does not absolve the government of its own responsibility in creating and sustaining the institutions to protect the quality of environment in the country (Dwivedi 1987).

The Emerging Administrative Style

There is no doubt that political will and political leadership have been the crucial factors in the kind of changes in administrative institutions, structures, style and cultures that have taken place in India after independence. However, the process of administrative development has been a continuous one. Although one can discern certain distinct changes occurring at some phases of the development of the polity, the emerging pattern has been the product of the totality of politico-administrative environment that has operated in the country so far.

The first ten years of the Republic represent a period of remarkably smooth change and adaption from the British Raj to a democratic parliamentary system during which a bold attempt was made by the political leadership to change the nature and values of the administrative system, while preserving its essential characteristics of an effective framework to cope with new problems and situations. There were no visible cracks in the system, rather it developed the necessary resilience, imagination, and the capacity to both mend, mold and build. The process of change from this situation was manifest in the next ten years of the growth of the Republic, which is up to the end of the period of Lal Bahadur Shastri's term as prime minister and the beginning of the Indira Gandhi era (1966). During this time, a new generation of politician emerged who was less affected by the liberal tradition and ways but clearly representative of the masses in objective and character. However, despite the many stresses and strains, the trend and temper of the administrative procedures and style of the preceding decade were substantially preserved.

It was after 1967 that most of the fundamental values of the administrative system consolidated during the earlier years of the Republic began to erode. That year marks the beginning of uncertainty and instability in the political will. This may be owing to personal struggle among leaders for consolidating and preserving power or to changing economic, local or institutional factors that did not result in appropriate directives to the administrative apparatus about policy-making. It remained disoriented and was replaced by a kind of a "shot-gun" approach. The administration and the administrators reached the lowest ebb in both their performance and their efficiency at the time of the heightened crisis posed by the imposition of the nationwide emergency in 1975. The post-emergency period also did not help in consolidating the erstwhile standards and morale of the public services to help solve some of the crucial emerging policy issues of the period. The coming to power of the youthful Rajiv Gandhi in 1984 raised substantial hopes for the emergence of a new administrative style having new vigor, new values of efficiency, technology and speedy service to the community, but soon such hopes seemed to have become dreams.

Basically, there have been a number of visible changes in the administrative system and style since the British times. The "district" as the fundamental unit of administration has undergone a metamorphosis, both in terms of its importance and its chief executive's position and stature. The importance of both the district and District Officer has weakened and disintegrated due to the vast expansion of governmental activities. The demands put forward by the local political leadership and the emergence of self-styled social and political workers who have the right political connections at the center and at times use antisocial elements for support, both have become a source of constant harassment to the District Officers' authority. Much of a District Officer's time is simply wasted in listening, persuading and arguing with these elements, while regular official work remains unattended without substantial accomplishment. These developments, coupled with the enormous responsibilities that are now put on a youngish District Officer, have eroded whatever autonomy and authority officers used to employ to their assigned duties in the past. An ambitious officer now wants to complete his compulsory tenure at the district as early and smoothly as he can and looks forward to the day he is posted to a position at the state capital away from the rough and tumble of district politics, with the result that district and local administration suffers much at the delivery point and at the cutting edge.

Along with the decline of the district as a level of administration, there has been a simultaneous decline in the strength and morale of the main public service—the so-called steel frame of the British administration. Although the Indian Administrative Service still maintains its dominant position despite the various attempts by the Administrative Reforms Commission and the Pay Commissions to water it down, its position and prestige in general has suffered, due to various sociopolitical factors referred to above. Public and political reactions, values, judgments, and even sentiments and prejudices have affected the performance and morale of public bureaucracy in India. There seems to be at present a strong reaction and suspicion against the power of the bureaucracy and the constant hammering that it has received at the hands of politicians. The bureaucracy earned the name of "villain" in the public eyes, who regard it as a big impediment in the attainment of the socioeconomic millennium promised to them by politicians. The ethical values of politicians, businessmen and bureaucrats have gone down so low that there is no aspect of public life today that is free from corruption or black money. The dual personality which each of these possess has enabled them to preach moral values in public but not hesitate to throw professional and individual morality behind the gaze of public eye for less or for more (Dwivedi and Jain 1985, p. 122–23).

The increased authority for "licensing" and "control and regulating" has earned the government the nickname of "license, permit, quota raj" which in addition has opened many areas and a multitude of opportunities for corruption, bribery and affluence through ill-gotten gains. Although at no time in the recent history of India did the public ever believe the administration was clean, there were times when the extent of suspicion was very low. All through these years, and particularly in the later period, corruption has almost become the way of life. A sort of cynicism seems to prevail that one has got to live with it. In the process, the one section of society that has suffered immensely is the poor citizen. He is devoid of proper means through which he can let himself be heard, or even put forward his complaint or grievance for any effective or speedy redress. The record of central and state governments in the post-independence period on the question of providing services that are "sensitive, courteous and satisfying" has been, to say the least, dismal. Even with the vast bureaucracy, the treatment of rank and file employees as compared to their high-ranked colleagues leaves much to be desired. The way they are huddled in dingy rooms overcrowded with dilapidated furniture, accumulated dust on files, cobwebs on the corners and cabinets, no proper sanitary or water arrangements, all these and much more speak about the prevailing duality in the administrative architecture and culture in India.

The officers' excessive dependence upon notations entered by the junior clerks on every file, the outdated administrative procedures and formalism, the excessive delay in forwarding an application and the infinite time taken to passing of the final order, the uncertainty in the application of rules or regulations but bending regulations for selective applications; the methods of flattery and encouraging subservience for obtaining service from the administrators, the lubrication required in the form of payment to powerful political or bureaucratic functionaries, the sight of an untidy, dirty public office with dust, vermin and the red stains of betel, have all become a part of administrative culture in India. Coupled with excessive "secrecy" and "mystique," such situations do not encourage any citizen even to attempt to seek what is legally due to him thereby generating a sense of indifference, apathy and resignation, which results in preferring to employ the services of so-called "intermediaries" on "payment" and get the work done rather than face the ordeal himself and get frustrated. In the government system of today's India, the hallowed tradition of continuity, hierarchy-based status and distance-based authority have become so important that the overall work ethic is usually one of apathy and indifference. The performance is at the level of lowest common denominator. There is no concern for the common man, his time, his difficulties, his inconvenience in coming to the office again and again. The lower hierarchy of employees has become so insensitive and unresponsive toward their duties and work that the public is no longer surprised. On the contrary, finding any exceptions to the above listed norm brings an element of surprise.

Finally, a part of the emerging administrative style is reflected in the erosion of the element of cooperation and esprit-de-corps not only between the superior and the subordinate but also within the members of one common service. The bonds of disciplinary control, supervision and disciplinary sanctions, and the bonds of attachment, interest and loyalty that were the hallmarks of cooperation between the various levels of authority in the past, have not only dissipated but, if invoked, remain attended without proper compliance among the erring officials or employees. Depending upon one's political linkages or the subordinate employees unions' political strength, even legitimate means of control have lost all sanctity and meaning in the administrative parlance. The emerging administrative style and culture of India does not seem to provide any positive help for the ordinary citizenry (Dwivedi and Jain 1987).

Conclusion

These above analyses of changes in the style and culture of administration in India may seem to be pessimistic. However, they are not meant to undermine the achievements and the performance of the administrative system. The administration in India has been a fine machine, capable of rendering some excellent performances in the sphere of policy-making and implementation. It has over the years sustained the working of the most populous democracy with the most politically conscious people anywhere in the world. It has been able to maintain its strength, and achieve a strong industrial base for the nation through a system of planned development. There has been an absolute growth in terms of literacy, education, scientific and technical knowledge, and even in relative prosperity. The bureaucracy in India has responded well in times of crisis and particularly when it was given clearly defined objectives and unambiguous priorities. All these give a ray of hope for further improvement in the style and operation of the administrative system in India. The need is to change the prevailing insidious subculture, and for this a change toward new ethos, new attitudes and a new work ethic is required at all levels of administration. As elaborated by Nitish De:

> We need a change process in the government with collective effort at the grass roots, the middle echelon, and the top level to ensure that quality of relationship at work is not vitiated by display of authority, arrogance and status. This is where task-oriented or goal-oriented management approach may go astray. Getting the task accomplished is as important as the processes that are initiated in getting it done . . . it is the quality of process that determines the quality of result (De 1985).

Clearly the administrative system in India, which has been assessed as a "plastic-frame" (Rai 1976, p. 147), is in need of nuts and bolts at points where the flows are stopped, reversed or increased. If administrators receive moral leadership from politicians, they then can provide the most effective, responsible and responsive service to the people they are there to serve.

References

Appleby, Paul H. *Public Administration in India: Report of a Survey.* New Delhi: Cabinet Secretariat, 1953.

_____. *Reorganization of India's Administrative System with Special Reference to Administration of Government's Industrial and Commercial Enterprises.* New Delhi: Government of India, 1956.

Ayyangar, N. Gopalaswamy. *Report on Reorganization of Machinery of Government.* New Delhi: Government of India, 1949.

De, Nitish. "Administrative Innovations: Technologies and Beyond." *Economic Times,* 25 Mar. 1985.

Dubhashi, P. R. "Administrative Reforms in Perspective." Dr. John Mathai Endowment Lecture, University of Kerala, 1985a.

_____. "Administrative Reforms: The Current Context." Lecture in the Indian Institute of Public Administration, New Delhi, 1985b.

Dwivedi, O. P. "India: Pollution Control Policy and Programmes." *International Review of Administrative Sciences* 43, no. 1 (1977):123–33.

_____. "Environmental Regulations in India." *The Environmental Professional* 7, no. 3 (1985):121–27.

_____. "Toxic Chemicals in the Environment: The Case of Canada and India." In *Perspectives on Technology and Development*. Edited by O. P. Dwivedi. New Delhi: Gitanjali, 1987, 241–59.

Dwivedi, O. P., and Jain, R. B. *India's Administrative State*. New Delhi: Gitanjali, 1985.

_____. "Bureaucratic Morality in India." *International Political Science Review* 9, no. 3 (1988):205–14.

Dwivedi, O. P., and Kishore, B. "Protecting the Environment from Pollution: A Review of India's Legal and Institutional Mechanisms." *Asian Survey* 22, no. 9 (1982):894–911.

Economist, 9 May 1987, p. 13.

Gorvine, Albert. "Administrative Reform: Function of Political and Economic Change." In *Administrative Problems in Pakistan*. Edited by Guthrie S. Birkhead. Syracuse, N.Y.: Syracuse University Press, 1966.

Gorwala, A. D. *Report on Public Administration*. New Delhi: Government of India, 1951a.

_____. *Report on Efficient Conduct of State Enterprises*. New Delhi: Government of India, 1951b.

Gould, David J., and Amaro-Reyes, Jose A. *The Effects of Corruption on Administrative Performance: Illustrations from Developing Countries*. Washington, D.C.: World Bank, 1983.

India. *Constituent Assembly Debates*. New Delhi, vol. 2, 4 Dec. 1947.

_____. *Report on the Public Services (Qualification for Recruitment) Committee*. New Delhi: Ministry of Education [Mudaliar Committee], 1956b.

_____. *Commission of Inquiry on Enrollments and Conditions of Service of Central Government Employees, 1957–59*. New Delhi: Ministry of Finance, [Second Pay Commission report], 1959.

_____. *Report on Indian and State Administrative Services and Problems of District Administration*. New Delhi: Government of India, [Krishnamachari Report], 1962.

_____. *Report of the Committee on Prevention of Corruption*. New Delhi: Ministry of Home Affairs, [Santhanam Committee], 1964.

_____. *Report of the Committee on the Indian Foreign Service*. New Delhi: Ministry of External Affairs, [Pillai Committee Report], 1966a.

_____. Ministry of Home Affairs, Department of Administrative Reforms, Resolution No. 40, 165-AR(P), dated 5 Jan. 1966b.

_____. *Report on Personnel Administration*. New Delhi: Administrative Reforms Commission, 1969.

_____. *The Administrative Reforms Commission and Its Work: A Brief Survey.*

New Delhi: Administrative Reforms Commission, 1970.

India, Planning Commission. *The Five Year Plan,* 1951–56. New Delhi: Planning Commission, 1953.

_____. *The Second Five Year Plan,* 1956–61. New Delhi: Planning Commission, 1956a.

_____. *The Third Five Year Plan,* 1961–66. New Delhi: Planning Commission, 1961.

_____. *The Fourth Five Year Plan,* 1980–85. New Delhi: Planning Commission, 1970.

_____. *The Sixth Five Year Plan,* 1980–85. New Delhi: Planning Commission, 1983.

_____. *Draft Seventh Five Year Plan.* New Delhi: Planning Commission, 1985.

International Bank for Reconstruction and Development. *World Development Report,* Staff Working Paper No. 583. Washington, D.C.: World Bank, 1983.

Jain, R. B. *Contemporary Issues in Indian Administration.* New Delhi: Vishal Publications, 1976.

_____. "Reverse Discrimination: A Dilemma, in Quest for Social Justice and Equal Opportunity." *Indian Journal of Public Administration* 27 (Jan.–Mar. 1981):181–98.

Jha, L. K. *Committee Report on Economic Administration.* New Delhi: Government of India, 1986.

Kothari, D. S. *Report of the Committee on Recruitment Policy and Selection Methods.* New Delhi: Union Public Service Commission, 1976.

Krueger, A. O. "The Political Economy of Rent Seeking Society." *The American Economic Review* 64, no. 3 (1974):291–303.

Maheshwari, S. R. "Administering the Planning System." *Indian Journal of Public Administration* 30 (July–Sept. 1984):603–12.

Mehta, Ashok. *Committee Report on Panchayati Raj.* New Delhi: Government of India, 1979.

Mishra, B. B. "Efforts for Administrative Reforms Before Independence." *Indian Journal of Public Administration* 9 (1963):311–55.

Narayanan, P. S. "ARC Goes: Core of Administration Remains Untouched." *Northern India Patri-Ka.* Allahabad: 1970.

Ozgediz, Selcuk. *Managing the Public Service in Developing Countries: Issues and Prospects,* Staff Working Paper No. 583. Washington, D.C.: World Bank, 1983.

Prasad, Kamta. Planning in India: Some Basic Issues Relating to Operational and Strategic Aspects. Presidential address to the 66th Annual Conference of Indian Economic Association. Bangalore, Dec. 1983.

Rai, E. N. Mangat. *Patterns of Administrative Development in Independent India.* London: University of London, 1976.

Sarkar, R. C. S. "Role of Government Departments in the Legislative Process." *Journal of Constitutional and Parliamentary Studies* 2 (1968):1–12.

Sharma, Keshav C. "Development Planning and Development Administration." *International Review of Administrative Sciences* 34 (1968):121–29.

Sivaraman, B. "Generalist and Specialist in Administration." *Indian Journal of Public Administration* 17 (July–Sept. 1971):383–96.

Taub, Richard P. *Bureaucrats Under Stress.* Berkeley: University of California Press, 1969.

Tottenham, R. *Reports on the Reorganization of the Central Government,* 1945–46. New Delhi: Government of India, 1946.

Weiner, Myron. "Preferential Policies." *Comparative Politics* 16 (Oct. 1983):35–52.

10

Administrative Reforms in Contemporary Japan

KU TASHIRO

Historical Perspective on Public Administration

Although the system of separation of powers was introduced immediately after the Meiji Restoration in 1868, the constitutional governmental system was actually established by the Meiji Constitution, which was enacted in 1889 and enforced the following year. Under this constitution, public administration based on and in compliance with the constitution was introduced in Japan. The power structure, however, was not always in line with the ideal of constitutionalism and the principle of administration by law. For example, the Emperor and his administrative agencies could enact orders or regulations without statutory authorization within a set range of administrative authority.

The present constitution, which was enacted in 1947, provides a solid ground of constitutionalism: the cabinet administers the law faithfully, and no administrative agency can institute any order or regulation without statutory authority. Administrative agencies, accordingly, carry out administrative actions strictly to execute the laws.

However, the scope of administrative actions had been expanded in order to cope with a variety of emerging administrative demands. As a consequence, the number and functional coverage of administrative organizations had to be increased. For example, the number of bureaus in the headquarters of central government rose from 90 in 1955, the year of economic recovery from war devastation, to the level before World War II, 133 in 1969, when Japanese export unprecedentedly exceeded the ten billion mark in U.S. dollars. The number of national public employees increased by 33.4 percent, or by approximately 225,000 persons, from 674,000 at the end of fiscal year 1957 to 899,000 at the end of fiscal year 1967. The number of advisory councils attached to ministries and agencies likewise increased from 208 in 1956 to as many as 277 in 1965.

In view of the need to streamline governmental administration for survival in the world arena, administrative reform has been the grand national policy in the last four decades. When Prime Minister Yasuhiro Nakasone, who had been one of reform's strongest supporters, assumed office in 1982, he clearly described his aim of effecting administrative reforms as "the clearance of the remnants of the past and the readiness and change for the future."

Administrative Reforms Since World War II

Japan had tried hard to catch up with the developed countries since the middle of the last century. The central government exerted strong leadership with effective guidance, control, and surveillance over local governments and the private sector. According to then Minister of State Nakasone, Director General of the Administrative Management Agency in 1982, this machinery "resulted in the compartmentalized and centrally lopsided system of the public administration with various field offices throughout the country for the implementation of administration."

During the period of accelerated economic growth after World War II, the role of the government expanded rapidly, which subsequently led to the proliferation of bureaucracy. After the strenuous effort of postwar reconstruction and industrial development, Japan entered into a period of stable economic growth. Thus, a new dimension of the need for administrative reform arose, while no previous administration had failed in tackling administrative reform in its own way. The history of administrative reforms during the period from 1945 to 1985 could best be explained and analyzed in four stages at ten-year intervals.

The First Stage (1945–54)

The first half of this stage saw the implementation of administrative reforms under the allied occupation. The enactment of the current constitution was the stimulus of reorganization and democratization of administrative institutions. Among the new legislation under the constitution, four important laws should be specified as follows:

THE CABINET LAW (1947). This law provided for the structure, authority, and management of the cabinet; the competence of the prime minister and other ministers; the relations with the administrative branches; the cabinet orders; and its auxiliary organs.

THE NATIONAL GOVERNMENT ORGANIZATION LAW (1948). This law provided the standards for the organization of administrative organs under the control of the cabinet.

THE NATIONAL PUBLIC SERVICE LAW (1947). The basic law on the civil service system was aimed at assuring the people democratic and efficient administration of their public affairs.

THE LOCAL AUTONOMY LAW (1947). Contrary to the aim of the previous centralized system, this law was oriented toward decentralization and contained elements of direct democracy. In addition, a series of related laws like the Public Office Election Law, Local Public Service Law, and Local Finance Law were enacted in order to strengthen local autonomous entities.

After the signing of the San Francisco Peace Treaty in 1952, some reforms were made to ameliorate controversial changes introduced during the occupation.

The Second Stage (1955–64)

The expansion of administration was inevitable to cope with the high rate of economic growth. Administrative machinery was expanded and public corporations grew in number. While the high economic growth necessitated the expansion of administrative institutions in the public sector, the private sector endeavored both technological innovation and rationalization of management. The wide difference between the efficiency of the two sectors was recognized by those concerned and subsequently in 1962 the First Provisional Commission for Administrative Reform was established in the Prime Minister's Office. The commission was headed by Kiichiro Sato, one of the most famous bankers, and consisted of 6 important members mostly from the private sector and a staff of 21 experts assisted by 70 researchers. After two years of intensive study, the commission submitted a report to the Prime Minister in 1964, the recommendations of which were as follows: (1) better coordination among public organizations, especially between the cabinet and ministries; (2) democratization of administration through strengthening of local autonomy; and (3) restraining the excessive expansion of public administration without failing to satisfy emerging needs for new services.

The Third Stage (1965–74)

The recommendations of the first commission were rigorously implemented. Administrative reform efforts were directed at elevating coordination between government organizations and on raising the efficiency and rationality of overall administration. For the improvement of efficiency and interministerial coordination, two new agencies were established: the Environment Agency in 1971, which was empowered with overall responsibilities for the implementation of environmental policies; and the National Land Agency in 1974 for overseeing land utilization.

In order to streamline public administration, a "shock treatment" including an across-the-board abolition of one bureau in each ministry and agency was introduced in 1968. The 131 bureaus of ministerial headquarters were reduced to 114 in the same year. The number largely remained stable thereafter, since a "scrap and build" approach was simultaneously employed.

The enactment of the Act on Total Number of Personnel in Administrative Organs in 1969 was another important cornerstone of administrative reform. The act stipulated that the total number of national service personnel, exclusive of those in both self-defense forces and governmental enterprises, could not exceed 506,571, which was the number of established positions for fiscal year 1967. The act also enabled the cabinet to determine the personnel levels of individual ministries and agencies and, thereby, the cabinet attained the power to manage governmental manpower in a much more flexible manner. In order to administer this act, the first national personnel reduction plan was also worked out by the government in the same year. Under the plan, the government could pool and redistribute personnel from inactive or redundant departments to ones that needed more personnel to meet new administrative demands. The combination of both the act and plan made by the government enabled it to eliminate a total of over 10,000 civil service positions in the central government in the intervening years.

The Fourth Stage (1975–85)

The reforms of the third stage resulted in a drastic reduction in governmental organizations as shown by the following: (1) 51 divisions in the headquarters of ministries and agencies (5 percent of total numbers then) were either dissolved or incorporated in other divisions in fiscal years 1978 and 1979; and (2) a total of 36 advisory councils were consolidated and/or abolished in 1978 and by this very reform about 1,000 council members were eliminated.

Apart from the staff reduction carried out under the combination of the act and plan, it was also decided that 18 public corporations should be consolidated or abolished. Approximately 1,000 licensing procedures (about 10 percent of Japan's roughly 10,000 procedures) were streamlined in the period of 1981–82. Over a four-year period starting in 1980, the reduction by a quarter of subsidy programs was also implemented.

Furthermore, in order to accommodate the younger generation in national government services to improve administrative efficiency, the National Public Service Retirement Law was enacted in 1981 — effective four years later in 1985 — to stipulate the retirement age, in principle, at sixty instead of the no-age-limit practice under postwar regulations.

A new wave of administrative reforms was triggered by the second oil crisis in 1979. The Second Provisional Commission was thus established in 1981. The commission aimed at overcoming the difficulties derived from environmental changes in both international and domestic affairs, in particular the discrepancy between an enormous accumulation of international trade surplus and internal deficits in government finance. The second commission, after two years of deliberations, submitted five consecutive reports. The characteristics of recommendations could be summarized as follows:

REFORM STRATEGY. While the reform proposals made by the first commission in 1962 were directed at making administrative procedures more comprehensive, more efficient, and more effective, the second commission concentrated its reform efforts on administrative policies and basic governmental systems and organizations. The commission was fully convinced that the primary goal of this society should be to produce a vigorous culture and a prosperous economy in the world arena. The reform strategy therefore emphasized: (1) further self-help efforts and mutual aids to secure education and welfare; (2) modifying the role of public administration to give the private sector a freer rein; and (3) making a positive contribution to the international community.

RECONSTRUCTION OF GOVERNMENT FINANCE THROUGH SPENDING CUTS. The commission advocated the reconstruction of central government finance through severe austerity measures. This policy was a major premise of efforts to overhaul public administration. In order to achieve the goal mentioned above, the commission recommended eliminating "big government," which was bloated with social welfare programs, and imposed large tax burdens. It was also suggested that financial rehabilitation should be accomplished without any undertaking of new taxation measures. If not done, the comparatively low rate of tax burden in Japan (25.4 percent of national income as of 1981) would inevitably increase. This was expressed very strongly by the commission in order to avoid the common problem of higher tax rates prevailing in most welfare states in developed democracies. In this connection, the commission believed that the reduction in the amount of government bonds — "special bonds" for making up the deficits in government finance in particular — should be of priority among other reform measures.

ATTENTION TO "SOFTWARE" MEASURES. While the first commission had maintained as its main reform target the "hardware" of government such as administrative organizations and the number of positions, the second commission paid more attention to "software." Measures aimed at improving government's relations with the public and securing public trust in the government were introduced. Among new measures, releasing public information more openly to the public, the rationalization of administrative procedures, and the introduction of an Ombudsman system should be noted.

The commission also recommended that the idea of turning over management of three major corporations to the private sector should be studied. The Japan Tobacco and Salt Public Corporation (TRSPC), the Japanese National Railways (JNR), and the Nippon Telegraph and Telephone Public Corporation were established to promote services to the public under the government's supervision in order to secure harmony between the enterprises' public and business characters. However, the combination of political involvement, intervention by supervisory organs, and the laxity in management and discipline undercut the profitability of these public corporations and threatened to ruin even their public character.

The commission also recommended that, in adherence to the principle of decentralization of functions between the central and local governments, administrative affairs directly related to local residents should be dealt with as much as possible by the local bodies to which they have access. With regard to the administration of local governments, the commission recommendations included two more important items: strict control of the number of local government workers by establishing maximum personnel levels for local public bodies; and holding down excessive salary levels of local public employees.

PROMOTION OF REFORMS. In coincidence with the establishment of the second commission, the Headquarters for the Promotion of Administrative Reform was established jointly by the government and the government party (the Liberal Democratic Party) in order to secure coordination of support for the recommendations of the commission toward implementation. The headquarters was headed by the prime minister and composed of the cabinet members and the executive officers of the government party.

The second commission submitted its recommendations as they were formed and the government responded with immediate action in support of them. This led to constant media coverage of reform issues and, as a result, the interest of the public in administrative reform was kept at a high level. Both the commission and the government then in turn were stimulated to promote further administrative reform.

Progress of Administrative Reforms

The Second Commission for Administrative Reform was dissolved in 1983 after two years' effort. It would be appropriate to summarize the activities of the commission before delving into the progress of recommended reforms.

The First Report (An Emergency Report)

When the commission was organized March 16, 1981, Prime Minister Zenko Suzuki requested the commission to submit its first report by the summer of 1981. In response to this request, the commission did so on July 10. This was an emergency report in which two specific recommendations were suggested for immediate implementation in view of the stringent financial conditions. The first was on the curtailment of expenditures and the reconstructuring of government finance. The second was on the streamlining and rationalization of public administration, in which four major areas were specified: governmental administration, public corporations, local public entities, and licensing administration.

The Second Report

The second report was submitted on February 10, 1982. It dealt with the reform of permits and licenses.

The Third Report (The Fundamental Report)

The third report was submitted on July 30, 1982, in which an outline of fundamental measures was shown. There were four areas of reform: public administration in general; governmental organization and the function of coordination; public personnel administration; and redistribution of administrative responsibility between central and local governments and local public finance.

The Fourth Report

The fourth report was submitted on February 28, 1983, and this recommended specifically the establishment of an oversight commission on administrative reform.

The Fifth Report (The Final Report)

The final report was submitted on March 14, 1983, before the dissolution of the commission. This recommended a package reform program in eight major fields as follows: (1) reform of central administrative organizations; (2) reform of governmental enterprises and public corporations; (3) reform of national and local relations and local public administration; (4) rationalization of the system of subsidies to local government and others; (5) rationalization of the system of permits and licenses; (6) reform of the public personnel system; (7) reform of budget, accounting, and public finance systems; and (8) reform of the system of releasing administrative information to the public, public administrative procedures, and related matters.

The responsibility for implementing reform recommendations was carried over to the new supervisory body, the Provisional Council for the Promotion of Administrative Reform, as recommended by the fourth report. Toshi Doko, honorary chairman of the Federation of Economic Organizations, was requested to maintain the chairmanship of both the commission and council. In addition to this continuity of reform machinery, there was another reform promotion body, the Headquarters for the Promotion of Administrative Reform, jointly established by the government and the Liberal Democratic Party. In other countries, administrative reforms often have been carried out when a new president took office or when the opposition party took over, but in Japan, the Liberal Democratic Party had been continuously in power for the last three decades and therefore the combination of the council and the headquarters was extremely effective in building up support for implementation of reform recommendations. As of the end of fiscal year 1984 (March 31, 1985), the administrative reform programs implemented pursuant to the recommendations of the second commission were as follows:

REORGANIZATION OF ADMINISTRATIVE INSTITUTIONS. For the enhancement of management and policy coordination functions in the central government, the Management and Coordination Agency was established in July 1984 with the merger of part of the prime minister's office and the Administrative Management Agency. The National Government Organization Law was also amended in order to increase flexibility of government organization. From July 1984, thanks to the amendment, the creation and reorganization of bureaus and the equivalent level of central government organizations came to be regulated by cabinet order instead of law. Major reshuffling of 20 internal bureaus and departments in 10 ministries and agencies was also made in the same period. The amendment stipulated further reorganization, including elimination of divisions of the headquarters of the national government. As many as 150 (10 percent) of all divisions were to be reorganized by 1988.

The local branch offices of the central government would be divided into three different levels, namely regional, prefectural, and municipal levels. (As many as 60 percent of national public servants were employed by these local branches.) During fiscal year 1984, 44 such branch offices were either consolidated, scaled-down, or eliminated. In 1985, three more reorganizations were made.

STAFF NUMBER CONTROL. Following the introduction of the first national personnel reduction plan in 1969, five consecutive plans were drawn up and actually about 16,000 positions were curtailed. (During the period from 1967 to 1984, reduction was made by some 170,000, but another 154,000 jobs were added in order to meet the emerging needs of universities, hospitals and sanataria. The balance was the rather small number of 16,000 but this implied some success in the "scrap and build" approach.) The sixth plan covering the 1982–86 period was drawn up which aimed at making a 5 percent reduction of posts: a 44,886 reduction in the 897,717 positions.

GOVERNMENT ENTERPRISES. Rationalization programs were introduced in four ailing government enterprises as follows:

Postal Service: (a) expansion of consignment coverage for collection and delivery of mail; (b) promotion of an on-line system for postal saving and insurance; and (c) rationalization of staff deployment.

National Forest Service: (a) amendment of existing improvement program; (b) improvement of business operation; and (c) rationalization of staff deployment.

Printing and Mint: (a) improvement of business operation; and (b) rationalization of staff deployment.

National Hospitals and Sanataria: Within a ten-year period starting in 1986, consolidation, abolition, and transfer of management to other institutions should be enforced as much as possible.

PUBLIC CORPORATIONS. Two major public corporations, Nippon Telegraph and Telephone Corporation (NTT) and Japan Tobacco and Salt Public

Corporation (JTSPC), were transformed to special companies effective April 1985. The heavily indebted corporation, Japanese National Railways, was to be divided into seven special companies in 1986 with the hope of recovering some 25 trillion yen of accumulated deficits.

Reform of other public corporations was also enforced through drastic measures: merger of 4 corporations into 2 in 1984, merger of 4 into 2 new ones again in 1985; and abolition of 2 corporations in 1985. Furthermore, privatization of 19 corporations was pushed forward; 12 were privatized by the end of fiscal year 1985. With regards to 46 corporations, reduction of business coverage was to be enforced from 1985. Periodical review and standardization of accounting were to be required in order to revitalize comprehensively the management of all public corporations.

ADMINISTRATIVE PROCESSES. The Diet passed related bills that would eliminate or curtail excessive regulatory measures. Some 191 among 253 cases pointed out by the commission were deregulated in line with the recommendations. Some 115 out of 496 statistical survey programs were to be either curtailed or rationalized during the 1984–86 period.

"Public watch and subsequent remedy systems" like the release of administrative information and the Ombudsman were to be examined for introduction.

NATIONAL-LOCAL GOVERNMENT RELATIONS. Fiscal year 1983 witnessed a comprehensive rationalization package that resulted in 55 regulatory functions being abolished or transferred to local governments. Furthermore, as many as 17 administrative involvements of the central government in local government affairs were either abolished or lessened by the end of fiscal year 1984. Rationalization of the system of subsidies to the local governments was also under way with main emphasis on consolidation and minimization of personnel costs and subsidies.

With regard to the abolition of the system of national government officials working in local government, those who had been engaged in land transport administration returned to national government service. Two more groups, social insurance and employment security, were to be redistributed to either national or local government services. When completed, the "temporary" system introduced in the difficult immediate post–World War II period (1947) will finally fade away.

While local governments were urged to have more self-evaluation capacity for their organizational and staff number control, the central government never failed to regulate them for more economy and efficiency. Measures to rectify excessive salaries and retirement allowances in the local governments had been strenuously enforced. Thus "administrative guidance" was extended in line with the Fundamental Principles of Administrative Reform in Local Government, which was approved by the cabinet on January 1985.

SUBSTANTIVE PROGRAMS.

Pension: The government launched the first reform drive (Public Employee's Mutual Aid Pension Scheme) in 1984 seeking to integrate public pension schemes by 1995.

Medical care: In line with measures to hold down the costs of medical care, both the medical insurance system and the provision of medical services were streamlined by the following measures: strengthening supervisory and audit functions for medical cost control; tightening checks on medical payment claims; and revising price standards for medicines. The controversial system of comprehensive health care for the elderly was finally introduced in 1983.

Agriculture: Rationalization of nationwide usage of paddy fields was carried out under the third program (1984–86) in order to attain balanced supply and demand of rice, the staple food of the Japanese. The reduction in expenditures of the Foodstuff Control System, which was introduced originally during the World War II period, was given priority in reform. Minimization of price discrepancy between purchase and supply and the reduction of personnel in the national network of food offices were among the major rationalization programs for rice production in Japan.

REFORM OF GOVERNMENT FINANCE. Following the enactment of the Special Act for Administrative Reform in 1981, which was incorporated into the first recommendation of the Second Provisional Commission for Administrative Reform, an emergency spending curtailment program was introduced. This program covered seven major items directly relating to 34 independent laws and was enforced strictly during the 1982–84 period. Along with this crash program, so-called zero-ceilings on ministerial requests for budget appropriations were enforced so rigorously that the growth of government expenditures was dramatically curtailed as follows: Fiscal year 1982, 1.8 percent; 1983, 0.0 percent; 1984, −0.1 percent; and 1985, 0.0 percent.

Grants and subsidies provided by the government added up to the enormous amount of about 14 trillion yen in fiscal year 1984, but strenuous efforts for their reduction and rationalization succeeded in saving a net 430 billion yen in the same fiscal year.

ORGANIZATIONS FOR ADMINISTRATIVE REFORM. The second commission was formed on March 16, 1981, and the Joint Headquarters for the Promotion of Administrative Reform was established on April 7 of the same year, only three weeks later, by the government and government party. This was a good testimony to the serious concern over administrative improvement by both politicians and bureaucrats. The creation of the Provisional Council for the Promotion of Administrative Reform, as recommended by the fourth report of the second commission, was another indication of enthusiasm for reform, and this was done on July 1, 1983, only three months after the dissolution of the second commission. For the controversial reform of the Japanese National Railways (a public corporation), the Inspection Commission for the Reconstruction of National Railways was established on June 10, 1983, by the Diet.

Analysis of Administrative Reforms

It is true that a combination of favorable conditions, internationally and domestically, enabled Japan to achieve rapid economic development in the last four decades. It is also true that no such striking performance could have been achieved without the stability of political leadership. Since its creation in 1955, the conservative Liberal Democratic Party (LDP) enjoyed the status of ruling party thanks to its absolute majority of seats in both houses, representatives (lower), and councillors (upper), of the National Diet. The LDP therefore had been monopolizing the premiership continuously since 1955 as shown in Table 10.1, because the president of the majority party automatically becomes prime minister under the constitution.

It was only in December 1983 when the LDP had to form a coalition with the New Liberal Club, a small secessionist group from the LDP, which

TABLE 10.1.   The Chronicle of LDP Administration

Number	Prime Minister	Period
1	Ichiro Hatoyama[a]	Dec. '54–Dec. '56
2	Tanzan Ishibashi	Dec. '56–Jan. '57
3	Nobusuke Kishi	Jan. '57–Jul. '60
4	Hayato Ikeda	Jul. '60–Nov. '64
5	Eisaku Sato	Nov. '64–Jul. '72
6	Kakuei Tanaka	Jul. '72–Dec. '74
7	Takeo Miki	Dec. '74–Dec. '76
8	Takeo Fukuda	Dec. '76–Dec. '78
9	Masayoshi Ohira	Dec. '78–Jun. '80
10	Zenko Suzuki	Jun. '80–Nov. '82
11	Yasuhiro Nakasone	Nov. '82–Nov. 87
12	Naboru Takeshita	Nov. '87–April '89

[a]Hatoyama was elected Prime Minister as the President of the Japan Democratic Party. The LDP was formed on Dec. 15, 1955, by the merger of the Japan Democratic Party and Liberal Party.

had been one of the opposition parties since its formation in 1976. Although these LDP administrations were not always diligent in tackling administrative reform, no single administration failed to address the subject. Why do conservative prime ministers behave consistently in favor of the idea? The answer is that the public has always supported reform plans one way or another. Their strong wishes in general enable the LDP to maintain a majority position continuously in the Diet, while the LDP's tactical success in election campaigns should not be disregarded. How strong the wishes of the public could be is attested by an interesting episode, Prime Minister Suzuki's unexpected announcement of retirement in 1982.

Prime Minister Zenko Suzuki was left the chance of premiership by the sudden death of Prime Minister Ohira during the election campaign in June 1980. Prime Minister Suzuki—who had been enjoying the reputation of troubleshooter—assumed the office by emphasizing the importance of "wa" (peace and harmony) among LDP members. He also made such public promises as "termination of heavy reliance on government bonds by 1984" and "reconstruction of government finance without any increase in taxes." However, these promises were gradually proven unlikely to materialize, due to a combination of emerging difficulties. Popular support for him—as measured by public opinion polls—declined dramatically as follows: December 1981, 40 percent support; March 1982, 30 percent support, 49 percent nonsupport; September 1982, 26 percent support, 52 percent nonsupport.

Even if factional opposition might occur among the LDP voters, he could have gained enough support for the reelection to the LDP presidency, and subsequently to the premiership. What actually happened behind the scene is not known, but it is clear that the public lost confidence in him. The public was disappointed by his indecisiveness on major pending matters, in particular his reform promises on government finance. He unexpectedly announced withdrawal from reelection on October 12, 1982, only four days before the closing date of candidacy.

Tripod Support for the LDP

Undefeated, the LDP enjoyed an unevenly shaped tripod support over the last three decades: financial support by financiers and industrialists; popular votes by farmers, fishermen, white-collar workers, and junior executives through the "koenkai" (supporters' society); and policy and legislative guidance by the bureaucracy. With regard to the relations to administrative reform of these three groups, each maintained its own stance.

FINANCIERS AND INDUSTRIALISTS. Either directly or indirectly through their organizations, both financiers and industrialists provide funds to politicians and parties. This is the major channel of political funds to the LDP, while the opposition parties receive funds by either individual donations or contributions from trade union federations. The financiers and industrialists form four major national economic organizations: "Keidanren" (The Federation of Economic Organizations), JCCI (The Japan Chamber of Commerce and Industry), "Nikkeiren" (The Japan Federation of Employers' Association), and "Keizai Doyukai" (The Japan Committee for Economic Development). The leaders of these organizations are the core of the "zaikai," which are considered to be influential to the LDP and often to the incumbent prime minister.

"Zaikai" have always been in favor of administrative reform by their preference for minimal and inexpensive government. The most symbolic fact in this context might be the selection of chairmen of both the first and second provisional commissions for administrative reform: Kiichiro Sato, chairman of the board of directors, Mitsui Bank, for the first commission; and Toshio Doko, honorary chairman of "Keidanren" and former president of both Ishikawajima-Harima Heavy Industry and Toshiba Inc., for the second commission.

FARMERS, FISHERMEN, WHITE-COLLAR WORKERS, AND JUNIOR EXECUTIVES. The constituencies of LDP's Diet members are mostly located in the rural areas where cottage industry dominates. The white-collar workers, and junior executives, though most of them are urban dwellers, support the LDP or other conservative parties, while the majority of blue-collar workers support the "progressive" camp including the socialist and communist parties. The "koenkai" of LDP's members was mainly composed of those influential persons in the local community. This system functioned well enough to collect the votes of farmers, fishermen, white-collar workers, and junior executives who would honor social traditions and family relations. Thus, the popular votes to the LDP had commonly matched or outnumbered those of "progressive" parties.

Dramatic economic development in the past three decades, however, encouraged the drift of population to cities. As of 1985, about 76 percent of Japanese were city residents. In 1955, it was only 56 percent. Accordingly the redistribution of the Diet's seats to each constituency emerged as one of the most controversial political problems after the mid-1970s in order to maintain fair representation throughout the country. The LDP had been cautious in initiating ameliorative measures but was forced to do so around the mid-1980s.

Another byproduct of economic development might be middle-class consciousness among Japanese people. After 1965, government surveys have never failed to show less than 90 percent identifying with this category.

This could imply people's reluctance to admit drastic changes, even in public administration. This coincided with the general support for the LDP by the people.

BUREAUCRACY. The bureaucracy worked closely with both politicians and businessmen in the course of economic development. It served the Diet members in general but particularly those who headed the administrative branches. The task of bureaucracy has been the execution of administrative policies formulated by politicians. Traditionally, however, it collected, processed and analyzed the data necessary for policy formulation. Furthermore, the bulk of government policies are designed to insure the health of the national economy, and therefore the bureaucracy has to establish close cooperative relations with both politicians and businessmen in drafting and implementing policies. The bureaucracy is also a major source of future politicians and business leaders. However, this is applicable only to a small portion of the bureaucracy, about 10,000 members of "kanryo" including 2,500-odd senior administrative officials at the headquarters of ministries and agencies and their heirs and heiresses. The relations of "kanryo" with the LDP have been comparatively good and sometimes senior government officials have been selected to be among future successors of LDP's Diet members.

"Kanryo" occupy most of the key administrative positions and are reinforced by as many as 400-odd new recruits every year through the highly competitive open entrance examination at the senior level. Most of them are graduates of recognized universities who specialized in law, the Law Department of Tokyo University in particular. They are recruited and trained primarily by the ministry or agency to which they belonged at the start of their career. They are called "career," an elite group among the national civil service, and given a combination of training and development programs including a wide range of job rotations, interministerial off-the-job training and study abroad. The work they are given is usually that relating to policy formulation and subsequent coordination for those concerned.

Accordingly, the career group of a specific ministry or agency is trained for the sake of their particular organization. The more they became knowledgeable about responsible administrative areas of the organization, the more they are likely to be involved in politics. Thus the "kanryo" as a whole are inevitably pro-LDP.

National Climate for Administrative Reform

Japan's unique government-business relations proved to be useful for explaining the reason for astonishing success in rapid economic growth. It was a story about the unique collaboration between government and business during the time before the first oil crisis when the "growth energy" outpaced opposing pressures. Labor-management relations during the period remained in the Japanese cooperative tradition. Referred to as "Japan Inc." by the U.S. State Department and others, this was the climate in this country.

With regard to administrative reforms so far enforced, the system of "Japan Inc." demonstrated its effectiveness in both working out and implementing reform plans. One of the examples could be the reduction of grants and subsidies provided by the central government. When the first (emergency) report of the second reform commission was submitted in July 1981, the total amount of governmental grants and subsidies was 13 trillion yen for the fiscal year: 36 percent for social security; 23 percent for education and science; 21 percent for public works; and the remaining 20 percent for miscellaneous purposes. Nearly 80 percent of the money was allocated to local governments and nearly the same percent was obligatory as regulated by relevant laws. Accordingly it was extremely difficult to curtail the funds and programs. However, across-the-board curtailment and other measures helped to reduce grants and subsidies as follows:

TABLE 10.2.   Grants and Subsidies, 1981–1985

Fiscal Year	Amount of Reduction (100 million yen)	Number of Cases Reduced
1981	1,668	1,329
1982	3,107	2,017
1983	4,007	1,631
1985	7,848	1,239

The government-business relations began to become more and more similar to other industrialized countries. For example, "zaikai" was not always happy to continue the "zero-ceiling" austerity budgets that were deemed imperative by the government. The huge international trade surplus resulted in strong pressures on the Japanese economy, but Prime Minister Nakasone's scenario for amelioration hardly produced visible improvement timely enough to convince the critics.

Another focus of administrative reform was something related to the administrative reforms carried out before the establishment of the second reform commission in 1981, which were mainly aimed at the improvement of administrative efficiency. The concept of inexpensive government was the key. Advanced technology was also employed. The implications of the second reform commission, however, seemed not necessarily the same as previous ones. The primary aim of the commission was to achieve financial reform. As the incumbent Prime Minister Suzuki promised to the public in 1980, it was the deteriorated government finance which was to be attacked.

The difficulty in public finance stemmed originally from the issuance of "special bonds" in 1975 for filling the financial gap. The total amount of both the "special bonds" and construction bonds has been around 10 trillion yen since then, which is roughly one-third of the annual general account budget. The miracle of quick recovery of the Japanese economy immediately after the first oil crisis could be attributable to this "special bond" issue. However, the recovery resulted in a huge accumulation of public debt — 70 trillion yen in 1980 — when the second reform commission was established. The commission, therefore, proceeded directly with the reconstruction of public finance.

The financial gap could be lessened, theoretically, by means of economizing and rationalization of outlays including revisions of the existing system. Practically, however, it should be adjusted during each year's budget compilation process by spending cuts, by revenue increase measures, or by the combination of these. The second reform commission followed this course of action. As far as the performance of previous administrative reforms was concerned, this orthodox approach had been effective enough but nowadays was not as clear as before. Three new pressures emerged related to reform: internationalization to meet global responsibilities; the aging Japanese population with bigger claims on the welfare programs; and individualistic claims on taste and value systems.

Conclusion and Perspective

It is true that a combination of favorable conditions enabled Japan to achieve rapid economic development. It is also true that no such splendid performance could have been achieved without the stability of political leadership. The world recognized the close collaboration between the government and "zaikai." Also, the world witnessed the existence of a well-managed public service in this country, as evidenced by the following data:

TABLE 10.3. Number of Public Servants per 1,000 Population

Country	Ordinary Services[a]	Defense Personnel	Total
Japan	42	3	45
U.K.	94	10	104
France	103	8	111
U.S.A.	64	14	78
F.R.G.	64	10	74

Source: Management and Coordination Agency of the Japanese Government, 1982.
[a]Ordinary services include both national and local services and also employees of national government enterprises.

While these figures entail the problem of comparability, particularly in the scope of public service, they are evidence of the efficiency of Japanese public administration. One of the reasons for such a high efficiency is the devotion of well-trained public workers. It would be appropriate to refer to their role in governmental decision making in order to show how they contribute to this efficiency. Actually, about 70 percent of the bills submitted to the Diet were originally drafted by the bureaucrats of ministries and agencies concerned and the great majority of them are eventually passed; only a small portion of the remaining 30 percent submitted by the members of the Diet are adopted. It is commonly understood by many foreign observers, therefore, that the key decisions in the central government have been made by the career bureaucrats rather than the politicians of the Diet and the cabinet. This kind of interpretation would have been valid until the mid-1970s. The dominant role of bureaucrats was challenged for the first time in postwar Japan when the Japanese economy encountered a new dimension of development. Stagnation in the early 1970s necessitated the introduction of an ambitious "Remodeling Plan of the Japanese Archipelago" by Prime Minister Kakuei Tanaka, which triggered galloping inflation reaching an unprecedented 30 percent rise in 1983. This coincided with the first oil crisis toward the end of the year. The bureaucrats could not handle the serious issues mushrooming from this and this inability caused some decline in the social status of the bureaucracy as well as the loss of their professional pride. Only political initiatives could lead to final resolution; for example, on the issue of the "special bond."

In addition to this change in politician-bureaucrat relationship, another factor to consider is the public, which was under the leadership of three major groups: constituency, journalism and "zaikai." "Zaikai" cultivated stronger self-confidence in their collective bargaining capacity after overcoming a series of difficulties in the first half of the 1970s. One of the most significant examples of their influence would be the privatization of three major public corporations as briefly described before.

Prime Minister Nakasone, whose tenure expired in November 1987, had been a major influence in promoting administrative reforms. This could be the most important reason why his administration had gained popular acceptance by the public. In this regard, administrative reform itself seemed to have been accepted favorably. However, there remained a dilemma in the process of implementing reform measures, because of the circular relations among the three major groups concerned with Japanese public administration. Politicians are stuck with bureaucrats but rather easily influenced by "zaikai." Bureaucrats are not so influenced by "zaikai" but are rather obedient to politicians. The "zaikai" listen rather cautiously to the views of bureaucrats but exercise their influence on politicians. This triangular relation does not guarantee that timely decisions can be implemented quickly. Whether the famous quotation "render unto Caesar the things that are Caesar's" can work or not is a big question. If it does, which party among the three would play a leading role in public administration hereafter?

References

Abegglen, J. C. *The Strategy of Japanese Business*. Cambridge: Berlinger, 1984.
Administrative Management Agency. *Administrative Management in Japan*. Tokyo: The AMA, 1982.
_____.*Administrative Reform in Japan*. Tokyo: The AMA, 1982.
Dowdy, E. *Japanese Bureaucracy: Its Development and Modernization*. Melbourne: Chesher, 1982.
Furuhashi, G. "Postwar Administrative Reform Efforts in Japan." Paper for Tokyo Roundtable of IIAS. Tokyo: The AMA, 1982.
_____. "Implementing Administrative Reforms: The Japanese Experience." Paper for Tunis Conference of IIAS, 1985.
Koh, B. C. "Stability and Change in Japan's Higher Civil Service." *Comparative Politics* 11 (1979): 279–97.
Koh, B. C., and Kim, J. O. "Paths to Advancement in Japanese Bureaucracy." *Comparative Political Studies* 15.3 (1982): 289–313.
Kubota, A. *Higher Civil Servants in Postwar Japan*. Princeton, N.J.: Princeton University Press, 1969.
Management and Coordination Agency. *Annual Report of the MCA*. Tokyo (yearly edition, original in Japanese), 1987.
Masujima, T. *Some Data for Reference on Public Administration in Japan*. Tokyo: The MCA, 1986.
McMillan, C. L. *The Japanese Industrial System*. Berlin and N.Y.: Gruyter, 1984.
Morita, A. *Made in Japan*. Tokyo: Asahi Shinbun, 1986.
Murakami, H., and Hirschmeier, J., eds. *Politics and Economics in Contemporary Japan*. Tokyo: Japan Culture Institute, 1979.
Ouchi, W. *Theory Z*. New York: Addison-Wesley, 1981.
Tashiro, K. "Productivity in Public Administration: Concept and Application in Japan." *Indian Journal of Public Administration* 28, no. 3 (1982): 458–65.
_____. "Career Executive Development in the Japanese Government." Paper for Boston Conference of American Society for Public Administration, 1987.
Tsuji, K., ed. *Public Administration in Japan*. Tokyo: The IIAS Tokyo Roundtable Organizing Committee, 1982.

11

Policy Developments and Administrative Changes in Latin America

J. NEF

Introduction

The issue of administrative reform in the Third World in general and in Latin America in particular has figured prominently in technical and political debates (United Nations 1971). It has also been a central theme in conferences related to strategies of development. There are abundant references that one of the greatest impediments to the achievement of self-sustained economic growth, social justice and democratic participation lies in the rigid structures and practices that characterize Latin America's administrative systems. The obvious, and almost platitudinal prescription arising from such discussions is the need to carry out an "administrative reform" to make the public sector more efficient and effective in the pursuit of its development goals. Generally, such a foregone conclusion is presented as a "technical problem." It is often perceived either as an instrumentality for the implementation of development plans or as a device to enhance the competence and professionalism of public servants, reduce corruption, and minimize the incidence of "political interference" in decision making.

Administrative Reform as a Political Process

I would like to offer an alternative view on administrative reform. I propose here that administrative reform in general, and especially in Latin

America, is eminently a political rather than a technical problem (Crowther and Flores 1970). Administrative reform, since the dawn of the overseas Spanish Empire to present-day Latin America, has been an attempt to manage political conflict. Its technical cloaking, in this context, could be understood more as an ideology to legitimate, in terms of logical absolutes, what is essentially an endeavor on the part of existing—and at times competing—elites to gain relational control or metapower; that is to regulate the power intercourse taking place in the society (Baumgartner et al. 1976). Substantively, no administrative reforms, nor the specific "technological package" (medical, military, educational) they support is apolitical although its rationalization is commonly expressed in antiseptic language (Israel 1984).

In very general terms, administrative reform has been equated with reorganization. The latter should be understood as a process whereby the relationship between administrative structures (or means) and administrative ends is brought into line with each other. Generally, reorganizations result from dramatic social transformation. When we talk about such reforms we refer to a planned and systematic attempt at altering structural and teleological relationships within the state apparatus in response to—or in the pursuit of—social change. For the sake of clarification, however, it is important here to differentiate between *reorganization* proper, where the ends and purposes of government are consciously (and at times profoundly) altered and *restructuring*. This notion refers to a conscious attempt to alter the means of government through which existing goals, purposes and policies are being implemented. In this sense, reorganization is a more fundamental type of reform involving redefinition of ends while restructuring is largely oriented to the maintenance of existing goals through a redeployment of means. Needless to say, since means and ends are closely interconnected, changes in the instrumentalities, or rationalization, may have unstated (and unintended) consequences for policies. But this is not to say that administrative rationalization will necessarily or even often have social impact. The opposite is commonly the case.

In Latin America, I think it is fair to suggest that administrative reform, except for some rare cases that we will mention below, has tended to be more oriented to affect the means of government rather than the ends. In most cases, reorganizations have responded to elite interests to modernize and strengthen the status quo. In this sense, the politics of administrative reform, excluding the rare cases of social revolution—such as Mexico in 1917, Bolivia in 1952, Cuba in 1959, or Nicaragua in 1979—has been colored by a distinctively conservative orientation.

A Theoretical Perspective

Taking a holistic or systemic approach, we can see administrative reform as part and parcel of an explicit, or implicit, political project supported by alliances and occurring in a concrete socioeconomic and political ambiance (Easton 1957; Stallings 1978). This process affects power relationships in the state: its structures, ends, modus operandi. It also has environmental consequences for the civil society. Reform always implies a form of technological innovation affecting either "hardware" or "gadget" technologies as well as (often implicit) social technologies of management and organization. But the technological packages referred to earlier do not exist in a vacuum (Nef and Dwivedi 1986). They are situated in a cultural, professional and ultimately political context. This means that any reform package reflects the nature of the political and social systems that created it in the first place, and that of the system in which it is being applied. It is important here to bear in mind that the ambiance of technology-generation and technology-application in Third World countries are not necessarily the same. Technological innovation, more often than not is exogenous, resulting from vogues and breakthroughs that have occurred in developed societies.

Administrative reform in Latin America has tended to reflect the nature of the region's political systems. Generally speaking, one could characterize the Latin American political process by five major recurring trends:

1. Latin American politics are essentially *fragmented* from a cultural and structural viewpoint.

2. The political process based upon such fragmentation tends to be predominately *conflictual* and punctuated by cycles of violence and instability.

3. Latin American politics have experienced a process of induced development and *modernization* that has severely disrupted traditional nonelite patterns and adversely affected their quality of life.

4. The political systems of Latin America have evolved essentially as *dependent* and penetrated political systems where external actors play important political roles.

5. Latin American politics are characteristically those of *underdevelopment* and where the issue of growth and distribution constitutes a central leitmotiv of political life. However, and despite the ubiquitous presence of political violence, elite socioeconomic structures have a remarkable degree of stability and continuity (Nef 1984).

From this sketchy characterization of Latin American politics, it is possible to suggest that the process of administrative reform has reflected the fragmented, conflictual, dependent and underdeveloped nature of Latin American politics and society. Likewise, in this context, external influences in the process of administrative reform have been paramount (Wahrlich 1978).

Presentation

For the purposes of simplification, we have divided this presentation into five major sequential periods. These entail a historical overview of the genesis and evolution of administrative reform in Latin America; each era of development is characterized by a specific type of administrative reform. The first is the transition from the patrimonial forms inherited from the colonial times to the modernization in the so-called export economy (1820s–1930s); the second period is the establishment of the state capitalist model with import substitution and populism (1930s–1950s); the third period is the era of crisis of import substitution and externally induced reform under the Alliance for Progress (1960s–1970s); the fourth era is the upsurge of bureaucratic authoritarianism and neodependency (1970s–1980s); and the last period involves the newly emerging forms of "restricted democracy" from the beginning of this decade to the present. The concluding section will briefly examine the main socioeconomic and political parameters of administrative reform with a special emphasis on the present socioeconomic and political configurations.

Historical Overview

One fundamental characteristic of administrative systems and administrative reforms in Latin America has been the exogenous nature of both administrative practices and innovation (Wahrlich 1978). Latin America was colonized by Spain and Portugal essentially in an attempt to expand the power and influence of the European metropolis. This was not only detrimental to the local populations but was discontinuous with political, administrative and even economic practices of the pre-Columbian era. The Aztec, Mayan and Incan empires had a fairly elaborate network of administrative practices. However, the role of colonial rule was not one of developing the indigenous societies but to subjugate them to a centralized will and insert them into a European-centered world system. The earlier administrative models of the House of Hapsburg (Charles V, Philip II) set the basis for a mercantile colonial economy. This system was streamlined, centralized and deprived of its "feudal trappings" by the Bourbon reforms undertaken in the mid-eighteenth century. Following the lines of similar absolutist and modernizing reforms in Europe (Frederick of Prussia, Peter and Catherine in Russia), the administrative reforms meant for the New World a drive toward greater centralization, professionalization and fiscal efficiency to facilitate accumulation. The old system based on "fueros" (special royal dispensations), town councils, and military governors as well as the all-encompassing House of Contracts (the equivalent of the British and Dutch East India Company), gave rise to a system of centralized accounting and management radiating centrally from Madrid, through the vice-royalties all the way down to the smallest units. All other autonomous social and political institutions, including the Catholic Church, were curbed. The foundations of an authoritarian colonial bureaucracy were laid down. The severance of colonial ties as a result of European events not only ruptured these ties but set in motion a power struggle between two types of administrative traditions: the earlier autonomous forms inherited from the Hapsburgs and the centralizing Bourbonic system. During the earlier part of the 19th century local warlords attempted to establish political dominance and order to the now independent and fragmented republics. Throughout this entire period, the Latin American state remained largely patrimonial: a booty of whichever *caudillo* sat in the saddle and enjoying an extremely limited degree of autonomy and professionalism (Zylberberg 1976). It was not until the end of an era of unifying dictatorships such as those of Rosas, the Portalean republic, or the Porfiato, that an enlarged and centralized state apparatus would be set in place (Burns 1986).

The Export Economy

The insertion of the Latin American economies into the world market resulted in a period of rapid economic expansion and modernization under the hegemonic leadership of an agroexporting and mining bourgeoisie. The introduction of new patterns of economic organization and production — such as the export of coffee, nitrates, wheat, meats or wool—constituted the backbone of a model of development better characterized as an *export economy*. The surplus generated by economic expansion was oriented to the importation of manufacture, both capital goods and consumer goods. It also provided for the expansion of the fiscal base of the state to coordinate the diverse fractions of the elite, to defend the countries against external competitors and most important, to protect the elite against lower-class mobilization. All these required a new and more efficient state apparatus. Administrative modernization was essentially national. It encompassed the classical "law and order" functions of the state as well as the spheres of education and the military (Johnson 1964). A consequence of these reforms was to set the basis for the professionalization and bureaucratization of the civil and military cadres of the state. It also facilitated in varying degrees, the emergence of a new white-collar petite bourgeoisie or state class, which from then on would buffer the establishment against pressures emanating from the subordinate strata of society (Johnson 1964). The educational reforms in particular opened mobility opportunities for immigrants, downwardly mobile members of the landowning classes as well as a few upwardly mobile members of the lower strata. In fact, it is here that the close connection between the state and the middle strata can be traced (Skidmore and Smith 1984; Burns 1986).

The export economy model began to falter shortly after World War I, when technological innovations in Europe and North America and a re-structuring of world markets negatively affected the Latin American econo-mies. With a shrinkage of economic surpluses, intra-elite conflict acceler-ated. Moreover, new subordinate social forces generated by the process of economic expansion began to pressure the exclusivist system of "gentlemen politics." In the more developed countries of South America and in Mexico the consolidation of the middle strata introduced a new element in the political game. This was the appearance of an administrative class and a state enjoying some degree of relative autonomy from the traditional upper classes. Thus, a tripartite arrangement of political actors began to take shape: the upper classes both "traditional" (landed gentry) and "modern" (bourgeois); the middle sectors articulated by intellectuals, civil servants and military officers; and the subordinate classes including a myriad of diverse social groupings from "integrated blue-collar workers" to marginal peasants, Indians and squatters.

The upsurge of the nonelites as political actors meant a growth of demands upon the governments. The central issue became the one of labor relations and the role of the newly emerging blue-collar and white-collar labor in national politics. The labor question was introduced in the political agendas of Argentina, Uruguay, Chile and Mexico. Its timing coincided with the first drives towards the university reform-movement. The reforms of labor legislation resulted in the creation of state-controlled systems of industrial relations and social security. These counted on the support of both organized labor as well as the white-collar bureaucracy. It is important to point out that the first labor reforms — as well as the aforementioned university reforms — in Latin America were enacted in favor of the middle classes. Only later did labor legislation expand to include the blue-collar workers. Even then, it did not include the vast majority of the urban poor and the peasants.

The labor reforms of the 1920s, like the educational and military re-forms of the 1880s and 1890s were also incremental. They had the effect of further expanding the role and size of the state. They also helped to diffuse revolutionary conditions in the countries of greater relative development.

In most of the less-developed Central American and Caribbean countries, with a small and fragmented white-collar class and limited social surplus, the state's repressive mechanisms rather than its distributive and legitimation functions were more directly affected by institutional modernization.

With the post World War I recession, compounded by the new cluster of policy objectives and social responsibilities attached to the state, effective fiscal management and accountability became important priorities. The first systematic attempts at introducing "scientific" methods of fiscal management and accountability were established by the U.S.-based Kemerer Commission hired by the governments of Chile, Peru, Bolivia and Colombia to set up mechanisms to secure efficient, honest and economical administration (Salgado and Valdes 1984). Resulting from the commission's work were the establishment of central banking systems, a rationalization of credit and currency, and the comptrollers-general office. The latter, inspired in the U.S. general accounting office, was for many years part of the standard package of administrative reforms to be transferred horizontally among Latin American countries. The Kemerer reforms preceded "scientific management." They were primarily centered on legality and accountability rather than on efficiency. Properly speaking they were more an attempt at restructuring than at reorganization. The long-term effects of this "technical" and legalistic attempt at administrative rationalization however, were far-reaching. They set the basis for the modern and accountable Latin American administrative state to emerge during the Depression.

The Great Depression accelerated the economic decline of the postwar years and broke the precarious social truce among the elites as well as the systems of labor relations brought about by social reforms. Political crisis followed on the heels of the economic crisis. In the less industrialized agricultural economies of Central America, the state ended up being controlled by professional soldiers, as in Nicaragua, El Salvador, Honduras and Guatemala. These new actors were called upon by the upper classes at the eve of the crisis to arbitrate intra-elite conflict and to repress brutally insurrectional attempts by the dispossessed peasantry. From then on, a form of condominium between the military and the landowning aristocracy would ensue. In some cases, this alliance has endured until the present. "Decompression" there was meant to buy time to provide for the eventual recovery of the export economy. Besides enforcement, the state did very little else.

State Capitalism, Import Substitution, and Populism

A different kind of alliance would emerge, after a brief period of demobilization in the more advanced countries (Mexico, Brazil, Argentina, Uruguay and Chile). This new strategy entailed a model of import substitution industrialization, supported by a coalition of industrialists, blue-collar workers and, most important, the bureaucratic middle classes that provided hegemonic leadership to the project (Furtado 1976). This political configuration has been referred to as populism (Zylberberg 1976). The state apparatus not only grew by leaps and bounds but new demands for managerial (or developmental) as opposed to "traditional" executive administration were put upon the state. Efforts towards sectorial planning, energy self-sufficiency, heavy industry, transportation, communication and, above all, financing of development activities became paramount functions of the state. These policies can be generally characterized as Keynesian. For as long as the economic recession, and subsequently the war, made it extremely difficult for Latin American countries to import U.S. and European manufactures, import substitution provided the impetus for national development. Moreover, with the outburst of the war, demands for Latin American raw materials augmented, increasing the internal flow of investment capital.

The era of import substitution industrialization constituted one of the most significant periods of administrative reorganization resulting from a fundamental reorientation of the role of the state. However, as with the earlier reforms, this tended to be largely haphazard, incremental and improvised. Despite its profound effects in society, import substitution policies with the exception of the Brazilian case, did not carry with them a comprehensive administrative reform package other than a kind of relentless incrementalism.

This is not to say that there were not some important innovations. The administrative legacy of the period of import substitution would be the creation of a large, professionalized and relatively autonomous state system in the Latin American republics. It would also leave a myriad of state enterprises, development agencies and corporations. The characteristics and basic orientations of state interventionism in Latin America essentially remained until the profound economic and political crisis of the 1970s, as we will see below.

With the exhaustion of import substitution, connected to a continual trend of deterioration of the terms of trade, the Latin American public sector became increasingly incapable of meeting the developmental goals set during the heyday of World War II. While social demands remained relatively high and a variety of nonelite groups expected to receive social benefits, the capacity for financing such programs laid far behind. Sunk costs, resulting from programs initiated during the "fat" years of Latin America's "New Deal" also put a heavy burden on the state. As social mobilization steadily increased although real mobility opportunities remained low, a social and political malaise set in that could be characterized alternatively as a crisis of over-participation, revolution of rising frustrations, or crisis of hegemony.

Crisis and Reformism

Governments found themselves ever more entangled with contradictory pressures leading to political immobilism and stalemate characterized by deficit financing and hyperinflation (Nef 1982). To compound the problems, social unrest of a potentially revolutionary nature sprouted in a number of countries. The explosion of these unfulfilled expectations was best exemplified by the Cuban revolution of 1959. The crisis of the 1960s was more a sociopolitical one than an economic crisis such as that of the 1930s. Unlike its predecessor, the new crisis was one where international politics and the Cold War played a disproportionate role in national politics. American efforts at preventing "communism" (ditto for Latin American nationalism) introduced a number of fundamental changes in Latin American societies. The ostensible goal of American-sponsored "reform mongering" was to stop actual or potential revolutions (Hirschman 1963). The most articulate expression of this policy was the Alliance for Progress, launched in 1961 in response to the Cuban Revolution. It presented economic development in classical Rostowian terms, as an antidote to insurgency (Rostow 1960; Dwivedi and Nef 1982). For Latin America, the Alliance meant the external inducement to reform the land tenure system, to rationalize fiscal policies, to usher in community development, and most important, the initiation of comprehensive administrative reforms along the lines of orthodox "development administration."

Nevertheless, the Alliance, whose historical antecedent had been the U.S.-initiated "Operation Bootstrap" in Puerto Rico in the 1950s, had built-in constraints. For one thing, it was an attempt to modernize and strengthen the status quo. Secondly, the process of induced development espoused by the Alliance remained conditioned to external (that is U.S.) needs, capital, technical assistance and expectations. Most important, however, was the fact that the Alliance carried with it a hidden agenda or "insurance policy package." This was the modernization and revamping of the defense and security establishments along the lines, or what has later become known as the counterinsurgency, civic action and national security doctrines (Weil et al. 1979). In sum, the administrative reforms undertaken during the period of the Alliance for Progress represented three somewhat contradictory trends.

First, there was a rather *substantive* drive to introduce social and economic reforms, such as agrarian reform and community development.

These brought about new administrative agencies, programs and management styles. Although the motivation for these reforms was largely to prevent the upsurge of radical movements and thus mainly to have a positive effect on the local elites, its unintended consequences were to enhance social mobilization. This was particularly the case with the attempts at integrating the peasantry and the urban poor into moderate antileftist movements.

In the second place, there were those "neutral" technical reforms, more appropriately classified as *re-estructuraciones,* which were oriented to improve the planning, organizational and managerial capabilities of the state. In a general sense, they were geared at improving the efficiency of the government bureaucracy in order to turn it into an administrative machinery for development. This is the aspect of the Alliance that is often referred to in the literature as the period of "administrative reform" (*la Reforma Administrativa*). The thrust here was purely formal and in a way, even contradictory with the substantive developments referred to above. It was a reform of administrative services: the creation and expansion of offices of organization and methods (O&M), personnel systems, (including career schedules), planning, programming and budgeting, and all the paraphernalia of scientific management (Salgado and Valdes 1984). Some of these trends of administrative reform had been in the cards since the 1950s when the United Nations and the U.S. Point Four program had introduced the idea of administrative rationalization. These early reforms, however, were imbued with a professional ethos of scientific management at odds with the "development administration" mood of the sixties. This reformist thrust also expressed itself in the expansion and creation of academic programs oriented to develop administrative cadres. Some of these had also been in existence since the 1950s such as ESAPAC (later ICAP) in Central America and EBAP in Brazil sponsored by the Getulio Vargas foundation. Schools of business, economics, public administration and planning also played an important role here by generating a new "technobureaucracy" (experts in scientific management and planning) of development managers.

In the third place, the reforms sponsored by the Alliance represented a less visible but highly significant counterinsurgent and repressive strain. This involved the modernization and coordination of the security establishments ranging anywhere from civic action to mass repression. These efforts that affected the military and police apparatus were a conscious attempt at demobilization, in fundamental contradiction with the manifest thrust of social reform present in the Alliance. In this respect they showed a remarkable resemblance with similar U.S. efforts in Southeast Asia, Korea and Iran (Dwivedi and Nef 1982).

Bureaucratic Authoritarianism

An important consequence of this third trend was a growing technical and ideological homogenization of the Latin American police and security forces. This process also enhanced a high degree of transnationalization of this most crucial element of the Latin American state (Nef and Rojas 1984). The counterinsurgency establishment, permeated with an American worldview where the "internal enemy" defined their very mission, increasingly displaced the drives toward substantive reform, as well as development administration. In fact it constituted a sort of "fail safe" mechanism against the failures of reformism to prevent social unrest. Moreover, since the Brazilian coup of 1964, and as the United States increasingly moved from a reformist to an outright conservative stand, the Latin American "new" military establishment with open American encouragement ended up displacing the civilian reforms (O'Brien 1972).

Also, as import substitution faded away and as transnational business further penetrated the Latin American economies, a new social alliance would come into being. These alliances — called by some "reactionary coalitions" — made up by the transnationalized business community and the equally transnationalized military elites ushered in a new model of economic development and accumulation (North 1978). This model was known as bureaucratic authoritarianism (O'Donnell 1977). Here, to facilitate private accumulation and foreign investment the state forcefully and drastically reduced the scope and extent of its activities in the areas of economic development and welfare. These functions were privatized and left to the "magic of the market." International competitiveness was enhanced by specializing in primary production along the lines of "comparative advantages"; almost a return to the "export economy." The latter also meant a drastic reduction of the cost of labor by cutting off social benefits, lowering tariff barriers and disarticulating labor organizations (Halperin 1976). Administrative reform in the civilian sphere implied a retreat of government activities from areas that had been traditionally in the domain of the administrative state (such as health, education, research, energy, transportation and financing). It also meant a greater emphasis on cost reduction, fiscal restraints and facilitation of private foreign investments following very closely standard IMF recipes. This was at the core of the so-called "global reforms" that replaced the old O&M, personnel management, program budgeting and development administration of the past.

There was an area, however, where government activity grew both in scope and intensity. This was the military and security areas. In fact, the total government expenditures for the region during the era of bureaucratic authoritarianism, either grew or remained constant. Since the economic and welfare functions of the state dramatically decreased, conversely, there was an equally dramatic increase of the repressive functions of the state. In the long run, authoritarian capitalism was thoroughly unsuccessful in bringing about economic development. True, for a short while Brazil and Chile could show accelerated rates of economic growth. Nevertheless, these rates did not mean the improvement of living conditions; the opposite was the case (Furtado 1979). It was also important to notice that generally when the GNP grew, this was more than matched by increases in foreign indebtedness. In sum, the price of the economic miracles was more poverty, an expanding foreign debt, greater marginalization, increased dependency and a huge and uncontrollable repressive apparatus to maintain "stability." In fact, by the late 1970s, the cost of repression had by far outweighed the benefits of the "economic miracles."

Redemocratization and Restricted Democracy

In the long run, social unrest had not been stamped out. Worse, it had been fueled by government attempts at forceful demobilization and widespread official terror. With economic successes withering away, an unmanageable debt burden, and with severe dislocations in the economy, the model of authoritarian capitalism could no longer buy legitimacy with economic effectiveness. The ensuing economic, political and social crises of the 1980s brought, once again, the spectre of revolution to the Latin American elites and their transnational associates. It is at this time that increased concern over *formulas de recambio* (exchange formulas) to recycle the crisis gained popularity among ruling circles in Latin America and the United States. The revolutionary upsurges in Nicaragua, El Salvador and Guatemala indicated that perpetual repression had serious limits. A new doctrine to overcome the crisis — referred to as "redemocratization" or the "theory of restricted democracy" — quickly became the dominant political discourse (Wolfe 1975).

With significant foreign inducement, the praetorian guards of the repressive 1970s retreated in order to their barracks. In their place, weak civilian regimes, some including the same U.S.-indoctrinated technobureaucracy and resulting from electoral processes, constituted a kind of receivership government charged with the balancing of almost unmanageable pressures. The military and police establishments across the board maintained a high degree of autonomy and veto power. On the other hand, the economic forces that controlled the commanding heights of society remained equally untouched; so were the transnational economic and military linkages established during the last two decades. By the end of the

1980s, there were scarcely any Latin American countries (Paraguay was a notable exception) under manifest military rule. All the rest, in varying degrees, had been "redemocratized" by regimes of limited or restricted participation.

Conclusions

Constraints on Administrative Reform in Contemporary Latin America

The historical analysis undertaken in the preceding presentation indicates a pattern of congruity between development projects and attempts at administrative reform. The political and developmental agenda present in this new phase of Latin American history presents a number of salient traits.

First, the present political projects in Latin America, far from being development projects, are more properly described as projects of survival. The issue at stake is how to manage the myriad of crises and prevent them from becoming one major explosion. Chief among these crises is the problem of the foreign debt. But there are important social crises brewing as well. These are related to the inability of these regimes to fulfill social demands postponed by 20 years of military repression.

A second characteristic is that the political agendas are severely restricted and limited. Many topics, issues and institutions remain outside the realm of "acceptable" political debate. Thus government maneuverability is severely restrained.

Third, the political coalitions supporting these alliances are fragile and unstable. On the one hand, numerous actors (the left, labor unions and grass- roots organizations) remain generally excluded from the formal political debate. On the other hand, the presence of an autonomous, powerful and externally controlled security apparatus further reduces the room for accommodation. This is compounded by the strong presence of external U.S. military and civilian constituencies that retain veto power over public policies.

Fourth, the administrative mechanisms to implement even these very limited policy packages are chronically underfinanced and heavily dependent on foreign aid and technical cooperation.

In sum, the present situation is one of extremely limited options and where the maintenance of formal electoral "democracy" rather than the satisfaction of basic needs is the only yet precarious objective. This, of course, makes more sense to the upper and middle sectors than to the marginalized poor. Moreover, under the present circumstances, it is not beyond the realm of possibilities that once redemocratization is exhausted, there would be a reversal to a form of repressive — yet not even rhetorically developmentalist — regime.

At present, as development strategies are being increasingly replaced by survival strategies, the options for substantive administrative reform in Latin America are being dramatically reduced. Inasmuch as participation, the issues and the breadth of sociopolitical alliances become more narrow and meaningless, there is a proclivity for administrative reform to engage in a symbolic game of "technocratic" adjustments without substance. Such reforms are by and large not oriented to alter the status quo or to produce developmental results. They constitute, at best, attempts at reinforcing and managing the present catastrophic equilibrium.

So far, and with the exception of the brief interlude between the post—World War I period, the Great Depression and the 1950s, Latin American development projects could be better characterized as projects of underdevelopment. Perhaps in this sense, one could argue that they were successful. They deepened and modernized underdevelopment while benefiting the social sectors, domestic and international, that they sought to benefit. They also fragmented national and regional unity. The effects on the majority of the population have been to foster underdevelopment. The overall characteristic of these projects at present could be summarized under four major headings.

Large scale: They have been capital intensive megaprojects oriented to satisfying the needs of those sectors that had a greater economic capacity to absorb these new developments. More often than not, these projects had been oriented toward cosmetic "modernization" without regard to the basic needs of the bulk of the Latin American population.

Dependent: Most development projects have tended to be dependent and imitative (Crowther and Flores 1970). They have resulted from external inducements and pressures. They have been heavily reliant on imported technology and capital, generally not the most appropriate mix to utilize internal resources. Their initiative has always laid outside Latin America.

Marginalizing: These projects have tended to benefit more the urban, integrated sectors of society than the vast majority of the rural poor and the marginal urban population. In fact, due to their limited coverage and accessibility, they have been most clearly confined to benefit the upper and middle strata of society.

Elitist: In connection with the above, most development projects have tended to be elitist, formulated and implemented in a top-down manner and with extremely limited incidence — if not outright exclusion — of popular participation.

None of these projects has reflected, even in recent years, development options such as "need orientation," "another development," "self-reliance" or "autonomy." More specifically, development projects in Latin America have reflected a fairly consistent conservative mode.

The politics of administrative reform in Latin America has followed the characteristics and directions of development projects. It is no wonder that, given these circumstances, most administrative reform efforts, especially in recent years, have tended to be devoid of substance. Worse, they have been used as a substitute for much-needed social and political reforms. They have also (and particularly in recent years) been determined by external initiatives, generally responding to external needs and definitions of problems. They have had a tendency to be divorced from a profound analysis of the concrete circumstances of the countries. They have concentrated as well more on the instrumentalities of government (budgets, personnel systems, formal accountability, etc.) than on the problems and the technologies appropriately devised to solve those problems. In this sense, there is a strong orientation towards the "politics of antipolitics." Reforms have also been strongly influenced by a view of development administration—and administrative development—which perceives the bureaucratic mode and scientific management as the epitome of administrative efficiency and effectiveness.

The formation of the cadres of administrators not only has been heavily influenced by foreign vogues and paradigms but also has lacked a coherent policy of research and development related to Latin American realities. Last but not least, efforts at administrative reform have been concentrated in the sphere of the central or national governments, with very little emphasis being placed upon lower jurisdictions. For instance, the area of local government has been hardly studied or understood. Worse, other modalities of administration that exist at the grass-roots level have been consciously excluded from any analysis, extension programs, or even as objects of study in public administration programs.

In fact, it is here that some of the most fundamental challenges to the status quo and to the administrative state have been generated. The peasant and Indian communities of *ejidatarios* was one of the social forces that started the Mexican revolution in 1910. It was the Cuban and Nicaraguan marginalized peasants who blended their natural and spontaneous organizations with the populist and revolutionary projects of the 26th of July Movement and the Frente Sandinista. It is the Indian communities in the Peruvian or Guatemalan highlands that have contributed in no small manner to alternative revolutionary projects of development in those societies. It is important to bear in mind that these embryonic forms of traditional survival, resistance and contemporary revolutions present not only valuable examples of self-administration, but an enormous potential for changing the status quo. These are, in their purest forms, modes of development administration (Dwivedi and Nef 1982). It may well be that once the present attempts at formal and status quo oriented administrative reforms without social substance run their course, these "subterranean" traditions and cultures would erupt on the political stage as full-fledged recognizable actors. This could have the most profound consequences in shaping not only the direction of administrative reform but Latin America's own history.

References

Baumgartner et al. "Meta-Power and the Structuring of Social Hierarchies." In *Power and Control: Social Structures and Their Transformation.* Edited by Tom Burns and Walter Buckley. Beverly Hills: Sage, 1976, p. 224–25.

Burns, E. Bradford. *Latin America: A Concise Interpretative History,* 4th ed. Englewood Cliffs, N.J.: Prentice Hall, 1986, p. 134–74.

Crowther, Win, and Flores, Gilberto. *Problemas Latinoamericanos y Soluciones Estadounidenses en Administración Pública.* Santiago: INSORA, 1970, p. 1–8.

Dwivedi, O. P., and Nef, J. "Crises and Continuities in Development Theory and Administration." *Public Administration and Development* 2 (1982):60.

Easton, David. "An Approach to the Analysis of Political Systems." *World Politics* 9, no. 3 (Apr. 1957):383–400.

Furtado, Celso. *Economic Development of Latin America: Historical Background and Contemporary Problems,* 2nd ed. Cambridge: Cambridge University Press, 1976, p. 107–17.

_____. "The Brazilian Model." In *The Political Economy of Development and Underdevelopment,* 2nd ed. Edited by Charles Wilber. New York: Random House, 1979, p. 324–33.

Halperin, Ernst. *Terrorism in Latin America.* Beverly Hills: Sage, 1976, p. 83–84.

Hirschman, Albert. *Journeys Toward Progress: Studies of Economic Policy-Making in Latin America.* Westport, Conn.: Greenwood Press, 1963, p. 276–97.

Israel, Ricardo. *Un Mundo Cercano: El Impacto Político y Económico de las Nuevas Tecnologías.* Santiago: Instituto de Ciencia Politica, Universidad de Chile, 1984, p. 25.

Johnson, John. *The Military and Society in Latin America.* Stanford, Calif.: Stanford University Press, 1964, p. 62–133.

Nef, J. "Stalemate and Repression in the Southern Cone: An Interpretative Synopsis." *New Scholar* 8 (1982):317–86.

_____. "Political Trends in Latin America: A Structural and Historical Analysis." In *Latin America: Its Problems and Its Promise.* Edited by Jan Black. Boulder, Colo.: Westview Press, 1984, p. 191–206.

Nef, J., and Dwivedi, O. P. "Science, Technology and Development in the Third World: Cultural, Professional and Administrative Circumstances." A background paper for the Pearson Fellowship Programme Seminar, IDRC, Ottawa, 1986.

Nef, J., and Rojas, F. "Dependencia Compleja y Transnacionalización del Estado en América Latina." *Relaciones Internacionales* 8–9 (1984):101–22.

North, Liisa. "Development and Underdevelopment in Latin America." In *Canada and the Latin American Challenge*. Edited by J. Nef. Guelph: OCPLACS, 1978, p. 79–80.

O'Brien, Donal Cruise. "Modernization, Order and the Erosion of a Democratic Ideal: American Political Science 1960–1970." *Journal of Development Studies* 1972:351–78.

O'Donnell, Gullermo. "Corporatism and the Question of the State." In *Authoritarianism and Corporatism in Latin America*. Edited by James Malloy. Pittsburgh: Pittsburgh University Press, 1977, p. 47–84.

Rostow, Walter. *The Stages of Economic Growth: A Non-Communist Manifest.* Cambridge: Harvard University Press, 1960.

Salgado, Ignacio Pérez, and Valdes, Mauricio. "Balance de los Movimientos de Reforma Administrativa en América Latina: Enseñanzas." In *Administracion Públical Perspectivas Criticas*. Edited by G. Flores and J. Nef. San Jose: ICAP, 1984, p. 91–120.

Skidmore, Thomas, and Smith, Peter. *Modern Latin America.* New York: Oxford University Press, 1984, p. 46–56.

Stallings, Barbara. *Class Conflict and Economic Development in Chile.* Stanford, Calif.: Stanford University Press, 1978, p. 10, 21, 51–52.

United Nations. *Public Administration in the Second United Nations Development Decade: Report of the Second Meeting of Experts 1971.* New York: United Nations, Department of Economic and Social Affairs, Public Administration Division, 1971. ST/TAD/M/57, p. 3–7.

Wahrlich, Beatriz. "Evolucion de las Ciencias Administrativas an America Latina." *Revista Internacional de Ciencias Administrativas* 12 (1978):70–71.

Weil, Jean Louis et al. "The Repressive State: The Brazilian National Security Doctrine and Latin America." LARU Studies. Toronto: DOC 3, no. 2 (1979):36–63.

Wolfe, Alan. "Capitalism Shows Its Face." *The Nation,* 29 Nov. 1975, p. 561.

Zylberberg, Jacques. "Etat-corporatisme-populisme: Contribution a una sociologie politique de l'Amerique latine." *Etudes internationales* 7, no. 2 (1976):215–20.

12

Administrative Policy in Southeast Asia

JON S. T. QUAH

Introduction

The Association of Southeast Asian Nations (ASEAN) was formed in August 1967 with Indonesia, Malaysia, the Philippines, Singapore and Thailand as its founding members. In January 1984, Brunei joined ASEAN as its sixth member. The purpose of this chapter is to describe and compare the nature of public personnel administration in the five founding ASEAN states. Brunei has been excluded from our discussion because of the scarcity of published data on its public bureaucracy.

The main thesis of this chapter is that the nature of public personnel administration in each of the five countries depends on its public bureaucracy and how it interacts with its policy context in the performance of its various personnel functions. To demonstrate this argument, we will begin with a brief description of the policy context in the five countries. A comparison will then be made of the growth of their public bureaucracies. This will be followed by a comparative analysis of the performance of the recruitment, selection, classification, compensation and performance evaluation functions in the five countries. We will conclude with an assessment of the extent to which the five public bureaucracies have succeeded in attaining the goals of productivity and excellence in the performance of the five selected personnel functions.

The term "public bureaucracy" as used here refers to the governmental bureaucracy or the civil service system found in most countries today (Peabody and Rourke 1965, p. 803). It excludes the military and the quasi-governmental bodies or public enterprises as these are usually not considered as part of the civil service.

Policy Context

The policy context in a country is important because it not only determines the nature and magnitude of the country's problems, but also influences the extent to which the public bureaucracy is able to cope with these problems and to contribute towards national development. We will now describe the policy context in the five ASEAN countries in terms of the geographical, economic, demographic and political aspects.

Geography

In terms of size, the five ASEAN countries differ a great deal. Indonesia has the largest land area (1,904,345 sq. km.) with its archipelago of 13,000 islands. Singapore, on the other hand, is the smallest of the five countries as it is a city-state with a total land area of 620 sq. km. Between these two extremes are Thailand with a land area of 542,373 sq. km., followed by Malaysia (330,434 sq. km.) and the Philippines (300,000 sq. km.). Thus, of the five countries, only Thailand is a mainland state, with the others being maritime states. According to Waddell (1972, p. 16–17), the mainland societies were static and "built on wet rice cultivation and a big population, producing great art and architecture at tremendous cost" while the maritime societies were "dynamic, sea-based and venturesome, making contact with the outside world and depending for its life on trade."

The archipelagic nature of the Philippines and Indonesia means that there are problems of communication and control between the central and provincial or state governments. Because of the vast distances involved, problems of logistics arise. For example, national elections are held over a period of time in these countries and the results are not known until several days later. Thailand and Malaysia encounter such problems too, but to a lesser extent. Unlike the neighboring countries of Indonesia and Malaysia, Singapore's smallness has contributed to a highly centralized public bureaucracy, which does not suffer from the same problems afflicting a federal public bureaucracy in its interaction with the state or provincial bureaucracies.

Except for Singapore, the other four ASEAN countries depend a great deal on agriculture and consequently have a sizable rural sector. This implies the existence of rural-urban migration to the capital cities as well as the necessity for the incumbent governments to formulate and implement rural development programs. In other words, the absence of a large rural sector in Singapore not only reinforces the centralized nature of the public bureaucracy, but also means that the latter is not burdened by problems arising from rural-urban migration or from initiating rural development programs because there is no need for such programs in the first place (Quah 1984a, p. 213).

Economy

There is also much diversity in the economies of the five ASEAN countries. The proportion of the economically active population that is engaged in agriculture in these countries ranges from 78 percent for Thailand, to 66 percent for Indonesia, to 59 percent for the Philippines, to 55 percent for Malaysia, and to 7 percent for Singapore. Furthermore, the five countries also produce very large amounts of some of the world's crops and its supplies of certain minerals, for example: 98.4 percent of the world's abaca fibre; 81.3 percent of its rubber; 64.2 percent of its copra; 53.4 percent of its coconuts; 33.8 percent of its palm oil; 62 percent of its tin; 6.6 percent of its chromium; and 3.4 percent of its bauxite (United Nations 1974, p. 7–8).

A country's level of economic development is important because it determines, among other things, the amount of resources that will be allocated by the government for the attainment of national development goals. Other things being equal, the more economically developed a country is, the greater will be the amount of resources devoted to national development efforts. Thus, in terms of per capita income, the range is from US$6,922 for Singapore at one extreme to US$566 for Indonesia at the other extreme. In between can be found Malaysia (with US$1,996), Thailand (with US$645.5) and the Philippines (with US$603) (FEER 1986, p. 6–7).

Demography

Two aspects will be discussed here: the size and nature of the population in the five countries. In terms of size, Indonesia has the largest population with 168.4 million in 1985. The Philippines ranks second with 56.8 million, followed by Thailand (52.7 million) and Malaysia (15.7 million). Singapore is the smallest with a population of 2.6 million (FEER 1986, p. 6–7). Needless to say, people constitute the most valuable resource of a country. However, if the population is very large in a country, this will stretch the country's resources and facilities and stress the need for family planning. On the other hand, if a country has too few people, it will have a manpower shortage. In short, the size of a country's population can be either an asset or liability depending on its resources and manpower requirements.

The degree of homogeneity or heterogeneity of a population is an important determinant of a country's success or failure in its nation-building efforts. All the five countries have heterogeneous rather than homogeneous populations. For example, the Indonesian population is characterized by ethnic and religious pluralism. The Javanese constitute nearly half of the population followed by the Sundanese (14.5 percent), Minangkabau (4 percent), Chinese (3 percent), the Makasarese-Buginese (4 percent), Bataks (2 percent), Ambonese (2 percent), Balinese (2 percent) and the Acehnese (1.4 percent). In terms of religion, about 90 percent of the Indonesians are Muslims. Among the non-Muslims, the Ambonese and Toba Batak are Christians, while the Balinese are Hindus (Suryadinata 1985, p. 110–11).

Malaysia, Singapore and the Philippines are also plural societies. In the case of Peninsular Malaysia, the Malays are the largest group as they constitute 56 percent of the population. The Chinese are the next largest group (33 percent), followed by the Indians (10 percent) and "Others" (1 percent). In Sarawak, the population is made up of Ibans (the majority), Malays, Chinese, Land Dayaks, Kelanaus and other minority groups. Similarly, in Sabah, the Kadazans are the largest group, with the rest of the population consisting of Chinese, Malays, Bajaus and Kedayans. While the Malays are Muslims, the Chinese are mainly Buddhists, Taoists or Christians. The Indians are mainly Hindus, but some are Muslims or Christians (Ministry of Finance, Malaysia, 1984, p. 7; Information Malaysia 1984 Yearbook, p. 306–9).

Singapore's population is multiracial, multilingual and multireligious in nature. In terms of ethnicity, the population consists of 76.7 percent Chinese, 14.7 percent Malays, 6.4 percent Indians (including those of Pakistani or Sri Lankan descent) and 2.2 percent of other ethnic groups. As far as language is concerned, there are four official languages: English, Malay, Mandarin and Tamil. Malay is the national language and English is the language of administration. There is also great diversity in religion among the population. Taoists are the largest religious group (29.3 percent), followed by Buddhists (26.7 percent), Muslims (16.3 percent) and Christians (10.3 percent). Atheists constitute 13.2 percent of the population (Quah 1984b, p. 110–11).

The Philippines has been described by David Joel Steinberg (1982) as "a singular and a plural place." According to him: "The Philippines is both a unified nation with a single people, the Filipinos, and a highly fragmented and plural society that is divided between Muslims and Christians, rural and urban, uplander and lowlander, and rich and poor and between the people of one ethnic, linguistic, or geographic region and those of another" (Steinberg 1982, p. xi). Seventy languages are spoken by the Filipinos, but nine languages—Tagalog, Cebuano, Ilocano, Hiligaynon, Bicol, Waray,

Pampango, Pangasinan, and Maranao—are used by 90 percent of them. The largest minority group is the Chinese, who number about 700,000. About 85 percent of the population is Catholic, 5 percent is Aglipayan, 5 percent is Muslim, and the rest is distributed among the Protestants (Steinberg 1982, p. 19, 22, and 77).

Finally, the population in Thailand is also heterogeneous, but to a lesser extent than the other countries. Sixty percent of the population is Thai, with the remaining 40 percent divided among the Lao (25 percent), Chinese (10 percent), Malays (3 percent) and Meo, Khmer and others (2 percent). The largest religious group in Thailand is the Buddhists, who make up 95 percent of the population. The remaining 5 percent of the population consists of Muslims (4 percent), Christians (0.6 percent), and Hindus, Sikhs and others (0.4 percent) (Office of the Prime Minister, Thailand, 1984, p. 284).

Politics

The nature of the political systems in the five ASEAN countries has been influenced to a greater or lesser extent by their colonial heritage. In terms of their former colonial background, it is well known that both Singapore and Malaysia have been colonized by the British, the Philippines by the Spanish and Americans, Indonesia by the Dutch; but Thailand has never been made a colony by a Western power. Frank C. Darling (1979, p. 242–44) has argued that the degree of harshness of the Western colonization process was low for the Philippines and Malaya (including Singapore) and high for Indonesia. However, it should be noted that Spanish colonial rule in the Philippines was harsh as the *Visitador General* and the *Residencia* were established by the metropolitan government in Spain to ensure effective control over the colonial officials working in the country. In between these two extremes of the harsh Spanish and the benign U.S. occupation can be found the Dutch and British methods of colonial administration. The Dutch system of indirect rule in Indonesia was a farce as all the native rulers "were reduced to mere servants of the colonial administration, inferior in everything except matters of ceremony." In contrast, the British system of colonial administration in Malaysia and Singapore was more complex and also more successful as it involved a combination of direct and indirect rule (Pluvier 1974, p. 14).

In terms of the formal political institutions, Malaysia and Thailand are constitutional monarchies, while Indonesia, the Philippines and Singapore are republics. Only Malaysia is a federal state, while the other countries are unitary states. All five countries have legislative assemblies and hold elections at periodic intervals. Except for Thailand, the other four countries have dominant party systems. The military plays an important role in politics in Indonesia and Thailand. Indeed, the president of Indonesia and the prime minister of Thailand were former army generals (Mauzy 1985, p. 6).

All the five countries have been quite stable politically. President Suharto of Indonesia has been in power since 1966, when he replaced President Sukarno. Prime Minister Lee Kuan Yew has been prime minister of Singapore for 27 years since June 1959. Ferdinand Marcos was president of the Philippines from 1966 until February 1986 when he was forced by "people power" to flee to Hawaii, and was replaced by Corazon Aquino. Although Datuk Seri Dr. Mahatir Mohamad has been prime minister of Malaysia only since 1981, the ruling *Barisan Nasional* (National Front) and its predecessor, the Alliance Party, have held the reins of government since the attainment of independence in August 1957. Perhaps, Thailand is the least stable of the five ASEAN countries because of the frequent occurrence of military coups.

Growth of the Public Bureaucracies

Gerald Caiden (1982, p. 102) has argued that the public bureaucracy has grown because it "has the power, coverage, resources, organization and professional competence to give it functional superiority." Indeed, according to him, the public sector has grown more rapidly than the private sector during the last century and will "remain a major instrument of social change and political socialization" as well as "the principal channel of economic and social mobility and advancement" (Caiden 1982, p. 102–3).

If we examine the actual dates of the founding of the public bureaucracies in the five ASEAN countries, it can be seen that these institutions were formed at different times. The Thai public bureaucracy is the oldest as it was founded by King Boromotrailokanat in 1448 (Siffin 1966, p. 17). The public bureaucracy in the Philippines was established in 1571 by Miguel Lopez de Legazpi and ranks second in age (Corpuz 1957, p. 15–19). The Indonesian public bureaucracy is the third oldest as it was created by William Daendels after the dissolution of the Dutch East India Company in 1798 (Hadisumarto 1974, p. 116–18). The public bureaucracies in Malaysia and Singapore are the youngest as both emerged after the period of private administration of the English East India Company in 1858 when the Company was dissolved (Tilman 1964, p. 40; Lee 1976, p. 88–90).

The public bureaucracies were set up at different times in the ASEAN countries because of the peculiar historical circumstances and environmental influences prevailing in each of these countries (Quah 1978, p. 427). Thailand was the first in establishing the public bureaucracy probably because of her noncolonial status. Thus, the public bureaucracies in the other four countries were foreign institutions introduced by the colonial powers for the attainment of a specific goal, namely, economic exploitation of the natural resources of the colonies for the benefit of the home governments. The public bureaucracies were established for the performance of such basic functions as "maintaining order, administering the law, and collecting taxes" (Steinberg et al. 1971, p. 203). In short, the public bureaucracies existed for the sole purpose of consolidating colonial rule and the attainment of its economic objectives.

However, as a result of economic growth, further expansion of the public bureaucracies was possible and desirable as this would not only reinforce but also accelerate the economic development of the colonial powers even further. The public bureaucracies in all the five countries grew quite rapidly especially after 1900 and were gradually entrusted with functions that had no local precedents. A variety of "specialist services" was provided by the public bureaucracies to the population at large in these countries. Some of these services such as geological services, postal, telegraph and telephone services, railways and censuses, had at best an indirect impact on the masses. Of more direct relevance to the villagers were the services provided to improve village life, namely, "a wide variety of public health programs, forest reserves to check erosion, village schools, rural credit services, cooperatives, agricultural extension services, the reorganization of village structure" (Steinberg et al. 1971, p. 203).

According to Emmerson (1978, p. 84–85), the Indonesian public bureaucracy grew at a much faster rate than the population in the country. He wrote:

> In Java in the late nineteenth-century less than a tenth of 1 percent of the inhabitants ruled over the huge remainder. By 1930 Java's government employees had increased to around 1 percent of its population. By the mid-1960s the percentage had more than doubled for the country as a whole and had risen even more steeply on Java because the central government was—and still is—located there. In the last hundred years the number of public employees in Indonesia has increased, very roughly, around five hundred-fold, compared to a "mere" five- or sixfold increase in the population (Emmerson 1978, p. 84–85).

During the Dutch colonial rule the goals of increased extraction and control led to the recruitment of 1,400 territorial native officials in Java during the late nineteenth century. The third goal of welfare was accepted by the Dutch colonial government in the twentieth century and justified the formation of schools and hospitals and the construction of railroads, roads and water works. Consequently, the size of the public bureaucracy rose to

250,000 by 1940 (Emmerson 1978, p. 86). After the attainment of independence on August 17, 1945, the nationalist government created eleven ministries: home affairs, foreign affairs, defense, justice, finance, economy, health, education and culture, social affairs, communications and information. Since then, the public bureaucracy has grown by about nine times in 1982 with 2,304,867 civil servants (Republik Indonesia 1983, p. 1373).

In the case of Malaysia, the public bureaucracy was concerned with the performance of such "housekeeping" functions as the maintenance of law and order and revenue collection before the attainment of independence in August 1957. However, during the postindependence period, the emphasis shifted to the performance of social and economic development functions by the civil service. The increase in the workload of the public bureaucracy gave rise to its rapid expansion. In his profile of the Malaysian administrative system in 1965, Esman (1972, p. 71) gave figures to show that there were 237,346 government employees in West and East Malaysia. By 1978, the public bureaucracy had grown to 405,164, with a total of 22 ministries and 68 departments at federal level and 348 federal departments at state level (Omar 1980, p. 254, 293). The latest figures provided by the Public Services Department (1984, p. 13) indicate that the Malaysian public bureaucracy had 665,265 employees in 1983.

This pattern of rapid growth of the public bureaucracy has also been repeated in the Philippines. Indeed, the Filipino public bureaucracy has doubled in size from about .6 million employees in 1972 to 1.2 million employees in 1983 (Endriga 1985, p. 17) in spite of the efforts of the Integrated Reorganization Plan (IRP) to trim its size. The IRP was the first major administrative reform introduced by President Ferdinand Marcos after martial law was declared on September 21, 1972. In terms of meeting its objectives, the IRP was able to reduce costs and simplify the government structure by reducing the size of the public bureaucracy from 19 cabinet-level departments, 79 bureaus, 307 agencies and 1,108 divisions to 16 departments, 72 bureaus, 193 agencies and 738 divisions (Quah 1985, p. 999). Some 40 million pesos were saved as a result of the IRP's cost-cutting measures (Endriga 1985, p. 7).

On the other hand, Presidential Decree (P.D.) No. 1 allowed the president to change and modify the IRP whenever necessary. This accounts for the creation of such new organizations as the National Economic and Development Authority (NEDA), the Department of Public Information (DPI), the Department of Tourism (DOT), Philippine Tourism Authority (PTA), the Ministry of Energy, and the Department of Human Settlements (DHS), which was created on June 2, 1978. Of all these agencies, perhaps the most well known was the DHS not only because it came under the charge of Imelda Marcos, but also because of its broad coverage of concerns envisaged in the New Society's eleven basic needs: water, power, food, shelter, medical services, education, sports and recreation, livelihood, mobility and ecological balance (Endriga 1985, p. 9–12).

Apart from the new ministries, other ministries were formed by splitting existing ones. For example, the Department of Agriculture and Natural Resources was split into two separate departments. Other examples of such splitting of departments to form new ones included the Department of Trade and Industry, and the Department of Public Works, Transportation and Communication. Thus, instead of reducing the number of departments from 19 to 16 as required by the IRP, the various departmental creations and splits had actually increased the number of departments to 21 (Endriga 1985, p. 13).

Before the advent of the People's Action Party (PAP) government in Singapore, the Singapore Civil Service (SCS) did not play an important role in national development as it was an instrument of the British colonial authorities and was under their control and policies. However, after June 1959, the SCS has grown not only in size but also in terms of its workload and responsibilities. More specifically, the SCS has grown both in terms of the number of ministries as well as the number of employees. In June 1959, the SCS was made up of nine ministries with a total of 28,253 employees. In addition to the Prime Minister's Office, the other ministries were the Deputy Prime Minister's Office, the Ministry of National Development, the Ministry of Health, the Ministry of Finance, the Ministry of Labor and Law, the Ministry of Culture, the Ministry of Home Affairs and the Ministry of Education. The Culture and National Development ministries were created by the PAP government for the purposes of nation-building and socioeconomic development respectively. In 1961, the Ministry of Social Affairs was established to take over the Social Welfare Department from the Ministry of Labor and Law. Three years later, the latter was reorganized and a separate Ministry of Law was created (Quah 1984c, p. 289).

After the attainment of independence in August 1965, the Ministry of Foreign Affairs and the Ministry of Interior and Defense were created to perform functions that had been undertaken before by the British and Malaysian governments. The Ministry of Home Affairs was given the additional function of defense and renamed the Ministry of Interior and Defense in 1966. This arrangement continued until August 1970, when the latter was divided into the Ministry of Defense and the Ministry of Home Affairs (Quah 1984c, p. 289).

The Ministry of Science and Technology and the Ministry of Communications were formed after the April 1968 general election because of the "growing importance of science and technology in the development of the economy" and the need to combine the vast transport and communications portfolio under one ministry. The Ministry of the Environment was created after the September 1972 general election to implement plans for the control and prevention of pollution and the preservation of public health. The Ministry of Trade and Industry was established in March 1979 to deal with "all economic matters and duties that were previously under the purview of the Development Division, Ministry of Finance." In March 1981, the Ministry of Science and Technology was dissolved and its functions were distributed between the Ministry of Trade and Industry and the Ministry of Education. Finally, after the December 1984 general election, the Ministry of Culture was disbanded and its Information Division was transferred to the Ministry of Communications, which was renamed the Ministry of Communications and Information. Similarly, the Ministry of Social Affairs was renamed the Ministry of Community Development.

In short, the public bureaucracy in Singapore has grown from 9 ministries to 14 ministries from 1959 to 1984. The number of civil servants has also increased by more than 45,000 as the SCS had 73,400 members in 1984 (Republic of Singapore 1985, p. 56). Thus, the increase in the SCS's workload and responsibilities during the same period can be attributed to Singapore's attainment of independence and success in promoting economic growth.

In Thailand, the public bureaucracy has expanded a great deal especially after the establishment of a constitutional monarchy in 1932 (Riggs 1966). The number of ministries has increased from 7 in 1933 to 13 in 1979. During the same period, the number of departments multiplied by three times from 45 to 131 departments. The rate of expansion of the divisions has been the most rapid as the number of divisions grew from 143 in 1933 to 1,264 in 1979 (Chandarasorn 1979, p. 4–6). Similarly, the number of government officials has increased from 220,252 in 1968 to 926,662 in 1982 (Chandarasorn 1985, p. 344).

A Thai scholar has provided two reasons for the rapid expansion of the public bureaucracy after 1932. First, the desire of the government agencies for autonomy and self-sufficiency has given rise to "the drive for larger budgets, greater powers, more positions, and more materials and equipment." Indeed, such "empire building" by the government agencies was difficult to control because of "the complexity of, and mystery shrouding, their work arrangements." The second reason for the rapid growth of the Thai public bureaucracy is the absence of any serious attempt to improve the system. According to the same scholar:

> Proliferation of agencies arises as a result of individual agencies' attempts to solve their own immediate problems. The parochialism inherent in the situation results in work overlap and duplication, and leads inevitably to jurisdictional disputes. In turn, this gives rise to work delays, displaced objectives, ineffi-

ciency, parochial perspectives, and refusal to accept responsibility. Agencies attempt to expand their own power and become self-seeking (Nakata 1981, p. 68).

In short, all the five ASEAN public bureaucracies have grown quite rapidly because of their increased workload and the widening scope of their activities. The growth rate of the public bureaucracy is the highest in Indonesia, followed by Thailand, Malaysia, Singapore and the Philippines in that order. More specifically, the Indonesian public bureaucracy grew by 9 times between 1940 and 1982; the Thai public bureaucracy expanded by 4 times during 1968–1982; the Malaysian public bureaucracy increased its size by 2.8 times from 1965–1983; the Singapore public bureaucracy grew by 2.6 times during 1959–1984; and the Filipino public bureaucracy doubled its size between 1972 and 1983. (See Table 12.1.)

TABLE 12.1.   Growth of the ASEAN Civil Services

		Civil Servants		Growth Rate
Country	Year Founded	(a)	(b)	(b/a)
Indonesia	1798	250,000 (1940)	2,300,000 (1980)	9 times
Malaysia	1858	237,346 (1965)	665,265 (1983)	2.8 times
Philippines	1571	600,000 (1972)	1,200,000 (1983)	2 times
Singapore	1858	28,253 (1959)	73,400 (1984)	2.6 times
Thailand	1448	220,252 (1968)	926,662 (1982)	4 times

Sources: Chandarasorn (1985, p. 344); Corpuz (1957, p. 15–19); Emmerson (1978, p. 86); Endriga (1985, p. 17); Esman 1972, p. 71); Hadisumarto (1974, p. 116–18); Lee (1976, p. 88–90); Public Services Department (1984, p.13); Quah (1978, p. 427); Quah (1984c, p. 289); Republic of Singapore (1985, p. 56); Republik Indonesia (1983, p. 1373); Siffin (1966, p. 17); and Tilman (1964, p. 40).

Public Personnel Administration

Public personnel administration is concerned with improving the productivity of civil servants and encouraging them to strive for excellence in the performance of their duties. It refers to those activities conducted by the central personnel agencies or government departments: recruitment, selection, classification, compensation, promotion, training, performance evaluation and disciplinary control of civil servants. Space constraints do not permit us to discuss all these functions (Quah 1986, p. 72–92). Accordingly, we will only deal with the performance of the recruitment, selection, classification, compensation and performance evaluation functions in the five ASEAN countries.

Recruitment

Instead of describing the recruitment process and identifying the criteria employed in recruiting civil servants in the five countries, we will consider whether they use the traditional or the realistic approach to recruitment (Quah 1986, p. 72–75). Traditional recruitment refers to the approach of selling the organization to outsiders by presenting only positive information and distorting information presented to emphasize the positive aspects. According to Wanous (1980, p. 34–35), "this selling of the organization involves two actions: (1) only positive characteristics are communicated to outsiders rather than those things insiders find dissatisfying about the organization; and (2) those features that are advertised may be distorted to make them more positive." In other words, traditional recruitment is designed to attract as many candidates as possible.

In contrast, realistic recruitment does not attempt to "sell" the organization, but provides "outsiders with *all pertinent* information *without distortion.*" Wanous (1980, p. 41) contends that realistic recruitment is superior to traditional recruitment because realistic recruitment not only increases job satisfaction, but also "reduces subsequent unnecessary turnover caused by the disappointment of initial expectations inflated by traditional recruitment." Indeed, realistic recruitment provides a "vaccination effect" since "job candidates are given a small dose of organizational reality during the recruitment stage in an attempt to lower initial expectations."

If we examine the five ASEAN countries in terms of their approach to recruitment, we will find that they emphasize traditional recruitment rather than realistic recruitment. This focus on traditional recruitment is understandable given the fact that as the civil service is the largest employer in these countries, it relies on traditional recruitment to lower the selection ratio (i.e., the proportion of job candidates who are hired) and to justify the budget of the central personnel agencies. Another advantage is that the low selection ratio gives the impression that only the "best" candidates are chosen since only a small proportion of those who apply are actually hired.

Furthermore, given the low salaries in the public sector jobs (especially in Indonesia, the Philippines and Thailand), it is easy to understand why the civil services in these countries rely on traditional recruitment to attract many applicants to apply for civil service jobs. The relatively higher salaries in the private sector jobs in all the five countries also means that there is constant competition between the public and private sectors for the best candidates. The traditional approach to recruitment is employed by the central personnel agencies in the five countries to enable them to compete with the private sector for competent personnel and to minimize the less attractive aspects of working in the civil service (i.e., low salaries, red tape, etc.).

While the emphasis on traditional recruitment in the five countries is understandable, nevertheless, the time is now opportune for these countries to reconsider their approach to recruitment. From the figures on the size of the five public bureaucracies in the previous section, it is obvious that there is no serious shortage of civil servants in the five countries. Traditional recruitment is more expensive in the long run if turnover is high. On the other hand, realistic recruitment will help to reduce turnover, as candidates recruited by this method tend to stay longer in the organization than those recruited by the traditional method (Wanous 1980, p. 42–43).

Selection

The two major selection methods of competitive examinations and/or interviews have been used by the central personnel agencies in the five ASEAN countries for selecting suitable candidates for the public bureaucracies. Indonesia, Malaysia and Thailand employ a combination of competitive examinations and interviews in the selection process. In contrast, both the Philippines and Singapore rely solely on a single method (either examination or interview) to select candidates for their public bureaucracies.

For entry into the Indonesian public bureaucracy, candidates must pass written examinations that test their general knowledge on Indonesia, their technical knowledge about the positions applied for, and their writing ability and style of language. If necessary, an oral examination may be held to supplement the written examination. Furthermore, a skill examination is required for those applying to become typists or drivers of motor vehicles. In some cases, candidates must also undergo a psychological test. To ensure objectivity, examination papers are graded by at least two examiners and oral examinations are conducted by at least two examiners also. A list of the eligible candidates is prepared in order of merit, and this list is submitted by the examination committee to the relevant agency to be used accordingly (Manurung 1980, p. 149–51).

Until recently, selection to the Malaysian public bureaucracy was by interviews only and candidates were assessed on the basis of their performance during the interviews. However, in 1977, the government stopped direct recruitment to the Administrative and Diplomatic Service (ADS) and candidates were appointed on a temporary basis as cadet ADS officers to undergo a one-year intensive training course at the National Institute of Public Administration (INTAN) before being appointed as probationary ADS officers (Omar 1980, p. 264, 274–75, 289). Thus, entry to the ADS is based on successful performance during the interviews and passing the examinations conducted by INTAN.

In Thailand, the combined use of examinations and interviews for selecting candidates to the public bureaucracy can be more clearly seen. The examination division of the Civil Service Commission first reviews all the applications submitted to identify eligible candidates as well as to eliminate unqualified candidates. The eligible candidates are required to take a written examination consisting of two parts: (1) the general ability part, which tests the candidate's general mental ability and his proficiency in the Thai language; and (2) the specific ability part, which assesses the candidate's aptitude, skill or knowledge appropriate to the position applied for. The final step in selection is the qualification appraisal interview, which is designed to examine whether the candidate possesses the qualifications required for the position and to assess such personal characteristics as his poise, attitude, adjustment, motivation and human relations. To gain entry into the Thai public bureaucracy, a candidate must obtain at least 50 percent for all parts and the total score must not be less than 60 percent (Singhawisai 1980, p. 68–137).

In the case of the Philippines, Article 12 of the 1973 Constitution specifies that all appointments in the public bureaucracy, with the exception of those appointments that are policy-determining, primarily confidential or highly technical in nature, are made only according to merit and fitness, which are determined as far as possible by competitive examinations. Selection in the Philippine public bureaucracy is decentralized as each department or agency evolves its own screening process, which includes tests of fitness in accordance with the standards and guidelines set by the Civil Service Commission (Fernandez 1980, p. 380).

In Singapore, the Public Service Commission (PSC) relies solely on interviews for selecting qualified candidates for Divisions I and II appointments to the public bureaucracy. To qualify for appointment, such candidates must fulfil these six criteria: citizenship, age, education, experience, medical fitness and character (i.e., no record of criminal conviction or corruption, and not being a security risk). (When there are no suitable citizens to fill the vacancies or when noncitizens are better qualified, the commission has appointed Malaysian citizens and others to Divisions I and II posts.) Candidates satisfying such criteria are interviewed by the PSC members. Letters of appointment are only issued to the successful candidates if they pass their medical examination and security screening and after their educational certificates and relevant documents have been verified (Quah 1982a, p. 51).

Classification

The five ASEAN countries have either adopted the British system of rank classification or the American system of position classification, or a combination of both. Malaysia and Singapore (being former British colonies) have retained rank classification; Thailand has shifted from rank classification to position classification on the advice of American consultants; and Indonesia and the Philippines have adopted a combination of rank classification and position classification.

In Malaysia and Singapore, the system of rank classification was originally based on the 1947 Trusted Commission's recommendation that the civil service be reorganized and divided into four divisions according to the duties and salaries of its members. Division I consisted of those in the administrative and professional grades, Division II the executive grades, Division III the clerical and technical grades, and Division IV, those performing manual tasks (Malayan Union and Singapore 1947, para. 44). The public bureaucracy in Singapore today still retains the fourfold division of work suggested many years ago by the Trusted Commission.

However, in Malaysia the Suffian Salaries Commission recommended in 1967 the replacement of Divisions I–IV with Categories A–D, with appropriate revisions of the salaries in each category. Category A, the managerial and professional group, includes those earning more than M$1,250 a month. Category B, the executive and subprofessional group, consists of those with monthly salaries between M$700 and M$1,250. Category C, the clerical and technical group, covers those with monthly salaries between M$250 and M$700. The industrial and manual workers come under Category D since they earn less than M$250 a month (Omar 1980, p. 257).

In Thailand, the traditional rank classification system was employed from 1928 to August 1975 as the basis for the compensation of civil servants. However, with the government's increased emphasis on national development programs and the resulting expansion of the public bureaucracy in the 1960s, the rank classification system "became a serious barrier to efficient management" (Boonprakob 1980, p. 548). In March 1964, E. J. Barbour, an American consultant, recommended, *inter alia,* the establishment of a system of position classification to replace the traditional rank classification system (Barbour 1964, p. 18). The Civil Service Improvement Committee, which was formed on November 20, 1964, recommended the adoption of a position classification system in the Thai public bureaucracy. The cabinet approved this recommendation and the United States Operations Mission of Thailand provided technical assistance from June 1965 to June 1971 for the development and installation of the position classification system. Implementation of the position classification plan began on

April 28, 1971; and full implementation throughout the public bureaucracy was finally completed on September 9, 1975. Today, the Thai public bureaucracy has a position classification system that divides the civil servants into eight occupational groups and 246 classes (Boonprakob 1980, p. 548–50).

In the Indonesian public bureaucracy, a combination of rank classification and position classification is used since civilian public servants are first ranked according to 17 levels, from the lowest rank (junior clerk) to the highest rank (senior administrator). The 17 levels are then divided into four groups, depending on the duties, responsibilities and educational qualifications. Levels 1–4 constitute Group I, which consists of the clerical workers; Group II (Levels 5–8) includes the supervisors; Group III (Levels 9–12) covers the superintendents; and the administrators come under Group IV (Levels 13–17) (Manurung 1980, p. 144–45).

Similarly, in the Philippines both rank classification and position classification are used in the public bureaucracy. However, it should be noted that before the restructuring of the public bureaucracy under the Integrated Reorganization Plan in 1972, only position classification was used. The Philippines public bureaucracy is divided into the career service and the noncareer service (for political appointments). The career service, which has three levels, has a mixed classification system because its first two levels are based on position classification, while the third level (i.e., the career executive service) employs rank classification (Fernandez 1980, p. 378–79).

Compensation

Compensation for civil service jobs in the five countries ranges from very low (Indonesia), to low (Philippines and Thailand), to adequate (Malaysia), and to high (Singapore). Low civil service salaries make it difficult for the central personnel agencies to compete in the labor market for competent and talented personnel. Low salaries also make the civil servants more vulnerable to corrupt activities and other forms of unethical behavior. On the other hand, the ability of each government to improve civil service salaries would depend on the country's level of economic development and the availability of funds for such an expensive undertaking.

Some scholars have argued that bureaucratic corruption becomes a serious problem in a society where civil servants are generally paid very low wages and where there is an unequal distribution of wealth (Braibanti 1962, p. 357–72). In other words, a civil servant might be forced by financial reasons to commit corrupt acts as he is not earning enough to support his family. The linkage between low salaries and bureaucratic corruption is best illustrated in Indonesia, where civil servants receive among the lowest salaries in the world. Each civil servant receives a basic salary and allowances for himself, his wife and children (Gray 1979). The basic salary of the most junior civil servant (a newly appointed junior clerk) is Rp. 12,000 (US$19.50) per month, while the most senior civil servant (a senior administrator with 24 years of experience) receives a monthly basic salary of Rp. 120,000 (US$195) (Manurung 1980, p. 162). (The 1980 exchange rate was used for all conversions.) The ratio of the monthly basic salary of the most senior civil servant to the most junior is 10:1. Thus, even though civil servants also receive a rice allowance and a functional allowance, it is difficult, if not impossible, for them to survive on their salaries and allowances because the latter amount to about one-third of the amount needed by them to sustain their families' standard of living (Smith 1971, p. 29). A survey of regional officials in Indonesia by Smith (1971, p. 30–31) has indicated that these officials consider low salaries to be the most important factor responsible for corruption in their country.

A second consequence of the low salaries of the Indonesian civil servants is that many, if not all of them, have a second job or take on additional work after the office hours of their first job. In fact, since the government has not been able to raise the salaries of civil servants in recent years, the working hours of civil servants have been adjusted to allow them to work elsewhere after their office hours. For example, for civil servants based in Jakarta, their working hours are: Monday to Thursday, 0800–1500; Friday, 0800–1130; and Saturday, 0800–1400. Thus, during each week Indonesian civil servants are required to spend 37.5 hours on their first job (Zainun 1982, p. 453). However, the need of these civil servants to hold more than one job means that their time and energies must be divided between their various jobs. This might lower their productivity and even commitment to their primary jobs, especially when their secondary jobs pay better. Thus, a great deal of moonlighting (holding a second job and putting in the contractual time on both) occurs. Indeed, according to Gray (1979, p. 92), "In Indonesia's public service many people hold two or more jobs, but those who put in the contractual time on each of one or more public sector appointments constitute a minority of dedicated souls."

Civil servants in the Philippines and Thailand also receive low salaries, but their salaries are much higher than those of their Indonesian counterparts. In the Philippines, P.D. No. 985 reduced the original 75 salary ranges and five salary steps formulated in 1957 to 28 salary grades with eight steps for each grade in 1976. The monthly salary of the most junior civil servant (Salary Grade 1, Step 1) is P286 (US$36) and the monthly salary of the most senior civil servant (Salary Grade 28, Step 8) is P5935 (US$747). The ratio of the monthly salary of the most senior civil servant to the most junior is 21:1. For those civil servants whose basic salary is low, substantial living allowances such as allowances for clothing, transport, children and representation expenses are given to help them cope with inflation. Moreover, overtime pay and partial coverage for hospitalization and medical fees are provided (Fernandez 1980, p. 389–94, 422).

In his study of the Thai public bureaucracy, Kasem Suwanagul highlighted the problem of low salaries of the civil servants during the postwar period and contended that such low salaries had contributed to an increase in bureaucratic corruption. In other words, civil servants' salaries could not keep pace with the rising cost of living after the war and were also lower than the salaries offered in the private sector (Suwanagul 1962, p. 79–80). Indeed, the situation has not improved very much since then as the salaries of Thai civil servants today are still inadequate despite some salary revisions, and frequently the only resort for many of them to make ends meet is to indulge in corrupt activities (Quah 1982b, p. 164). According to the Schedule of Civil Service Salaries (No. 3), 1980, the monthly salary of the most junior civil servant (Level 1, Step 1) is B1,255 (US$46) and the monthly salary of the most senior civil servant (Level 11, Step 9) is B17,745 (US$657). The ratio of these two salaries is 14:1. Since their salaries are inadequate to meet inflation, Thai civil servants are provided with other benefits and services. Employee benefits given include retirement benefits, cost-of-living allowances, health benefits, children's allowances, special allowances and leave with pay. The services provided to civil servants include housing facilities for provincial officials, medical services, educational assistance, and social and recreational programs (Boonprakob 1980, p. 555–57).

In contrast to the three countries discussed above, civil servants in Malaysia and Singapore enjoy much higher salaries. Following the salary revision recommended by the Cabinet Committee Report II in July 1980, the monthly basic salary in Malaysia for the most senior position is M$6350 (US$2886) and the corresponding salary for the most junior position is M$250 (US$114) (Public Services Department 1984, p. 36). The resulting ratio of both salaries is thus 25:1. Malaysian civil servants also receive such fringe benefits as eligibility for government housing, medical benefits and car loans (Omar 1980, p. 267).

Civil servants in Singapore have the highest salaries among the five countries under discussion. When the PAP government assumed power in June 1959, it was determined to eradicate corruption in general and in the public bureaucracy in particular. Apart from taking various anticorruption measures, the government also minimized the need to be corrupt among civil servants by constantly improving their salaries and working conditions. Another important reason, which surfaced subsequently, for improving the salaries and working conditions in the public bureaucracy was the need to stem the exodus of competent senior civil servants to the private sector by offering competitive salaries and fringe benefits to reduce the gap between the public and private sectors (Quah 1984c, p. 296). Accordingly, the salaries of civil servants were revised in 1972, 1973 and 1979. In 1981, a survey on the employment and earnings of 30,197 graduates found that graduates in the private sector earned, on the average, 42 percent more than those in the public sector. At the same time, figures provided by the Public Service Commission showed that many senior civil servants had left the public bureaucracy for more lucrative jobs in the private sector.

To deal with these twin problems of wide disparity in pay between graduates in the public and private sectors and the serious brain drain of senior civil servants from the public bureaucracy to the private sector, the government further revised the salaries of those in the Administrative Service and other Professional Services in April 1982. Consequently, the monthly consolidated salary for the most senior position (Staff Grade III) is S$21,700 (US$9,864). If all the allowances are included, the total salary would be S$25,112 (US$11,415) per month. At the other extreme of the scale, the most junior position (Bilal) carries a monthly salary of S$380 (US$173) (Republic of Singapore 1985, p. 509–11). The ratio of the highest salary to the lowest salary is 57:1. In addition to their monthly basic salary, civil servants in Singapore also receive a National Wages Council allowance and such fringe benefits as housing loans, car loans and microcomputer loans. Senior civil servants such as permanent secretaries are provided with a Mercedes Benz each for their use, and they are also appointed as directors of various government companies. In short, the extremely high salaries of civil servants in Singapore can be attributed to the government's desire not only to curb bureaucratic corruption, but also to minimize the brain drain of senior personnel from the public bureaucracy to the private sector.

Performance Evaluation

In comparing the systems of performance evaluation in the five ASEAN countries, we will not describe these systems in detail, but simply focus on the criteria employed in such evaluation and consider whether the methods used are modern or traditional.

In Indonesia, each civilian public servant is evaluated by his or her direct superior in terms of six criteria and a service test for appointment in certain ranks. The six criteria are: (1) work capability; (2) diligence; (3) work discipline; (4) cooperation; (5) initiative; and (6) leadership (Manurung 1980, p. 164). The report on the performance and personal qualities of a civil servant and the service test are traditional methods of performance evaluation, and are therefore more vulnerable to the various rating errors.

Similarly, traditional methods of performance evaluation are also used in the public bureaucracies in Malaysia, Thailand and Singapore. In Malaysia, Administrative and Diplomatic Service officers are evaluated for promotion on the basis of their performance during training and during the interviews by the promotion board as well as the assessment of his or her superior officer as reflected in the annual and special confidential reports. In Thailand, the consideration of annual salary increments and the promotion of civil servants are at the discretion of the appointing authority and are based on a man-oriented assessment. As in the case of promotion, both favoritism and merit are important criteria in assessing the performance of Thai civil servants (Boonprakob 1980, p. 559).

The Singapore Civil Service relies on traditional methods of performance appraisal for assessing its members. The Shell staff appraisal scheme, which has been incorporated in the Staff Performance Report (SPR), is confined to members of the Administrative Service. Part II of the SPR, which seeks to identify the personal qualities and performance of the officer being evaluated, is basically a graphic rating scale and it is therefore vulnerable to rating errors. Similarly, the bulk of the Staff Confidential Report (SCR) G259, which is used for the professional grades, is based on the traditional graphic rating scale. The remaining Division I and II officers are assessed by the SCR G205, while all Division III and IV civil servants are evaluated by the SCR G206. Both the SCR G205 and SCR G206 also use the graphic rating scale and are therefore not immune to rating errors (Quah 1984c, p. 308).

The Philippines is the only country among the five under study to adopt a modern method of performance evaluation. After nearly two years of study among five pilot agencies in 1976, a Performance Appraisal System (PAS) was developed to minimize subjectivity in performance evaluation. From January 1979, the PAS was used to assess the performance of Filipino civil servants. In the PAS, emphasis has been placed on output results rather than input or character traits. The weightage is now 75 percent for output factors (quantity, quality and timing of results) and 25 percent for input factors (public relations, punctuality, attendance and potential). The PAS is a modern method of performance evaluation because it is based on the concept of Management by Objectives (MBO). According to a member of the Civil Service Commission, the PAS has improved the quality of performance evaluation in the Philippines public bureaucracy in three ways: it promotes constant dialogue between supervisors and supervisees, thus providing feedback; it improves efficiency; and it also enhances employee motivation (Fernandez 1980, p. 396–97).

Table 12.2 summarizes the preceding discussion on five selected aspects of public personnel administration in the five ASEAN countries. The public bureaucracies in Indonesia, Malaysia, Singapore and Thailand should follow the example of the Philippines public bureaucracy in adopting the PAS, which is a modern method based on MBO. Thus, instead of relying on traditional methods, more modern methods like MBO, Behaviorally Anchored Rating Scales (BARS) and the Assessment Center Technique could be suitably modified for use by these civil services. Modern methods of performance evaluation are expensive to develop, but are much more accurate than traditional ones. On the other hand, traditional methods are easy to develop and administer, and are cheap, but are inaccurate because of the various rating errors. If the choice is between using a cheap but inaccurate method of performance appraisal and an expensive but accurate method, there is really no choice at all if the concern is to improve the quality of performance appraisal in the Indonesian, Malaysian, Singaporean and Thai public bureaucracies.

TABLE 12.2. Comparative Analysis of Some Aspects of Public Personnel Administration in the ASEAN Countries

	Indonesia	Malaysia	Philippines	Singapore	Thailand
Recruitment	Traditional	Traditional	Traditional	Traditional	Traditional
Selection	Combination[a]	Combination[a]	Examinations	Interview	Combination[a]
Classification	Mixed[b]	Rank	Mixed[b]	Rank	Position
Compensation	Very low	Adequate	Low	High	Low
Performance Evaluation	Traditional	Traditional	Modern	Traditional	Traditional

[a]This indicates that a combination of examinations and interviews is employed in selecting civil servants.

[b]This indicates that a mixed system, which combines both position classification and rank classification, is used.

Conclusion

In this chapter we began by describing the policy context in the five ASEAN countries in terms of their geography, economy, demography and politics. The purpose of this description was to illustrate the differences in the policy context in these countries. On the one hand, there is Indonesia, which is a large archipelago with a relatively low standard of living, heterogeneous population and quite stable political system. On the other hand, Singapore is a city-state of 2.6 million people, with the highest standard of living, a multiracial population and a high degree of political stability. Thus, comparing the two countries, it is obvious that the policy context in

Singapore appears to be more conducive than that in Indonesia for the effective performance of the various personnel functions.

Like public bureaucracies in other parts of the world, the ASEAN public bureaucracies have also expanded a great deal, albeit at different rates of growth. The Indonesian public bureaucracy has grown the fastest, followed in turn by the Thai public bureaucracy, the Malaysian public bureaucracy, the Singapore public bureaucracy and the Philippines public bureaucracy. Needless to say, such rapid expansion of these public bureaucracies has not only enlarged the scope of their activities, but also increased the burden of performing the various personnel functions. Other things being equal, the more rapid the expansion of a public bureaucracy, the greater would be the scope of its activities and its workload in personnel administration.

Our comparative analysis of public personnel administration in the five ASEAN countries indicates that the record of their public bureaucracies in attaining the goals of productivity and excellence is a mixed one. Needless to say, all the five public bureaucracies profess their commitment to these twin goals. For example, during the First ASEAN Conference on Reforms in the Civil Service held in Manila in July 1981, the three workshops dealt with career development, productivity in the civil service, and training for organizational effectiveness in the civil service. Similarly, each ASEAN country prepared a country paper on productivity improvement of its own civil service for the Second ASEAN Conference on Reforms in the Civil Service, held in Kuala Lumpur in August 1983.

At one extreme, it can be seen that Indonesia, the Philippines and Thailand appear to be facing more problems in meeting the goals of productivity and excellence. The Indonesian public bureaucracy has the heaviest burden since it is the largest public bureaucracy in the five countries. Furthermore, the salaries of civil servants are extremely low, thus giving rise not only to corruption, but also to moonlighting, inefficiency and lack of job commitment. Low salaries do not promote productivity or excellence. Traditional methods are employed in recruitment and performance evaluation. Even though the classification system is mixed, there is little or no job analysis in the Indonesian public bureaucracy.

The Thai public bureaucracy is similarly plagued with the problems of corruption, low salaries, traditional recruitment and traditional methods of performance evaluation. Moreover, the promotion of Thai civil servants is based on merit and favoritism. In the same way, the public bureaucracy in the Philippines suffers from low salaries, widespread corruption and reliance on traditional recruitment. To compensate for these weaknesses, the Philippines public bureaucracy encourages job analysis, and uses a modern method of performance evaluation. The bureaucracy functions basically the same even after the overthrow of Marcos.

At the other extreme, Malaysia and Singapore appear to be more likely to meet the goals of productivity and excellence. Apart from being smaller countries, both are not affected by low salaries or corruption. However, their public bureaucracies rely on traditional recruitment and traditional methods of performance evaluation. Moreover, there is little or no job analysis in the Malaysian and Singaporean public bureaucracies because they use the rank classification system.

In Malaysia, the merit principle has not been adhered to fully, especially in the case of recruitment and selection to the Administrative and Diplomatic Service (ADS), where a quota system of four Malays to one non-Malay has been practiced since 1952. According to the Malaysian Constitution, there should be no discrimination against citizens "on the ground only of religion, race, descent or place of birth . . . in the appointment to any office or employment under a public authority" except in the case of the reservation of positions in the ADS for the indigenous group, that is, the Malays or Bumiputras (Omar 1980, p. 256). Thus, the quota system not only gives rise to "protective discrimination" for the Bumiputras but also ensures that they will be recruited in adequate numbers into the ADS. However, the quota system used in the ADS has reduced the chances of non-Malays to enter the ADS and has created problems of morale among them.

Given the extremely high salaries in the public bureaucracy in Singapore, the Public Service Division should not rely solely on salary revisions to keep people from leaving the civil service as this might encourage the development of a mercenary attitude among the civil servants. Indeed, the Singapore Civil Service should not rely mainly on financial incentives to attract, motivate and retain talented people in the public bureaucracy. Nonfinancial rewards (such as giving letters of appreciation and providing recognition for work well done) can help to increase the civil servant's commitment to his job and organization.

In sum, the public bureaucracies in the five ASEAN countries should focus on realistic recruitment rather than traditional recruitment. With the exception of the Philippines, traditional methods of performance evaluation should be replaced by modern methods whenever possible. Indonesia, the Philippines and Thailand have public bureaucracies that have been adversely affected by low salaries and the widespread corruption and moonlighting that result. Finally, more job analysis should be introduced especially in Malaysia and Singapore, which have the rank classification system.

References

Barbour, E. J. "The Needs of the Thai Civil Service System." Bangkok: Public Administration Division, United States Operations Missions of Thailand, 1964.

Boonprakob, U. "The Civil Service System in Thailand." In *Asian Civil Services: Developments and Trends,* p. 539–68. Edited by A. Raksasataya and H. Siedentopf. Kuala Lumpur: Asian and Pacific Development Administration Centre, 1980.

Braibanti, R. "Reflections on Bureaucratic Corruption." *Public Administration* 40 (Winter 1962):357–72.

Caiden, G. E. *Public Administration,* 2d ed. Pacific Palisades: Palisades Publishers, 1982.

Chandarasorn, V. "Patterns of Organizational Expansion in the Thai Public Bureaucracy: A Study of Agencies' Functional Responsibilities, 1969–1982." Ph.D. dissertation, New York University, 1985.

Corpuz, O. D. *The Bureaucracy in the Philippines.* Manila: Institute of Public Administration, University of the Philippines, 1957.

Darling, F. C. *The Westernization of Asia: A Comparative Political Analysis.* Boston and Cambridge: G. K. Hall & Co. and Schenkman Publishing Company, 1979.

Emmerson, D. K. "The Bureaucracy in Political Context: Weakness in Strength." In *Political Power and Communications in Indonesia,* p. 82–136. Edited by K. D. Jackson and L. W. Pye. Berkeley: University of California Press, 1978.

Endriga, J. N. "The Bureaucracy in an Authoritarian Political System: The Case of the Philippines." Paper presented at the 13th World Congress of the International Political Science Association, Paris, July 1985.

Esman, M. J. *Administration and Development in Malaysia: Institution Building and Reform in a Plural Society.* Ithaca: Cornell University Press, 1972.

Far Eastern Economic Review (FEER). *Asia 1986 Yearbook.* Hong Kong: FEER, 1986.

Fernandez, F. U., Jr. "The Civil Service System in the Philippines." In *Asian Civil Services: Developments and Trends,* p. 363–430. Edited by A. Raksasataya and H. Siedentopf. Kuala Lumpur: Asian and Pacific Development Administration Centre, 1980.

Gray, C. "Civil Service Compensation in Indonesia." *Bulletin of Indonesian Economic Studies* 15 (Mar. 1979):85–113.

Hadisumarto, D. "The Indonesian Civil Service and Its Reform Movements." D.P.A. dissertation, University of Southern California, 1974.

Information Malaysia 1984 Year Book. Kuala Lumpur: Berita Publishing Sdn. Bhd, 1984.

Lee, B. H. "The Singapore Civil Service and Its Perceptions of Time." Ph.D. dissertation, University of Hawaii, 1976.

Malayan Union and Singapore. *Report of the Public Services Salaries Commission of Malaya.* Kuala Lumpur: Malayan Union Government Press, 1947.

Manurung, C. "The Public Personnel System in Indonesia." In *Asian Civil Services:*

Developments and Trends, p. 135–77. Edited by A. Raksasataya and H. Siedentopf. Kuala Lumpur: Asian and Pacific Development Administration Centre, 1980.

Mauzy, D. K. "Introduction." In *Politics in the ASEAN States,* p. 1–12. Edited by D. K. Mauzy. Kuala Lumpur: Marican & Sons (Malaysia) Sdn. Bhd., 1985.

Ministry of Finance, Malaysia. *Economic Report 1984–85.* Kuala Lumpur: National Printing Department, 1984.

Nakata, T. "The Thai Political System in the 1980's: Significant Issues, Problems and Prospects." In S. Xuto et al., *Thailand in the 1980's: Significant Issues, Problems and Prospects,* p. 55–81. Bangkok: The Thai University Research Association, 1981.

Office of the Prime Minister, Thailand. *Thailand in the '80s,* rev. ed. Bangkok: National Identity Office, 1984.

Omar, E. B. "The Civil Service Systems in Malaysia." In *Asian Civil Services: Developments and Trends,* p. 253–99. Edited by A. Raksasataya and H. Siedentopf. Kuala Lumpur: Asian and Pacific Development Administration Centre, 1980.

Peabody, R. L. and Rourke, F. E. "Public Bureaucracies." In *Handbook of Organizations.* Edited by J. G. March. Chicago: Rand McNally, 1965.

Pluvier, J. *South-East Asia from Colonialism to Independence.* Kuala Lumpur: Oxford University Press, 1974.

Public Services Department: Organization and Functions. Kuala Lumpur: Information and Documentation Unit, PSD, 1984.

Quah, Jon S. T. "The Origins of the Public Bureaucracies in the ASEAN Countries." *Indian Journal of Public Administration* 24 (Apr.–June 1978):400–429.

_____. "The Public Bureaucracy and National Development in Singapore." In *Administrative Systems Abroad,* p. 42–75. Edited by K. K. Tummala. Washington, D.C.: University Press of America, 1982a.

_____. "Bureaucratic Corruption in the ASEAN Countries: A Comparative Analysis of Their Anti-Corruption Strategies." *Journal of Southeast Asian Studies* 13 (Mar. 1982b):153–77.

_____. "Public Administration in a City-State: The Singapore Case." In *Comparative Study on the Local Public Administration in Asian and Pacific Countries,* p. 206–16. Edited by K. Hanaoka. Tokyo: EROPA Local Government Center, 1984a.

_____. "The Public Policy-making Process in Singapore." *Asian Journal of Public Administration* 6 (Dec. 1984b):108–26.

_____. "The Public Bureaucracy in Singapore, 1959–1984." In *Singapore: Twenty-five Years of Development,* p. 288–314. Edited by P. S. You and C. Y. Lim. Singapore: Nan Yang Xing Zhou Lianhe Zaobao, 1984c.

_____. "Bureaucracy and Administrative Reform in the ASEAN Countries: A Comparative Analysis." *Indian Journal of Public Administration* 31 (July–Sept. 1985):987–1015.

_____. "Towards Productivity and Excellence: A Comparative Study of the Public Personnel Systems in the ASEAN Countries." *Asian Journal of Public Administration* 8 (June 1986):64–99.

Republic of Singapore. *Economic Survey of Singapore, 1984*. Singapore: Ministry of Trade and Industry, 1985.

Republik Indonesia. *Pidato Pertanggungjawaban*. Jakarta: Majelis Permusyawaratan Rakyat, 1983.

Riggs, Fred W. *Thailand: The Modernization of a Bureaucratic Polity*. Honolulu: East-West Center Press, 1966.

Siffin, W. J. *The Thai Bureaucracy: Institutional Change and Development*. Honolulu: East-West Center Press, 1966.

Singhawisai, W. "Recruitment and Selection in the Thai Civil Service." In *Asian Civil Services Technical Papers*, vol. 2, p. 68–137. Edited by A. Raksasataya and H. Siedentopf. Kuala Lumpur: Asian and Pacific Development Administration Centre, 1980.

Smith, T. M. "Corruption, Tradition and Change." *Indonesia* 11 (Apr. 1971):21–40.

Steinberg, D. J. *The Philippines: A Singular and a Plural Place*. Boulder, Colo.: Westview Press, 1982.

Steinberg, D. J. et al. *In Search of Southeast Asia: A Modern History*. Kuala Lumpur: Oxford University Press, 1971.

Suryadinata, L. "Indonesia." In *Politics in the ASEAN States*, p. 109–37. Edited by D. K. Mauzy. Kuala Lumpur: Marican & Sons (Malaysia) Sdn. Bhd., 1985.

Suwanagul, K. "The Civil Service of Thailand." Ph.D. dissertation, New York University, 1962.

Tilman, R. O. *Bureaucratic Transition in Malaya*. Durham, N.C.: Duke University Press, 1964.

United Nations. *Economic Co-operation among Member Countries of the Association of Southeast Asian Nations: Report of a United Nations Team*. New York: Department of Economic and Social Affairs, United Nations, 1974.

Waddell, J. R. E. *An Introduction to Southeast Asian Politics*. Sydney: John Wiley & Sons Australasia Pty. Ltd, 1972.

Wanous, J. P. *Organizational Entry*. Reading, Mass.: Addison-Wesley Publishing Co., 1980.

Zainun, B. "Effective and Efficient Utilisation of Civil Service Working Time: Indonesian Case." *Indian Journal of Public Administration* 28 (July–Sept. 1982):452–57.

13

Policy Developments and Administrative Changes in the United Kingdom

ANDREW DUNSIRE

THE THEORETICAL BASIS of this chapter is that policy developments and administrative changes in the United Kingdom in the last century have taken place against the background of four major social trends, which have provided conflicting paradigms or ways of seeing public administration in their era. The first of these social trends was the explosion of manufacturing technology in the mid-nineteenth century, which both attracted population to the cities and enabled authorities (eventually) to cope with it — at the cost of greatly increased complexity and the virtual abandonment of the unskilled lay performance or "do-it-ourselves" ethos that had underpinned local self-government in the eighteenth century, and persisted much longer in central government. The outcome was the merit appointment of trained and expert officials supervised by elected representatives, under what Schaffer (1973, p. 252) called the "public service bargain." Top civil servants offered loyalty, proficient performance, anonymity, and sacrifice of some political rights, in return for permanency, adequate remuneration and pension, and honorable social status. This can be matched quite closely with Weber's bureaucratic ideal-type, once that came to be known in the 1940s; and could even accommodate the injection of "Rationalization" (the European term for Scientific Management) in the 1920s, as the tool of expertise and proficiency in administrative tasks.

I am greatly indebted to Christopher Hood for many of the ideas in this paper, and for comments upon an earlier version.

261

This, then was the dominant paradigm in British public administration for the first half of the twentieth century, persisting even now. Its values include neutrality, anonymity, objectivity, long-term views, and emphasis on feasibility rather than mere desirability; but above all, administration as paternalist vis-à-vis the people, and towards the political arm, ancillary and subordinate but professionally so — somewhat as enshrined in Wildavsky's (1979) aphorism about policy analysis: "speaking Truth to Power." This paradigm can thus be named the *public service paradigm,* and it dominated traditional public administration as an academic discipline.

The second social trend began very soon after the beginning of the century, with the first moves towards the welfare state. An enormous increase in the interface between civil servants and citizens took place with its full flowering after World War II; bureaucratic encounters became the normal image of public administration for most members of the public. One outcome was a change in the values it was increasingly felt should govern the behavior of civil servants — felt not only by citizens and their representatives but also by many civil servants themselves, especially the growing numbers of professional civil servants. These were the un-Weberian values of "humaneness," "compassion," "client-centered orientation," "treating people as people, not cases," and so on (Blau 1955). In recent decades these values were the basis of the New Public Administration movement in the U.S. (Marini 1971), though these enthusiasts would have gone farther and have public servants act always so as to reduce social disparities in the society — denounced by Thompson (1975) as "theft of the public domain." This set of values can perhaps be called the *community service paradigm,* and it dominates the academic disciplines of social administration and social policy, as well as the implementation theory approach to public administration (in its "bottom-up" version).

The third social trend to be noted is the universal spread of general education coupled with the increase in the speed of communications, leading (particularly after World War II again) to greatly increased political awareness and activism, and the view that participation in and influence over public decision making was something to which people were entitled, directly and not merely via their elected representatives. Elective organs indeed were seen to be inadequate channels of communication with officials, and to the bureaucratic encounter interface there was increasingly added the lobby or interest-group activity, where the views and demands of citizens and their (nonelected) representatives, and of business and other groups, could be put directly to officials. Values of representative bureaucracy, adversarial bureaucracy, responsiveness, and a duty to consult affected parties before regulative or other administrative action, began to permeate public administration; and notions of open government, freedom of information, and access to files upon oneself became the currency of criticism from the civil liberties standpoint. This set of values can be named the *public participation paradigm,* and it dominated the systems and public policy-making approaches to public administration.

A fourth social trend modifying the nineteenth century administrative culture gave rise to the *new political economy paradigm.* There were perhaps three elements to this trend. First, the finiteness of material resources (including natural resources) was increasingly recognized, especially after the oil price rise of the early 1970s. Second, the enormous sunk costs and increasing commitment of budgets on social welfare provision began to be highlighted. Third (partly arising out of the second), larger and larger numbers of citizens were paying income and other taxes at relatively high levels, including increasing numbers of married women, so that tax liability of families became much more noticeable (Hood 1986). Such trends created a potential constituency for a political party willing to espouse a "roll back the State" platform, and when in office to initiate a quite conscious and articulated attempt to change the values of British civil servants away from their traditional ones, and towards more businesslike attitudes: an attack on waste, value-for-money audit, shifting costs on to the user, and so on. While the public service paradigm had embraced *input efficiency* as one of its values, it had sat rather uneasily with the values of *output efficiency.* The *new political economy paradigm* can be seen in emphases on contracting-out, privatization, and public choice theory generally, and it dominates the "inside bureaucracy" and economics approaches to public administration.

These, then, are the underpinnings of the paper. However, not all of this ground can be covered adequately in one paper, and I shall be selecting only some aspects of each paradigm to discuss, under these four headings: administrative rationality; administrative civility; administrative responsiveness; and administrative economy. A concluding section will deal with administrative legitimacy.

Administrative Rationality

The continuing debate about improvement of administrative organizational structure can be said to be a perennial demonstration of the triumph of hope over experience. The expert world is divided between those who hold, and those who deny, that administrative organization is a rational matter, subject to principles susceptible of test and proof by the hypothetico-deductive method like any other aspect of human ordering. Maybe it is a matter of emphasis: the rationalists speaking normatively (people ought to look at administrative organization as a matter of discoverable principle, and hence of correctibility); the skeptics speaking empirically (organization is always the instrument of the powerful, and their objectives always overwhelm any principles there may be). Schaffer (1973, p. 57ff), however, questioned the very possibility of universal principles in a field like this. Pollitt, in the most recent full-scale analysis of British central government organization (1984) shows that the majority of top-level changes in structure in the last few decades in Britain have owed less to rationality than to party faction and the distribution of power in Cabinet. From a different angle, my colleagues and I, in a quantitative analysis of all British central departments, failed to find any significant backing for the predictions of the contingency theory school of organizational analysis about the relationships between structure, task, technology, and environment (Hood and Dunsire 1981).

Pace Pollitt, it would be a mistake to think that administrative change in Britain over the past century or so has been entirely a matter of party and personal advantage, or short-term manipulation. Doctrine has played an important part. Doctrine stands halfway between scientific theory and mere pragmatism. It motivates by its apparent logic, but it does not encourage or welcome test and proof. As many commentators have pointed out, reform has often been its own justification, the rewards taken by the reformers upfront, as insurance people say, whatever the results or outcomes (Caiden 1970; March and Olsen 1983). It is not then in their interests to find out whether the changes made have in fact produced the results promised.

Administrative reorganization in nineteenth-century England, as in other European countries, was dominated by two great debates: that about centralization versus local self-government (or bureaucracy versus rule by elected representatives); and that about the single-headed structure versus the collegiate form, or boards (Dunsire 1973a, ch. 4). (The early part of the century was characterized by a proliferation of ad hoc statutory authorities, formed piecemeal to cope with urbanization.) These dilemmas of doctrine were (totally subconsciously) resolved by English compromise: at national level, the multiplicity of ad hoc boards would go, and there would be centralization, but under a single-head structure to maximize accountability (the ministerial department); whereas at local level, there would be local self-government, under a collegiate structure (the elected council and its committees) to maximize representativeness; and nothing in between.

The doctrine of the ministerial department held sway from the 1850s for the rest of the century. No more nonministerial bodies were created (Schaffer 1973, p. 4). The parallel doctrine of ministerial responsibility was the British solution to bureaucracy, and along with the doctrine of collective responsibility of the cabinet, formed what Mackintosh (1977) called the Westminster Model of parliamentary democracy. The apotheosis of the doctrine of the ministerial department as the single acceptable form of administrative organization at national level was found in the report of the (Haldane) Machinery of Government Committee (1918). Most people expected that, just as the Great War of 1914–18 had been fought administratively by a proliferation of ministries, so after the war the railways and the electricity industry, coal mining and the ports, would (like the Post Office) be run by ministries. There were anomalies, such as the Road Board and the National Health Insurance machinery; but it was held that these, and some older bodies like the Stationery Office and the Charities Commission, should eventually be assimilated to the ministerial pattern. The doctrine was still being enunciated confidently in 1928 and 1939 with respect to Scottish administration (Milne 1957, p. 18). But rival doctrines were by then in the field.

One such doctrine took as model a type of public sector organization that had emerged in the capital city to transcend the territorial limitations of the local authorities (the Metropolitan Water Board, the Port of London Authority, the London Passenger Transport Board [LPTB]), and generalized it (the Central Electricity Generating Board, British Overseas Airways Corporation). This form became known as the public corporation, and through the influence of Herbert Morrison (father of the LPTB) was the vehicle for nationalization of major industries by the Labour government after World War II. Trading enterprises, it was held, could not successfully be run by ministerial departments, because of the limitations of the traditional civil service style of working and the responsible minister's political answerability for every detail. Thus trading enterprises in the public sector had to be "at arm's length" from the political arena.

There were some public tasks that should be kept at arm's length for another kind of reason: as the economist J. M. Keynes put it in a lecture originally given in 1924, they should be: "semi-autonomous bodies within the state—bodies whose criterion of action within their own field is solely the public good as they understand it" (Keynes 1926, p. 41; quoted in Shonfield 1965, p. 233). The most celebrated such body is probably the British Broadcasting Corporation (created 1926), which has had a continuous struggle to preserve its semiautonomy. Governments, conversely, have set up such bodies to relieve themselves of the responsibility of decisions that might have unwelcome political repercussions: the Royal Fine Art Commissions, the Arts Council, the Horse race-betting Levy Board, and many others.

The Second World War, like the First, was run administratively mainly by ministries, including a number of new ones (supply, aircraft production, food, information, etc.), some with trading functions—arm's length being a dispensable luxury in war mobilization. Restructuring after the war saw no dominant doctrine emerge, as Haldane had done. As well as the public ownership doctrines (which are not administrative), Labour's nationalization measures contained an implicit centralization doctrine: operational control over the whole territory of the kingdom (the very opposite of the rival Labour doctrine of workers' control, defeated in intraparty struggles in the 1920s) implied a search for, not exactly economies of scale, but perhaps potencies of scale. The National Health Service (NHS) was organizationally *sui generis:* in form an executive agency of a ministry, not different from the Prisons Department of the Home Office, or the Royal Ordnance Factories, but immensely larger in scale, with well over a million employees. The bulk of these were in the hospitals, grouped territorially under ministerially appointed regional hospital boards; the general practitioner and the dental and ophthalmic services, though also under the minister, were assimilated organizationally to the local government pattern, as were the environmental health services and the personal social services — not on doctrinal grounds, but on mere pragmatism. The other nationalizations, conforming to the public corporation rule-configuration (or charter), were tidier, though the arm's length bit proved problematic: ministers could not keep their fingers out of the pie.

Many other doctrineless governmental and quasi-governmental forms of organization emerged in the postwar decades, and quite suddenly became a political and academic issue in the 1970s. The acronyms "quago" and "quango" (short for quasi-governmental and quasi-nongovernmental organization) were adapted from UN usage (NGO = nongovernmental organization, e.g. International Red Cross), but were soon rendered useless for technical description by the mistake of a journalist, who decided that "quango" meant "Quasi-Autonomous National Government Organization" and applied the term indiscriminately to almost any body that was not a ministry. "Quango-hunting" became a political blood sport, on the suspicion that such bodies were a source of too much ministerial patronage and financial irresponsibility (Holland and Fallon 1978), and their numbers did decline to a small extent, briefly; but in their rich variety such bodies (advisory councils, producer associations, minor regulatory bodies like the Plant Variety Rights Tribunal, major distributory agencies like the Arts Council, state-funded but entirely nonpublic bodies like the Family Fund for handicapped children, and so on) are far too valuable to government to be done without, and they are still being created. They became an academic issue because the field resisted classification. No one has worked harder at the task of finding patterns in the chaos of ministerial departments, nonministerial departments, nondepartmental public bodies, quagos and quangos, and whatever other beasts may be discovered in this wild, than Christopher Hood (1973; 1975a; 1975b; 1978; 1981; 1982; etc.). But his general conclusions can be stated thus: there is no theory (or doctrine) you can put forward to explain why agencies of a certain type are used in a given situation, without it being possible to find instances of agencies of that type being used in different situations, and instances of agencies of different types being used in that given situation. Not even a theory of random selection, or of generational or other fashion, or purely political or expedient explanations, will account for a significant amount of the variance.

The decade 1965–75 saw the high-water mark of administrative rationalism in postwar Britain. The (Fulton) Committee on the Civil Service (1968) crystallized a sentiment that managerial skills were undervalued and existing structures not adapted to the facilitation of good management in the civil service. Almost in reversal of the nineteenth-century doctrine (as if the less ministerialization the better) the Report suggested that wherever a block of executive work could be identified, it should be "hived off" from the mainstream of policy-oriented tasks and given to a nonministerial agency, or at least made the responsibility of an accountable management unit within the ministry. In this spirit the entire Post Office, hitherto a ministerial department, was turned into a public corporation in 1969; the regulation of air traffic was removed from a ministry to a separate Civil Aviation Authority in 1971, and the major airports likewise to a British Airports Authority. The Procurement Executive within the Ministry of Defense (1971) and the Property Services Agency within the Department of the Environment (1972), both enormous spenders and property owners, are expressions of the "hiving-off" doctrine. Her Majesty's Stationery Office and the Royal Ordnance Factories, manufacturing and retailing organizations, were put on a trading fund basis: that is, they operate under a profit-and-loss account, and are intended not to call on the national budget for their funding. Many other such administrative changes, avowedly doctrine-based, could be listed from this period.

The clearest statement of the ruling doctrines came in the White Paper *The Reorganisation of Central Government* in 1970 (Cmnd 4506). Space cannot be taken here for a full analysis of this document (see Johnson 1971; Clarke 1971; Dunsire 1973b). But the spirit that animates it is clearly that of rational planning, clearly defined objectives, overall strategies, comprehensive approach, longer-term aims, and the other terminology of scientific managerialism. In particular, the White Paper commits itself to reorganizing central government department responsibilities around "coherent fields of policy and administration," on "the Functional Principle," and to a policy of "unification." What this meant in practice was fewer and larger ministries; continuing a trend begun under the previous government, which had unified the Ministry of Defense and the Department of Health and Social Security, there now appeared the Department of the Environment

(DOE) and the Department of Trade and Industry, each merging two or three former separate ministries. It was not size as such that was seen to bring advantages; indeed, gigantism was recognized as a management and control problem. But unification would reduce the number of policy fields the cabinet would have to survey, and thus ease the tasks of overview and long-term strategy.

Even more massive restructurings were in preparation. April 1, 1974, was "vesting day" for the most wholesale administrative reorganization of government services seen in any country at any time — to my knowledge at least. The entire system of local authorities was changed from top to bottom. The National Health Service was completely changed. And so was the whole water industry — supply, sewerage and waste disposal, and drainage and flood protection. We cannot go into detail, but a word on the doctrines involved may be apposite.

The nineteenth-century settlement of multipurpose local authorities collegiately controlled endured into the second half of the twentieth century remarkably without basic change, though modified in four ways. Some services were taken away, and others developed (gas, electricity, and hospitals to nonlocal authorities; social welfare services and land-use planning acquired). Second: since the drawing of the map of counties, cities, boroughs, urban and rural districts, and parishes, in the last decades of the nineteenth century, massive growth and shifts in population had taken place, transport revolutionized, and so on. By 1930 there was general agreement that (in the words of a later official paper) there were: "too many authorities and many of them too small in area and resources to support the operation of services to the standard which people nowadays have the right to expect" (Cmnd 4584 1971, para. 4). There were now doctrines of *size,* of *standards,* of *expectations.* But despite several Royal Commission and other reports, no reform took place until 1974, when the number of top-tier authorities in England and Wales outside London was reduced from 141 to 53, and second-tier authorities from 1,250 to 369, with similar reductions in Scotland.

Third: collegiality has been retained, in that the council is still itself the executive body in local government, acting through committees of its membership — it is not a legislature only. But the 1974 doctrines of size and standards were accompanied by doctrines about *management;* in remarkable unanimity considering that there was no statutory requirement for it, almost all of the new top-tier authorities and many of the second-tier authorities adopted the recommendations of a report commissioned by the associations of local authorities (The Bains Report 1972) for a single-headed officer structure, under a chief executive, to replace the previous system where independent specialist chief officers reported to their own committees, only loosely coordinated by a *primus inter pares* town clerk or county clerk who was also legal officer. Along with this change went doctrines of corporate planning and corporate management, impressing on councils the need to consider their budgets and their policies holistically, and not (as before) service by service (Greenwood et al. 1980). The extent to which councils have persisted with these reforms varies greatly. Many chief executive posts have since been abolished.

Fourth: although in the White Paper that preceded the changes there was a commitment to "return power to those people who should exercise decisions locally" (Cmnd 4584 1971, para. 3), there would be virtually complete agreement among observers that the period since 1974, and especially since 1979, has seen central government controls over local spending and tax-levying grow tighter and more draconian than ever before, with central government intent on preventing local authorities from increasing the Public Sector Borrowing Requirement, or overcoming reductions in central grants by raising the level of their taxes on property (which the Conservative party has committed itself to abolish in any case). In this and some other ways the party traditionally associated with anticentralism, in favor of local self-government, finds itself the most centralist government this century. (In a voluminous literature, see e.g., Dearlove 1979; Rhodes 1981; Dunleavy and Rhodes 1984.)

Doctrines embodied in the 1974 reorganization of the National Health Service were a little confused and not always free from internal contradiction (Dunsire 1973b; Klein 1983), but the main thrust was again unification accompanied by a sound management structure at all levels. All health services (hospitals, GPs, dentists, etc., and local authority environmental and personal health services) were brought under the same roof: that of the Area Health Authority, whose boundaries in most cases ran with those of the corresponding top-tier local authority. Great stress was laid on the planning process, an annual cycle updating a rolling ten-year plan, district plans nesting in area plans nesting in regional plans nesting in the national plan, all done by "critical appraisal and agreement at each level" (Cmnd 5055 1972, App III, para. 8). And collegiality at the lower levels (beginning with the district management team comprising the chief consultant, the chief nurse, the chief accountant, the chief administrator, the chief GP, and so on) was to be reconciled with the overall accountability to Parliament of the Secretary of State for everything except clinical judgments. The success of this particular reform can perhaps be judged by the facts that in 1982 the 93 Area Health Authorities were abolished, simply swept away without replacement; and collegiality was replaced by the appointment to each remaining health authority in 1985 of a professional general manager—not always from within the National Health Service.

Restructuring in the water industry (a phrase not used until this era) was equally massive. Laymen soon learnt about the hydrological cycle, the essential unity of all water-borne services, and the overriding need for a national plan for water, backed up by a national water grid to maximize the utilization of this surprisingly scarce resource, given Britain's annual rainfall (Funnell and Hay 1974). Water supply, including collection and storage, had been the responsibility of the local councils of individual cities, boroughs, and districts, as was sewerage and sewage treatment. Drainage and flood protection had been carried out by separate river boards and conservancies, levying their own rates on landowners. These bodies were abolished and all these tasks given to each of only ten Regional Water Authorities, covering England and Wales, with a membership heavily dominated by professional water engineers. It is now the most technocratic of all government services.

The period of Conservative government under Mr. Edward Heath and his Head of the Civil Service Sir William (later Lord) Armstrong was thus a markedly rationalist one, evincing strong belief in the structure/performance hypothesis, and in particular, in unification and managerialism. The period of Labour government that followed saw no great changes in administrative structure; and the Conservative government that came into office in 1979 under Mrs. Margaret Thatcher has shown itself anything but rationalist in this sense. Salvation is not to be found, for Mrs. Thatcher, in "getting the structure right." When she tackles structure, it is by way of abolition: an entire tier of the National Health Service, an entire tier of local government (the Metropolitan County Councils in the conurbations of e.g. Merseyside, Tyneside, the West Midlands and West Yorkshire, and the Greater London Council, ceased to exist at the end of March 1986); an entire grade of the civil service (the under-secretary rank), if her advisers had not managed to persuade her of the impracticality of the proposal (Fry 1985, p. 40). She also abolished the Central Policy Review Staff (the cabinet think tank), and the Civil Service Department; as well as some quangos. There is, of course, a rationality in what she does; but it is not an administrative rationality in the sense we are using it here, or in that which explains Mr. Heath's reforms. We shall go into Mrs. Thatcher's doctrinal bases in a later section.

Administrative rationalization at meso- and micro-level, however, does go on. For instance, the regional structure of the Department of Health and Social Security was reduced from twelve regional offices to seven, as part of a Rayner scrutiny (see below) of the flow of business or traffic between local, regional, and headquarters offices. A very careful and interesting analysis of the exercise by the civil servant who carried it out (Warner 1984b) lists nine effects or outcomes of the change—a welcome disproof of the charge that reforms of structure are never followed up to see whether they are delivering. But it is noticeable, nevertheless, that the outcomes listed are all effects upon costs, and upon the organization itself or other departments watching it; none are concerned with better service to the client.

Administrative Civility

The acceptability of public administration once it had become centralized and bureaucratized was a question the Victorians did not ask; the public service ideal (a form of *fonctionnesse oblige*) was their substitute. Once contacts between civil servants and ordinary citizens multiplied with the growth of government and its expansion into so many more fields of activity, the question of acceptability (not at all the same thing as accountability) became pressing. We can conceptualize this at three levels: (1) at micro-level, or individual case level, the so-called citizen/state interface, where acceptability requires *civility,* a degree of mutual comprehension and decent interpersonal behavior; (2) at meso-level, the level of policy and program, where the client is more often a group than an individual, and the quality looked for is *responsiveness;* and (3) at macro-level, the level of institutions and regime, where the client is society at large, and acceptability is in terms of *legitimacy.* We shall look at civility in this section, responsiveness in the next section, and legitimacy in the concluding section.

To recapitulate: the only acceptability known to the constitution under the nineteenth century settlement was parliamentary acceptability; ministers answer to one House or the other for their conduct of administration, and front-line or street-level public servants are not accountable to their clients, only to their superiors and hence to their minister. The public service bargain (and it is a myth, not historical fact) was, however, struck when there was no interface to speak of: virtually the only civil servants the nineteenth century ordinary citizen would meet were postmen and excisemen. It was somewhat different at local government level (teachers, policemen, roadmen, etc.), but there the elective councillors themselves were more easily available immediately behind the interface, as it were.

It was the welfare state, the two World Wars and the environmental planning movement that enormously widened the interface: the local "High Street" offices of central ministries became as familiar a part of everyone's experience as the Town Hall offices. The networks of regional and local offices, whose staffs often collectively outnumbered headquarters staffs, were perhaps a necessity of efficacy more than of acceptability; but they could be seen as bringing case-decisions close to the individual citizens concerned, enabling actual discussion of a problem face-to-face (indeed, "putting a face on" the otherwise "faceless bureaucrat") and obliterating remoteness. In terms of acceptability, however, this was far from being pure gain, as we shall see in a moment.

The rationalizing spirit of the 1960s manifested itself in this area in two ways. First, Whitehall (it was said) discovered the regions. (It is a standing witticism about senior civil servants that few of them have ever been north of Watford, a town on the fringe of London.) There had, of course, been regional policies for industrial location and so on long before this; but each ministry had its own ideas, and the region, as such, had no collective cross-ministry voice. The 1950s saw attempts to get all the ministries to adopt the same regionalization pattern, based on the wartime civil defense regions (themselves said to be based on a contingency plan for ensuring communications if the General Strike of 1926 had been successful); but these Treasury Regions were slow to take on. The political importance of regional identity was first recognized in respect of the North East (Tyneside) by Harold Macmillan; but under Harold Wilson and George Brown in the first Labour government for 13 years, a fully-fledged National Plan in which coherent regional bodies would play a large part was developed.

The country was divided up into Economic Planning Regions each with a Regional Economic Planning Council comprising local manufacturers, councillors, and other dignitaries, charged with making and implementing a regional plan, with the aid of a Regional Economic Planning Board comprising representatives of all the ministries with an interest, under a chairman from the new Department of Economic Affairs (DEA), of surprisingly high rank (under-secretary) for a nonheadquarters office. Each region did produce its plan; some boards were more effective than others; but the Treasury's heart was not in the DEA's National Plan, and the economic situation was also unfavorable. The Department of Economic Affairs was wound up in 1969. The regional councils and boards hung on, without doing much good work, until finally killed off by Mrs. Thatcher in 1980.

The other rationalizing move in the 1960s, mainly in the interest of economy but also showing an acceptability aspect, was the effort to bring the local offices of different ministries in a town together, in a single building where feasible, and in some places, into experimental joint offices where civil servants of one ministry would carry out interviewing and application-processing for another. This experiment was not entirely successful but the idea was good. By these means the government saved money in rents, heating costs and the like, and some citizens were saved time and temper when (as often happens) more than one office had to be visited, or when it was not clear which ministry was the appropriate one.

The lengthening of the interface had counteracceptability effects also. The million-fold increase in number and frequency of bureaucratic encounters multiplied also the occasions for error and misunderstanding and dispute. Yet initially the formal machinery for registering and dealing with complaints remained linked to the nineteenth century formulae. Lacking any real administrative law tradition (a situation profoundly exacerbated by A. V. Dicey's (1885) misreading of what administrative law implied in Europe), Britain stumbled about for most of the twentieth century, creating ad hoc and piecemeal remedies, some structural, some procedural: nonjudicial tribunals, public hearings, citizens' advice bureaus, ombudsmen, immigrant advisory services, and so on — a patchwork designated as *bureaucratic justice* (Mashaw 1983), but regarded as in principle complementary to the time-honored doctrines of redress of grievance as the prerogative of members of parliament, and to the remedies available at common law for those who had the time and resources to seek them.

Official doctrine was eventually changed, following the Report of the (Franks) Committee on Administrative Tribunals and Inquiries (Cmnd 218 1957), and one part of this twilight world, that containing the jumble of adjudicating bodies set up separately to deal with individual disputes in literally hundreds of distinct fields of regulation, alphabetically from agriculture to wireless telegraphy, was recognized as part of the judicial system, rationalized, and brought under a degree of centralized control, by the setting up of a Council on Tribunals (see e.g., Griffith and Street 1973; Wade 1982).

The absence of any such system of tribunals would certainly render the modern citizen/state interface unacceptable; but whether it is the best that might be devised to maximize acceptability is doubtful. For the unaided citizen, its complexities are impenetrable; insofar as the tribunals are known about at all, they are regarded as simply another manifestation of the authorities. The structure of ombudsmen (Parliamentary Commissioner for Administration, 1967; Northern Ireland Parliamentary Commissioner, and Commissioner for Complaints [Northern Ireland], 1969; the Health Service Commissioners, 1973; the Commissioners for Local Administration, 1974 and [Scotland] 1976) has had a slightly better reception; but it is still somewhat remote, and suffers from a lack of teeth, in particular when confronting recalcitrant local councils (Stacey 1978).

At the micro-level, a considerable amount of effort has been put into nonstructural means of increasing mutual comprehension between citizen and bureaucrat; for example, by the improvement of official forms and documentation of all kinds. Examples of "officialese" and unfathomable bureaucratic prose still abound; but the problem is well recognized, and for important changes, or for propaganda campaigns, the skills of advertising copywriters and designers are employed. It remains the case, however, that information (even of benefits available) can fail to get through to a percentage of the target population in spite of all-media coverage. One of the indicators that gauge this is *take-up rate:* that is, the proportion of an eligible population that actually receives a particular benefit. To a degree, government is in command of this: by what Hood (1983, p. 27) calls "privishing" information rather than publishing it (showing minimum zeal in calling attention to it), government can practically ensure take-up by only the most active searchers. Claimants Associations and other self-help groups have burgeoned in the United Kingdom since the 1960s to supplement official publishing of entitlements, and to press for more publishing of internal codes of regulations and the like — with some success (Donnison 1982).

But the major obstacle to acceptability of public administration at the "sharp end" — where citizen as welfare supplicant meets official as rule-follower — remains the social ambiguity of the interpersonal encounter itself. However obscurely and inarticulately, the supplicant resents his posture (the two most frequently heard expostulations are "My father [or I] fought in the war to save you lot," and "You forget we pay your wages"); and the official on his part is deeply suspicious of fraud. The grossly unfair tag of "welfare scrounger" is indiscriminately applied (when the real incidence of abuse is, though never negligible, quite low); and the middle-class myths of, for example, the public-housing tenant on subsidized rent with four wage-earning adults in the family and three cars parked outside, sustain hostility on all sides. The face-to-face interview over the Social Security office counter, far from increasing the total amount of acceptability in the system, frequently increases the degree of misunderstanding, incomprehension, and multiple unacceptability (Hill 1972; 1976).

A recent brief and localized experiment in computerization of the Social Security encounter had remarkably suggestive results. Clients were offered the choice of consulting an official in the normal way about their entitlement to benefit, or sitting on their own learning how to consult a computer via a normal keyboard by following its instructions on the screen. Not only did many people choose to consult the computer though they had never used one before, but they professed to understand it better — and said it gave them fuller information about their eligibility for benefits they did not know about than any official would have given them.

Some headway has been made in eliminating encounters, or defusing them. The function of offering employment was separated from the function of paying out unemployment benefit (the former going into a "High Street" Job Shop). Many vehicle-licensing and other local offices have disappeared, their functions being done by mail or by local post offices. Flat-rate universal benefits such as Child Benefit, run centrally from a single office using post offices as the local point, cause very little angst compared with means-tested benefits subject to high local discretion. The field needs much more thought along these lines and less resort to special forces of fraud investigators (Donnison 1982, p. 209).

Some changes at the interface, like that one, have proved unacceptable to liberals. The most controversial have involved the police: unpunished though admitted misconduct by individual officers, allegations of endemic and ineradicable racism, misgivings about complaints machinery, anxieties about the use to which the Police National Computer is put, worries about the role and discipline of certain special riot control forces and their methods, and so on (Ackroyd et al. 1977; Kettle 1984; Sked and Cook 1984, p. 350). One interesting development went under the innocuous name of the National Reporting Centre.

There are in England and Wales 47 separate police forces, each under a Police Authority, most covering a single county, some an amalgamation of counties; and each commanded by a chief constable. In law these forces are all autonomous, although the Home Secretary has some supervisory powers, and the Metropolitan Police in London (whose police authority is the Home Secretary himself) provide certain common services and consultancy services on request (to Scotland Yard, their headquarters). Similarly, one force will often help out another on request, by loan of men or equipment, when large-scale ceremonies or events such as World Cup football matches place a strain on a particular force's resources. In 1972 these interforce arrangements were strengthened by the setting up (in London, but not by the Home Secretary or the Metropolitan Police, rather by the collective action of the Chief Constables) of a National Reporting Centre, through which the deployment of manpower could be coordinated. The Centre played some small part in localized disturbances in London and provincial cities in 1974 and in 1980, but was effectively used during the extensive inner-city riots of 1981 (Taylor 1985). Then in 1982 it came into more peaceful prominence, during the first visit to Britain of His Holiness, the Pope.

When in 1984 the National Union of Mineworkers went on strike against the threatened closure of coal mines, and began to send "flying pickets" to different coal regions in the country, the police were able to respond in kind. The telephones in the National Reporting Centre were again busy, and the blue transit vans filled with policemen became a common sight on the roads of Britain. Picket lines in Yorkshire were policed by constables from Devon and Somerset, from Surrey, from Manchester, and from many other areas; and similarly elsewhere. The national deployment of local police resources was consolidated over more than 12 months of continuous operation; and it can no longer plausibly be held that in Britain we do not have a national police system. In such ways does administration change in Britain, more typically than by reform.

The improvement of the *acceptability* of public administration is not an aim that administrative reformers have had constantly before them (though it might be said to be the main aim of social policy and social administration reformers). The main aim of the administrative reformer has conventionally been the improvement of effectiveness, or possibly efficiency. But if I may repeat a thought I have recently published elsewhere (Dunsire 1985, p. 69), a newish development in implementation theory seems to offer advance in the direction of acceptability. Renate Mayntz (1981), Christopher Hood (1983) and others have pointed out that instruments of governing (e.g., the choice between using propaganda, or grants and rewards, or regulations and licensing, or direct bureaucratic labor) can often be substituted for one another without apparent loss of effectiveness, and that the use of a particular instrument is often a matter of mere habit, or style, or lack of awareness of alternatives. If so, and if there is as Adam Smith (1776/1910, II, p. 309) held, an obligation on governments to visit on the people at large no more trouble, vexation and oppression than is absolutely necessary to achieve the aim in view (quoted by Hood 1983, p. 142), then administrators could perhaps consciously select more acceptable instruments, what Mayntz calls the "softer" tools, before resorting to the harsher ones. Hood hypothesizes that where governments are trusted and compliance is high, the softer tools will work; but where consensus is low and recalcitrance rises, government is obliged to turn more and more to the "harder" instruments, regulation and sanctions – and in this way exacerbating the social climate that made them necessary in the first place.

Civility in administration, you may think, is a kind of moral imperative for governments, at least in regimes claiming to be democratic. If the analysis is correct, it may also have survival value.

Administrative Responsiveness

Traditional public administration in the U.K. based on the Weberian/rationalist organizational model and the Westminster model of constitutional relationships, tended to define public administration in terms of central government (ministerial departments), local government (counties, cities, and districts), and the public corporations (mainly the utilities and transport bodies). These entities or congeries do exist; but they do not very well map the administrative terrain. Presenting a fuller picture of administrative organization, at least for the post-1945 period, requires in addition a mapping of the relationships between central and local government, for example, and of the relationships between the public sector and the private sector—the public corporations themselves almost disappearing into the quagmire of bodies that are not-central, not-local, and perhaps only quasi-governmental at all. Where so many bodies have to be designated as hybrid, the distinction between public and private loses all edge. It is a sign not only of a more aware and more active population, but also of a more pluralist society than existed in nineteenth century Britain, that even for those concerned with structure, academic interest has very largely shifted away from categorizing and describing the organizations in public administration, towards understanding the connections between them, the ways they link together to make a system.

Much work has been done on *central-local relations* in recent decades (see Dunleavy and Rhodes 1983; Goldsmith 1985; Rhodes 1986, etc.). Two major features of this system emerge. First: there are three ways in which local authorities are linked with central government; one, directly between Whitehall and Town Hall; two, between Town Hall and the regional offices of one or more ministries; and three, between Whitehall and one or other of the representative (or *peak*) organizations of local authorities (associations of county councils, etc.). Second: neither central government nor any local authority is a monolith, a single terminal for communications; both are multiorganisations. Communications typically flow between a department of a local authority and a department of central government, or in an even finer discrimination, between sections of the respective departments. Communications may be denser along such channels than they are among the various departments of a single local authority or among the ministries of central government. Communications also flow between one department of one local authority and the corresponding department in other local authorities; and also along professional networks, trade union networks, party networks, social membership group networks (Rotary, Freemasons, etc.); and so on.

If we focused instead on government-industry relations, we should find much the same patterns: direct links between firm and ministry, links via regional offices, links via peak associations; interfirm linkage, interest group and trade union linkages; professional, party, and social links: a very similar pattern. And likewise with government and the voluntary sector—churches, youth clubs, community organizations, sporting clubs and arts associations and hobby societies from angling (the largest!) to zoology. Some such groupings would be but weakly interlinked among themselves, perhaps only weakly linked to local government and hardly at all to central government; others would have well-established national associations but not much traffic with government; others still, both strongly interlinked and strongly linked to government, local or national or both.

Focusing on communication nets highlights not so much what public administration is as what it does; and not so much what its processes are as what its functions are, its roles in society. A shift in the number of linkages and in the traffic they carry will signal a shift in the role of public administration. The system responds to its environment. Each node and net was designed for some specific purpose at the time: historians of central-local relations commonly trace many such origins and developments—in the default powers of ministers, in grants and subventions for specific purposes and then for general purposes, in central inspections, etc. The two twentieth-century world wars were prolific creators of bodies and linkages, many of which survived the ending of hostilities, and were put to peacetime use. But we can perhaps now see that it was what has come to be called the "long boom" in the sixties and early seventies, postwar prosperity, which is associated with the greatest intensification of communications between tiers of government (intergovernmental relations) and between government and other sectors.

It is unnecessary to decide whether the wartime consensus and all-party postwar vogue for consultative planning created the long boom or were merely contemporaneous with endogenous factors. But certainly, the richly interconnected system described above, however generated, was used and developed in the post-war settlement, rooted in Keynesian economic theory and government intervention in the interests of economic stability and social equity. Some of the networks were the structures of the so-called partnership between central and local governments (really a complex bargaining relationship); others, especially the peak associations in several policy fields, and the evolution since 1961 of the peak economic planning forum the National Economic Development Council (NEDC), were the instruments of "neocorporatism" (Smith 1979), and of decision making in "policy communities" (Richardson and Jordan 1979), giving rise to fears about the bypassing of Parliament and the electoral machinery.

Any observer of the same macroscopic system today and over the last few years must have noted a marked reversal of the development: a decrease in interconnectedness, a decline in the volume and frequency of communications, the atrophy of many linkages. It is universally complained that communications in central-local relations have become almost one-way traffic, not bargaining but central determination. Channels between government and the peak associations of industry, both of employers and of trade unions, have fallen into comparative desuetude—the NEDC has all but ceased to meet. The same phenomenon can be found in the community sector. Whatever kind of regime we are moving into, it certainly is neither a consensus one nor a corporate state.

Mrs. Thatcher's government has its own style. It does not bargain, it does not even consult any more than it absolutely has to; it prefers to decide what is best to be done, and announce it. In April 1984 the Prime Minister said on television: "I go for agreement for the things I want to do. Consensus is too wishy-washy." Recently this style has come under fire from her own side, and backbench revolts on a succession of issues (parental contributions to student maintenance grants, the Sikorsky takeover of Westland Helicopters, the sale of Leyland Trucks and Land Rover to General Motors, and other matters) have perhaps modified the reality though not the rhetoric of "conviction politics." Sponsorship and other official government-industry linkages remain in place and are routinely used; but the omission of the consultation phase in the preparation of new developments is distinctly noticed.

For all her emphasis on economy and the elimination of waste (see later), Mrs. Thatcher knows when to throw dollars at a problem. The defeat of the National Union of Mineworkers is a case in point: the cost of police deployment through the National Reporting Centre mentioned earlier was enormous. Another is the job creation scheme and its successors (Ridley 1980; 1984). The scheme was begun under the Labour government in Autumn 1975, via the newly created Manpower Services Commission (Howells 1980), and was succeeded by a number of programs with slightly different titles and aims (Youth Opportunities Programme, Training Opportunities Programme, Youth Training Scheme), but with one feature in common: they had apparently unlimited resources, for the purpose of providing alternatives to unemployment for young people. The Manpower Services Commission (MSC) itself became a growth industry, establishing its own countrywide network of regional and local offices.

Mrs. Thatcher adapted this machinery to bypass the normal channels of the educational system in launching, with great speed and directness, a completely new program for children aged 13 to 18, called the Technical and Vocational Education Initiative. Under it local education authorities can draw upon funds administered by the MSC (not the Department of Education and Science [DES]) to provide teachers, equipment, and allowances (on scales more liberal than under any DES scheme) for the technical education of school-age boys and girls. Staff in DES and in the local education authorities were apparently as surprised as everyone else by the announcement of the initiative; they had not been consulted (Moon and Richardson 1984).

What we have seen is, seemingly, a decline in administrative responsiveness at the program or policy level. Other straws in the wind bend the same way. Ministers have long had the power to seek advice from the public on some matter of public policy, via public hearings or the submission of written memoranda to a Royal Commission or other committee of inquiry (Chapman 1973). In the 1960s and 1970s there were a number of important Royal Commissions, on local government reform, on the press, on broadcasting, on trade unions, on the National Health Service; and departmental or other committees on the civil service, on education, on personal social services. These illumined some part of the policy scene more or less brightly and briefly; but it is an open question whether they are regarded as having contributed to increased responsiveness of public administration. They are commonly seen as devices used by ministers either to avert the personal opprobrium of a difficult choice or to put off decision for another year or two. (They are often of immense help to teachers, however, because of the wealth of material they make available in more-or-less handy form.) It is not universally expected that the government will be seriously influenced by the recommendations of a Royal Commission or departmental committee. But for what it is worth, the present government has appointed significantly fewer such commissions than did its predecessors.

In some fields of government, particularly land-use planning, statutes require relevant ministers to appoint an inspector and hold a local inquiry in certain circumstances (for example, an opposed compulsory purchase order), and enable them to do so in other circumstances (Boaden et al. 1982). There has been a general liberalization of such inquiries since the original legislation, allowing voice to people with a personal though not a legal interest in the matter, and allowing the inquiry to hear objections not only to the specific proposal in question but also to the policy involved — for instance, not only where a new road should go, but also whether it was needed (Tyme 1978). Such planning inquiries are not much loved, but they are undeniably mechanisms of administrative responsiveness; and misgivings were expressed in July 1985 over a government White Paper, which, under the rubric of "reducing burdens on business," proposed the creation of "Simplified Planning zones" where local authorities could publish specifications of what types of development could be carried out within their area; developers would not then be required to submit planning applications at all if their schemes fell within the specifications. This might seem, and be, a desirable adjustment to land-use planning regulations; but environmentalists are wary of this government's intentions with regard to a number of the foundations of British environmental protection, such as erosion of the Green Belt policy, and what is seen as apathy over pollution control. However, a broad review of the whole field by the Central Policy Planning Unit (CPPU) of the Department of the Environment, released in March 1986, proposes several changes in the direction of reaffirming and consolidating existing green policies and coordination of present diverse departmental inspectorates and controls under a single corps of Her Majesty's Environmental Inspectors, with environmental impact accounting on all new developments and greater force behind the "make the polluters pay" principle. The DOE CPPU document also, however, declares for greater freedom of information and other principles not dear to present ministers, so it cannot be said (or even hoped) to represent current government policy.

As well as the local planning inquiry, ministers under the Town and Country Planning (Amendment) Act 1972 (which followed the wide-ranging but extrastatutory Roskill Inquiry into the Third London Airport 1967–70) may set up a public inquiry into strategic plans without many of the legal limitations of a local inquiry. The device of the open inquiry has been used, most notably, into the need for a new nuclear processing plant at Windscale (Pearce 1979), the expansion of Stansted Airport near London, and the building of a nuclear reactor plant at Sizewell in Suffolk (Sieghart 1979; Williams 1980). The Sizewell Inquiry took more than two years of almost daily hearings, with hundreds of witnesses heard and literally tons of paper generated, at a public cost of several million pounds (the report is awaited). There is no question but that such mammoth inquiries enable enormous volumes of steam to be released relatively harmlessly into the atmosphere, which might otherwise build up dangerous pressures. To that extent, they increase public acceptance, or make public policies that are short on acceptability at least procedurally more tolerable. Groups are able to mount protests that fall within the pale of what governments find acceptable (Ryan 1978), and obtain a measure of media coverage that would be impossibly expensive otherwise, even if they have to struggle to employ the barristers who alone can make best use of the opportunity, in the forensic (though far from fully judicial) procedures adopted. The bigger and longer the inquiry, the less easily can government set aside the recommendation of its own inspector. They are, therefore, important if rather rare mechanisms of administrative *responsiveness* at program or group-pressures level.

Consultative committees were set up in many of the original statutes effecting the nationalization of an industry in the 1940s, in the public utilities field—coal, gas, electricity, transport, and (later) postal services. They are broadly representative of consumers in composition, and exist to be consulted by the corporation board on important changes, for example, in charges or levels of service, and to receive complaints. Although the Transport Users' Consultative Committees were originally active in holding public hearings about railway branch line closures, none of the consultative committees has evolved in any significant way since their inauguration; they have never been of much importance to the boards themselves, and their existence is largely unknown to the majority of customers, who complain (if they do) to the staff in the local showroom and office of the industry itself. As devices designed to render the public bodies concerned more publicly acceptable and responsive, they must be judged a failure. Only the Post Office Users' National Council regularly achieves a newspaper headline, and that usually because of the trenchant style of its chairman. More acceptance is engineered by the public relations departments of the industries, who are well skilled in corporate advertising and image-building (Tivey 1973, 1982; Pryke 1981).

There are similar consultative bodies in the National Health Service, now called Community Health Councils, which in fact play a quite active role in representing patients' interests in some areas (Brown 1975; Bates 1982), but are otherwise subject to the same criticisms as the public utilities' consumer representative organizations: not widely known, not seen to be independent, not seen to be effective. And the NHS perhaps suffers from having *no* public relations departments to man its interface with the public, save that of the Department of Health and Social Security (DHSS) itself in London. It will be ironic, while not at all unwelcome, if one of the results of the managerialization of the health service under the present government is an improvement in civility at hospital level, through more professional public relations, even if not in responsiveness as defined here.

On the face of it, however, lay or democratic participation in the running of health, local authority, and water services has markedly declined in recent decades. The main representative bodies in the line management of the NHS, the Area Health Authorities, were simply wiped out in 1982. The reorganization of local government in 1974 saw large increases in the area and population over which the most local of local authorities exercises authority and provides services, and consequently a diminution in the ability of smaller groups of citizens with territorial affinities (neighbors, villagers, fellow-townsmen) to make their own decisions in matters that affect only or primarily themselves. Yet awareness of this loss of democratic participation does not seem widespread, and there is no popular clamor for its restoration. It is possible that the reorganization has raised the local standing and influence of the most immediate rural representative organ, the parish or community council, which has never had any significant executive or financial power but which has voice, and the right to be consulted on planning and other proposals affecting its territory.

In the water industry, regional authorities now control the entire water cycle in their regions, from the gathering and treatment of drinking water to the maintenance of river basins and agricultural drainage and flood prevention measures. But they are unelected bodies, save at one remove for part of their membership (local authority appointees), and subject to no regional or local control over their charging and taxing powers or their expenditure, only to oversight by the Secretary of State for the Environment. Moreover, more recent legislation has removed the obligation on regional water authorities to admit the public and press to their meetings. So far, however, this situation appears to be unacceptable only to a few academics and organs of the press. The water authorities are now on the government's list for privatization, with questions about their monopoly status, their taxing powers, and their regulatory functions, quite unresolved.

To sum up on the responsiveness of public administration in the United Kingdom today: it would seem that much of the organizational and structural change that has occurred in the last 15 years or so has actually reduced the responsiveness of administration quite markedly, and that the country has become significantly less *pluralist* than it was in the years of the long boom. Whether economic decline and retrenchment causes centralization and increased authoritarianism is another question.

Administrative Economy

It is perhaps not a deep paradox, that Mrs. Thatcher's government constantly denigrates bureaucracy and bureaucratic methods of doing things (much preferring the market way), while demonstrating the strongest of centralizing and regulating tendencies itself. It may merely be that it is consistently market-oriented where market provision is feasible and more efficient, and consistently rationalist, elitist and control-minded where the market fails or is not appropriate. What Mrs. Thatcher is not is conspicuously community-minded or pluralist in outlook.

The public service paradigm is no stranger to the search for efficiency as an administrative value. It is difficult to deny that description to the work of the Health of Munition Workers Committee in 1915–18, or the work of Treasury Organization and Methods teams from the 1920s onwards (Chester and Willson 1968, p. 292). There is a very sophisticated and theoretical article under the title "Efficiency as an Alternative to Control" in the 1928 volume of *Public Administration* written by a serving British public servant (Bunbury 1928), which discusses the application of scientific management thinking to public service operations. The movement that produced PPBS (Planning, Programming, Budgeting System) in the United States, and PAR (Program Analysis and Review) and the PESC system (Public Expenditure Survey Committee) in the United Kingdom, in the 1960s, was more of a departure from the public service paradigm; it was clearly said that they were attempts to bring business methods into bureaucracy. PAR was a procedure whereby departments in turn presented to cabinet an analysis of a specific program they were running (e.g., the motorways construction program, the adult literacy program), attempting answers to questions such as "Why are we doing this at all? Could we get the same results with fewer resources? Could the same resources produce better results?" The PESC system, following the Plowden Report on Control of Public Expenditure (1961), was an annual projection of expenditures, program by program, for five years into the future (with decreasing firmness), for review together; something that was, incredibly, new at the time, although the idea of reviewing taxation proposals together in a bundle or budget was considerably older.

PAR has by now been abandoned, and the reasons exhaustively studied (Gray and Jenkins 1983, 1985; Richardson 1982; Plowden 1981; etc.). The conclusion seems unavoidable that ministers simply did not take to the idea of having their departmental programs scrutinized in cabinet by their political rivals, or of scrutinizing other ministers' work. They saw the cabinet as a place for bargaining, not for planning. PESC as a planning device foundered on the reefs of galloping inflation, the oil price rise, and the resort to the IMF in 1976 (though it still exists in more modest form). But for the new government of Mrs. Thatcher in 1979 perhaps their greatest shortcoming was their association with the "synoptic planning" doctrines of Edward Heath, her Conservative predecessor. One of her first actions was to abolish the cabinet think tank, the Central Policy Review Staff, bringing together bright young civil servants and imported experts and academics, which had had under Mr. Heath the function of setting all departmental program objectives, clearly and unambiguously stated, into a system of priorities within an overall comprehensive strategy (Plowden 1981; Hennessy 1984). Mrs. Thatcher simply does not believe in this kind of thing. She has no wish to use the powers of government to achieve programmatic objectives, except insofar as they may be steps towards her overall aims: to "roll back the State," to withdraw from as many fields of government action as may be feasible, to halve the numbers of public employees, to end government trading and public enterprise, and to wean the country away from its enervating dependence on state-provided health and welfare services. Positively, she believes in market mechanisms and sees the role of the state as providing the conditions in which enterprise can flourish—including the preservation of external security and internal order.

These, of course, are the doctrines of the New Right, associated with the names of Hayek and Friedman, and founded in classical economic theory. But this is not merely a political platform, the manifesto of one side in standard adversarial politics. In the form of *public choice theory* it can fairly be said to offer a new paradigm, a way of seeing from a different standpoint the whole of the phenomena of public administration (Ostrom and Ostrom 1971; Mueller 1979; Whynes and Bowles 1981). In the form of the *economic approach to bureaucracy* it opened up a startling challenge to conventional Weberian and public service views of the motivation of civil servants (Niskanen 1971). There is no space here to go more deeply into the theoretical underpinnings of these positions than to say that they depend fundamentally on neoclassical economists' arguments about *allocative efficiency*—the least-cost arrangement for matching supply and demand; and on an axiom that bureaucrats like any other organizational actors maximize their own interests.

Two very influential propositions have been drawn from these arguments. First, that financing through a block budget drawn from a general fund by annual negotiation will result in a higher level of provision of any service than will revenue financing from user charges. Block-budget financing sets up incentives to spend rather than to save, since savings typically cannot be appropriated by the spending unit but are "clawed back," and may in any case weaken the unit's claims in future budget negotiations. Second, transferability of ownership rights and the possibility of bankruptcy or insolvency limits allocative or X-inefficiency. If an enterprise is being operated at other than the least-cost combination of inputs, there is a surplus available for extraction by whoever has or can gain control of it. Where there is no transferability of ownership, not only is there no incentive for anyone to attempt to gain control in the hope of producing more cheaply, but the interests of the current operators lie in continuing to operate inefficiently. This is precisely the situation of "bureaucracy."

Hood summarizes the normative implications of public choice theory for the organization of public services thus: a bias toward small-scale rather than large-scale enterprise in public service provision; a bias towards performance contracting rather than direct labor through open-ended employment contracts; a bias towards multiple-provider structures of public service provision (preferably involving rivalry among competing providers) rather than single-provider structures; a bias towards user charges (or at least earmarked taxes) rather than general tax funds as the basis of funding public services other than pure public goods; and a bias towards private or independent enterprise rather than public bureaucracy as the instrument of service provision (Hood 1986).

The present Conservative government in the United Kingdom has put all of these biases into practice, though not altogether consistently. Thus the telephone system has been privatized but not broken up; proposals for the privatization of British Gas and British Airways likewise do not envisage any reduction in scale of operation. Examples of contracting-out concern the cleaning of government offices, hospital laundry work and some NHS nursing, much government catering, and even security at immigration control reception centers. All licensing of scheduled bus services has been abandoned and anyone may start up a service on a new or an existing route.

Charges for medical prescriptions have risen by 1000 percent since 1979. State companies now wholly or predominantly in private ownership include British Aerospace, Britoil, Jaguar Cars, National Freight Consortium, Sealink, and several others.

But even more striking results have been achieved in two other directions: first, a reduction in the number of nonindustrial (white-collar) civil servants from 548,500 when Mrs. Thatcher took office in 1979, to 448,500 in January 1985 (and still falling); second, a change in the culture of the British Civil Service — by no means complete, but quite marked.

The Conservatives pledged themselves before the election in May 1979 to wholesale reversal of recent trends in many respects, including reductions in public expenditure and the level of taxation, and above all, reduction in the number of civil servants. This is not the place for detailed evaluation of the outturns to date; but in general, it can be shown that neither the level of public expenditure nor the level of taxation has been reduced, or even contained at their 1979 levels (see graph in Appendix comparing actual government expenditure with the rate of inflation); and it can be shown that some of the staff reductions are not really savings but number-massaging. But it would be hard to show that removing employees at the rate of 320 per week for six years is in any sense a "phony cut."

Some programs and departments suffered more than others, and a table in the Appendix indicates which ministries were cut either deeply or regularly or both, and in either budget or staff or both, between 1976 and 1983. The ministries least affected included Health and Social Security, Employment, the Home Office and the Justice department (Lord Chancellor); those most severely cut included Agriculture and Fisheries, the Environment, Trade and Industry, and National Savings. (This data is still being worked on by my colleagues in a research project into "Whitehall in Retrenchment" supported by the U.K. Economic and Social Research Council at the Institute for Research in the Social Sciences at the University of York.) Another table distributes staff cuts (over only three years because of difficulties of data comparison) by grade levels and by occupational group. Here it can be seen that the heaviest losses came in the top ranks, not at the bottom. In another analysis, by proportions of staff in top, middle, and bottom grades between 1976 and 1983, the main relative gainers in reducing totals were the middle ranks. (The same was reported for the U.S. by Martin 1983.)

By occupational group, the heaviest losers were the scientific and other specialist groups, and the relative winners the administration and related groups. But it is to be noted that grade level and occupational group are interdependent; you cannot protect the lowly in rank, and protect the specialists and professionals at the same time.

Another analysis on which we are engaged is into the *dynamic* of the cuts over the last decade in Britain. Some retrenchment theorists (Levine 1978, 1981; Beck Jørgensen 1987a) discern a process that progressively pushes a system from one style of cutback to another—usually from decrementalism to quantum cuts, or in Beck Jørgensen's formulation, from incrementalism through managerialism to strategic. (Charts in the Appendix spell out what these mean.) We used figures supplied to the House of Commons by the Treasury on the sources of cuts, under the following categories: (1) increases and decreases arising from change in work loads (including revised economic assumptions); (2) carrying out work more efficiently by a major change in method; (3) general streamlining (including lower standards of service) and other minor changes; (4) increases arising from major new activities; (5) dropping or materially curtailing a function; (6) privatization, including contracting out; and (7) hiving-off to a new or existing body. Over the years 1980–84 the big shares of staff saving were produced by lower standards of service and dropping functions (27 percent for each); each of change in work loads, increased efficiency, and privatization/contracting-out/hiving-off, accounted for about 15 percent.

Ignoring the sources for increases in staff, and taking (1) with (3) as indicating *incrementalism,* (2)/(6)/(7) together indicating *managerialism,* and (5) as representing a *strategic* type of cut, we simulated an *expected dynamic* for the years 1980–84 (see charts in Appendix). It can be seen that whereas the 1980–84 picture for Whitehall as a whole does not entirely contradict the theoretical dynamic, the pictures for several individual ministries are very varied indeed—that for Trade and Industry, for example, being the complete reverse of the expected pattern. We are of the opinion that dropping functions is quite frequently seen as the easiest route to demanded staff cuts, and that the style of last resort is more likely to be that called managerial here. But we are still working on that.

Just as retrenchment did not begin in 1979 with Mrs. Thatcher, neither did the change in civil service *culture* mentioned above. Indeed, the culture (or basic assumptions, ways of seeing and knowing, and ways of communicating) of the British Civil Service (by which, in such discourse, is usually meant the top one percent of the half-million or so civil servants) is something that has changed more than once before. Nineteenth-century top civil servants tended to see themselves as experts in the subject matter of their departments, and resisted the idea of a service-wide promotion field. It was the explosion of ministries in the welfare area and in wartime, coupled with a flood of retirements of Permanent Secretaries who had stayed on during the war, that made cross-ministry promotions and postings a necessity in the first two decades of the twentieth century (Fry 1969), followed by the discovery that if you had learned your trade of advising ministers in one department, you could take it with you to another. Thus was born in the early 1920s the *cult of the generalist,* which survived the expansion of the professional and scientific civil service in the 1930s to become an administrative wonder of the world in the postwar era. Americans and Australians and all sorts visited Whitehall, to see how these "mandarins" (private school, Oxbridge, top drawer persons all—or so was the myth) ran a welfare state for Socialist politicians; and the French founded their École Nationale d'Administration to turn out a corps of *administrateurs civils* like the administrative class in Whitehall.

Later, the British turned against their mandarins, first on the grounds of their exclusivity, and the rules and practices of the Civil Service Commission were altered to try to widen the field of recruitment to the administrative class. After that, it was their isolation and ignorance of the real world that came under fire; and in the early 1960s a Treasury Centre for Administrative Studies was set up, to run courses in economics for senior civil servants. This was the background to the blistering attack on the whole ethos of the administrative class (unhistorically calling it a nineteenth-century one) in the first chapter of the Report of the (Fulton) Committee on the Civil Service (1968), and of the creation of the Civil Service College and the unified grading system (now extended to Grade 7, Principal level) wiping out distinctions between administrators, professionals and specialists and making any occupational group eligible for the top jobs. At this time also (the early 1960s) was heard the view that senior civil servants had to learn to become managers of their departments, not just advisers to ministers on policy; and the Fulton Report contained recommendations about hiving-off and identification of accountable management units, as mentioned under Administrative Rationality above.

Similarly, it was under Harold Wilson that the phrases "output budgeting" and "performance measurement" began to be heard in Whitehall as well as in the universities, and that auditors began talking about VFM (value-for-money); and it was Edward Heath who invited a team of businessmen to work in the Cabinet Office and act as a yeast to spread the new outlook. So it cannot be said that the Conservative government of 1979 onwards under Mrs. Thatcher is responsible for any culture-change that may now be detectable. As a respected British journalist put it recently: "Just as she herself is a symptom as well as a cause, an expression of what the electorate felt had to happen next, so the idea of a more responsive, less self-contained Civil Service run on managerial lines had been mooted before 1979" (Whitehorn 1986). But she is presiding over the development, which is entirely in tune with her own predilections, and also her style. The same journalist began the piece quoted thus: "Whitehall is not what it was. The days when all civil servants were suave, silent and faceless have plainly gone; even obedience is now in question. There's a new, cruder atmosphere; more vigour, more excitement – but a good deal of unease and disillusion too." An assistant secretary was quoted: "Before, you got good marks for elegant midfield play; now, only if you score goals." The enormously successful television comedy series *Yes, Minister* is popular not only with Mrs. Thatcher (for whom the exquisitely finessing Sir Humphrey is proof of everything she always thought about Permanent Secretaries) but also with the mandarins, or some of them at least, who can now laugh at themselves because the parodies are less near the bone than they would have been 10 or 15 years ago. (Even now, however, Sir Humphrey surfaces regularly during confrontations between senior civil servants and parliamentary committees.) Those top men who have genuinely adopted the new outlook can feel themselves to be in the mainstream, going with it, and not fighting against it all the time.

The major initiatives in this area have been the creation in Downing Street itself of the Efficiency Unit originally under Sir Derek (now Lord) Rayner, the former head of one of Britain's most successful retail enterprises, Marks and Spencer; and the Financial Management Initiative, a system of standard costing and management controls. There is a large literature on the impact and style of "Raynerism" (Gray and Jenkins 1983, 1985; Warner 1984a; Metcalfe and Richards 1984). The Rayner scrutinies, in contrast to the goal-oriented rationalism of earlier Program Analysis and Review (PAR) exercises, revert to an older style of the search for economy; less emphasis on policy objectives and integration, more on the simple uncovering of waste, by the microscopic investigations that are the stuff of old-fashioned work study. A measure of the culture change is the extent to which waste-hunting has become an acceptable enthusiasm for younger high-fliers, though they may still meet with the same kind of obscurantist recalcitrance that has been reported by such gadflies since the eighteenth century (Chapman 1978; Ponting 1985).

The Financial Management Initiative, too, is the latest in a line of attempts to provide better management information to top civil servants and their ministers (Cmnd 8616 1982; Cmnd 9297 1984; RIPA 1983; Lee 1984; Gray and Jenkins 1985; etc.). But of even greater significance for present purposes are developments in personnel management and training. The Treasury and the management and personnel office of the cabinet office have set up a joint management unit whose job is the promotion of just such a change in management outlook as we are discussing; or, in the kind of second hand buzzwords that swiftly become current, to act as product champion of a number of ideas. One of these is the idea of separating running costs from program costs in any ministry or agency. Program costs are not to be ignored, but they are the province of ministers, and policy-linked. Running costs, on the other hand, are the province of civil servants, and managerial attention should be devoted to reducing them. Running costs include wages and salaries, personnel overheads like travel and subsistence allowances, accommodation costs, office services, and contracted-out services.

At present, the central departments (Her Majesty's Treasury [HMT] and Management and Personnel Office in the Cabinet Office [MPO]) maintain controls both on manpower and on expenditure. But the illogic of this is recognized; it may not always be feasible to meet targets on both expenditure and manpower separately; managers need power to deal with both, together. So, although it may be difficult for a while yet to drop controls on manpower, that is the aim; manning levels will be an outcome of expenditure decisions. Although it is not yet said openly, the obvious next target after that for the product champions is the rigid grading and salary structure; merit bonuses are already being experimented with, and scarcity allowances are already paid (in considerable amounts) to staff in occupational groups in high demand outside.

Another product to be championed is *policy evaluation,* to take care of program costs. The delineaments of this have been well enough known to academic policy analysts for a decade and more; but now it is being preached in Whitehall, and the cabinet secretariat will not allow papers concerning new policy initiatives to go to ministers unless they conform to the approved pattern: "All proposals with VFM implications should state: what is to be achieved, by when, at what cost, and how that achievement is to be measured." Policy evaluation—the designation of what shall count as failure at the time of policy choice—is now mandatory for all new policy initiatives and policy reviews, at whatever level, and is encouraged for public expenditure survey bids and current programs and policies (JMU 1985).

A third product is the creation in May 1984 of the Consultancy, Inspection and Review Service (CIR)—encouraging departments to regard as a single resource all the previously separate units like the staff inspectorate, economists, internal auditors, accountants, work study people, and the like. This service will have two functions: to help line management with advice and undertake surveys, and to act as the instrument of top management, in monitoring and inspecting. A central CIR, similarly, offers consultancy services and keeps tabs on departmental CIRs. Some of the professional officers involved have received these developments less than warmly.

Finally, not under the JMU but following the (Cassells) Review of Personnel Work in the Civil Service (Cassells 1983), annual staff appraisal has been rethought. Until recently, when staff were reported on formally once a year, they were appraised in terms of their *qualities,* and in terms of their fitness for promotion. But the great bulk of civil servants can expect a promotion only two or three times in their careers, and to judge all only by their prospects of a distant and statistically unlikely promotion is not only a waste of time but potentially disruptive and dispiriting. Now staff are appraised on their *performance,* according to a series of mutually agreed targets. Again, this is old-hat theoretically; but it is now current practice in the whole of the British Civil Service.

It cannot be said that there is nothing left of the public service paradigm in the hearts and minds of British civil servants — by no means, as we shall see in the next section. But a considerable change has undoubtedly taken place; the middle and upper-middle ranks of civil servants do now see themselves as managers of public enterprises (even if not in a trading context), rather than as mere administrators of government policy (Johnson 1985). The individual accountability of the manager of an accountable unit for the performance of the tasks and for the spending capacity entrusted to them is a concept not only accepted by ministers (encouraged by the PM) but now effectively worked into the ethos of the service. Yet such a concept is unknown to the British Constitution, and is bound to cause trouble sooner or later (Plowden 1985).

Administrative Legitimacy

This aspect of the relationship between the responsibilities of civil servants and the responsibilities of ministers has not yet been seriously examined by any official body (though it may well be on the agenda of the inquiry into just this subject now in train by the Treasury and Civil Service Select Committee of the House of Commons). But another aspect of that relationship has been a current political issue for the last 18 months or so: arising out of a number of cases of leaked documents, the question asked is "To whom or what is a civil servant responsible?"

The Ponting Affair was not the first such case but it is the most celebrated and important. Clive Ponting was a senior civil servant in the Ministry of Defense who, when he felt that his minister was misleading parliament on a material point, sent a copy of a secret document to a member of parliament. This MP gave the document to the Chairman of the Commons Defense Committee, who returned it to the Ministry of Defense and Ponting's hand in the matter was revealed. He was sent for trial under the Official Secrets Act of 1911. The judge took a high view of the phrase in the act "the interests of the State," holding that it could only mean the policies of the government of the day, and it was no part of Ponting's duties to go beyond these. The jury seemingly took a different view, for they acquitted

Ponting of any criminal offense. The outcome was seen as public approval for the doctrine that civil servants have a loyalty higher than that to their ministers (Ponting 1985).

The official position on that had already been stated by the head of the civil service, Sir Robert Armstrong, during the trial. A civil servant's ultimate loyalty was to the government of the day, and his duty was first and foremost to the minister in charge of his department. Ministers, and ministers alone, were responsible to parliament. If a civil servant were asked to do something of which he seriously disapproved, he should take the matter to his departmental superior, and then, if necessary, to the Permanent Secretary. If the problem were still unresolved, the civil servant should resign, but still keep silent on the matter. This is in fact the historical tradition, in line with the mythical public service bargain struck by the nineteenth-century inheritors of the Northcote-Trevelyan reforms of 1854. There is no historical or, indeed, legal room for any doctrine of a civil servant's responsibility to the State, or the Crown, or Parliament, much less the people. Those who brought forward such arguments during the Ponting trial were inventing doctrine, not reporting it. Yet at a deeper level, what the constitutional position *should be* depends upon what the British Constitution *is*. And that is not such a simple matter as it sounds.

Constitutionalism is something more than the law: it means that government itself acknowledges that its authority is derived from, and must be exercised in accordance with, rules that government may not amend or dispense with (even though, formally, any statute in Britain can be amended by another statute, by the ordinary process of legislation). It is the concept of constitutionalism that, to my mind, embodies the supreme manifestation of the Rule of Law, perhaps the highest achievement of human society in the civilizing of the imperium. But there is no doubt that in Britain what the British Constitution is is less a legal than a political question, and prudent jurists do well to say that in law there is no such thing. I have much sympathy with the positivist view, which holds that the British Constitution is what the politicians of the day can get away with. So, in the present discussion, there are those who say that if the Constitution is taken to be the Westminster Model described earlier, including the political neutrality of civil servants, then the Constitution has already been changed by the present government, and the actual role of senior civil servants today is not that envisaged in the Westminster Model.

Political neutrality is the phrase most often used in this context: but it may need clarification. It would be generally accepted that what the mythical public service bargain required of top civil servants was not neutrality as between government and opposition, but unstinted loyal service to the government of the day, *whatever its party color.* There are three kinds of departure from this position alleged. First: a spate of books and articles by ex-Labour ministers (e.g., Benn 1980, 1982) has claimed that top civil servants obstructed and frustrated their wishes while in office, echoing (Fry 1985, p. 17) assertions of the 1930s by Laski and others about the impossibility of people with the social background and training of the mandarins being able to implement Socialist policies. Second: many writers have almost routinely alleged that civil service departments have programs of their own, and have effectively dictated the policies of all governments since the War—an assertion made by a minority of a House of Commons Committee (HC 535-I 1976; quoted in Fry 1985, p. 20; and see Young and Sloman 1982). This claim is given color by the ill-advised remarks of a retired Permanent Secretary: "The Civil Service always hopes that it's influencing Ministers towards the common ground. Now that's not to say influencing them towards some piece of ground which the Civil Service has itself constructed; it is the Civil Service trying to have a sense of what can succeed for Britain, and trying to exercise its influence on Ministers to try to see that they do capture the common ground with their ideas, from whatever origin they start" (Part 1980, p. 132; quoted in Fry 1985, p. 27). But the charge being leveled now is a third one: that what is being required of top civil servants today is not mere professional loyalty, but political commitment, something approaching party-card bureaucracy.

This charge rests on a few unchallenged facts and a great deal of unfavorable construction, rumor, and alleged intention. It is the high standing of some of those making the charge—former Permanent Secretaries and Heads of the Civil Service, no less—that require it to be taken seriously. The facts concern mainly two episodes (this is not the place for a longer catalogue): one, the appointment by the prime minister of an outsider (Mr. Peter Levene, a former defense contractor) to the civil service post of head of the Defense Procurement Agency at a nonstandard salary, by a method that was later judged by the government's own lawyers to be illegal, since it quite bypassed the Civil Service Commission's rules; the other, an order given by Mrs. Thatcher personally to the head of the Civil Service in December 1983, without cabinet approval, to ban trade unions in the Government Communications Headquarters (the GCHQ case), on the grounds that security required that GCHQ civil servants should not be subject to divided loyalties—the implication being that civil servants could not be members of a trade union and loyal to the government or the state at the same time. Civil servants at GCHQ were thereupon offered a sum of £1,000 in return for the surrender of their rights to join a trade union, and most accepted. What is to happen to those who did not leave their union, or having accepted the £1,000 then rejoined the union, was undecided.

The allegations are that the prime minister has taken a much closer interest in the opinions of candidates for high civil service posts than has ever been normal before, and that her famous question "Is he one of us?" has been applied not only to parliamentary private secretaries and junior ministers, but to deputy under secretaries and perhaps even lower ranks of the civil service. Now this may be sinister or not, according to construction. When selecting between two candidates for a permanent secretaryship, one of whom has fully internalized the managerial approach while the other is still steeped in the public service approach, it may not be a political choice at all to select the first. As the journalist quoted earlier put it: "There's no doubt that promotions have gone to those who are right-minded, who are seen to be 'one of us', but that doesn't mean that Tory hacks are being promoted over redder heads. It's more a matter of those who fit the flavour of the times doing better, and that has always been so" (Whitehorn 1986). It may be different, however, if the officer is expected to share the prime minister's rooted antipathy to public sector trading of any kind, or her distrust of trade unions, or her impatience with pressure groups and indeed the consultation mode of doing business; commitment to such attitudes on the part of a senior civil servant might well render him or her unfit to serve under a successor government of a different color. The line can be fine. Here is where we have to pay attention to who they are who are saying such things.

Lord Bancroft, a former head of the Civil Service, said in the House of Lords in February 1986 that the nonpolitical civil service, built up over a century and a quarter, could be destroyed in a decade by ministerial hostility, misuse, and indifference. He was referring to the government's record as an employer, and suggesting that no government could expect loyalty if it did not give loyalty. A former Downing Street adviser and confidant, Sir John Hoskyns (Hoskyns 1984), and a former Permanent Secretary to the Treasury and joint head of the Civil Service, Sir Douglas Wass (Wass 1984), have both predicted the creation of a cadre of party-political mandarins, coming in and going out with their ministers, as the solution to the impossible position many senior civil servants feel themselves to be in. In May 1985 senior civil servants in a conference organized by the First Division Association (their trade union) heard their chairman, an assistant secretary in DHSS, refer to the emphasis the government placed on commitment and conviction, and to the "increasing suspicion — whether or not true — that the way to the top is unquestioning delivery of predetermined government policy." The conference went on to endorse by a large majority a call for an independent complaints body to which troubled civil servants could take a Ponting-type problem, a call repeated by Sir Douglas Wass in an article in July 1985, suggesting an "Inspector-General," and suggesting further a

Royal Commission to look into the question of civil service loyalty, ministerial involvement in appointments and the public accountability of Whitehall officials (Wass 1985).

The need for a code of ethics for civil servants had been voiced for many years, notably by the FDA, and several drafts have appeared, but ministers remain quite unconvinced of the need, since ministerial responsibility to the House is complete and sufficient. But the unease occasioned by another leak—this time, one authorized by a minister—in the Westland Affair has reopened the controversy. Westland Helicopters, a private company although a defense contractor, was to be taken over (with the agreement of its board of directors) by Sikorsky International; the British Defense Secretary (Mr. Michael Heseltine) opposed this move, and advocated a joint European consortium. Although the government's formal position was one of utter neutrality in the bid, the sympathies of Mrs. Thatcher and of the Secretary of State for Industry (Mr. Leon Brittan) were with the Sikorsky deal (as were those of the Westland workers). Probably in order to discredit Mr. Heseltine's activities, Mr. Brittan caused his head of information section (a civil servant) to leak a confidential letter from the government's lawyers to Mr. Heseltine. The civil servant checked with the prime minister's private office and got what she thought was Mrs. Thatcher's approval of the move; but later, amid great confusion, this was denied; and Mr. Brittan's taking on the full responsibility did not prevent the names of all the civil servants being known, or their being effectively rebuked by Sir Robert Armstrong for not consulting their permanent secretaries (before obeying the minister's instruction, presumably). Both Mr. Brittan and Mr. Heseltine resigned over the affair, but the future of the civil servants involved is unclear.

A related issue (in that it too challenges the central doctrine of ministerial responsibility) is that of a Freedom of Information Act for the United Kingdom, advocacy of which also has a long history but has escalated in recent months, enjoying the endorsement not only of the First Division Association and of such bodies as the Royal Institute of Public Administration, but also of an even larger number of recently retired mandarins, the latest being a rather surprising convert, Sir Frank Cooper (lately Permanent Secretary at Defense, now holding the job Mr. Peter Levene vacated to join the Ministry of Defense).

Evidence that relations between the government and its civil servants are now worse than at any time before comes out week by week. Ministers have tried to dissuade civil servants from voting (in a ballot the government has imposed on all trade unions) to continue with a political fund—money set aside from subscriptions for the running of campaigns not directly related to terms and conditions of employment. Here is the deputy general secretary of the Civil Service Union, representing mainly manual and lower-paid personnel:

> It is the Government that has politicised the Civil Service. It was the Government, not the unions, that elevated public service pay and conditions to matters of party dogma. It was the Government that made reductions in Civil Service manpower a totem of ministerial virility. And it is the Government that, shamelessly, has wheeled its senior officials into the political cauldron of the Westland affair. It ill becomes them now to complain when civil servants seek a voice to answer back (Randall 1986).

The Treasury and Civil Service Committee of the House of Commons here reported on all these matters. It may all, from the hindsight of five years hence, seem merely a troubled episode stemming from personalities and not principles. But it may not: and certainly, the sense that the rules are changing under our feet (whether or not we can say that the government is breaking the rules) is very strong at present. We shall see.

That is not exactly a conclusion from the arguments of this paper; but insofar as it has been my argument that paradigms, or ways of seeking public administration, have been associated with underlying major social trends, then if the debates reported in this final section, under the heading of Administrative Legitimacy, do portend a new way of seeing public administration in the United Kingdom, we should search for the associated social trend. But my own view is that the present crisis (if it is one) arises out of the combination of the working out of the political economy paradigm and the presence in No. 10 Downing Street of a conviction politician with deep-rooted prejudices against bureaucrats as such. The British Constitution is not in peril.

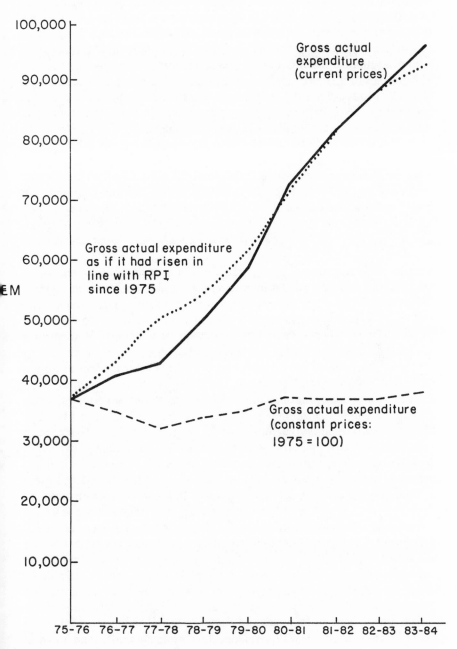

Figure 13.1. Total Government Expenditure,
1975–1983

TABLE 13.1. Departments and Departmental Groupings Used in Survey, with Conventional Initial Codes and Staff Numbers, Ranked by Gross Expenditure (£M) in 1976.

		£M	Staff (thousands)
DHSS	Department of Health and Social Security	8,518.2	91.60
DOE	Department of the Environment (including Proprietary Services Agency)	8,378.5	57.90[d]
MOD	Ministry of Defense (including Royal Ordnance Factories)	5,465.9	261.20
SO	Scottish Office[a]	2,027.3	10.80
DIn	Department of Industry	1,909.7	10.10
DES	Department of Education and Science (including Arts/ Libraries)	1,433.6	4.10
DTp	Department of Transport	1,131.4	13.50[d]
HO	Home Office	1,031.2	32.50
DE	Department of Employment[b]	760.2	45.50
FOO	Foreign and Commonwealth Office plus Overseas Development Administration	666.2	12.60
MAFF	Ministry of Agriculture, Fisheries and Food	517.5	15.60
ECGD	Export Credits Guarantee Department	504.9	1.90
DTr	Department of Trade (including Prices)	488.0	8.10
NIO	Northern Ireland Office	467.2	0.30
WO	Welsh Office	436.7	1.50
IR	Board of Inland Revenue	308.8	79.10
DEn	Department of Energy	301.4	1.40
TCC	Treasury (HMT), Civil Service Department (CSD)[c], Cabinet Office (CabO), Civil Service Catering Organization	264.0	5.60
C&E	Board of Customs and Excise	128.1	29.30
HMSO	Her Majesty's Stationery Office	123.9	7.40
LCD	Lord Chancellor's Department (including Public Trustee)	93.5	10.40
DNS	Department for National Savings	71.8	13.60
IBAP	Intervention Board for Agricultural Produce	58.7	0.50
COI	Central Office of Information	21.4	1.40
OS	Ordnance Survey	18.6	4.40
LR	Land Registry	17.9	4.90
OPCS	Office of Population Censuses and Surveys	9.6	2.70
PCO	Privy Council Office	0.3	0.05

[a]Includes: Central Services, Scottish Development Department, Scottish Economic Planning Department, Scottish Education Department, Scottish Home and Health Department, and Department of Agriculture and Fisheries for Scotland.

[b]Includes: Manpower Services Commission, Health and Safety Executive/Committee, and Advisory, Conciliation and Arbitration Service.

[c]Management and Personnel Office (MPO) from 1981.

[d]1977 figures (DOE & DTp were one department in 1976).

TABLE 13.2. Departments Arrayed by Frequency and Extent of Reductions in Budget and Staff, 1976–1983

STAFF/BUDGET	Neither continuous nor deep	Continuous squeeze on budget	Deep cuts in budget	Both continuous and deep
Neither continuous nor deep	DHSS LR HO DE LCD WO	DTp IR SO C&E IBAP FOO	ECGD	
Continuous squeeze on staff				
Deep cuts in staff	OPCS			
Both continuous and deep	MOD COI DEn PCO TCC DES	NIO	HMSO	MAFF OS DNS DOE DIn DTr

Continuous squeeze = budget cuts in four or more years out of seven, staff cuts in six or more years out of seven.

Deep cuts = budget overall reduction in real terms over period, staff overall reductions of more than 15%.

TABLE 13.3. Non-industrial Home Civil Service by Group and Grade Level, April 1, 1980, and April 1, 1983

	Administrative Group (including related departmental classes)	Science Group and related grades	Professional and Technical Group and related grades	Other specialist groups	Total
Open structure levels (US & above)					
1980					811
1983					690
Change (%)					(−14.9)
Assistant Secretary and grades between AS and US					
1980	1,300	950	850	2,100	5,200
1983	1,210	850	730	1,750	4,540
Change (%)	(−6.9)	(−10.5)	(−14.1)	(−16.7)	(−12.7)
Principal and Senior Principal					
1980	7,100	2,500	2,500	6,000	18,100
1983	6,560	2,250	2,250	6,000	17,060
Change (%)	(−7.6)	(−10.0)	(−10.0)	(−5.7)	
Executive Officer to Senior Executive Officer					
1980	122,200	10,800	37,400	44,800	215,200
1983	116,700	9,900	32,600	41,850	201,050
Change (%)	(−4.5)	(−8.3)	(−12.8)	(−6.6)	(−6.6)
Clerical Officer and below					
1980	244,000	3,200	300	53,900	301,400
1983	235,850	2,450	150	50,250	288,700
Change (%)	(−3.3)	(−23.4)	(−50.0)	(−6.8)	(−4.2)
Totals					
1980	374,600	17,450	41,050	106,800	540,711
1983	360,320	15,450	35,730	99,850	512,040
Change (%)	(−3.8)	(−11.5)	(−13.0)	(−6.5)	(−5.3)

Sources: HC 423, 1980–81; MPO report to Treasury and Civil Service Committee, 1983, 207, Note 4, no date.

TABLE 13.4. The Beck Jørgensen Model: Style of Cutbacks

Climate	Process	Operation	Style

Cuts temporary
Tighten belts
Growth psychology
  retained
	Prune estimates
	Superficial
	  search
	  process
	Seize on any
	  excuses for
	  cuts
		Cash limiting
		Defer capital expenditures
		Recruitment clampdown
		Reduce service standards
			Incremental

Could be long haul
  to recovery
Build-up of
  detrimental effects
  of incremental cuts
  noted
	Stress
	  efficiency
	Emphasize
	  structural
	  reorganization
	Reform training
	Accept higher
	  search and
	  disruption
	  costs
		Improve methods
		Program analysis, import
		  consultants
		Charge for services
		Shift burdens to clients,
		  suppliers, etc.
		Hiving off
		Privatization
			Managerial

Belief in eventual
  regrowth gone
Skepticism on value
  of "efficiency"
	Comprehensive
	  political
	  evaluation of
	  role of
	  public sector
	Search for cuts
	  with
	  increasing
	  returns
		Shutdowns
		Dropping functions
		Legislative redrafting
			Strategic

Source: Adapted from Beck Jørgensen (1987a).

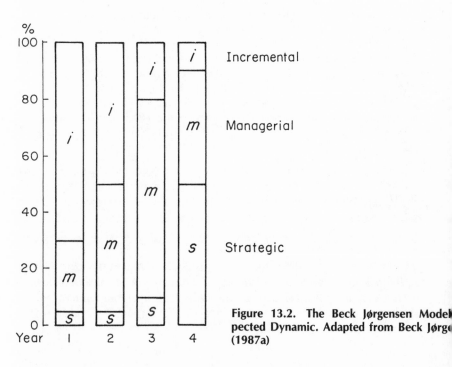

Figure 13.2. The Beck Jørgensen Model Expected Dynamic. Adapted from Beck Jørgensen (1987a)

References

Ackroyd, C.; Margolis, K.; Rosenhead, J.; and Shallice, T. *The Technology of Political Control.* Harmondsworth: Penguin Books, 1977.

Bates, E. "Can the Public's Voice Influence Bureaucracy? The Case of Community Health Councils." *Public Administration* 60, no. 1 (1982):92–98.

Beck Jørgensen, T. "Models of Retrenchment Behavior." *Working Paper No. 24.* Brussels: International Institute of Administrative Sciences, 1987a.

———. "Financial Management in the Public Sector." In *Managing Public Organizations.* Edited by J. Kooiman and K. A. Eliassen. London: Sage, 1987b.

Benn, A. "Manifestos and Mandarins." In W. Rodgers et al., *Policy and Practice: The Experience of Government.* London: Royal Institute of Public Administration, 1980.

———. *Arguments for Democracy.* Harmondsworth: Penguin Books, 1982.

Blau, P. M. *The Dynamics of Bureaucracy,* 2d ed. Chicago: University of Chicago Press, 1963.

Boaden, N.; Goldsmith, M.; Hampton, W.; and Stringer, P. *Public Participation in Local Services.* London: Longman, 1982.

Brown, R. G. S. *The Management of Welfare: A Study of British Social Services Administration.* Glasgow: Fontant/Collins, 1975.

Bunbury, Sir Henry. "Efficiency as an Alternative to Control." *Public Administration* 6 (1928):96–105. Reprinted in *Style in Administration: Readings in British Public Administration,* p. 32–44. Edited by R. A. Chapman and A. Dunsire. London: George Allen and Unwin, 1971.

Caiden, G. *Administrative Reform.* London: Allen Lane, 1970.

Cassells, J. *Review of Personnel Work in the Civil Service.* Management and Personnel Office. London: Her Majesty's Stationery Office, 1983.

Chapman, L. *Your Disobedient Servant: The Continuing Story of Whitehall's Overspending.* London: Chatto and Windus, 1978. Also Harmondsworth: Penguin Books, 1979.

Chapman, R. A., ed. *The Role of Commissions in Policy Making.* London: George Allen and Unwin, 1973.

Chester, D. N., ed., and Willson, F. M. G. *The Organization of British Central Government, 1914–1964.* London: George Allen and Unwin, 1968.

Clarke, Sir Richard. *New Trends in Government,* Civil Service College Studies no. 1. London: Her Majesty's Stationery Office, 1971.

Dearlove, J. *The Reorganisation of British Local Government.* Cambridge: Cambridge University Press, 1979.

Dicey, A. V. *Introduction to the Study of the Law of the Constitution,* 10th ed. London: Macmillan, 1959.

Donnison, D. *The Politics of Poverty.* Oxford: Martin Robertson, 1982.

Dunleavy, P., and Rhodes, R. A. W. "Beyond Whitehall." In *Developments in British Politics.* Edited by H. Drucker et al. London: Macmillan, 1984.

Dunsire, A. *Administration: The Word and the Science.* London: Martin Robertson, 1973a.

_____. "Administrative Doctrine and Administrative Change." *Public Administration Bulletin* 15 (1973b):173–88.

_____. "The Moral Dimension of Administrative Reform." In *Life in Public Administration*. Edited by L. Klinkers. Amsterdam: Kobra, 1985.

Efficiency and Effectiveness in the Civil Service. Cmnd 8616. London: Her Majesty's Stationery Office, 1982.

Expenditure Committee 1976–77, 11th Report. *The Civil Service*. HC 535-I. London: Her Majesty's Stationery Office, 1976.

Financial Management in Government Departments. Cmnd 9058. London: Her Majesty's Stationery Office, 1983.

Fry, G. K. *Statesmen in Disguise: The Changing Role of the Administrative Class of the British Home Civil Service, 1853–1966*. London: Macmillan, 1969.

_____. *The Changing Civil Service*. London: George Allen and Unwin, 1985.

Funnell, B. M., and Hay, R. D., eds. *The Management of Water Resources in England and Wales*. London: Saxon House, 1974.

Goldsmith, M. J., ed. *New Research in Central-Local Relations*. Farnborough: Gower, 1985.

Gray, A. G., and Jenkins, W. I., eds. *Policy Analysis and Evaluation in British Government*. London: Royal Institute of Public Administration, 1983.

_____. *Administrative Politics in British Government*. Brighton: Wheatsheaf Books, 1985.

Greenwood, R.; Walsh, K.; Hinings, C. R.; and Ranson, S. *Patterns of Management in Local Government*. Oxford: Martin Robertson, 1980.

Griffith, J. A. G., and Street, H. *Principles of Administrative Law,* 5th ed. London: Pitman, 1973.

Hennessy, P.; Morrison, S.; and Townsend, R. *Routine Punctuated by Orgies: the CPRS, 1970–83*. Glasgow: University of Strathclyde, 1984.

Hill, M. J. *The Sociology of Public Administration*. London: Weidenfeld and Nicolson, 1972.

_____. *The State, Administration and the Individual*. Glasgow: Fontana/Collins, 1976.

Holland, P., and Fallon, M. *The Quango Explosion: Public Bodies and Ministerial Patronage*. London: Conservative Political Centre, 1978.

Hood, C. C. "The Rise and Rise of the British Quango." *New Society,* 16 Aug. 1973.

_____. "Government by Other Means." In *WJMM: Political Questions*. Edited by B. C. Chapman and A. M. Potter. Manchester: Manchester University Press, 1975a.

_____. "Keeping the Centre Small: Explanations of Agency Type." *Political Studies* 26, no. 1 (1978):30–46.

_____. "Axeperson, Spare That Quango. . . ." In *Big Government in Hard Times*. Edited by C. C. Hood and M. Wright. Oxford: Martin Robertson, 1981.

_____. "Governmental Bodies and Government Growth." In *Quangos in Britain: Government and the Networks of Public Policy Making*. Edited by A. Barker. London: Macmillan, 1982.

_____. *The Tools of Government*. London: Macmillan, 1983.

_____. "British Administrative Trends and the Public Choice Revolution." In *Bureaucracy and Public Resource Allocation.* Edited by J. E. Lane. London: Sage, 1986.

Hood, C. C., and Dunsire, A. *Bureaumetrics: The Quantitative Comparison of British Central Government Agencies.* Farnborough: Gower, 1981.

Hood, C. C., with Mackenzie, W. J. M. "Appendix III: The Problem of Classifying Institutions." In *Public Policy and Private Interests: The Institutions of Compromise.* Edited by D. C. Hague et al. London: Macmillan, 1975b.

Hoskyns, J. "Whitehall and Westminster: An Outsider's View." *Parliamentary Affairs* 36 (1983):137–47.

_____. "Conservatism Is Not Enough." *Political Quarterly* 55 (1984):3–16.

Howells, D. J. "The Manpower Services Commission: The First Five Years." *Public Administration* 58 (1980):305–32.

Johnson, N. "The Reorganisation of Central Government." *Public Administration* 49 (1971):1–12.

_____. "Change in the Civil Service: Retrospect and Prospects." *Public Administration* 63 (1985):415–33.

Joint Management Unit. *Policy Work and the FMI.* HM Treasury. June 1985. London: Her Majesty's Stationery Office.

Kettle, M. "The Police." In *Developments in British Politics,* p. 197–208. Edited by H. Drucker et al. London: Macmillan, 1984.

Keynes, J. M. *The End of Laissez-Faire.* London: Hogarth Press, 1926.

Klein, R. *The Politics of the National Health Service.* London: Longman, 1983.

Lee, M. "Financial Management and Career Service." *Public Administration* 62, no. 1 (1984):1–6.

Levine, C. H., ed. "Symposium: Organizational Decline and Cutback Management." *Public Administration Review* 38, no. 4 (1978):316–25.

Levine, C. H.; Rubin, I. S.; and Wolohojian, G. C. *The Politics of Retrenchment: How Local Governments Manage Fiscal Crisis.* Beverly Hills: Sage, 1981.

Local Government in England: Government Proposals for Reorganisation. Cmnd 4584. London: Her Majesty's Stationery Office, 1971.

Mackintosh, J. P. *The Government and Politics of Great Britain,* 4th ed. London: Hutchinson, 1977.

March, J. G., and Olsen, J. P. "Organising Political Life: What Administrative Reorganization Tells Us About Government." *American Political Science Review* 77 (1983):281–95.

Marini, F., ed. *Toward a New Public Administration.* Scranton, Pa.: Chandler, 1971.

Martin, S. *Managing Without Managers.* Beverly Hills: Sage, 1983.

Mashaw, J. L. *Bureaucratic Justice: Managing Social Security Claims.* New Haven: Yale University Press, 1983.

Mayntz, R. "The Changing Conditions of Effective Public Policy: A New Challenge for Policy Analysis." Forschungsgruppe 1981–2, Preprint Series no. 9. Bielefeld: ZiF Universität Bielefeld, 1981.

Metcalfe, L., and Richards, S. "The Impact of Efficiency Strategy: Political Clout or Cultural Change." *Public Administration* 62, no. 4 (1984):439–54.

Milne, D. *The Scottish Office.* New Whitehall Series. London: George Allen and Unwin, 1957.

Moon, J., and Richardson, J. J. "Policy-Making With a Difference? The Technical and Vocational Initiative." *Public Administration* 62, no. 1 (1984):23–33.

Mueller, D. *Public Choice.* Cambridge: Cambridge University Press, 1979.

National Health Service Reorganisation: England. Cmnd 5055. London: Her Majesty's Stationery Office, 1972.

The New Local Authorities: Management and Structure (The Bains Report). Department of the Environment. London: Her Majesty's Stationery Office, 1972.

Niskanen, W. A. *Bureaucracy and Representative Government.* Chicago: Aldine Atherton, 1971.

Ostrom, V., and Ostrom, E. "Public Choice: A Different Approach to the Study of Public Administration." *Public Administration Review* 31 (1971):302–16.

Plowden, W. "The British Central Policy Review Staff." In *Policy Analysis and Policy Innovation,* ch. 4. Edited by P. R. Baehr and B. Whittrock. London: Sage, 1981.

———. "What Prospects for the Civil Service?" *Public Administration* 63, no. 4 (1985):393–414.

Pollitt, C. *Manipulating the Machine, Changing the Pattern of Ministerial Departments, 1960–83.* London: George Allen and Unwin, 1984.

Ponting, C. *The Right to Know: The Inside Story of the Belgrano Affair.* London: Sphere Books, 1985.

Progress in Financial Management in Government Departments. Cmnd 9297. London: Her Majesty's Stationery Office, 1984.

Pryke, R. *The Nationalised Industries: Policies and Performance Since 1968.* Oxford: Martin Robertson, 1981.

Randall, J. "The Servants Answer Back." *The Guardian,* 21 Feb. 1986.

The Reorganisation of Central Government. Cmnd 4506. London: Her Majesty's Stationery Office, 1970.

Report of the (Franks) Committee on Administrative Tribunals and Inquiries. Cmnd 218. London: Her Majesty's Stationery Office, 1957.

Report of the (Fulton) Committee on the Civil Service. Cmnd 3638. London: Her Majesty's Stationery Office, 1968.

Report of the (Haldane) Committee on the Machinery of Government. Cd 9230. London: Her Majesty's Stationery Office, 1918.

Report of the (Plowden) Committee on the Control of Public Expenditure. Cmnd 1432. London: Her Majesty's Stationery Office, 1961.

Rhodes, R. A. W. *Control and Power in Central-Local Relations.* Farnborough: Gower, 1981.

———. *The National World of Local Government.* London: George Allen and Unwin, 1988.

Richardson, J. J. "Programme Evaluation in Britain and Sweden." *Parliamentary Affairs* 35 (1982):160–80.

Richardson, J. J., and Jordan, A. G. *Governing Under Pressure: The Policy Process in a Post-Parliamentary Democracy.* London: Martin Robertson, 1974.

Ridley, F. F. "The Job Creation Programme: Administrative Problems in Implementation." *Public Administration* 58 (1980):261–85.

_____. "Employment: The Job Creation Programme." In *Policies Into Practice: National and International Case Studies in Implementation.* Edited by D. Lewis and H. Wallace. London: Heinemann, 1984.

RIPA. *Management, Information and Control in Whitehall.* London: Royal Institute of Public Administration, 1983.

Ryan, M. *The Acceptable Pressure Group: Inequality in the Penal Lobby; A Case Study of the Howard League and RAP.* Farnborough: Saxon House, 1978.

Schaffer, B. B. *The Administrative Factor: Papers in Organization, Politics, and Development.* London: Frank Cass, 1973.

Shonfield, A. *Modern Capitalism: The Changing Balance of Public and Private Power.* London: Oxford University Press for RIIA, 1965.

Sieghart, P. *The Big Public Inquiry: A Proposed New Procedure for the Impartial Investigation of Projects with Major National Implications.* London: Outer Circle Policy Unit, 1979.

Sked, A., and Cook, C. *Post-War Britain: A Political History,* 2d ed. Harmondsworth: Penguin Books, 1984.

Smith, A. *An Inquiry Into the Nature and Causes of the Wealth of Nations* (1776). Two vols. London: Dent, 1910.

Smith, T. *The Politics of the Corporate Economy.* London: Martin Robertson, 1979.

Stacey, F. *Ombudsmen Compared.* Oxford: Oxford University Press, 1978.

Taylor, A. J. "The Politics of Coal: Some Aspects of the Miners' Strike." *Politics* 5, no. 1 (1985):3–9.

Thompson, V. A. *Without Sympathy or Enthusiasm: The Problem of Administrative Compassion.* Tuscaloosa, Ala.: University of Alabama Press, 1975.

Tivey, L. *Nationalization in British Industry.* London: Jonathan Cape, 1973.

_____. "Quasi-government for Consumers." In *Quangos in Britain: Government and the Networks of Public Policy Making.* Edited by A. Barker. London: Macmillan, 1982, p. 137–51.

Tyme, J. *Motorways versus Democracy.* London: Macmillan, 1978.

Wade, H. W. R. *Administrative Law,* 5th ed. Oxford: Clarendon Press, 1982.

Warner, N. "Raynerism in Practice: Anatomy of a Rayner Scrutiny." *Public Administration* 62, no. 1 (1984a):7–22.

_____. "The DHSS Social Security Regional Organization – An Exercise in Managerial Change." *Public Administration* 62, no. 3 (1984b):251–71.

Wass, D. *Government and the Governed.* London: George Allen and Unwin, 1984.

_____. "The Civil Service at the Crossroads." *Political Quarterly* 56 (July 1985).

Whitehorn, K. "Whitehall's New Wave." *Observer,* 16 Mar. 1986.

Whynes, D. K., and Bowles, R. A. *The Economic Theory of the State.* Oxford: Martin Robertson, 1981.

Wildavsky, A. *The Art and Craft of Policy Analysis.* London: Macmillan, 1979.

Williams, R. *The Nuclear Power Decisions: British Policies, 1953–78.* London: Croom Helm, 1980.

Young, H. and Sloman, A. *No, Minister: An Inquiry into the Civil Service.* London: British Broadcasting Corporation, 1982.

14

Policy Developments and Administrative Changes in the United States

KEITH M. HENDERSON

AN OUTSIDE OBSERVER of American policy developments and administrative changes over the last decade or two could be easily perplexed by the myriad interpretations and viewpoints available in the scholarly literature, the press, and public discussion. Much attention is centered on presidents and their policies with careful analysis and discussion of budgetary and civil service reduction-in-force proposals, pronouncements on the bureaucracy, cutback strategies, and Supreme Court decisions or legislative actions. Every informed citizen has heard of supply-side economics and the debate over Defense Department expenditure levels. Scholarly discussion has shed light on the effects of the 1978 Civil Service Reform Act (CSRA) and the various Congressional actions to curb executive powers: the War Powers Act, the Budget and Impoundment Act, and similar measures. Out of this welter of conflicting and confusing dialogue, it is difficult for a reader interested in the U.S. as a point of reference for comparative public administration studies to extract meaningful insights.

This chapter attempts to assist in that regard and to highlight — from a public administration perspective — some of the salient recent developments. These might be summarized under several headings: organization and reorganization; policy processes; budget; and personnel. Such a classificatory scheme of necessity neglects numerous policy fields, as well as detailed analysis of institutional changes and social trends. However, it does provide a possibly useful guide through the labyrinthian corridors of the American public administration establishment — an establishment that is constantly under surveillance from a critical press, interest groups, and the general public, as well as the scholarly community.

The perspective adopted here encompasses the political atmosphere of administration and the implications of administrative actions for the broader social and economic spheres. It also incorporates academic thinking on these topics as of the mid and late 1980s.

Organization and Reorganization

The strategy of fundamentally restructuring the executive establishment to accomplish goals of efficiency and economy as well as streamlined service delivery, has not been used in the '60s, '70s, and '80s to the extent it once was. The tendency in the Kennedy and Johnson presidencies — particularly the latter — was to add new agencies to accomplish Great Society or War on Poverty programs without affecting existing operations. Most of these agencies were outside the traditional line departments and reported directly or indirectly to the president rather than to a department head. For example, the Economic Opportunity Act of 1964 created the Office of Economic Opportunity within the executive office of the president with program responsibility for Operation Headstart (for preschool children), the Neighborhood Youth Corps (for teenagers), and the well-known Community Action Programs. Associated with the new agencies and programs were requirements for program evaluation necessitating considerable emphasis upon policy analysis performed by quantitatively sophisticated analysts. The resulting studies or their by-products, when published, have provided a rich literature on these agencies and programs.

The Nixon/Ford years — 1968–76 — witnessed a number of policy developments and administrative changes but no fundamental restructuring of the executive branch. One of President Nixon's first administrative actions was to create a mechanism for studying and implementing reorganizations and management improvements by revamping the Bureau of the Budget into the Office of Management and Budget. A reorganization plan in 1970 established — within the increasingly important executive office of the president — a "bifurcated structure" with stress upon both management and budgeting. In his 1968 campaign, Nixon had proclaimed the need for reform of administrative practices and this was to be the institutional mechanism for such reform. Later, an attempt was made to more closely integrate the management control and budget functions. President Nixon's attention to administration was reflected in a subsequent attempt to induce Congress to fundamentally reorganize existing government departments: four new departments — community development, natural resources, economic affairs, and human resources would replace the existing departments of interior; commerce; health, education, and welfare; housing and urban development; and transportation. That this had been proposed once before by the Nixon administration and followed a similar plan by President Johnson illustrated the difficulty of implementing a reorganization strategy. Congress has resisted such proposals with a high degree of consistency; the famed "iron triangle" of interest groups, Congressional representatives, and concerned bureaucrats has typically been mobilized to counter a threat to an existing institutional arrangement.

President Carter also encountered "iron triangles" in his quest to reform the bureaucracy but was able to oversee the creation of two new cabinet-level departments: energy and education. The former involved a drawing together of existing programs scattered throughout the government and was a timely political response to the perceived need to address the energy crisis of the time. The education department was carved from the health, education, and welfare organization (HEW), which was renamed health and human services. "Welfare" had long been a target for reform and the symbolic changing of name to "human services" appeared to be a step in the right direction. Administrative logic might decree a smaller operation than the massive HEW, which sandwiched education between two more compelling functions, but the real explanation for the creation of a new department of education may be found in candidate Carter's campaign pledges to the National Education Association—a powerful interest group representing teachers and one interested in independent status in the cabinet. It is interesting that President Reagan at one point proposed abolishing both the energy and education departments but as his presidency moved forward he gradually abandoned the idea.

Reorganization proposals are usually preceded by prestigious blue ribbon studies sometimes of major proportion. Every American student of public administration has heard of the comprehensive Brownlow Commission under President Roosevelt and the two Hoover Commission studies in the post-World War II period. In more recent times, President Kennedy established the Landis Commission to examine federal regulatory commissions and under President Nixon, Roy Ash—head of giant Litton Industries—was named chair of a study commission and later himself became director of the Office of Management and Budget, presumably placing him in a position to carry out his own recommendations. Although his major contribution was in the area of civil service reform, President Carter also sponsored other reorganization studies. Some studies are focused on particular agencies or arms of government such as the Packard Commission's concern—during the Reagan era—for the defense department; others are systemwide. Far surpassing the Landis Report, the Ash Council, and the

Packard study—in the scope and boldness of its proposals—was the Grace Commission study.

Under the feisty leadership of its chairman, J. Peter Grace, the President's Private Sector Survey on Cost Control issued a 47-volume report to the president in early 1984, which recommended far-reaching program and management changes that would save the astronomical sum of $424 billion over a three-year period, rising to $1.9 trillion per year by 2000. According to the controversial Grace Report, one-third of all taxes collected is consumed by waste and inefficiency, and much additional tax that is owed is not collected. Press, public, and the academic community, as well as government officials themselves, took a close look at the more impressive Grace suggestions and debated their merits. Grace himself went on the lecture circuit as a spirited defender of the report and critic of government spending. The sentiment was compatible with President Reagan's emphasis upon "getting government off our backs" (Grace 1984; Kennedy and Lee 1984).

The biggest target of all, the Pentagon, came under additional attack in another commission report, the President's Blue Ribbon Commission on Defense Management, known as the Packard Report for its chairman, former deputy defense secretary, David Packard. The commission recommended reducing interservice rivalry in weapons procurement by creating a civilian procurement chief with considerable power. It also sought to change the role of the Chairman of the Joint Chiefs to reduce "end runs on the Congress made by the individual services" (Final Report 1986).

Management improvement efforts attributable to outside investigations or internal review efforts are described, in terms favorable to the administration, in the yearly *Management of the United States Government:* Fiscal Year, 1987; 1988; 1989. Productivity improvements, paperwork reductions, credit management, and other public administration changes are accounted for in various publicity releases and in the budget documents, as well as the above publication. The independent General Accounting Office (GAO) reports provide a different version of organizational changes by critiquing the heavy administration stress on centralized controls (through the Office of Management and Budget; Office of Personnel Management; and General Services Administration) rather than reliance on the operating agencies themselves. The National Academy of Public Administration has been similarly critical of the administration's organizational improvement efforts, which often are imperfect adaptations from the business sector and may be demoralizing to the professional administrator (NAPA 1983).

During the 1960s, 1970s, and the Reagan years, American presidents have used their authority to secure a variety of policy changes in all areas of government. Although their memoirs and post-presidential pronounce-ments tell of the difficulties and frustrations of getting organizational pro-posals adopted by Congress and then properly implemented and of the obstacles to their decision making, presidents have fundamentally in-fluenced the federal structure during their terms of office. Agencies and programs once created tend to be self-perpetuating and, even if modified, to continue to address their original purposes. The Peace Corps still ex-ists — out of the limelight — as does the Environmental Protection Agency under less controversial leadership. The National Aeronautics and Space Administration was carefully scrutinized and heavily criticized following the disaster in which seven astronauts were killed but continued with its responsibilities for the space program. Only history will judge the time period in recent memory that contributed the most lasting organizational efforts.

Policy Processes and Developments

Shrinking the size of the federal government has been a major theme in public administration in the 1980s. Excepting defense and certain entitle-ment programs (such as Social Security), the attempt has been to reduce the rate of expansion in government which characterized the 1960s and early '70s, indeed, which has been a consistent pattern since the 1930s. The origi-nal impetus for reducing government intervention in the economic/social sphere came from the state level in the guise of a "taxpayers' revolt." In 1978, California passed a citizen-sponsored measure that would restrict property taxes and, hence, lessen revenues available to local governments. Proposition 13 as it was called was fortunately enacted at a time the State of California had a large revenue surplus in its treasury which could take some of the slack. Nevertheless, the impact was dramatic and was the harbinger of much that followed — similar ballot proposals in other state and local elections, many of them successful although most of them were of lesser magnitude than Proposition 13.

At approximately the same time, a corresponding attempt to reduce the amount of federal regulation was underway and, in 1978, the airline industry was substantially deregulated. The arguments for deregulation were similar to those for tax reduction: (1) Government is too costly — technically, many policy areas are not managed in a cost-effective manner; (2) government is attempting to do what the private sector can do better; (3) government interference does not contribute to a productive, expansive economy.

To those familiar with past efforts at reform, these arguments were not unusual. Numerous studies had called for emulation of the business model and for businesslike techniques in government. It was suggested that policy processes should be businesslike, properly evaluated, and nonpolitical; bureaucratic procedures should be simplified.

The new emphasis, however, went further by calling not so much for change in government programs as for their elimination or at least curtailment. The airlines would regulate themselves in a free-market environment; the State of California would get by with lower tax revenues.

Nevertheless, in the 1980s as in the 1970s social problems in the United States continued to crowd the public agenda. Legislative solutions were sought for the needs of the poor, sick, elderly, homeless, ill-housed, high-school dropouts, unemployed, working mothers, and other categories. Most domestic policy areas aroused differing responses among Democrats and Republicans, urban and rural interests, the liberal and conservative, and by region. Welfare — rechristened Human Services — was generally regarded to be in need of reform but the direction of reform was disputed. Health priorities turned towards specific problems (such as AIDS) at the same time as efforts were underway to curtail the rapidly escalating costs of programs such as Medicare. Housing policy shifted from large-scale construction projects to use of subsidies and vouchers. Education and training — from the standpoint of the federal government — were regarded as inadequate and incentives were provided to state and local governments and to the private sector for upgrading.

Some policy processes seemed to fail regardless of the level of expenditure. The most rapidly growing segment of the federal government in terms of rate of increase of funding was not defense or social service or debt service but agriculture. No matter what the government did during this period, agriculture seemed to remain in a state of perpetual crisis. The 1981 farm bill, which was intended to reduce the impact of inflation on farm commodity prices, actually priced farmers out of the world market with its generous subsidies and price supports and encouraged such overproduction that a large commodities glut resulted. Additional subsidy and trade legislation followed on an almost yearly basis.

In analyzing policy developments during the Reagan presidency, many ironies are evident. Agricultural policy may turn out to be the most expensive mistake but others of magnitude will undoubtedly surface. The overall cutback strategy, divorced from subsidy and support programs or entitlements, has the effect of indiscriminately cutting services. Moderately successful agencies may be cut back while badly run agencies are left alone (Rubin 1985, p. 199). Cutting from a base point uniformly across agencies does not require a justification of the quality of services provided at that base point and exempting programs for political reasons negates the president's claim to act cost-effectively.

Administrative Federalism

Another arena of policy developments concerned the nature of intergovernmental relations. In his 1982 State of the Union message, President Reagan proposed a New Federalism that would shift approximately 40 social, transportation, and community-development programs from the federal government to state governments. In return, the federal government would assume responsibility for the full cost of Medicaid health programs. The Food Stamp program and Aid to Families with Dependent Children would go to the states as well. Nothing much came of this particular proposal but the agenda had been set for changes in intergovernmental relations leading to a shift in responsibilities to the state level. Symptomatic of this shift was the abolishing through executive order of the Federal Regional Councils, which had coordinated grant applications for federal funds at a suprastate level, in 1983 and the redirecting of this activity to the state level. The argument was that the states should be full partners in a strengthened federal system but the overall effect was to begin to undo many of the policy initiatives of previous years. Many intergovernmental programs that could not be assumed by lower levels of government were significantly reduced in scope.

Through federal legislation, executive orders, and court decisions, state governments (and local governments within them) have been required to undertake an increasingly large number of tasks from toxic waste cleanup (Resource Conservation and Recovery Act of 1976) to prevention of discrimination based on age in state and local government employment (Age Discrimination in Employment Act of 1967 made applicable to state and local governments in 1974). Court decisions have defined the proper role of government and in many instances have required mechanisms of compliance or adjustments in funding. In turn, some local governments, in New York for example, have complained of the double burden of federal and state mandates. Complicated grant formulas, which were arrived at after political bargaining and compromise, have favored certain sections of the country at the expense of others: the Snow Belt of the Northeast and North Central states sometimes benefited from need formulas and the Sunbelt areas of the South and Southwest benefited from population formulas since a major demographic shift was the movement of people towards the South and West. Balancing or redistributing the federal largess has always been a political problem with elaborate mechanisms worked out for fair or equitable benefit. Critics point to the "pork-barrel" style of determining who gets what as members of Congress, interest group representatives, and bureaucrats themselves attempt to devise formulas. The character of the American political system stresses grouping according to single interest and free exercise of intentions to influence policy processes within a framework of agreed laws and rules. Most interests are represented but not with equal power.

Public Budgeting

In the United States, the budgetary process and its end result, the implemented federal budget, are critical elements not just in government financing but in macroeconomic impact. The federal budget and the process of formulating, adopting, and presenting it affect the entire economy—indeed, the international economic system—and contribute along with funding activities of the Treasury, decisions of the Federal Reserve Board, and other actions to overall fiscal and monetary policy. In recent years, there have been some significant budgetary changes with far-reaching implications: supply-side budgeting; the Gramm-Rudman-Hollings deficit reduction act (partially invalidated by Court decision but still applicable), and the Budget and Impoundment Act that created a new Congressional Budget Office (CBO), budget committees in both houses of Congress, a new budget timetable including a new budget year beginning October 1 instead of July 1, and restrictions on the president's ability to impound funds without Congressional notification.

Since 1921, the U.S. Federal Government has had an executive budget prepared by a centralized budget office and then submitted to Congress. The historical pattern has been for agencies to request increases in funding for the forthcoming fiscal year, which are reduced by the central budget office acting on behalf of the president, and then to have partial restoration of requested funds for favored agencies in the Congress, where final decisions on authorizations and appropriations are made.

Ronald Reagan became publicly committed to supply-side economics during his presidential campaign in 1980. The basic idea that tax reduction, as well as reduced government spending, would spur savings and investment and stimulate economic advance was put into effect in the 1981 Economic Recovery Tax Act. Subsequent economic recovery was attributed by political leadership on the Republican side to the tax-reduction measures and investment incentives, but it was certainly facilitated by fortuitous circumstances such as falling oil prices and lower interest rates. The total Reagan package of tax reduction, spending cuts, bigger defense programs, and economic expansion proved to be unrealistic as deficits (inherited from the Carter spending programs according to the Republicans) mounted higher and higher. The proposal for a balanced budget at the federal level, as found in state governments, did not make headway, but a measure calling for fixed deficit reduction targets elicited bipartisan support. The resulting Gramm-Rudman-Hollings Act establishes statutory ceilings on federal deficits. For fiscal year 1986, the maximum allowable was $171.9 billion (the actual deficit turned out to be $220 billion); for 1987, $144 billion; for 1988, $108 billion; for 1989, $72 billion; for 1990, $36 billion; and for 1991, 0. These original targets were later modified. Automatic spending cuts were to be triggered when the deficit ceiling was exceeded by a certain amount. It was the mechanism for putting into effect the automatic cuts that was challenged in a federal court and judged unconstitutional based on the Separation of Powers doctrine; nevertheless, both Congress and the president remained committed to the purposes of the act. For the president, it was one of several desirable budget reforms along with a balanced budget act, a line-item veto, and a separation of capital spending for construction and large acquisitions from the operating budget.

Under the Gramm-Rudman-Hollings bill (1985), the president is required to submit early in the calendar year a budget that does not exceed the deficit target. President Reagan, in his 1987 Budget Message, stated: "By submitting this budget, I am abiding by the law and keeping my part of the bargain" (Budget for Fiscal Year 1987, M-4). The president further indicated that it would be possible to eliminate the deficit without raising taxes (a campaign promise), without sacrificing defense preparedness, and without cutting into "legitimate programs for the poor and elderly" (Budget, M-4). The 1988 and 1989 Budget Messages of the President (M-5) repeated that sentiment. The Gramm law established not only the goals to be met but the enforcement procedure. In August of each year, following Congressional drafting of the budget blueprint, the White House Office of Management and Budget (OMB) and its counterpart in Congress, the Congressional Budget Office are required to make reports on the fiscal year scheduled to begin October 1, stating the projected budget deficit and the gap—if there is one—between that figure and the mandated statutory deficit. These reports would be sent to the General Accounting Office (GAO) for review as an auditing agency (the GAO is in the legislative branch), and it would prepare a list of cuts to be made according to Congressional guidelines. These cuts would be sent to the president who would issue instructions making them applicable by October 15. The Gramm law requires that cuts in equal amounts be made for military and nonmilitary purposes. Exempt from automatic cuts are Social Security retirement and disability payments, Medicaid (the federal-state program providing health care for those of low incomes), food stamps (subsidizing food purchases for the poor), veterans' pensions and payments, and several other human services (welfare) and child nutrition programs. Reductions for certain human services programs are limited to one percent in the first year and two percent in subsequent years. Recessions or wars are the only periods when the plan can be suspended.

In a pattern that does not vary drastically from year to year, a substantial portion of revenue is raised from the individual income tax and the largest appropriations are for entitlement programs and defense.

The budgetary process in the United States has traditionally been highly fragmented and has called forth various proposals for greater rationality. Several years ago, students of Public Administration often spent considerable time studying Planning, Programming, Budgeting System (PPBS), and more recently Management By Objectives as applied to budgeting or, under President Carter, the Zero Based Budget (ZBB) concept, which was designed to list policy priorities and alternatives (such as having a program performed by the private sector) with justification from ground zero. Previous nonpolitical formats such as the original performance budget proposals of the First Hoover Commission in 1949, predate all of these. Most of the formats improved considerably on the old line-item process (still used in some local jurisdictions) but suffered from common weaknesses: they required much analytical work by highly trained specialists; they required a high degree of centralization; and they were executive branch dominated. These problems were also their strengths since the basic purpose was to achieve greater rationality, cost-effectiveness, and meaningful decision-making desiderata apart from political considerations. As A. Wildavsky, A. Schick, R. Lee, T. D. Lynch and others have carefully documented, the politics of administration and the influence of political actors in the American system were not to be ignored (Wildavsky 1984, 1988; Schick 1980; Lee 1983; Lynch 1985). In an attempt to assert greater Congressional control over budgeting (instead of simply reacting to the OMB's budget submitted to it on behalf of the president and acquiescing to impoundment actions), an act was passed in 1974 creating a new budget timetable, Congressional budget committees and an office for budgeting, and restrictions on the impoundment of funds.

The Congressional capacity to examine the budget as a whole has been significantly strengthened since passage of the Budget and Impoundment Control Act even though many aspects of the act have not been followed. The numerous analytic reports of the highly skilled Congressional Budget Office attest to this small organization's usefulness as a counterweight to the powerful OMB. Differing estimates on figures such as the deficit are based on different assumptions about economic conditions and do not reflect lesser analytic abilities than found in the OMB.

In addition to the new Congressional budget committees, the Joint Economic Committee, the House Ways and Means Committee, the Senate Finance Committee, and the House and Senate Appropriations Committees remain critically important in the budget process.

On the executive side, additional efforts have been made to further strengthen OMB. While its principal mission remains budgetary, allied functions have also moved to the fore. Reform 88, the much heralded management improvement plan for federal procedures, was to be coordinated by the OMB. It would serve as an umbrella for a variety of actions including federal debt collection improvements, elimination of travel abuse, and forms control, as well as provision of assistance to the President's Council on Integrity and Efficiency (Benda and Levine 1986, p. 386).

A final and little noticed change in the Office of Management and Budget occurred in 1981 under Executive Order 12291. The OMB was given additional legislative review functions to provide clearance for all regulatory changes proposed by federal agencies. This power was particularly important in relationship to entitlement programs.

The yearly struggle over the budget continues with Congress inclined to consider narrower constituency interests and to resist efforts to curb spending in favored programs. Legislation providing for major tax reform in 1986 was a conspicuous success for the president and its "revenue neutral" stipulations allowed the Republicans to remain within their guidelines for not raising taxes. Coupled with the earlier tax reductions, it was politically popular but did not alter the traditional need to balance interests and compete for resources.

The election of George Bush in November 1988 promised continuity in policy but few easy solutions to mounting deficits, Third World debt problems, and a growing crisis in the nation's savings and loan industry.

Managing the Public Services

Unlike the budget process, public personnel administration (frequently called human resources administration or management) remains largely in the background, unaffected by public scrutiny. Episodic accounts in the media concerning dismissals, whistleblowing, conflict of interest, or striking employees mask the real behind-the-scenes drama of government officials on a daily basis pursuing their duties and responsibilities. They also mask the story of slowly evolving struggles to modernize the merit system — a staple of American public administration since 1883 — and to adjust to new developments in the area of Equal Employment Opportunity and Affirmative Action beginning with the civil rights developments of the 1960s.

The reformist actions of the Carter years, culminating in the Civil Service Reform Act of 1978, are the result of many years of debate and dissatisfaction over the operation of the Civil Service Commission (CSC), the traditional guardian of the merit system originally designed to "keep the rascals out." The CSC had not failed so much as fallen out of step with the demands of modern personnel practice and the needs of a complex bureaucracy. Under President Eisenhower, the chairman of the CSC was given a new role as presidential advisor (Truman and Roosevelt had personnel liaison officers) and with Presidents Kennedy and Johnson, the CSC Chair was used informally to recruit high-level appointees. It wasn't until 1966, however, that a prestigious task force was convened to make recommendations and propose legislation on more fundamental modifications in the CSC. Convened by John Macy, a Civil Service Commission member, the task force incorporated a fundamental recommendation of the Second Hoover Commission (1955) in its suggestions—a federal executive service modeled on the British generalist pattern. The ideas of the task force— representing a consensus of numerous forward thinkers in public personnel administration—became politically controversial and although President Nixon supported the recommendations when they were finalized in 1970 his support was not enthusiastic enough to win passage; nothing happened. Meanwhile, the Watergate episode was beginning to unfold and by the time its implications had been assimilated (including the related manipulations such as the so-called Malek Manual, a guide for circumventing the restrictions of the Civil Service System by the politically appointed deputy director of OMB), the time was ripe for change. President Carter came to office on a tide of disaffection with the federal government establishment and made commitments to introduce a new style of administration not based on Washington insiders' ways. One of his early efforts was to sell the bureaucrats themselves on the need for basic changes in the federal government's civil service organization and procedures. Town meetings with civil servants, public support building, and Congressional suasion were used simultaneously to pave the way for the Civil Service Reform Act, which became law in 1978.

The CSRA contained a wide number of provisions, the most important of which were as follows:

1. It abolished the Civil Service Commission and in its place created two separate agencies: an Office of Personnel Management and a Merit Protection Board.

2. It created a senior executive service.

3. It provided for merit pay for employees in Grades GS-13 through GS-15.

4. It required meaningful performance appraisal systems in agencies.

5. It protected whistleblowers.

6. It established the labor relations program of the federal service on a statutory basis.

In general, there was a major restructuring of the entire federal civil service system with additional protection for employee rights coupled with greater flexibility for management. Some of the traditional rigidities such as inflexible salary schedules with guaranteed advancement were relaxed and opportunities for lateral movement and reassignment were increased. Perhaps the two most significant parts of the act are the two new agencies and the Senior Executive Service (SES).

The Office of Personnel Management advises the president on personnel matters and coordinates government-wide personnel programs.

The Merit Systems Protection Board is the new appellate arm of the Civil Service System. It is given authority to hear disputed issues concerning merit system principles and to rule on them in quasi-judicial fashion. (Decisions, of course, under certain circumstances can be appealed into the federal courts.) The board may also conduct studies and review rules and regulations of the Office of Personnel Management (OPM). The effect is to have a separated appellate body apart from other programs previously conducted by the single (and now abolished) Civil Service Commission. Those programs are now in the Office of Personnel Management along with new coordinative activities created by the CSRA. The OPM got off to a poor start since the transition from the Carter to the Reagan presidency interfered with the implementation of its designs and political considerations in the appointment of its directors (especially Donald Devine) caused considerable backlash (Ingraham and Ban 1984; Levine 1985).

The establishment of the SES addressed a long-felt need within the federal service to provide greater mobility and flexibility for high-level executives. The common refrain was that a restrictive civil service system prevented the opportunities for reassignment and career advancement based on recognition of true merit that were found in large-scale businesses and in British government. Freeing up salaries and career paths it was argued would improve the quality of the federal service. Those who perform especially meritoriously receive cash bonuses and awards; those dismissed from the SES are entitled to a lower-level position in an agency. SES is applicable to grades GS-16, 17, and 18, and executive levels IV and V. The "rank in man" concept, as in British public administration, rather than "rank in job" is used; presumably, the federal government is better served with flexible conditions of employment designed to attract and retain the very best individuals.

The record on SES (like the OPM) is mixed but it is clear that it has fallen far short of its goals. Between July 1979 and March 1983, more than 40 percent of the SES left government service (Levine 1986, p. 200). Several surveys have shown a decline in morale among the higher levels of the federal service.

Both the Carter administration and Congress found the first SES bonuses too ample and too widely distributed (up to 50 percent of the career executives could receive awards in amounts up to 20 percent of base salary; 5 percent may receive the rank of "meritorious executive" with a $10,000 payment, and one percent a $20,000 award). Consequently, steps were taken to restrict the payments by reducing to 20 percent the number eligible. Similarly, the merit pay provisions for mid-level administrators (GS13–GS15) were not fully funded, in this instance by simply not appropriating enough money.

Other aspects of the Civil Service Reform Act also encountered difficulties between the design and the implementation. Of particular note is the new performance evaluation system that altered past practices by eliminating the time-honored three category rating system (outstanding, satisfactory, unsatisfactory) and requiring more sophisticated arrangements linking ratings to individual performance and using this as a basis for personnel actions such as promotions. The Office of Personnel Management as the standard setter assists agencies in devising new rating procedures and approves each agency's system prior to implementation. One of the difficulties encountered in implementation was a very early deadline for establishing the required appraisal systems (July 1979). Both the General Accounting Office and the prestigious National Academy of Public Administration expressed doubts about the feasibility of such an early date. Another problem was the perceived politicization of the appraisals since political appointees who rate higher-level bureaucrats have additional power over bonuses, which are tied to the ratings. Surveys of federal employees revealed that only a small percentage believed that performance appraisals were helpful in measuring effectiveness (OPM surveys 1980).

Two aspects of public personnel administration addressed in part by the Civil Service Reform Act but also subject to other important influences are collective bargaining and affirmative action. The former involved some changes in the government's labor relations programs and the latter recruiting programs for minorities and women and a strengthened and coordinative power for the Equal Employment Opportunity Commission (EEOC).

Government labor relations have undergone many changes in recent years. Within the broader context of recession and recovery, public employee unions have attempted to recapture a momentum that was lost in the early 1980s, if not before. One major setback for all federal unions was the well-known confrontation between the Reagan administration and the Professional Air Traffic Controllers' Association (PATCO) in 1981. PATCO, which had been granted exclusive recognition as the sole bargaining agent of the nation's air traffic controllers, won a number of favorable contracts in the 1970s and developed a confrontational style that involved job actions and ongoing conflict with the Federal Aviation Agency. In 1981, the membership overwhelmingly rejected a management offer for a $40 million settlement and on August 3, officially struck against the government. Such strikes, of course, are illegal and the President of the United States not only fired the controllers but also took steps to have the union decertified. His action was successful, if forceful, and served to remind other unions of the hazards of confrontational actions.

Public employee unions had gained in membership and in political power throughout the 1960s and 1970s, lagging by a few years the same accomplishments in private sector labor relations. At the state and local levels, even more than at the federal, powerful unions were obtaining gains in salary, benefits, and working conditions during this period. Gradual changes began to occur before the PATCO strike but that signaled the end of an expansionist era for public unions for at least the immediate future; membership declines and frustrated efforts in organization drives followed.

The newer emphasis in collective bargaining is towards cooperative union relationships with participatory arrangements for union involvement in decision making, grievance procedures, and protection of employee rights. Productivity bargaining has been required by some jurisdictions with specific linkages between salary and benefit increases and measurable improvements in productivity.

Equal Employment Opportunity and its more forceful supplement Affirmative Action have an even more checkered recent history than government labor relations. Efforts to redress discriminatory practices and affirmatively move towards goals of representativeness in employment have involved legislative, executive, and judicial actions at the federal level — some of them aimed at extension to the state and local levels — and many of them applicable to all employment situations. The Civil Rights Act of 1964 had prohibited discrimination based on race, religion, national origin, or sex; age discrimination was explicitly outlawed in the Age Discrimination in Employment Act of 1967. Women and men were required to be paid the same if the work was the same at an even earlier date, 1963 (Equal Pay Act). However, having the laws on the books was not sufficient and numerous implementing mechanisms were drawn up along with challenges in the courts. An ambiguous and confusing picture emerged as specific enforcement actions and court cases decided on an individual basis presented a patchwork of viewpoints. Three Supreme Court cases in the 1970s generated particular influence. Griggs et al. v. Duke Power Company (1971); Regents of the University of California v. Bakke (1978); and United Steelworkers of America v. Weber (1979). Interpreting the 1964 Civil Rights Act (Title VII), the Court unanimously found in the Griggs case that not only overt discrimination but practices that are discriminatory in effect (disproportionate impact) are improper. Examinations that are not directly related to job requirements and exclude minorities disproportionately are inherently discriminatory. This decision was applicable to the private sector but, in 1972, the Equal Employment Opportunity Act extended Title VII to the public sector as well. The Bakke case was widely discussed in the media because of its implications for reverse discrimination actions such as hiring quotas. Allan Bakke had been denied admission to the University of California Medical School at Davis even though his test scores were higher than minority applicants who were admitted on a quota basis. The Court held that although race could be a factor in admissions, it should not be the sole factor and Bakke was entitled to admission. The effect of this case was to call into question the many arrangements and Department of Justice compliance regulations that were then used to advance the cause of Affirmative Action. The Weber case—also a split decision by the Court—determined that preferential hiring and promotion plans do not necessarily violate the Civil Rights Act.

Other cases were also influential. For example, the 1984 decision in Firefighters Local Union v. Stotts held that, in the absence of proof of actual discrimination, a last-hired, first-fired seniority system is permissible. In 1986, the Supreme Court found sexual harassment in the workplace to be a violation of Title VII of the Civil Rights Act of 1964, which prohibits racial and sexual discrimination and in two cases concerning the legality of Affirmative Action plans upheld a plan in Cleveland that reserved about half the promotions in the city's fire department for qualified minority candidates and, in the second instance, required a union representing sheet metal workers in New York and New Jersey to significantly raise its nonwhite membership. Hiring goals that correct sex bias (in the Santa Clara County California transportation agency) were supported in a 1987 case. Other cases, however, required that plans to help minorities do not also give preferential treatment at the expense of whites.

Advocates of traditional examinations, hiring and promoting according to quotas, and dismissal on a representational rather than seniority basis have not abandoned their struggle. The federal government was not successful in finding a satisfactory service-wide entrance examination following the demise of, first, the FSEE, and then the PACE exams. Similarly, individual departments and agencies remained uncertain as to the appropriateness of their usual hiring, promotion, and dismissal procedures. In the mid to late 1980s, the Attorney General and Justice Department (and the Reagan appointed Civil Rights and Equal Employment Opportunity Commissions) seemed to be taking a different position than that of liberal civil rights advocates. In no area was this clearer than on the issue of comparable worth.

Comparable worth refers to payment of equivalent salaries for traditionally female jobs that are rated the same as traditionally male jobs. For example, if secretaries or nurses — jobs usually held by women — are given an objective job evaluation rating them at the same level as labor supervisors or telephone linemen — jobs usually filled by men — then they should be paid the same, according to the protagonists. President Reagan, the Equal Employment Opportunity Commission, and the Civil Rights Commission have all contended that comparable worth will be both disruptive and expensive, frustrating the demands of the marketplace and upsetting generally acceptable job evaluation practices. Advocates of comparable worth contend that inequities in pay are not justified for jobs of comparable worth and just as equal pay for equal work is required so too should equal pay for comparable work. Several court cases, actions by a number of state governments, and mounting pressure by feminist and civil rights groups add to the heat of the controversy. The example of those state governments that have adopted comparable worth laws or have study groups underway and of foreign governments, such as the Canadian, that may have made greater progress is cited by the advocates in making their case to the federal government.

Another emotionally charged issue of fundamental concern to women employees is sexual harassment, which, in 1980 in a legally binding ruling by the Equal Employment Opportunity Commission, was held to be sex discrimination as defined by Title VII of the Civil Rights Act. Later, the Supreme Court agreed. Employers have a legal responsibility to create a working atmosphere that is free of sexual harassment or intimidation and many have taken the requisite steps to provide and publicize the procedures for redress by affected employees.

Public personnel administration (human resources administration) in the remainder of the 20th century will be a field of considerable controversy and interest. New concerns may emerge and new perspectives will undoubtedly develop on the above-named issues. If past trends continue, however, there will be no expansion in the Federal work force (see Table 14.1) nor any radical retrenchment; contrary to popular opinion the numbers have remained fairly constant for many years.

TABLE 14.1. Government Civilian Employment

	Employees (in thousands)[a]			
Year	Total	Federal	State	Local
1940	4,474	1,128	3,346	
1945	6,677	3,496	3,181	
1950	6,402	2,117	1,057	3,228
1955	7,432	2,378	1,199	3,855
1960	8,808	2,421	1,527	4,860
1965	10,589	2,588	2,028	5,973
1970	13,028	2,881	2,755	7,392
1972	13,759	2,795	2,957	8,007
1975	14,973	2,890	3,271	8,813
1976	15,012	2,843	3,343	8,826
1977	15,459	2,848	3,491	9,120
1978	15,628	2,885	3,539	9,204
1979	15,971	2,869	3,699	9,403
1980	16,213	2,898	3,753	9,562
1981	15,968	2,865	3,726	9,377
1982	15,841	2,848	3,744	9,249
1983	16,034	2,875	3,816	9,344
1984	16,436	2,942	3,898	9,595
1985	16,690	3,021	3,984	9,685

Source: U.S. Bureau of the Census, *Public Employment.*
[a]Full-time equivalent.

Other Policy Developments and Administrative Changes

A number of important recent trends and tendencies in American public administration are not directly encompassed in the foregoing categorization. These include ethical issues; privatization; deregulation; blurring of public/private distinctions; multiple service-delivery systems; and the computerization of government. Other more dramatic concerns are also important. Episodic stresses on various crises: urban, intergovernmental, energy, environmental, economic, and foreign policy tend to overshadow long-term developments and focus discussion on the immediate. The 1986–87 crisis over foreign policy is a case in point. Media disclosures concerning shipments of arms to Iran and the diversion of arms-sale revenues to the contras in Nicaragua appeared to signal a major disaster within the Reagan White House. Traditional rivalries between the National Security Council (NSC) (in the Executive Office of the President) and the State Department over the conduct of foreign policy became public with the resignation of the NSC chief, Admiral Poindexter, and disavowals from the Secretary of State, George Shultz, of complicity in the questionable arms transactions. Internationally televised hearings treated the public to a detailed account of the events in an attempt to clarify the record and establish responsibility. At the time, these incidents appeared to rival the Watergate disclosures of the early 1970s as the credibility of top-level officials was challenged and the Congressional committees conducting the investigation—as well as a Watergate-style independent investigator and a presidentially appointed group known as the Tower Commission—all sought the truth concerning elaborate operations originally designed to free American captives held in Lebanon, establish contacts with Iranian moderates and simultaneously assist the contras (Freedom Fighters) in Nicaragua. Once again, the American politico/administrative process had become high drama.

Ethical concerns, in general, have remained a dominant theme in the federal government. Opinion polls have revealed a decline in confidence and trust, and new legislative, executive, and judicial actions have addressed the public anxiety. Similarly, the public perception of governmental inefficiency has been assuaged with a variety of actions designed to improve productivity. Academic attention has also been directed at ethics and productivity with newer textbooks devoting sections to both. Program evaluation, which was required in legislative acts creating the Johnson Great Society programs, continued to be important, reflecting a greater analytic capacity within the government. Outside the government itself, citizen or public interest watchdog groups monitor and comment upon governmental activities. Advisory groups associated with certain agencies and other mechanisms for wider citizen participation may be found at all levels: federal, state, and local. Regional, cross-jurisdictional, and functional agencies outside the public sector or with quasi-public status contribute to a heightened degree of scrutiny along with the specialized and mass media. Congress itself, of course, oversees the executive branch at the federal level and exercises its right to hold hearings, conduct inquiries, and otherwise provide checks upon the other branch. Until a Supreme Court decision in 1983 outlawing the practice, a legislative veto could be used by Congress to express its displeasure at executive action if provided for in the original legislation. "Sunshine" laws were designed by Congress, state legislatures, and local legislative bodies to further the goal of open meetings and public access. Important in this regard, also, was the Freedom of Information Act as used by those seeking factual data on government operations (Feinberg 1986). "Sunset" laws, which provide for the automatic termination of programs unless explicitly renewed, have a similar purpose in keeping government accountable and responsive within a democratic framework.

Privatization involves the turning over to private industry of government-run programs based on the argument that the private sector is better equipped to perform businesslike functions. Quasi-governmental boards or commissions may also be empowered to operate programs; the removal of the Post Office from departmental status and its designation as an "independent establishment" of the federal government in 1970 is an example of this. Sale of government assets or contractual relationships seem to be cost-effective for many operations at all levels of government. Citizens at the local level may have little difficulty with proposals for private refuse collection (if paid for by the local government) or snow plowing. Operation of prisons and police forces by private contractors is more controversial as is sale of major federal government public works such as Naval Petroleum Reserves or Power Marketing Administration hydroelectric projects. The sale of CONRAIL was completed and was followed by a proposal to sell AMTRACK, thereby getting the government out of the passenger train business.

Deregulation — as alluded to before in the case of the airlines — removes government controls from private sector activities and allows freer play of the marketplace. Few would want all regulations removed involving safety, the environment, and consumer protection; in fact, many pressures exist for increased regulation in some areas. Particularly from a conservative point of view, however, less regulation by bureaucrats has great political appeal. In the 1970s and 1980s, deregulation was undertaken not only for the airlines and air cargo, but also for railroads, over-the-road trucking, banking, energy, telecommunications, and health care.

Many observers have commented on the blurring of public/private distinctions (e.g., Mosher 1980, p. 543–46; Starling 1986, p. 528–36; Waldo 1980, p. 164, 165) and the corresponding intermix of functions. Some see this as an opportunity for public-private partnerships that go beyond the usual regulating, subsidizing, purchasing role of the government. Others talk of the necessity of loans and loan guarantees by the federal government (such as the bailout of the Chrysler Corporation). New industrial policies have been touted, often with the Japanese model in mind. More conventionally, observers point to the numerous existing public-private ventures in economic development, job training, research and development, trade programs, and procurement strategies. In addition, other mechanisms to improve upon existing arrangements have been suggested.

Long-term trends and tendencies appear to include a penchant for different organizational forms than the conventional government department. Quasi-governmental corporations (known as parastatals in many countries); semipermanent boards and commissions; agencies that provide specialized financing; and numerous other structures have been created. In addition, cross-agency coordinating mechanisms (from the Domestic Council and its successors to the intelligence oversight committees and counter-terrorism groupings) have been adopted.

The trend towards multiplicity of service-delivery arrangements is not inconsistent with that towards a slower rate of growth for government at all levels. The complexity of forms and modalities increases but the number of public officials does not. In some of the arrangements, wide public participation is provided or, as in the case of special districts at the local level, control devolves to the interest groups affected (private aviation interests run airport districts; medical officials control hospital districts). Many of the service-delivery systems that are unconventional are far from new but, as Frederick Mosher points out for the federal government, they imply the carrying out of responsibilities through and interdependently with nonfederal institutions and individuals (Mosher 1980, p. 541).

The computerization of government operations needs to be noted in any listing and analysis of policy developments and administrative changes. Virtually every program has now been impacted by mainframes, minis, and microcomputers. Vast numbers of government officials have micros on their desks and numerous systems have been computerized. Computer literacy is required for many positions, at least to the extent of knowing how to operate a word processor, spreadsheet, or retrieval system.

Conclusion

American public administration has been through a period of turmoil in the last two decades as declining trust in government; legislative and judicial enactments; presidential proclamations, and the legacy of Vietnam, Watergate, and Irangate complicate the jobs of officials. Media attention has focused on the dramatic and newsworthy and both the political right and the political left have targeted public officials (bureaucrats in the pejorative sense) for attack.

America remains an open society and its institutions and practices are fair game for criticism. External assaults are complemented by internal problems including the inevitable inter- and intra-organizational conflict over turf protection and turf expansion; competition for prestige and resources; factionalism; and personal rivalries. Perhaps the genius of American public administration is its capacity for overcoming enormous dislocations and morale-depressing periods and emerging seemingly unscathed from the fray. Stability, as in other Western democracies, seems to triumph.

There is no agreement as to whether the negatives outweigh the positives nor about the directions and significance of American public administration. Many informed observers are highly critical of the curtailment of government programs for society's needy in the 1980s; others regard the reduction in government expansion as long overdue and highly desirable. One thing that is clear is the visibility and impact this trend has had worldwide; from Great Britain, through Europe, and into the Second and Third

Worlds, there is awareness of American domestic policy (particularly economic policy) and there are attempts to assess and emulate it.

Although free-market economic policies may be copied, American public administration is no longer looked upon as a model for the remainder of the world; technological transfers of budgetary formats or civil service practices appear less feasible from the standpoint of both donor and recipient. Whether this is a short-term or long-term effect remains to be seen.

It is hazardous to project what American public administration will be like in the early years of the 21st century; one guess is a stable model of structures and persons not radically different in number or kind than in the late 1980s. (The size of the federal work force has been remarkably stable for many years.) Another guess is that the pendulum will swing back to the liberal policies and expansionist tendencies of earlier years, reflecting internal and external needs and demands, with a variety of new public/private modalities and a new pattern of subsidies, grants, guarantees, insurance programs, and intergovernmental sharing that will usher in a new era perhaps even without increasing the number of federal employees. One thing is probable—that by the beginning of the 21st century public officials will be more technologically sophisticated and computer-oriented; more aware of practices in the business community; and more attuned to developments in the world at large.

References

Aberbach, J. D., and Rockman, B. A. "Clashing Beliefs within the Executive Branch: The Nixon Administration Bureaucracy." *American Political Science Review* 70 (June 1976):456–68.

Adams, G. *The Politics of Defense Contracting: The Iron Triangle*. New Brunswick, N.J.: Transaction Books, 1982.

Arnold, P. E. *Making the Managerial Presidency, Comprehensive Reorganization Planning, 1905–1980*. Princeton, N.J.: Princeton University, 1986.

Arnold, R. D. *Congress and the Bureaucracy*. New Haven: Yale University Press, 1979.

Bardach, E. *The Implementation Game: What Happens After a Bill Becomes a Law*. Cambridge, Mass.: MIT Press, 1977.

Barrett, P. M. "Refund? What Refund?" *The Washington Monthly*, Sept. 1985, p. 26.

Barrett, S., and Fudge, C., eds. *Policy and Action: Essays on the Implementation of Public Policy*. London: Methuen, 1981.

Baumer, D. C., and Van Horn, C. E. *The Politics of Unemployment*. Washington: Congressional Quarterly Press, 1984.

Benda, P. M., and Levine, C. H. "OMB and the Central Management Problem: Is Another Reorganization the Answer?" *Public Administration Review* 46 (Sept.–Oct. 1986):379–89.

Brunner, R. D. "Decentralized Energy Policies." *Public Policy* 28 (Winter 1980):71–91.

Bullock, C. S. III and Lamb, C. M., eds. *Implementation of Civil Rights Policy.* Monterey, Calif.: Brooks/Cole, 1984.

Campbell, C. *Managing the Presidency: Carter, Reagan, and the Search for Creative Harmony.* Pittsburgh: University of Pittsburgh, 1986.

Chubb, J. E. *Interest Groups and the Bureaucracy: The Politics of Energy.* Stanford, Calif.: Stanford University Press, 1983.

Clinton, C. A. *Local Success and Federal Failure: A Study of Community Development and Educational Change in the Rural South.* Cambridge, Mass.: Abt Books, 1979.

Cole, R. L., and Caputo, D. A. "Presidential Control of the Senior Civil Service: Assessing the Strategies of the Nixon Years." *American Political Science Review* 73 (June 1979):399–413.

Dan-Cohen, M. *Rights, Persons, and Organizations.* Berkeley: University of California Press, 1986.

Derthick, M. *New Towns In-Town.* Washington, D.C.: Urban Institute, 1972.

Dommel, P. R., and Associates. *Decentralizing Urban Policy: Case Studies in Community Development.* Washington, D.C.: Brookings Institution, 1982.

Feinberg, L. E. "Managing the Freedom of Information Act and Federal Information Policy." *Public Administration Review* 46 (Nov.–Dec. 1986):615–22.

Final Report. *President's Commission on Defense Management (Packard).* Washington, D.C.: Government Printing Office, 1986.

Grace, J. P. *War on Waste, President's Private Sector Survey on Cost Control.* New York: Macmillan, 1984.

Heclo, H. *A Government of Strangers: Executive Politics in Washington.* Washington, D.C.: Brookings Institution, 1977.

Henderson, K. *The Study of Public Administration.* Washington, D.C.: University Press of America, 1983.

Herken, G. *Counsels of War.* New York: Oxford, 1987.

Ingraham, P. W., and Ban, C., eds. *Legislating Bureaucratic Change: The Civil Service Reform Act of 1978.* Albany: State University of New York, 1984.

Kaufman, H. *The Administrative Behavior of Federal Bureau Chiefs.* Washington, D.C.: Brookings Institution, 1981.

Kennedy, W. R., and Lee, R. W. *A Taxpayer Survey of the Grace Commission Report.* Ottawa, Ill.: Jameson, 1984.

Lane, F. S., ed. *Current Issues in Public Administration,* 3d ed. New York: St. Martin's Press, 1986.

Lee, R. D. *Public Budgeting Systems,* 3d ed. New York: Marcel Dekker, 1983.

Levine, C. "The Federal Government in the Year 2000: Administrative Legacies of the Reagan Years." *Public Administration Review* 46 (1986):195–205.

_____. *The Unfinished Agenda of Civil Service Reform.* Washington, D.C.: Brookings Institution, 1985.

Lipsky, M. *Street-Level Bureaucracy: Dilemmas of the Individual in Public Services.* New York: Russell Sage Foundation, 1980.

Lynch, T. D. *Public Budgeting in America,* 2d ed. Englewood Cliffs, N.J.: Prentice Hall, 1985.

Meier, K. J. *Politics and the Bureaucracy.* North Scituate, Mass.: Duxbury, 1975.

_____. *Regulation: Politics, Bureaucracy, and Economics.* New York: St. Martin's Press, 1985.

Meier, K. J., and Nigro, L. G. "Representative Bureaucracy and Policy Preferences: A Study in the Attitudes of Federal Executives." *Public Administration Review* 36 (July–Aug. 1976):458–69.

Mosher, F. C. "The Changing Responsibilities and Tactics of the Federal Government." *Public Administration Review* 40 (Nov.–Dec. 1980):541–48.

National Academy of Public Administration. *Revitalizing Federal Management.* Washington, D.C.: NAPA, 1983.

Navarro, P. "The Politics of Air Pollution." *The Public Interest* (Spring 1980):36–44.

Newland, C. A. "Federal Government Management Trends." In *Current Issues in Public Administration.* Edited by F. S. Lane. New York: St. Martin's Press, 1986.

_____. "A Mid-Term Appraisal: The Reagan Presidency." *Public Administration Review* 43 (Jan.–Feb. 1983):1–21.

Nice, D. C. *Federalism.* New York: St. Martin's Press, 1987.

Pearce, J. L., and Perry, J. L. "Federal Merit Pay: A Longitudinal Analysis." *Public Administration Review* 43 (July–Aug. 1983):315–25.

Pechman, J. *Federal Tax Policy,* 4th ed. Washington, D.C.: Brookings Institution, 1984.

Rabin, J., and Lynch, T. D., eds. *Handbook on Public Budgeting and Fiscal Management.* New York: Marcel Dekker, 1983.

Randall, R. "Presidential Power versus Bureaucratic Intransigence: The Influence of the Nixon Administration on Welfare Policy." *American Political Science Review* 73 (Sept. 1979):795–810.

Ripley, R. B., and Franklin, G. A. *Congress, the Bureaucracy, and Public Policy,* 3d ed. Homewood, Ill.: Dorsey Press, 1984.

Rohr, J. *To Run a Constitution, the Legitimacy of the Administrative State.* Lawrence: University of Kansas, 1986.

Rose, R. *The Welfare State East and West.* New York: Oxford, 1986.

Rosen, B. "Crises in the Civil Service." *Public Administration Review* 46 (May–June 1986):207–14.

Rourke, F. E. "Bureaucratic Autonomy and the Public Interest." *American Behavioral Scientist* 22 (May–June 1979):537–46.

Rubin, I. *Shrinking the Federal Government: The Effect of Cutbacks on Five Federal Agencies.* White Plains, N.Y.: Longman, 1985.

Salamon, L. M., and Lund, M. S., eds. *The Reagan Presidency and the Governing of America.* Washington, D.C.: The Urban Institute, 1985.

Schick, A. *Congress and Money: Budgeting, Spending, and Taxing.* Washington, D.C.: The Urban Institute, 1980.

Starling, G. *Managing the Public Sector,* 3d ed. Homewood, Ill.: Dorsey Press, 1986.

Straussman, J. D. *Public Administration.* New York: Holt, Rinehart, and Winston, 1985.

Szanton, P., ed. *Federal Reorganization, What Have We Learned.* Chatham, N.J.: Chatham House, 1981.

Tolchin, S., and Tolchin, M. *Dismantling America, The Rush to Deregulate.* New York: Oxford, 1986.

U.S. Congressional Budget Office. *The Industrial Policy Debate.* Washington, D.C.: Government Printing Office, 1983.

U.S. Congressional Budget Office and General Accounting Office. *Analysis of the Grace Commission's Major Proposals for Cost Control.* Washington, D.C.: Government Printing Office, 1984.

U.S. General Accounting Office. *Hatch Act Reform.* Washington, D.C.: Government Printing Office, 1979.

_____. *Difficulties in Evaluating Public Affairs Government-Wide and at the Department of Health, Education, and Welfare.* (LCD-79-405). Washington, D.C.: Government Printing Office, 18 Jan. 1979.

_____. *Increased Use of Productivity Management Can Help Control Government Costs.* (AFMD-84-11). Washington, D.C.: Government Printing Office, 10 Nov. 1983.

U.S. Office of Management and Budget. *Budget FY 1985, 1986, 1987, 1988,* 1989. Washington, D.C.: Government Printing Office, 1985, 1986, 1987, 1988.

_____. *Management of the U.S. Government.* Washington, D.C.: Government Printing Office, 1987, 1988, 1989.

Ventriss, C. "Emerging Perspectives on Citizen Participation." *Public Administration Review* 45 (May–June 1985): 433–40.

Voss, L. E., and Eikmeier, D. "Microcomputers in Local Government." *Public Administration Review* 44 (Jan.–Feb. 1984):60–63.

Waldo, D. *The Enterprise of Public Administration.* Novato, Calif.: Chandler and Sharp, 1980.

Walker, D. B. *Toward a Functioning Federalism.* Cambridge, Mass.: Winthrop, 1981.

Wildavsky, A. *The New Politics of the Budgetary Process.* Glenview, Illinois: Scott Foresman, 1988.

_____. *The Politics of the Budgetary Process,* 4th ed. Boston: Little, Brown, 1984.

Wilson, J. Q., ed. *The Politics of Regulation.* New York: Basic Books, 1980.

Yarwood, D. L., ed. *Public Administration, Politics, and the People.* New York: Longman, 1987.

3

Internationalization

15

Rethinking the Comparative Experience: Indigenization versus Internationalization

KEITH M. HENDERSON

THE INTENT OF THIS CHAPTER is to briefly identify and clarify two contradictory trends in comparative public administration around the globe and to suggest the desirability of one of them. It is hoped that this somewhat controversial interpretation will stimulate debate and provoke reactions in a continuing dialogue on the orientation, assumptions, ideology, cultural bias, and usefulness of comparative public administration study. Essentially, the argument is between indigenization and internationalization: the former position advocating a basically nationalistic or regional perspective on study and application in public administration and the latter a worldwide study and international application. This discussion is implicit in much of the current research and commentary in the field including the accounts in this volume. This chapter was originally written in Adana, Turkey, in the Spring of 1986, and therefore some Turkish examples are used.

The term "indigenization" has been used in the literature in a somewhat different sense than here. It generally refers to what used to be called "localization," or in the case of Africa, "Africanization," and is concerned with the process of replacing expatriates with native-born officials in both the public and private sectors. Similarly, internationalization may be used in different senses to indicate a shift in focus or direction towards the global and away from the parochial.

The specific concern here is the study of public administration and the application of ideas.

Indigenization

There are those who reject everything Western. The presumably universal scientific method, the search for theory in social science, the reliability and validity of carefully derived statistical data, the attention to possible biases, the open-mindedness of the Western spirit of inquiry, and even the very essence of intellectual understanding may all be rejected in the most extreme form of indigenization. The integrity as well as motives and ideologies of outside investigators and "appliers" are questioned. All is distorted; all is self-seeking; and all is irrelevant in this view. Less virulent, but as insistent, Communist-bloc intellectuals have long made a case against Western intellectual modes as we have of theirs.

At a series of conferences in the 1970s, the "academic colonialism" based on the "Western paradigm of development" began to emerge as a dominant theme for scholars from the Third World. It was heard at the UNESCO Conference on Teaching and Research in Social Science held at Simla, India, in 1973; at the 1976 UNESCO Conference on Interregional Cooperation in the field of Social Sciences, Paris; at a Korean Social Science Research Council seminar in 1979; and later in the same year at the Third International Federation of Social Science Organizations Conference in Manila.

As a corollary to condemnation of foreign academic colonialism, there has been an attendant return to native categories of thought, glorification of tradition, paradigm replacement, localization, and de-emphasis upon foreign language. Some aspects of this are well summarized in an article by Yogesh Atal:

> 1. Indigenization is a plea for self-awareness and rejection of a borrowed consciousness. It emphasizes the need for an inside view. Its proponents wish to stimulate such scholarly endeavors so as to promote thoughtful analysis of their own societies to replace the existing trend of knowing these via the West.
> 2. Indigenization advocates the desirability for alternative perspective on human societies with a view to making the social sciences less parochial and enriching them. This would, it is believed, emancipate the mind and improve the quality of professional praxis, so that society can be examined through new lenses.
> 3. Indigenization draws attention to historical and cultural specificities and argues for the redefinition of focus, with a view to developing dynamic perspectives on national problems.
> 4. Indigenization should not lead to narrow parochialism, or to the fragmentation of a single discipline into several insulated systems of thought based on geographical boundaries. It is opposed not only to false universalism but also to false nationalism. Reduced to the level of national narcissism, indigenization would be rendered futile (Atal 1981).

The attitude of Turkish officialdom is not atypical. The strong political commitment at the top level to economic and social development using indigenous personnel and institutions supplemented by external aid is complemented by academic programs and approaches that emphasize Turkish values and traditions. The leadership disagrees, however, on the question of how much traditionalism is desirable: "Turkey's body politic is almost evenly divided between those who are conservative and frequently traditional in outlook and those who seek more rapid implementation of the secular, Westernizing, statist philosophy propounded by Ataturk" (Gale Research Co. 1984).

As in the Arab world, the debate between modernizers and traditionalists dissolves into an administrative issue concerning the extent that Islamic laws and customs should be preserved in governmental administration as opposed to Westernized patterns (see Al-Buraey 1989). For example, in selecting officials, should merit and technical abilities be stressed or indigenous values? (Global Network 1985).

In the Islamic world, the most conspicuous recent example of thorough indigenization of the public service and the study (or lack thereof) of public administration is found in Iran. The return to fundamentalism associated with the Islamic Revolution brought an explicit denial of usual Western ideas and practices of administration and the substitution of a purified Islamic version. Islamic self-awareness and rejection of a borrowed consciousness as well as the need for an inside view are proclaimed.

Also on the continent of Asia is the well-known example of China at the time of the Maoist "reforms" (1960s). Foreign advisors and ideas (in this case Russian) were rejected. (See Laaksonen 1987.)

Other historical and contemporary instances of indigenization—many less dramatic—also reveal the implications for study and practice of administration. The orientation of the cadres (civil service or otherwise) changes along with subject matter studied and strategies for advancement or continuation in government employment. Contact with outsiders and their ideas is not rewarded nor are foreign modes of education prized. Even the technology may be rejected as in China's experiments with deep-plowing or Iran's new forms of crop cultivation. The bureaucracy is purged of foreign influence; the academic system becomes closed to the outside.

The concern with indigenization is informed both by a theoretical underpinning in dependency analysis—sometimes within a broader Marxist theory of imperialism—and the widespread observation that neither sympathetic reports to international agencies nor policy recommendations to governments have made much fundamental difference. Self-reliance becomes the key idea, ranging from attempts at radical economic and social change to self-help projects within the existing governmental framework.

One strong line of argument reflected in the two selections here on Africa is that underdevelopment becomes the true goal of those who espouse development since their basic purpose is to sustain the bureaucratic status quo by fostering continued dependency. Those in power in the bureaucracy are coopted by or align themselves with outside interests and seek to maintain or strengthen their own power. Proposals to strengthen the bureaucracy through the modernizing assumptions of comparative public administration and development administration are welcomed since they can be used to the officials' own advantage. "West African public administration, like others that have evolved out of a colonial past, is still basically despotic and authoritarian in its character and relationship with the people it is supposed to serve. Any attempt to improve the public service by making more resources available to it (including the power of control) only strengthens this despotic character" (Olowu, this volume).

Fortunately, there is some recent empirical evidence on the question of whether African managers (primarily public managers) serve developmental goals. The Southern Africa Development Coordinating Conference in 1984 generated a large number of critical incidents of managerial behavior and while providing some confirmation of the tendency to frustrate developmental goals ("the intensely internal preoccupation of these supposed entrepreneurs of development is not a good sign") (Montgomery 1987) also found no reason to conclude that the managers studied (in nine Southern Africa countries) are very different from their counterparts elsewhere.

The best case for indigenization is not made by reference to its extreme forms. The well-reasoned position of many scholars and practitioners around the world is that Western and neocolonial influences in all forms have had their day and the new hegemony lies in the Third World. This sentiment is supported by the rationale Atal suggests as well as the increasing levels of self-sufficiency in many countries. It may be reinforced by lack of concern for the Third World in foreign policy decisions by Western countries (and Eastern).

Internationalization

Internationalization may be thought of as the process of participating in and contributing to the development of the worldwide study and practice of public administration. For a given country, it can be a series of conscious choices or a function of incremental program and institutional changes; it may be reversed fairly rapidly as in the case of Iran's expulsion of advisors and self-imposed exclusion from the international public administration community at the time of the Islamic Revolution.

The enlarging public sector in many countries, the growing complexity of public tasks, and the increased importance of competent administration world-wide are reasons to consider internationalization.

The internationalization of public administration involves a common core of knowledge about bureaucratic characteristics, familiarity with Western academic ideas, specialized skills that are intelligible to colleagues, and some willingness to share knowledge, skills, and experience. It espouses concern for improved administration, whatever its form; a commitment to social and economic change, and a quest for objective knowledge. If this sounds Western, it needn't be construed as such; it encompasses the Communist orbit and potentially most of the Third World.

The argument for internationalization in comparative public administration is well stated by Gerald and Naomi Caiden in their selection in this book and is implied in most of the other material in this book. They point out that policymakers need to know more of the world than what lies on their doorstep. Exposure to foreign practice teaches better ways of doing things; through observation of other systems one can sift out what is applicable and what is suitable. The Caidens are quoted here:

> The gradual emergence of an international culture—which makes young people quickly at home whether they are in Amsterdam, Singapore, Rio de Janeiro or Toronto—highlights the similarities and differences among national cultures and administrative systems. If American organization and management could not be exported without some strange and unexpected results, could the Japanese economic miracle and needless to say Japanese management methods? . . . To neglect comparative analysis is to be chained to amateur dilettantism.

Earlier in their article, the Caidens point out that CPA is already more universal than its American-dominated predecessor and less concerned with technical assistance, American sponsorship, and Western concepts of development and bureaucracy.

Recognition of the deficiencies of the earlier approaches has stimulated newer emphases upon institution-building, basic needs, bottom-up development strategies, what the Caidens call "collective self-reliance," Emanuel de Kadt's "equity, pluralism and tolerance," (1985) and other pragmatic techniques referred to elsewhere in this volume. It is now understood by many American comparativists that their ideas and schemes were perceived by the intended Third World recipients as "foreign values and objectives, foreign technology, foreign organization and methods, which would tie the Third World into an international system not of its making; that development administration legitimized governmental control and authority, political elites, and a public bureaucracy."

The field of comparative public administration now numbers among its adherents participants from many of the world's countries. Much of the advantage of internationalization derives from cross-jurisdictional contact among Third World scholars and practitioners themselves without the need for outside intervention. Networks and inter-relationships may develop spontaneously on a regional, multilateral or bilateral basis. Universalistic methodologies for accounting, data-gathering and dissemination, and statistics may be used without an aura of Western domination. Many administrative matters — legal, transport, communication, trade, energy, weather reporting, etc. — are covered by existing international agreements and conventions and are subject to extensive reporting.

The minimum for successful internationalization is a fourfold commitment to the following essentials:

1. *Communication.* Beyond reporting data to international authorities on a standardized basis, it is desirable to share information on policy development and implementation including successes and failures. (Hale reports that Turkey has used two sets of figures on wheat production: one from the State Planning Office and the other by the State Institute of Statistics. This confounds the purposes of data-gathering and dissemination [1984].) Communication unfettered by noise or ideology should help move scholars and practitioners towards cumulative understanding and application. The key to open communication would be more an attitude or predisposition than the proliferation of conferences, seminars, and meetings.

2. *Appropriate Information Technology.* Closely related to the other three factors here is the technology used for information flows. Both telecommunications and computer technology — and combinations — are available at various levels of sophistication. For example, user-friendly microcomputers with modems enable scholars and practitioners to engage in monitoring, assessment, prediction, communication, and research and generally to have an additional tool for decision making. The important ingredient is not the hardware as such nor data accumulation but the development of systems and the pursuit of competent use of information. Good decisions require good information. (For a good analysis of technological dependence and self-reliance see Stover 1984.)

3. *Research.* Antipathy towards social science and applied research using survey methodologies and nonlegal/formal techniques is widespread. "Look up the codes; ask the expert; we already know that," are not adequate responses to clearly formulated questions. Feedback on government programs is often quite inadequate at the time it is most needed. In Turkey, for example, there is limited opportunity to conduct public opinion surveys. Program evaluation and systematic analysis of policy in many countries is either absent, unreliable, or restricted to certain fields. Research is

not encouraged or rewarded. My 1969 comment that problems of access, language, poor statistics, and hostile or indifferent governments severely inhibit research unfortunately still seems to be applicable (Henderson 1969). The need remains for relevant research based in the country under study. If, as we are sometimes told, 70 percent of sponsored research in the Western countries deals with defense, space, and nuclear energy, then it is clear that another type of research emphasis is needed in the Third World.

4. *Training.* Training of all kinds is essential for public officials and is more widely appreciated than the need for research. In addition to skill development and acquisition of usable knowledge, training may serve the purpose of socialization or reorientation—even what Anthony Downs describes as indoctrination; permanently altering deep level goals (1967). Ethical behavior, capacity for innovation, and entrepreneurship and leadership skills are desirable but elusive end products of training. Training should not be confined solely to local materials and sources but, by the same token, it should not be Westernized.

Reconciliation?

The two contradictory approaches—indigenization and internationalization—may be an inevitable aspect of an endemic North/South conflict.

The rules of the game are set by the North and efforts to change them are met by frustration, even when successful in the short term (the anti-Western information policy adopted by UNESCO was countered by withdrawal of the U.S. and its resources from the organization) (Krasner 1986). Under these conditions, extending the opportunity for interaction in broadened North/South academic forums will simply increase the number and range of opportunities for conflict.

An approach to reconciliation of Western (Northern) and non-Western approaches, is taken by Dwivedi and Nef (1982) who offer encouragement to a measure of autonomy in the study of administration and development in different societies by pointing to and criticizing the restricted cultural assumptions built into the study and arguing for the importance of heretical models. They suggest that development thinking and practice in India, China, Tanzania, and elsewhere has rejected Western thinking and been based on indigenous approaches. They stress that only through open examination of these nontraditional approaches can the struggle for a successful development strategy ensue.

One hopes for convergence of the two tendencies, and the experience of some countries offers hope. Japan, India, and Israel among others have emerged from foreign academic hegemony to establish their own traditions in their own very distinctive ways. Australia and Canada—within the original Northern orbit—along with other countries have developed their own literatures and applications without being submerged under outside influences (Henderson and Dwivedi 1987). All of these countries—as is clear in the selections in this volume—are also participants in the international public administration community and have made important contributions.

Conclusion

It is important to identify and clarify the difference between indigenization and internationalization since the dominance of one or the other will determine the future of comparative public administration.

The implications of indigenization include greater fragmentation of study and application, with little exchange of expertise, and few cumulative understandings. No worldwide study would emerge but rather separate national or regional enterprises focused on local problems. The danger of domination by an external ideology would be eliminated along with exclusion from an international system.

Internationalization on the other hand bears promise of beneficial participation in a wider enterprise after neutralizing the related problems of dominance by exogenous forces. The later could be eliminated by modifying Western or other external ideas and practices to suit particular circumstances and in turn contributing from each nation's experience information and skills valuable to others. Nontraditional and Marxist models pose a special challenge to the internationalization of study since they are particularly antagonistic to the West and involve a different concept of state action, mass mobilization, and political oversight. At the level of communication and exchange of technical ideas, however, the possibility of joint participation in an international system exists and in fact is now being experienced in some fields. Cultural exchanges of various kinds are currently being undertaken across ideological lines. (It is interesting to note that the prestigious International Centre for Public Enterprises, which provides a common forum and issues publications, is located in Ljubljana, Yugoslavia.)

In summarizing the arguments devoid of nationalistic, anti-colonial, anti-Western fervor, the case for internationalization seems persuasive. Increased amounts of inter-dependence and inter-connectedness in a complex modern world argue strongly for internationalizing.

References

Al-Buraey, M.A. *Administrative Development: An Islamic Perspective.* London: Kegan Paul, 1989.

Atal, Yogesh. "The Call for Indigenization." *International Social Science Journal* 33 (1981):192–93.

de Kadt, Emanuel. "Of Markets, Might and Mullahs: A Case for Equity, Pluralism and Tolerance in Development." *World Development* 13, no. 4 (1985):549–56.

Downs, Anthony. *Inside Bureaucracy.* Boston: Little, Brown, 1967, p. 233–34.

Dwivedi, O. P., and Nef, J. "Crises and Continuities in Development Theory: First and Third World Perspectives." *Public Administration and Development* 2 (1982):59–77.

Gale Research Co. *Countries of the World and Their Leaders, Yearbook 1985.* Detroit: Gale Research Co., 1984, p. 1165.

Global Network. "IIAS Roundtable in Tunis." Report on Arab Organization of Administrative Sciences. *Global Network* 6, no. 4 (Fall–Winter 1985–1986):1.

Hale, William. *The Political and Economic Development of Modern Turkey.* New York: Praeger, 1984, p. 154.

Henderson, Keith. "The Identity Crisis in Comparative Public Administration." *Journal of Comparative Administration* 1, no. 1 (May 1969):69.

Henderson, Keith, and Dwivedi, O. P. "Comparative Public Administration: The Canadian Case." *Proceedings of the IV Conference on Public Policy and Administrative Studies.* Guelph University, Apr. 1987.

Krasner, Stephen. *Structural Conflict: The Third World Against Global Liberalism.* Berkeley: University of California Press, 1986, p. 300.

Laaksonen, Oiva. *Management in China During and After Mao.* Berlin: W. de Gruyter, 1987.

Montgomery, John D. "How African Managers Serve Development Goals." *Comparative Politics* 19, no. 2 (1987):347–60.

Olowu, Dele. "Policy Developments and Administrative Change in West Africa." This volume.

Stover, William J. *Information Technology in the Third World.* Boulder, Colo.: Westview Press, 1984.

16

Management Training Methods for Third World Development

WILLIE CURTIS

Management Development Training

For the developing countries, the problem of insufficient managerial capacity is critical. "Throughout the world, trained, experienced managers are being seen increasingly as a resource, the supply of which is critical to the survival and further development of an organization or a nation" (Lippitt and Taylor 1975, p. ix). Not only must training programs address the problem of insufficient numbers of managers, the issue of managerial efficiency must become paramount, Lippitt and Taylor continue for "it is becoming apparent that the difference in performance between countries and the competitive advantages of business enterprises, rests not so much on their supply of natural resources—or even on technological expertise—but on the ability of their people to manage these resources and to utilize new technology through efficient and innovative organizations."

The International Labor Office (ILO) has defined management development as "the activity directed towards the further development of the knowledge and skills of practicing managerial personnel and modification of their concepts, attitudes, and practices" (Black, Coleman, and Stifel 1977, p. 4). For the purposes of this chapter, the definition of management development by Robert L. Desatnick (1970, p. 11) provides a more workable although somewhat cumbersome description of the concept: "Manage-

This article is adapted from a study prepared by the author while serving as an NASPAA/AID intern in Washington, D.C., during 1982. I am indebted to Dr. William Boyer of the University of Delaware for his comments on an earlier draft of this paper. The views and conclusions expressed here are those of the author and not necessarily those of NASPAA or AID.

ment development is an individual process involving the interaction of a man, his job, his manager, and the total work environment. Individual development then results in the acquisition of new knowledge, skills, and attitudes in a planned, orderly manner to improve present job performance while accelerating preparation for advancement into more responsible positions."

This definition includes a number of elements not specifically addressed by the ILO definition, namely the work environment, the manager's superior and the process of advancement. Therefore the important elements of job environmental impact and motivation based on the hope of advancement are viewed as important factors impinging on individual manager responsiveness. Both definitions imply that through a planned and deliberate activity certain skills and attitudes are influenced positively, thus producing an increase in managerial effectiveness. If we accept Desatnick's definition, namely that managerial development is an individual process leading to the acquisition of new knowledge, skills and attitudes in a planned and orderly manner designed to improve managerial effectiveness, the next logical question is how are these desired acquisitions brought about? The obvious answer is through some type of management education or training program.

The ILO has distinguished between education and training, defining the first as "the teaching of management as part of an institutional curriculum leading to a formal degree and would normally occur in a university or an institution devoted specifically to management activities (Black, Coleman, and Stifel 1977, p. 4). Management training is defined as "an institutional program that does not result in a formal degree. Training may be conducted by universities, management institutions, or other types of organizations." In the final analysis, whether one chooses management education or management training programs, the basic objectives are the same, to improve managerial effectiveness through a systematic and deliberate learning process.

How effective are present training methods in developing the knowledge, skills, and attitudes that improve on-the-job performance and thereby insure development program success through better management? It is this question this chapter addresses.

As indicated earlier, the consequence of heightened concern for management development has been a proliferation of training programs designed to increase managerial capability in the public sector. The rapid growth has led to mixed results, however, and given rise to two very different views of training effectiveness. One view suggests that training is the only solution to the problems confronting development administrators, while at the other extreme training is seen as not very useful. Both views are insupportable and the true value of training may lie somewhere near middle ground. Training is just one approach to the multitude of problems facing developing countries as they seek to take full advantage of development assistance programs. As Berkman (1974, p. 169) suggests:

> Training by itself is not and cannot be a panacea and, it should not be viewed as such. Training does not immediately or automatically produce more productive and effective administrators . . . more training does not necessarily imply that a more capable group of administrators or managers will emerge. . . . It is just one piece in the puzzle for improving performance. Other pieces of the puzzle must be secured and put into place.

If training is truly one piece of a puzzle, it is essential to understand clearly just where it is to fit. Management training cannot operate in a vacuum. External political, social, and economic factors may increase or decrease the effectiveness of training programs, and internal organizational structure and atmosphere may enhance or impede goal attainment.

> AID [Agency For International Development] has sent individuals abroad to regional or incountry management training programs. These individuals often return to their respective ministries only to find that he *alone* can have little effect, even if well trained, on the improvement of management there. Often, his attempts to use good management techniques are misunderstood by his superiors and co-managers, resulting in confusion and minimal output (Berg 1981, p. 1).

Consequently, for the developing countries, management training programs should seek objectives that aim at "develop[ing] a broad range of skills, attitudes and knowledge which will enable the manager to perform effectively and efficiently in a number of different organizational and situational contexts" (Bohdan 1975, p. 169).

Without a clear understanding of what training can accomplish, programs designed to improve managerial capacity will yield unsatisfactory results. Training may not be a panacea for solving development administration problems, but as William B. Berg (1981, p. 1) suggests, "it is the best and fastest known method to improve management." Yet, as Lippitt and Taylor (1975, p. 3) argue, "We know more about management development techniques and tools than about their effectiveness, and in any case, little is known about application in an international [developmental] perspective."

Management Training in Developing Countries

Management training programs in developing countries are influenced by the premise upon which the programs are based. Program premises may be developed from either a universalist or a cross-cultural perspective. The universalist position is that there are no real differences in management principles that govern practices around the world. Managers do the same things everywhere, or at least good managers do, and therefore there is a universal appropriate managerial behavior. In contrast, Negandhi (1974, p. 59) suggests the cross-cultural approach assumes that cultural differences have a profound effect on managerial behavior from one country to another, and that there are few universal principles if any.

Most studies of cross-cultural transfer of management know-how to developing countries appear to be influenced by the cross-cultural perspective. For example, Redding and Casey's (1976, p. 353) study of the managerial attitudes of 800 managers throughout South and East Asia reported the need for methods that are "appropriate both to the belief systems of the managers concerned and the relatively autocratic systems in which they are likely to work. The simple transferring of the Western participative approach could be dangerously dysfunctional for the organization and puzzling for the individual." A 1979 study by M. K. Badawy of the managerial leadership styles and attitudes of 248 Middle Eastern executives from Saudi Arabia, Kuwait, Abu-Dhabi, Bahrain, Oman, and the United Arab Emirates recommended the following for managers of multinational corporations: "[One] should not expect Mid-Eastern managers to abandon their culture as pride is a large part of their heritage. Rather, management should work with this heritage in order to cultivate useful qualities inherent in the Mid-Easterner's personality" (Badawy 1979, p. 353).

The findings of Griffith et al. (1980, p. 66) suggest that management training programs should take advantage of research findings of both the universality and cross-cultural schools. They indicate that "cross-national differences mainly reflected differences in job satisfaction, while organizational perceptions such as role overload and perceived organizational structure were relatively similar across managers from different nations." They concluded that:

> Those that argue [that] no real difference in attitudes and managers all over the world are engaged in essentially the same activities . . . and those who argue that cultural differences are the major sources of variation in cross-national managerial attitudes and behaviors (the "Cultural Cluster" school) may both be correct. The validity of either argument depends on what is examined (Griffith et al. 1980, p. 66).

Whether the premise of a developing country's management training program is based on the universality or a cross-cultural perspective, historically management training approaches used in developing countries have been grouped into three major categories: formal training, on-the-job training, and nonformal training. Since the mid-1970s, action training, a combination of formal training and on-the-job problem solving has become the fourth and most recent developed approach to management training.

Management Training Strategies in Developing Countries

In a survey of 236 institutions in 91 developing countries providing public administration and management training (PAMT), the International Labor Office (ILO) found that government institutions of training (those primarily engaged in nondegree training programs) made up 45 percent of the institutions providing PAMT in developing countries. The ILO survey indicates that in the three developing regions, Africa, Asia and Latin America, PAMT institutions are about evenly distributed in numbers and that only "in Latin America, [did] university-related institutions form the single largest group" (Paul 1983, p. 42).

Training provided within these government institutions were pre-entry training (PET), in-service training (IST) and nondegree and field work. The target groups were new recruits to public service and middle and senior level personnel of ministries/departments. Furthermore these institutions were staffed by civil servants and academic trainers. While management institutes provided PET, IST, project-related training and field projects, they constituted only 4.5 percent, with university-related institutions and autonomous institutions providing 35.5 percent and 15 percent respectively.

Samuel Paul's (1983, p. 86) findings suggest that "[t]he training infrastructure in LDCs is highly skewed in favor of elites in public service and, in many cases, the utilization of existing facilities is poor." He further suggests that: "Training resources are allocated chiefly to meet the entry-level needs of public servants. . . . This has led to the relative neglect of in-service training in general, and of the training needs of lower-level personnel . . . [and] the failure of training designs (curricula, methods, and so forth) to match the real training needs of public servants" (Paul 1983, p. 86).

Consequently, management training in developing countries tends to emphasize the formal training approach with most training taking place in the classroom. Within this environment pre-service training is conducted almost exclusively as formal training and the lecture method predominates, despite its vulnerability to serious criticisms. One factor suggesting the continued popularity of the lecture method in developing countries is its tendency to reinforce the formal relationship that exists between the trainer and participant.

Historically, on-the-job training (OJT) was used to provide indigenous managers in developing countries after colonial independence. However, OJT has been viewed as a relatively unsuccessful approach to developing managers in developing countries because as a training intervention strategy it depended on such factors as a high-quality top management and a significant number of competent middle-level managers. For many developing countries these conditions do not exist, therefore OJT as a management training strategy is seldom a viable option.

Nonformal training, the third training approach, involves a learning situation where a group of managers with common interest, experience and needs meet in an essentially self-directed learning environment to exchange information and techniques. Nonformal training emphasizes learning from organizational experience and focuses primarily on information exchange. Nonformal training will have particular relevance to the senior and executive levels of management in developing countries, because top executives do not readily participate in formal training, on-the-job training or action training. They may choose to use informal training for information exchange, peer support or social affiliation. A variety of methods may be used in nonformal training — study circle, managerial support groups, panel discussion or conference meetings. As a management development strategy nonformal training has high potential for improving managerial techniques in developing countries.

A more recent trend in management training has been the action-learning or action-training approach used in training managers engaged in rural development. This approach grew out of the organizational development strategies for improving organizational health projects, and one of the key elements in action-training is that needs assessments and problem analyses accompany the training intervention. The Jamaica National Planning Project in 1977 was an early model of the action-training approach "based primarily on concepts developed by Morris J. Solomon, coordinator of USDA's Development Program Management Center (DPMC)" (Ingle et al. 1983, vol. II, p. 2).

> The central idea of "action-training" is that the concepts and skills included in any training effort be those which relate directly to a real need on an actual live project. In other words, training should result in immediate action and that action itself should become the content for learning. Results of training are immediately applicable to the task at hand and training success is measured in terms of progress made on actual project-performance.

As Paul suggests, this approach differs significantly from the three general approaches. Formal training, which is the most common training approach aimed primarily at pre-entry training for public service, within a classroom setting remains the dominant approach in developing countries. Nef and Dwivedi (1985, p. 243) concluded that rather than "provid[ing] standard education and training for development managers, [t]raining has tended to concentrate upon generalists. . . . Training for very specific and circumscribed developmental tasks has been rather scarce." Widespread concern for project-related training is reflected in the following statement of an Agency for International Development's (AID) *Management Development Strategy Paper:*

> A review of the developmental progress achieved during the decade of the 1980's will conclusively demonstrate that the next ten years may be referred to as the Management Decade. The importance of improved management of scarce human and physical resources in the pursuit of development objectives is the inescapable conclusion implied by numerous AID project impact evaluations, donor organization sector assessments, management improvement initiatives undertaken by the World Bank, UNDP, ILO, and FAO, feedback from AID project officers and host country project directors. . . . One of the fundamental challenges to those interested in supporting economic and social development in Third and Fourth world countries is overcoming the gap in managerial resources which now frustrates the aspirations of a large majority of development policy makers (U.S. Agency for International Development 1981, p. 1).

In India, according to Samuel Paul (1983, p. 75), a third of training programs organized by the Central Personnel Division during the 1970s focused on specialized, development-related subjects.

This resulting shift in emphasis necessitated a shift in target groups and methods of management training. Increased attention to project-related training meant "widening the target group to cover field project personnel such as planners and project managers." Yet, Paul's observations indicate that, despite this noticeable shift in target group and focus, training approaches and methods continue to emphasize the "individual and the development of his skills, attitudes, and ability to perform the defined tasks" with "[s]ome attention to team work and group performance" (Paul 1983, p. 77). It is questionable that the dominant management training approach, formal training with its emphasis on developing individual skills at the expense of group-related skills, its elite orientation and continued reliance on the classroom methods will be effective in meeting the evolving management training needs in developing countries.

If, as Paul suggests (1983, p. 78) "a shift in focus toward project appraisal and project management training [will] lead to a more analytic rather than descriptive emphasis in teaching and possibly increased . . . use of field work, group projects, and problem solving methods," developing countries face a number of problems. *First* — government institutions emphasizing pre-entry training will play an increasingly limited role in project-related management training. With few exceptions (Francophone Africa) the emphasis remains on training individuals in classroom settings, and not on the newer management training approaches, i.e., action-training with its group orientation; *second* — diversification of training methodologies must occur in all levels of management training institutions, for recent surveys by the ILO and Commonwealth Secretariat indicate that a mix of teaching methodologies are gaining in popularity while "T-groups and programmed instructions are seen as among the least useful methods" (Paul 1983, p. 77–78); and *third* — additional research must be conducted to identify those training methodologies that are successful in the initial phases of management training intervention in project-related programs.

In sum, since the decade of the 1970s the growing awareness of the importance of development administration and project-related training suggests that management training structures and approaches in developing countries, with their emphasis on pre-entry training, require a new approach to providing the managerial expertise necessary for successful project implementation.

As the target group shifts from the individual in a formal setting to field project personnel and project managers, training methodologies must also reflect such changes. The present domination of developing countries' training programs by the formal training approach with its emphasis on the lecture method in a classroom setting will not provide for the complex skills associated with group work essential for project implementation. Thus, the field of management development training would be best served by developing management training intervention strategies and teaching methods that provide a degree of success in achieving project-related management objectives.

Relative Effectiveness of Management Training Methodologies

Recent expansion of the management training target groups in developing countries to include field project personnel and project managers has necessitated a shift in training focus. Increased attention must now be paid to team work and group performance. Increased emphasis on people-centered project management and new management training intervention strategies, such as action-learning, have shifted the focus of training from the individual to the organization. As Paul (1983, p. 77) suggests "the target is no longer the individual or persons in the same level or category, but all members of the organization who are relevant to the total performance."

Paul cites a number of studies that suggest that in developing countries "teaching methodologies associated with the conventional approaches . . . continue to dominate even though significant shifts have occurred in the concepts and task of training." He goes on: "A recent survey of PAMT institutions in different parts of the world shows that the lecture method still dominates training. However, another survey—one by the Commonwealth Secretariat—finds there is no single dominant method of training in most of its member countries" (Paul 1983, p. 77). Trainers and educators have indicated that there are nine training methods preferred for teaching purposes. These are case study, conference (discussion) method, lecture, business games, films, programmed instruction, role playing, sensitivity (T-group) and television lecture. While the management training literature suggests that all nine methods are in use, it appears that in academic circles there is a tendency to rely very heavily on the lecture method as a means of providing instruction to students. In a survey of approximately 500 trainers, Neider (1981) sought to determine if there had been a shift in attitude about the relative effectiveness of teaching methods over the past decade. By using a questionnaire modeled after Carroll, Paine and Ivancevich (1972), Neider built on the findings of earlier research. In assessing the responses of trainers on the relative effectiveness of various teaching methods for attaining commonly agreed objectives (e.g., knowledge acquisition, knowledge retention, attitudinal change, development of problem-solving skills, developing interpersonal skills and participant acceptance), Neider concluded that "taken as a whole, data from the current survey indicate experts have not changed dramatically in their perceptions of different training procedures" (1981, p. 26). (See Table 16.1 for rankings of effectiveness of various training methods for various training objectives.)

In the area of management training, a 1980 study prepared for the U.S. Bureau of Mines by Joseph A. Olmstead and Devah R. Galloway surveyed more than 500 titles in a broad selection of literature (behavioral science, education, business, and training literature). Using a framework for analysis closely resembling that of Carroll, Newstrom, and Neider, their findings were rather inconclusive. Five questions were asked within the context of the study:

1. Does the training increase knowledge, awareness, and sensitivity to problems and issues involved in management and supervision?

2. Are participants' attitudes and self-insight influenced by the training?

3. Does training improve problem-solving skills?

4. Are participants' skills in leadership and interpersonal relations improved by training?

5. Is performance on the job improved through the training?

TABLE 16.1. Rankings of Training Directors on Effectiveness of Teaching Methods for Various Training Objectives

Training Method	Knowledge Acquisition 1972	Knowledge Acquisition 1981	Changing Attitudes 1972	Changing Attitudes 1981	Problem Solving Skills 1972	Problem Solving Skills 1981	Interpersonal Skills 1972	Interpersonal Skills 1981	Participant Acceptance 1972	Participant Acceptance 1981	Knowledge Retention 1972	Knowledge Retention 1981
Case study	2	4	4	4	1	1	4	5	2	2	2	4
Conference	3	3	3	3	4	3	3	3	1	1	5	3
Lecture	9	2	8	6	9	5	8	6	8	3	8	6
Business games	6	8	5	5	2	2	5	4	3	4	6	5
Films	4	7	6	7	7	8	6	7	5	6	7	7
Programmed instruction	1	1	7	9	6	6	7	9	7	7	1	2
Role playing	7	5	2	1	3	4	2	1	4	5	4	1
Sensitivity training	8	9	1	2	5	7	1	2	6	9	3	8
TV lecture	5	6	9	8	8	9	9	8	9	8	9	9

Sources: 1972 rankings are from S. J. Carroll, F. T. Paine, J. J. Ivancevich, "The Relative Effectiveness of Training Methods—Expert Opinion and Research." *Personnel Psychology* (1972): 495–509. 1981 rankings are from Linda Neider, "Training Effectiveness—Changing Attitudes." *Training and Development Journal* (Dec. 1981): 24–28.

Olmstead and Galloway's findings led to the following conclusions:

1. Lecture-discussion, conference method, and case analysis may all be effective in knowledge acquisition.

2. Changes in attitudes, as measured by written test, can be achieved by mixed training methods, i.e., lectures with heavy group discussion, role playing, case analysis, etc. However, little evidence exists to support the view that on-the-job behavior can be affected through training designed to achieve this objective.

3. It appears that training can produce improved problem-solving skills; however, the methods selected and used, such as case analysis, business games, and small group discussion reflect no significant difference in improving these skills.

4. Under proper training conditions interpersonal skills can be developed; however, much longer training time than is normally provided is required, and carefully structured training situations designed specifically to provide intensive practice of skills, as well as systematic feedback to the trainee are necessary.

5. No consistent evidence concerning the impact of training on the job performance exists (Olmstead and Galloway 1980, p. 19).

Olmstead and Galloway found in their survey of the literature that very little systematic guidance is available to trainers as to the potential value of the various training methods or their relative effectiveness in relation to particular objectives. They also noted that there are about as many methods as there are programs, each with its group of adherents, and the literature is full of unsupported claims as to their relative efficacy.

The Olmstead and Galloway analysis supports the conclusions of Newstrom (1975) and Neider (1981). The latter suggest that there is no one best teaching methodology, and, as Newstrom (p. 15) argues, the one-best-method syndrome "needs to be laid to rest early because it implies that there is an all-around 'best' method for use in most training programs." The evidence from Olmstead and Galloway supports this argument. This is not to imply that trainers should disregard the comparative data on training methods, even though they are far from definitive. These findings are still helpful in training design, particularly in selecting instructional methods other than those based on a particular trainer's personal preference or intuition.

As suggested by Bela Gold (1966, p. 71), "One way to avoid the futility of most past controversies about teaching methods . . . is to begin by recognizing that teaching may serve a variety of purposes; that any given teaching method may be better suited to some objectives than others; and that the development of new objectives or new kinds of content may counsel changes in instructional methods." However, too much latitude in this area may simply mean that the trainer will acquire a "pet" method or continue to mimic the method of a favorite professor.

In responding to the findings of the Commonwealth Secretariat's survey, Paul (1983, p. 77–78) suggests that the survey "probably points to the emergence of a shift in the mix of methods being used in some countries."

A 1982 Management Development Program Review conducted by the U.S. Department of Agriculture, Development Program Management Center of six different major management development programs in developing countries since 1970 suggests that even when a specific management training teaching method is used, eventually a mix of teaching methods will dominate (Ingle et al. 1983, p. II–3).

The International Training Division (ITD) of the Office of International Cooperation and Development of USDA's course on managing agricultural project implementation, for example, was aimed at mid- and upper-level managers actually involved in implementing agricultural projects, and it used case studies, team exercise, formal presentations and field trips in its six-weeks-long structured seminars. The USDA/DPMC Assisted Jamaica National Planning Project (1976–80) used the action-training approach "incorporat[ing] a range of methodologies . . . seminars, lectures, surveys, courses, workshops and consultations" (Ingle et al. 1983, p. II–4) to provide for "continual focus on real project results [with] . . . emphasis on learning through the experience of applying new skills and concepts." The Practical Concept Incorporated Training of Trainers in Management (TTM) Program (1976–81) sponsored by AID "relied on intensive . . . four to six week seminars in developing countries as the principal instructional method" (Ingle et al., p. III–1). This learning-by-doing approach to training includes exercises, games, simulations, video programs and video-assisted feedback sessions and field trips. Clearly there is a move toward less emphasis on the lecture method and increasing evidence to suggest that trainers should include a mix of methods to achieve management training objectives.

As the most influential actor in the training process, the trainer's decisions to apply a particular teaching methodology are often made without benefit of rigorous analysis, relying on individual preference, based on past experience, organizational pressures, outmoded educational philosophies or incompatible training intervention strategies. "What is needed is systematic guidance for trainers that will permit them to select methods appropriate for specific objectives and use them in accordance with instructions designed to get best results" (Olmstead and Galloway 1980, p. 19).

Criteria for Management Training Methods

As Andrzej Huczynski (1983, p. 7) cautions, "there are numerous criteria which one can use in order to choose between different teaching and learning methods." For the trainer, faced with a variety of conditions in developing countries, the necessity to be creative is increased. While the trainer is primarily concerned with the immediate task of teaching for results, national policy and strategy are important factors impinging on management training effectiveness. In project-related or project management training for developing countries the trainer must be cognizant of a number of factors that will enhance or constrain his effectiveness. This is not to suggest that the trainer must be involved in planning at the national level, it does suggest that factors such as national training policies, strategy and program design criteria are particularly relevant when selecting a teaching method. At a minimum the trainer must develop strategy, program design criteria, and teaching methods (see Table 16.2). While national training policy is important, trainers will have less input and control over this element of the selection process because training policies spelling out the institutional arrangements for meeting the management training needs in a developing country are frequently made at the national level. Therefore, assessment of training needs at the institutional and individual levels must be made within the context provided by the central government. Assuming that a developing country has established a national training plan, and that management training priorities have been selected, the trainer can then focus on *strategy* and *program design criterion,* two elements having a direct impact on selection of teaching methods.

TABLE 16.2. Strategy, Program Design Criteria, and Teaching Methods

Strategy	Program Design Criteria	Methods
Management training intervention	Learning objectives	
Formal training	Priority target	
Nonformal training	Target groups	Teaching method mix
On-the-job training	Target group size	
Action training		

Strategy: Management Training Intervention

Recent research suggests that each of the four management training approaches have potential for achieving different management training objectives. The formal training approach has been quite successful in obtaining the objectives of knowledge acquisition and understanding concepts and technique. On-the-job training can increase skills acquisition, and learning transfer, while the nonformal approach increases knowledge acquisition, learning transfer and interpersonal skills. Action training has a high potential for knowledge acquisition, understanding concepts, understanding techniques and skills acquisition. While neither of the four training interventions are all-encompassing in their inherent abilities to obtain all the objectives, the crucial issue for the trainer is to develop a program that reflects the proper balance of methods.

PROGRAM DESIGN CRITERIA. For the trainer, Andrzej Huczynski's recent study of management development methods will be quite valuable. When using learning objectives as a basis for choosing a teaching method, Huczynski (1983, p. 8) proposes to use Pedler's scheme as a basis for thinking about objectives in management development. As Huczynski (p. 10) cautions "Pedler's [has] offered a classification . . . [system] which [relates] objectives to method. He offered it with the proviso that it should not be taken too literally." Pedler's scheme added two additional domains to Bloom's three original areas of learning. The resulting five learning areas are psychomotor, cognitive, affective, interpersonal and self-knowledge. To this horizontal division was added a vertical division that represented four levels of learning division dealing with the cognitive aspects of learning. Hierarchically ordered, the levels of learning division are: 4 — Transfer, values and self expression; 3 — Application; 2 — Understanding; and 1 — Memory. Huczynski (p. 10) defines the memory level (level 1) or knowledge level as the ability to recall knowledge, recognize basic facts, procedures, principles and methods . . . memory level objectives frequently need to be achieved before the student can progress to higher levels of learning. Understanding (level 2) involves integrating or relating bits of knowledge; application (level 3), often termed skills level, deals, with understanding through doing, while transfer (level 4) represents the learner's ability to select and use the appropriate skills and knowledge in a range of new and different situations.

Huczynski noted that as one moves up through the levels, it was more difficult to select the appropriate methods. He suggests that:

> In the first three levels, traditional learning sequences appeared to work as one moved from the rules of theory to practice; from the learning of parts to an understanding of the whole; from simple to complex learning. At these levels one can distill the theory from the experiences of practice. Whereas at the first three levels of learning methods dictated the nature of the learning, at the fourth, it was the nature of the learning which dictated the method (Huczynski 1983, p. 11).

Pedler's scheme suggests that the hierarchy of cognitive learning objectives may be used to select teaching methods that are generally successful in their application. Briefly he suggests that the lecture method, talks and programmed learning are useful for enhancing memory (level 1). Talks, discussion and case studies are useful for (level 2) understanding; demonstration and practice, role play, simulations and discussions are useful for (level 3) application; and discussion, sensitivity training and group exercises are quite useful for (level 4) transfer. Yet, to apply this scheme as the sole classification criteria for selecting a method is to overestimate its impact. For management behavior will span all levels of learning and no single level exists in isolation. Therefore the trainer must consider other factors such as priority target, group size and target groups.

PRIORITY TARGET. Samuel Paul suggests that upgrading the management skills and abilities of mid-level project personnel including management staff and low-level managers should be given higher priority by developing countries. Therefore, a priority target for trainers should be providing the type of management training that will enhance those managerial skills that relate to project success. This is not to imply that management training programs must be narrowed in scope, for as argued in a 1981 AID, *Management Development Strategy Paper:*

> We must recognize that the domain of management skills development is now far broader than that originally posited by classical management theorists. In addition to the basic planning, organizing, and control functions, we have come to recognize team building, joint problem solving, organization design, organization change, information system design, role negotiation, and coalition and relationship management, action research, and resource mobilization as critical skills for public service managers (U.S. Agency for International Development 1981, p. 36).

TARGET GROUP. Walsh (1984, p. 10) concluded that "[t]he most severe shortage of managerial technology in the Third World societies is in the rural areas and at the grass roots level" while Nef and Dwivedi (1984, p. 246) suggest that "training . . . should be oriented to two types of clientele. One is made up of grass roots organizations." They further argue that "[t]raining here would involve the expansion of simple technical know-how into management for change and problem-solving—a sort of 'barefoot manager' " (1985, p. 245). While Nef and Dwivedi see a second clientele as essentially at the more professional level, they emphasize that "both sectors aim at the formation of a cadre of technicians able to see in perspective, and apply, basic management and organizing skills to very concrete and specific problems" (Nef and Dwivedi 1985, p. 245–46).

However, for the trainer the problem at hand is to select a teaching method with a high probability of success in obtaining the desired learning objectives. Given developing countries' priorities the present target group should consist of first line managers and middle-level project managers.

TARGET GROUP SIZE. Again, the Huczynski study will be of value to the trainer. He suggests that "the size of group is a second and equally important dimension against which a choice of methods is to be made" (1983, p. 12). Huczynski uses a modified version of Gage and Berliner's work, which was done in the American secondary schools. Recognizing that management training groups tended to be smaller, Huczynski classified groups in the following manner: 25 or more students, aggregate; 17–24 students, large group; 3–16 students, small group; and 1–2 students, individual/ dyad. Huczynski provides the trainer with the following guidelines in selecting teaching methods based on group size: with individual/dyad (1–2 persons), typical teaching methods are development assignment and programmed learning; with small groups (3–16), typical teaching methods are role playing and some experiential exercises. Huczynski (p. 14) selects the number 16 as the upper limit because "small group work which involves four groups reporting back in a plenary session is just possible within a ninety-minute class session." Large groups (17–24) is seen as the upper limit of group work, with typical teaching methods such as case study and the syndicate method. The largest and most impersonal situation is the aggregate group (25 plus) and the teaching method best suited for large groups is the lecture method.

To this point the trainer has accumulated information that will assist him in selecting a combination of teaching methods having a high probability of obtaining the desired learning objectives. Identifying the management training intervention approach allows the trainer to adapt the program design criteria (learning objectives, priority target, target group and target group size) to the constraints of the local environment resulting in a basic framework that brings a measure of order to teaching method selection.

This framework may also be useful in selecting a management training intervention strategy. The elements of the program design criteria will impact both teaching method selection and provide feedback as to the best approach to the overall training program.

At this point the trainer can select the methods to use in obtaining the desired result. Again Huczynski has made a major contribution to the field of management development training with his book *Encyclopedia of Management Development Methods* (1983). He provides a directory listing approximately 385 methods from which the trainer may select methods suitable for his individual training needs. Huczynski's directory of methods will allow the trainer to take advantage of recent research in the field of management training and yet be innovative in adapting techniques to the local environment. This encyclopedia of management training methods should become an essential addition to the library of trainers in the various countries. The field of management training is suitable for innovations, offering the trainer the opportunity to make a major contribution to successful project implementation in the developing countries.

Conclusions

Training may not be a panacea for solving the developmental and administrative problems of developing countries; however, management training has assumed increased importance as a strategy for assisting developing countries confront their massive economic and managerial problems. Lack of management skills in developing countries is a major factor identified by the World Development Report 1983 as limiting development. However, the shift in focus and emphasis identified by Samuel Paul suggests that the conventional approaches to management training in developing countries signal a need to reassess the effectiveness of many of the training programs, which appear to be inappropriate for obtaining developmental objectives in rural development projects.

A number of projects have been funded by both private and international organizations to improve management training programs in developing countries and a number of emerging methods show great promise. The action learning approach, and the Coverdale method, are just a few of the contributions made in the past decade to providing alternatives to conventional approaches to management training.

One has only to contrast the present understanding of the relative effectiveness of different training strategies with the dismal conclusions of two decades ago.

In his 1970 study of management training methods Campbell summarized the state of knowledge then prevailing:

> What do we know? We know that management development can change managers toward more employee centered attitudes. We know that laboratory education probably can change behavior in the work role, but the nature and implications of these changes are unclear. We know that P.I. [Programmed Instructions] is at least as effective as conventional institutional methods in some situations and is probably faster when used appropriately. . . . In sum, we know a few things but not very much (Campbell 1971, p. 593).

A decade later, Olmstead and Galloway made a similar observation:

Lecture-discussion, conference method, and case analysis may all be effective in improving knowledge and increasing awareness and sensitivity to the human element in work situations, and evidence suggests that changes in attitudes, as measured by written attitude test, can be achieved through training. It appears that training can produce improved problem-solving skills, and under proper training conditions, it is possible to improve the interpersonal skills of trainees, and that only a few studies have examined the effects of training on managerial performance with no consistent evidence concerning the impact on job performance (Olmstead and Galloway 1980, p. 19).

Since the Olmstead and Galloway study in 1980, a number of studies indicate that certain management development approaches do work in the developing countries. The Management Development Center of USDA's Management Development Program Review suggests that certain combinations of teaching methods are quite successful in obtaining learning objectives. Samuel Paul's review of *Training for Public Administration and Management in Developing Countries* offers the trainer "the results of a survey of the trends, developments, and problems in public administration and management training (PAMT) in developing countries" (Paul 1983, Abstract).

However, Paul has identified a number of lingering problems in management training. He cites in the 1983 Abstract "weaknesses in the design and management of training institutions, and failure to match faculty (trainers) resources, curricula, training materials and methodologies relevant to the emerging needs of developing countries" as limiting the effectiveness of management training in developing countries.

Marcus D. Ingle (Ingle letter 1985) of the International Development Management Center (IDMC) suggests that "the key issue [today] . . . seems to be in getting the state-of-the-practice to be more in line with the state-of-the-art." The framework proposed in this chapter is aimed at providing the trainer, the essential actor in the management training process, a simple guideline for selecting teaching methods in the field that present a high probability of obtaining the desired learning objectives within the confines of the local environment. While it is difficult to assess fully the effectiveness of present training methods in developing the knowledge, skills and attitudes that improve on-the-job performance, we can, based on recent studies, make a number of assumptions as to the usefulness of various methods. Management development training is a field ripe for innovation and development and the adaptation of new techniques is taking place in many areas. This is not to suggest that trainers have a free hand in selecting methods, since this process may be constrained by management training intervention approaches, the learning objective sought, target priority and target group size in addition to a developing country's national priorities. In the final analysis the trainer must select the teaching method that has the greatest potential for success. There is no one best criteria for method selection just as there is no one best teaching method. However, the trainers should be given some systematic guidance permitting them to select the methods most appropriate for their situation. Realizing that there is no one best method, the trainer must use criteria other than face value or tradition to provide guidance in selecting appropriate teaching methods. The framework presented in this paper will provide the trainer with a simple means of developing the criteria for selecting teaching methods. Huczynski's *Encyclopedia of Management Development Methods* offers the trainer 385 teaching methods to choose from. This provides the trainer with a source for decision making and the opportunity to be innovative in the field.

While there is room for optimism today, the problem of effective project implementation remains. It will require innovative approaches and flexibility on the part of donor agencies, developing countries and trainers if the managerial capacity of developing countries is to be improved.

Appearing before the Subcommittee on Foreign Operations of the Senate Appropriations Committee, M. Peter McPherson, the AID administrator, emphasized the importance of technology development and dissemination in developing countries: "Sustained development requires an indigenous capacity to adopt, create and apply a continuing stream of appropriate technologies to the problems of health, population growth, hunger, illiteracy, unemployment, and labor productivity" (Department of State Bulletin 1984, p. 63). Management development training plays a critical role in this process, for it absorbs substantial budgetary resources in donor agencies and the developing countries. Despite the progress made in the past decade, the conditions in many developing countries are best described by Bryant and White (1982, p. 23) as "[a]lthough administrative capacity is in short supply everywhere, its serious scarcity in the Third World is particularly crippling."

To remedy this problem increased emphasis on management training represents an attempt to upgrade the administrative capacity in developing countries and to eliminate a condition further described as follows:

> Buried in the thousands of pages of five-year plans throughout the Third World are programs that purport to bring development to rural regions—to expand the economy and to increase the income of the people who live there. But once the political battle to gain power, formulate the plan, and raise the funds is won, the next phase is less clear. . . . Conversely, the fact that development often does not happen, or is very uneven, is partially rooted in management and organizational problems (Bryant and White 1982, p. 23).

References

Badawy, M. K. "Managerial Attitudes and Need Organizations of Eastern Executives: An Empirical Cross-Cultural Analysis." *Academy Management Proceedings* 297 (1979).

Berg, William B. "An Immediate and Wide Impact Approach to Management Improvement." Unpublished paper. USAID/Ghana, 1981.

Berkman, Ali. "Comments." In *Public Administration Training for Less Developed Countries.* Edited by Irving Swerdlow and Marcus Ingle. Syracuse: Maxwell School of Citizenship, 1974.

Black, Joseph E.; Coleman, James S.; and Stifel, Lawrence D. *Education and Training for Public Sector Management in Developing Countries.* New York: Rockefeller Foundation, 1977.

Bohdan, Hawryshyn. *Management Development and Training Handbook.* New York: McGraw Hill, 1975.

Bryant, Coralie, and White, Louise G. *Managing Development in Third World.* Boulder, Colo.: Westview Press, 1982.

Campbell, John P. "Personnel Training and Development." *Annual Review of Psychology* 22 (1971):593.

Carroll, S. J.; Paine, F. T.; and Ivancevich, J. J. "The Relative Effectiveness of Training Methods—Expert Opinion and Research." *Personnel Psychology* 25 (1972).

Department of State Bulletin. *Request for Economic Assistance Program.* Volume 84, No. 2086. Washington, D.C.: Government Printing Office, 1984.

Desatnick, Robert L. *A Concise Guide to Management Development.* New York: American Management Association Inc., 1970.

Ferrari, Sergio. "The Open Problem of Management Training Evaluation." *Management International Review* 10, no. 4–5 (1970):39.

Gold, Bela. "Adjusting Teaching Methods to Changing Objective Management Education." *Management International Review* 1 (1966):71.

Griffith, Rodger W.; Hom, Peter W.; Denisi, Angelo; and Kirchner, Wayne. "A Multivariate Multinational Comparison of Managerial Attitudes." *Academy of Management Proceedings* 66 (1980).

Huczynski, Andrzej. *Encyclopedia of Management Development Methods.* Aldershot, England: Gower, 1983.

Ingle, Marcus D.; Owen, Wilfred, Jr.; Spears, Donald; and Bordelon, Marvin. *Management Development in Agriculture Program Review and Workshop.* Development Management Center (DPMC), Washington: U.S. Department of Agriculture, 1983.

_____. Letter to author, 1985.

Lippitt, G. L., and Taylor, B. *Management Development and Training Handbook.* New York: McGraw Hill, 1975.

Nef, J., and Dwivedi, O. P. "Training for Development Management: Reflections on Social Know-How As A Scientific and Technological System." *Public Administration and Development* 5, no. 3 (1985):235–49.

Negandhi, Annat R. "Cross-Cultural Management Studies: Too Many Conclusions, Not Enough Conceptualizations." *Management International Review* 14, no. 6 (1974):59.

Neider, Linda L. "Training Effectiveness-Changing Attitudes." *Training and Development Journal* 35 (Dec. 1981):26.

Newstrom, John W. "Selecting Training Methodologies." *Training and Development Journal* 29, (Oct. 1975):15.

Olmstead, Joseph A., and Galloway, Devah R. *Management and Supervisory Training: A Review and Annotated Bibliography* (Special Report 80–8). Alexandria: Human Resources Research Organization, 1980.

Paul, Samuel. *Training for Public Administration and Management in Developing Countries: A Review.* World Bank Staff Working Papers Number 53, Management and Development Series Number 11. Washington: World Bank, 1983.

_____. *Educating Managers for Business and Government.* Washington: World Bank, 1988.

Redding, Gordon, and Casey, Terry. "Managerial Beliefs Among Us Managers." *Academy of Management Proceedings* 353 (1976).

United States Agency for International Development. "Management Development Strategy Paper: AID's Response to the Implementation Needs of the 1980's." Washington: Office of Rural Development and Development Support Bureau, 1981.

_____. "Performance Management." (Mimeographed report) Project No. 936–5317, 1982.

Walsh, A. M. "Public Administration and Development." *IPA Report* 1 (1984).

17

Towards the Future of Comparative Public Administration

GERALD and **NAOMI CAIDEN**

OF ALL SOCIAL SCIENCES, public administration remains the least universalistic and comparative. Perhaps the planning and execution of public policies, services and programs are by their very nature so idiosyncratic, particularistic and contextual that the attainable level of generalization and nomothetic theory is relatively low. Perhaps the action-oriented activities of public administrators, like lawyers and doctors, have not yet attracted an intellect to match an Aristotle in politics or an Adam Smith in economics or a Max Weber in sociology or a Sigmund Freud in psychology, someone who could provide a general framework, as did Newton and Einstein in physics, within which succeeding generations of theorists could guide practitioners in the field. Yet the vision of a universalistic and comparative science of public administration still allures generation after generation of researchers in public administration, dating as far back as the cameralists.

Here is not the place to describe in any detail the many attempts to evolve a truly universal and comparative discipline of public administration and the host of reasons and explanations why they have failed to achieve the critical mass necessary to make the crucial breakthrough. Suffice to say that interest in evolving such a science has ebbed and flowed, with each wave advancing the frontier but falling still short of the goal. The latest and most significant of these waves emerged just after World War II and surged to its peak in the mid-1960s with its institutionalization in the Comparative Administration Group (CAG) under the auspices of the American Society for Public Administration (ASPA). Led by its most productive, ambitious and original theorist, Fred Riggs, and financed in large part by the Ford Foundation, CAG built up a belief in comparative administration that no previous wave had done. It stimulated much intellectual excitement in the comparative side of public administration. It led to a voluminous literature, unmatched in quantity and possibly quality too, producing at least one classic (Riggs 1964), alas now out of print, among its many books, papers and bibliographies. And it planned ambitious research and educational projects, such as an international center for development administration that might, if funded, have succeeded eventually in attaining the goal of comparative administration.

Unfortunately, the funding could not be found and just as quickly as CAG crested, so it ebbed and diminished in force and influence through the 1970s. Yet, building up behind it another wave seems now to be gathering strength and is sweeping forward. This new and most current wave is more universal than its American-dominated predecessor. It is less concerned with technical assistance programs as such, with American research designs and American institutional sponsorship, with administrative development and development administration, or rather Western conceptualizations of development administration and development goals, and Western-style public bureaucracy. It is just as concerned about administrative stability and administrative change, institution-building and institutional develop- ment, with social values as well as managerial processes, although the em- phasis may differ. More significantly, it is more concerned with practicality and implementation than theory building and abstractions, with public pol- icy and administrative organization than societal context and administra- tive ecology, and with administrative substance than intellectual concerns. It is altogether more pragmatic, more practitioner-oriented, more down to earth and no longer hungers after a universal discipline of public adminis- tration that fired many adherents of CAG.

The Legacy of the Comparative Administration Group

Looking back at CAG, Peter Savage had suggested that fads and fancies in the social sciences lasted about a decade (1976). Either they made it or they were dropped and replaced by fresher ideas, theories and perspectives. Comparative administration had by then enjoyed its decade in the sun. Not only had it failed to provide a unified framework or theory or paradigm for the discipline of public administration but it had failed even to provide much social knowledge with social utility. On the one hand, comparative administration had made a lasting impact, its concerns and perspectives had become a part of the discipline, its legacy was alive and flourishing, and the problems of public policy and human betterment that had given life to comparative administration would continually pose a challenge to the discipline's theorists and practitioners. On the other hand:

> "The auguries for Comparative Administration are not good. *The Journal of Comparative Administration* has gone. The Comparative Administration Group . . . has . . . disbanded. . . . The Duke University Press series in Comparative Administration has come to an end. . . . Gone too are the fecund "summer seminars," the easy assurance of panels devoted to the field at professional meetings, and the receptivity of scholarly journals to articles in Comparative Administration. My own experience [is] of dwindling classes and the lessening appeal of course work to American . . . students" (Savage 1976, p. 415).

Such pessimism turned out to be warranted; within five years, a survey of MPA programs in the United States had shown a drastic decline in the study, teaching and research of international and comparative public administration (Mohapratra 1983). Actually, interest had begun to wane long before that. A CAG survey in 1963 had shown increasing interest (1960), confirmed by a better response in 1966 (1967), but a poor response in 1970 indicated that several old-timers who had moved into the field as a result of the U.S. technical programs abroad had drifted out again and that the growing neoisolation sentiment had shifted interest to domestic concerns. (See also Gable 1971.)

Comparative administration rarely appeared in the core and it had been dropped as an option in many programs because of lack of student demand. "It appears many MPA clientele did not perceive these courses to be very relevant" (Mohapratra 1983). Indeed, most of Savage's fears were confirmed as publications on comparative administration dropped sharply. The Section on International and Comparative Administration of the American Society for Public Administration, which had inherited the Comparative Administration Group, lost half its membership, and it became quite difficult to raise any interest and funds for comparative administration. The ten good years reviewed by Peter Savage were followed by ten lean years.

Yet comparative politics, which had similar beginnings to comparative administration and for an initial period shared much the same concerns, both theoretical and pragmatic, and even the same researchers, has meantime fared considerably better. Comparative politics (rather than comparative government) has established itself in the core of political science. The comparative method has displaced description with "cross-nationally applicable explanatory generalizations" (Mayer 1983), encompassing:

> (1) the search for more comprehensive scope—an effort to break away from parochialism and ethnocentrism; (2) the search for realism—an attempt to escape from formalism and examine all the structures and processes involved in

politics and policymaking; (3) the search for precision—a commitment to conceptualization and to theory building and testing rather than simple description. What had once been a "descriptive, largely classificatory, and sometimes normative enterprise" was now being infused with explanatory and predictive pretensions (Sigelman and Gadbois 1983).

As a result of this transformation and consequent centrality, comparative politics can boast a plethora of major texts for compulsory core courses. Major publishing houses compete among themselves for the most popular choice, and at least two major journals, *Comparative Politics* and *Comparative Political Studies* whose contents are "more theoretically and conceptually attuned, more sophisticated in terms of their approach to data collection and analysis, and more likely to incorporate explicit comparative elements into their design," cater to comparative studies (Sigelman and Gadbois 1983). Comparative politics has moved away from its former narrow focus "on the institutions, rules, and procedures through which governments operated" to a wide array of issues in pursuit of a science of politics that endeavors to achieve unity through mastering diversity.

The Elusive Search for a Science of Public Administration

This goal common to both comparative politics and comparative administration had first been brought to the attention of public administration in 1947 by Robert Dahl's critique of pre-World War II efforts to seek a science of public administration with universal laws "independent not only of moral and political ends, but of the frequently nonconformist personality of the individual, and the social and cultural setting as well" (Dahl 1947). He identified three fundamental problems. First, it was impossible to exclude normative considerations from the problems of public administration. Public administration could not avoid concern with ends, moral purposes and values. Second, apart from the methodological problems arising from the diversity, complexity and nonrepeatability of the subject matter, it was wrong to depend on an oversimplified view of human nature, an abstract mechanized "Administrative Man." Third, the social setting could not be ignored because public administration was conditioned by it and could not be independent of and isolated from it.

> At the same time as value can be gained by a comparative study of government based upon a due respect for differences in the political, social, and economic environment of nation-states, so too the comparative study of public administration ought to be rewarding. Yet the comparative aspects of public administration have largely been ignored; and as long as the study of public administration is not comparative, claims for "a science of public administration" sound rather hollow (Dahl 1947, p. 8).

In short, "we need many more studies of comparative administration before it will be possible to argue that there are any universal principles of public administration" (Dahl 1947, p. 11), or, in Dwight Waldo's words, *"through mastering diversity we shall achieve unity"* (Waldo 1964, p. 7). Comparative administration should take the world as its canvas, to discover what could be compared, to develop criteria that could be used to make valid comparisons, to employ scientific methods in making comparisons, and to validate hypotheses about the real world of public administration so that the discredited principles of public management might be replaced with a truly comparative public administration. In this, comparative politics has largely convinced its audience, even if the practice falls well short of the promise. But comparative administration has largely failed to convince. Consequently, it is at the periphery of public administration, a supplement, even an afterthought, and few today can recall that its motivation was once to "facilitate the development of a practical, or applied, science of administration" (Kaufman and Sayre 1953).

That the original promise of comparative administration had been dashed can be illustrated by comparing the initial optimism of the comparative administration movement in the late 1950s and early 1960s with the often bitter and acrimonious observations after the Comparative Administration Group (CAG) became the Section on International and Comparative Administration (SICA) of the American Society for Public Administration in the early 1970s, well illustrated in the Symposium on Comparative and Development Administration: Retrospect and Prospect in the last issue of the 1976 volume of *Public Administration Review*. Nonetheless, as early as 1966 Milton Esman had already guessed that comparative administration would not convince public administration. Despite all the good things it was doing, such as "expanding the substantive horizon and the methodological sophistication of academic public administration in the United States," it was too diverse and vacuous, too far removed from the compelling problems of action, too distant from sensitive practitioners, altogether too ambitious in grand designs, general theories, new typologies, new terminology, in short, too far ahead of itself. "Our ability to raise questions, to pose hypotheses and to state insights has far outrun our capacity and perhaps even our inclination to test them empirically" (Esman 1966). What was needed was more empirical data, more relevance to the pressing developmental issues of the day, and less faith in the public bureaucracy to overcome development problems and obstacles. He concluded: "We are still at the stage of searching for hypotheses rather than testing them and we have few new prescriptions which we can confidently offer to supplement our intuitions and our educated judgments" (Esman 1966). As research proposals that would have ameliorated the situation were not financed, CAG could only do more of the same. So when its modest funding by the Ford Foundation ran out, its efforts floundered, the momentum dropped, and the many disappointed faithful whose hopes had evaporated turned on one another, especially on the leading CAG figure, Fred Riggs, for the decline in comparative administration fortunes.

Article after article appeared lamenting the failure of the comparative administration movement and variously attributing the blame. Possibly the most damaging psychologically for CAG was Warren Ilchman's attack on the "uninspired and uninspiring performance of the CAG" (Ilchman 1971, p. 6) at CAG's Grand Central Conference at Syracuse in April 1971 from which comparative administration has never quite recovered. Against conventional wisdom Ilchman evaluated CAG's contribution to comparative administration by analyzing its answers to five questions relating to the power, productivity, structure (or organizational form), role congruence and capacity for maintenance and adaptation of public organizations, using a resource exchange model to understand the answers. He believed that CAG had made no theoretical advance, a damaging conclusion to an audience that judged its own performance on advancing theory beyond conventional wisdom. Further, it had failed "to live up to the promise of discovering through comparative analysis methods and approaches that would be useful in developmental situations" and as it "did not produce a body of empirical materials," it was unlikely "to say anything of value for those people who dwell in the world. There were theories, theories about theories, analysis of other's theories . . . we find each other much more interesting than our subject matter" (Ilchman 1971, p. 44–45). He did concede that CAG may have begotten some unconventional departures; it may have impressed the importance of the public bureaucracy on political scientists; and it may have made its members more thoughtful. With Ilchman's puncturing of the CAG balloon, other critics became bolder as exuberance gave way to introspection (Heady 1978, 1984).

CAG Shortcomings

Hindsight now suggests that CAG could never have reconciled the conflicting parties, on the one hand those who wanted help with the practical problems of development, demanded workable prescriptions and pressed for immediate results and on the other those who sought a genuine universal science of public administration. Broadly, there were six major CAG shortcomings. First, *it was too academic,* suffering from overly detached scholarly objectivity. Its work was too abstract, encompassing whole systems as units of analysis so that much of it lost any theoretical meaning and was impossible to operationalize and irrelevant to the practical needs of the day. Its typologies were unemployable and its classifications too complex—just names "and names do not provide any basis for research" (Landau 1969). By concentrating on the ecological approach, it lacked administrative substance so that it was indefinite and undelimited, abounding in undefined conceptualizations, and lacking in focus and therefore in accumulation. It produced no universal models of modernization or development. Much of this was the result of CAG's deliberate choice to follow the original 1953 Sayre-Kaufman outline to stress scholarly research, to map a scientific understanding of administration systems and develop the field on the basis of uniform checklists, and CAG's modus operandi copying that of the Committee on Comparative Politics of the Social Science Research Council though without "the use of a consistent theoretical model by which to order knowledge" (Ilchman 1971, p. 8–9).

Second, *it was insufficiently empirical.* Theory building requires empirical testing and validation. Although at the outset, William Siffin and others had tried to follow a consistent model and to test it empirically (1957), CAG did not indulge in much systematic testing or attempt to build data banks shaped by a consistent model for comparative purposes. Its members preferred grand theory building to field work or even to assimilating field work into their theory building. On a 1966 CAG questionnaire, Peter Savage reported that "There was not a consistent, sustained, widespread, or strongly stated appeal for linking the theoreticians with the practitioners under the aegis of the CAG nor for an investment of resources in stimulating empirical research" (Savage 1967, p. 12). Later, Keith Henderson commented:

> Neither students nor scholars seemed inclined, on a large scale, to face the perils of field research, which on any rational cost-benefit calculus was not worth the effort. Inadequate statistics, problems of access, language barriers, expenses which foundations seemed reluctant to share, hostile or indifferent governments and study subjects, and other obstacles conspired to frustrate would-be researchers who could not operate from some firmer base than comparative public administration. When obstacles were partially overcome, the results were sometimes disastrous nonetheless (Henderson 1969, p. 69).

He diluted his criticism by admitting that some good empirical work had been and was being done by CAG members and that CAG had outlined a rather elaborate prospectus for empirical research across the board even though it had failed to obtain funding for field work.

Third, *it was still too culture-bound.* While professing to combat the ethnocentricity of American public administration, CAG itself was more culture-bound and ethnocentric than it would acknowledge. Indeed, it was often wrongly accused of being an arm of the U.S. government and of being geared to U.S. foreign policy. CAG itself took pains to dissociate itself from the U.S. government and CAG members could never resolve the issue whether or not they should accept funds from the technical cooperation and assistance programs of the U.S. government. Not until the Ford Foundation funding ran out did CAG scramble around for other action-oriented projects. Nonetheless, to obtain the Ford Foundation funds CAG adopted the term "development administration" in place of comparative public administration and thus became associated with U.S. government efforts to modernize several alleged backward countries through the transfer (imposition?) of Western institutions and values. Many CAG members had been employed in previous and continuing U.S. technical assistance programs and it was expected that CAG research would have beneficial impacts on such programs that were experiencing difficulties in the field. Consciously or not, CAG supported efforts to modernize, i.e. Westernize, the Third World, to speed up development in poor countries, to use government and public organizations as spearheads in developmental efforts, and to transform (reform) public bureaucracy into a progressive force. Public administration to CAG was not just nuts and bolts management of public organizations or the transfer of American administrative know-how, but the administrative state in action, the shaper of societies, capable of changing its context, determining public policy, and overcoming resistance from traditionalists (antimodernizers).

In fact, CAG was divided over the goals, strategies and instruments of development. No doubt there was a faction that identified itself with U.S. foreign policy, that did seek to provide "an intellectual grounding for American foreign policy in the 1960s" (Loveman 1976, p. 618), that sought to win over the Third World for the West against Marxism, that did emphasize *economic* development over social and political development, that did exaggerate the role of the administrative state, that did believe in inducing, imposing and managing change through state-controlled instruments, that did push for industrialization, urbanization, and bureaucratization, that did see their expertise as creating effective public administrative instruments, that did support authoritarian regimes that would employ them as advisors or adopt their managerial reforms, and that saw development administration largely in terms of physical facilities (preferably built by Americans). But there was another faction that opposed U.S. foreign policy, that attacked the Cold War and would have no part of it, that stressed social and political development as well as economic development, that feared the dominance of the bureaucratic state, that preferred a democratic ethos, that sought public participation in and control of developmental efforts, and that refused to assist authoritarian regimes and enhance their repressive capability.

Yet neither faction adequately recognized that development administration involved for the Third World foreign values and objectives, foreign technology, foreign organization and methods, which would tie the Third World into an international system not of its making; that development administration legitimized governmental control and authority, political elites, and a public bureaucracy, which would tie poor peoples into a political-administrative system not of their making; and that development administration, despite much empirical evidence, ignored how Western institutions, particularly the Weberian bureaucracy, were not necessarily effective in the West and much less so when transplanted into the Third World. Other than through personal contacts, CAG as a whole was insensitive to counterparts elsewhere that did not share its outlook and cultural norms and could not communicate in English. It was essentially an American group rather than an international group and it remained apart from other organizations, such as the International Institute of Administrative Sciences (IIAS) based in Belgium, with which it might have combined efforts on behalf of comparative administration. However, the blame was not wholly CAG's, as the IIAS was unsympathetic to the American group.

Fourth, *it was too isolated.* Just as CAG did not forge an international movement, it failed to forge any coalition within the United States. Originally, comparative administration could have gone with either the American Political Science Association or the American Society for Public Administration. After the political scientists failed to show sufficient enthusiasm, reflecting their general disdain for public administration, the American Society for Public Administration parented CAG and the political scientists were increasingly outnumbered. Although CAG's switch to development administration emphasized its multidisciplinary nature, CAG could not attract other social scientists, with the exception of some internationally renowned sociologists. For its part, CAG seemed to ignore comparative studies in other disciplines. No reference was made to cross-cultural research in comparative management (Nath 1968, p. 35–62; Udy 1965, p. 678–709) and almost no mention was made of the role of business in economic development. Indeed, CAG seemed to ignore development economics altogether, as it did social change literature and comparative studies outside political science.

Even less excusable was CAG's isolation from administrative practitioners, causing Bernard Schaffer to remark that its members "had their conferences and wrote their papers, but the practitioners did not seem to take much notice and changes in developing countries did not seem to be directly affected" (Schaffer 1971, p. 330). Its members were always "getting ready to get ready — exploring epistemological matters, debating the boundaries of the field, and surveying the manner in which concepts have been used" (Sigelman 1971, p. 330) and spending too "much time and energy debating issues of comparison, putting forth general analytic frameworks, and sketching out the environment of administration that we have been diverted from the study of administration itself" (p. 623). Consequently, CAG gave no help in solving practical problems or providing meaningful advice to practitioners. It failed altogether "as the overseas extension of traditional public administration concerns such as control and responsibility, personnel, budgeting, and organization and methods studies" (Henderson 1969, p. 72) and provided no guidance to troubleshooters removing administrative obstacles to nation-building, economic advance and modernization. "Little has been contributed to the expert in the field" (p. 73), a point conceded by Fred Riggs who readily admitted that CAG had "contributed very little to AID's public administration program" (Riggs 1976, p. 649).

Fifth, *it had too few academic payoffs.* Paradoxically, although CAG concentrated on scholars, it had few successes among them. Its theories were neglected. Even the critics, like Ilchman, who offered different schema had little impact on research.

> Comparative Administration started with no paradigm of its own and developed none. . . . [Its] literature displays an exchange of idiosyncratic theoretical formulations and organizing perspectives, many of which have more to do with academic or personal fancy than with any generally acceptable cumulative purpose . . . what was fabricated were often not so much theories, in any scientific sense of the word, as they were fantasies (Savage 1976, p. 417).

The theories, models, concepts and speculations did not speak, commented Peter Savage, to the reality of global problems and issues that first gave rise to the field. "It did not produce much in the way of socially useful knowledge" (p. 419). It did not bring practitioners into the classroom and it did not even attract students. In short, it failed "to correct the inadequacies of parochial, unsystematic, noncomparative study" (Henderson 1969, p. 67), and the "various earlier hopes have not materialized, such as attainment of a higher degree of cumulative knowledge, more direct relevance to programs of technical assistance and the conduct of more extensive and well-coordinated data collection and field research activities" (Heady 1978, p. 358).

Sixth, *it was too idiosyncratic.* Although initially CAG started off with a common agenda, it soon came apart as its members went their own ways. If there was a center, it was at Indiana University where William Siffin began by sticking to the original agenda and produced the first teaching materials for the new comparative administration (Siffin 1957). When Fred Riggs, who had participated in the original Sayre-Kaufman outline, assumed the chairmanship of CAG in 1959, he put his energetic, versatile, productive and liberal stamp on the whole movement with the help of Peter Savage. Fred Riggs became, if anyone did, the intellectual guru of CAG. But neither Riggs nor Savage was able to contain the centrifugal forces within CAG. At the University of Michigan, Ferrel Heady and Nimrod Raphaeli contributed a general text and an accompanying reader (Heady and Stokes 1962; Heady 1966; Raphaeli 1967). At each major school of public administration, a different intellectual leader pursued a different path.

As Warren Ilchman has pointed out, at least two quite incompatible strategies emerged involving different conceptions of science, knowledge and explanation, and also different conceptions of character. While Riggs pursued an essentialist strategy of pure social science, others such as Milton Esman and Joseph La Palombara, pursued existential applied social science. "Briefly put, the antithesis was between those who thought political man would cheat unless he were watched and those who thought political man was deserving of the public trust. . . . Mistrust and trust got woven into the theory of comparative administration" (Ilchman 1971, p. 417). Apart from sharing a common interest in stimulating comparative theory, members of CAG had no other central focus. They were confused and confusing. No wonder that comparative administration had not "isolated and identified a manageable and distinct piece of the terrain of human political behavior, posed an agenda of compelling questions and problems within the terrain, and established an appropriate logic of inquiry" (Savage 1976, p. 417).

Comparative Administration Survives CAG's Demise

In response to the attacks on CAG and the comparative administration movement, and implicitly his own centrality, Fred Riggs (1964, p. 648–54) was quick to point out that the critics had offered little to take CAG's place. He claimed that CAG had been institutionally constrained by its place within ASPA (whose leadership was none too sympathetic with CAG's avowed aims of finding more appropriate paradigms of public administration then current), its need to survive somewhere, and its inability to raise funds for empirical research (regarded as the function of regular academic institutions rather than a professional society). While CAG had wanted to study all aspects of public administration, the terms of its grants had constricted it to development administration. In no stretch of the imagination had it been a tool of the establishment; on the contrary, its members had been "more often critical than supportive of the way AID carried out its public administration programs" (Riggs 1964, p. 649). While it had not directly undertaken empirical research, it had encouraged and supported its members in conducting field research and he cited several instances.

Fred Riggs further argued that the collapse of the movement, if indeed it had collapsed, which was not so evident from the vigor that continued in SICA, might be more a signal of success than failure. CAG had changed the American paradigm of public administration. It had made scholars and practitioners aware of the world of public administration outside the United States. It had entrenched international, comparative and development administration within public administration research and instruction. It had reduced the ethnocentricity and determinism in development administration. Most importantly, it had revealed that the most compelling problems of mankind and therefore of public policy and administration were global and could not be solved in a narrowly American framework. He remained optimistic that: "A new framework of 'comparative' administration will evolve—not as a 'subfield' but as the master field within which 'American public administration' will be a subfield . . . 'Comparative' [means] the generalized or global framework for thinking about problems . . . since [their] solution will require increasing communication between scholars and practitioners in all countries" (Riggs 1964, p. 652).

Two other former CAG members posited a less ambitious future. Keith Henderson (1969, p. 76–81) foresaw two probable futures and one desirable future. One probable future might be the decline of comparative administration into relative obscurity and the other might be its subordination (incorporation?) into comparative politics. A more desirable future would be for comparative public administration to assume the intellectual leadership of public administration as "the study of the real and proper structure and functioning of government executive organizations—and the behavior of organizational participants, in various environments" (Henderson 1969, p. 80). CAG's reservoir of intellectual capacity should be marshalled for invigorating public administration. Public administration would not survive unless it became more relevant to contemporary problems, something that could not be done until its major academic strengths were brought into contact with the practitioners, primarily urban administrators.

Ferrel Heady's analysis of the possible future ahead for comparative administration began with an annotation of the prescriptions of CAG's critics (1978, p. 361–64). He found little new in them and saw no consensus emerging. In their eagerness to score points the critics had not done their homework properly. They had sometimes set up straw men for easier attack. They, themselves, had failed to follow through on their own suggestions. "At this juncture what comparative public administration needs is not prolonged postmortems of past contributions but vigorous pursuit of attractive new opportunities" (Heady 1978, p. 364). The scene was by no means bleak. A great deal of work, accumulating work, had been done and was still being done in comparative administration. He would abandon the search for a synthesizing theory, an all-inclusive framework, for the avowed preference for the bureaucratic model within middle-range theory. This was the most manageable for comparative study providing that bureaucracy was defined in terms of its basic structural characteristics so that attention could be centered "on differences in patterns of behavior among diverse bureaucracies." He believed that:

> The day is gone when study and research in public administration could be confined within the traditional parochial national boundaries. The comparative perspective inevitably will become more prominent, enriching general public administration by widening the horizon of interest in such a way that understanding of one's own national system of administration will be enhanced by placing it in a cross-cultural setting (Heady 1978, p. 365).

His, then, was "an outlook of anticipation rather than disenchantment." In this vein he undertook the revision and updating of his original comparative administration text, still at that time (1978) the only available general text in comparative public administration.

But too much damage had been done to stop the exodus from comparative administration. Riggs' vision of the bold, new world of public administration did not materialize. On the other hand, comparative administration did not decline into oblivion nor was it absorbed by comparative politics from which it has remained very much apart and separate. Whatever vigor was exhibited by the younger CAG members went into the New Public Administration movement of the 1970s and was lost. Comparative administration scholars did not assume the leadership of American public administration. Instead, they showed greater enthusiasm to get out into the field and mix with the practitioners. Heady's sound, middle-of-the-road prescription based on a more detached view of CAG's successes and failures, seemingly won out. The grand theories were put aside for more conventional and traditional foci of public administration although the development administration tail still continued to wag the comparative administration dog. A new text by Guy Peters appeared more in the style of comparative politics (1978), with "an emphasis on the role of public bureaucracy in making public policy and on the institutional politics of policy making," and reflecting the emergence of yet another thrust, that of comparative policy-making. While the momentum generated by CAG had slowed, it remained significant, well above the pace that had preceded CAG, and within a decade of the transition of CAG into SICA, a substantial literature had accumulated, set out in several bibliographies (Honadle 1984; Huddleston 1984; Miewald 1984). It had not floundered (Sigelman 1976) or fallen by the wayside (Honadle 1982).

The Value of Comparative Administration

Comparative administration has never been center stage in public administration. Even in the heyday of CAG and U.S. technical assistance programs, American public administration remained largely parochial, as it was elsewhere around the globe. For a time, it was a star-studded show heading towards the top but the New Public Administration movement took top billing during the 1970s with its search for relevance, its attempt to capture the dominant paradigm, and its advocacy of social equity as *the* major value in public administration. Comparative administration was relegated to an interesting side show with its regular devotees. To make the really big time, it would need to consolidate and regroup, reassess which of its many thrusts would produce the best return, and take advantage of continuing opportunities.

The Need for Comparative Administration

The circumstances that gave rise to a strong comparative public administration movement after World War II have, if anything, strengthened. Warren Ilchman had found an apt quotation from Schelling's *Philosophie der Mythologie* to head his critique of CAG: "The question is not how the phenomenon must be turned, twisted, narrowed, crippled so as to be explicable, at all costs, upon principles that we have once and for all resolved not to go beyond. The question is: to what point must we enlarge so that it shall be in proportion to the phenomenon" (Ilchman 1971, p. 5). The growth and entrenchment of the administrative state, the enlargement of the public sector, the bureaucratization of the world, the merging of public and private policy-making, the tripling of the number of independent states, the spread of multinational and international public organizations, are just among some of the factors that have transformed public administration and impelled it to enlarge its vision and abandon its parochialism. "We Are the World," the concept of spaceship Earth, and similar expressions of popular realization that no peoples anywhere are immune from what happens somewhere else on the planet show that people can make a difference to other people if they can get organized, be constructive and exert pressure on public authorities. More people than ever are traveling and traveling further and quicker than ever before. Modern technology brings virtually instantaneous news — news as it is actually happening — to every person with a transistorized receiver.

The gradual emergence of an international culture — which makes young people quickly at home whether they are in Amsterdam, Singapore, Rio de Janeiro or Toronto — highlights the similarities and differences among national cultures and administrative systems. If American organization and management could not be exported without some strange and unexpected results, could the Japanese economic miracle and needless to say Japanese management methods? Are there any universals in administrative science? If so, what are they? If not, why not? What can be expected if one borrows somebody else's practices? Are they necessarily better? If so, how? If not, why not? What can be done to improve administrative performance? So why doesn't anyone act accordingly? What makes for administrative inertia or change? How can any of these questions be answered without comparative analysis? If such questions are important, and there can be no doubt in modern society that they are increasingly important, then comparative analysis is unavoidable and inescapable and must constitute a crucial part of professional training and practice. To neglect comparative analysis is to be chained to amateur dilettantism.

One mistake that CAG may have made was to overemphasize the theoretical rather than the practical benefits of comparative analysis. Perhaps first among practical considerations is that of effective policy-making. As the affairs of the world become increasingly complex and increasingly interconnected, it becomes more and more important for policy-makers — whether politicians or public servants — to know more of that world than what lies on their own doorstep. Parochialism is seldom a good atmosphere for decision making. It is increasingly necessary for those with power to understand the potentialities, constraints, modes of thought and means of making and implementing decisions of their counterparts in other countries. It is also of benefit if thereby they come to appreciate better the particularistic framework within which they themselves operate. The old adage "travel broadens the mind" applies equally well to comparative studies.

Connected with the policy-making consideration is that of general improvement in one's own arrangements. In homely terms again, example is the best means of teaching, and we can learn better ways of doing things by exposure to foreign practices. This is the path to enlightenment and innovation: by sharply observing methods of others, we may find it possible to incorporate some of them and to experiment in our own domain. In terms of administration, observation of systems other than our own gives us the opportunity to sift out what we like and what we think would suit us, and possibly to discover general principles of good administration.

Finally, the argument may, and has been, turned the opposite way around. Comparative study is essential in efforts to export our own methods or institutions in an attempt to improve the ways in which things are done in other countries. The historical context is, of course, the extensive international aid and technical assistance efforts that have been frequently, despite their good intentions, of little impact. The administrative factor is now seen as a crucial variable in the implementation of development plans. Even if it is assumed that the donors have the administrative know-how necessary, it is still essential to take account of local conditions, to adapt so-called Western expertise to the rationale of indigenous ways of doing things. One response of aid administrators has been simply to label local administrative methods as "wrong," and insist upon adoption of their own prescriptions for technical and administrative success.

Difficulties in eradicating local methods, the frustrating tendency of well-tried formulas at home to produce unexpected, and sometimes disastrous effects abroad, and the failure of development aims that did not take into account either the full ramifications in terms of social and economic change they brought about or the preferences of the people for whom the plans were made, have resulted finally in a welcome change of direction. First, it has become necessary to study local administrative mores, to find out in what ways and why they work and why people prefer to handle their business in this fashion. Second, it has become necessary to evaluate Western administrative methods, not only in terms of their impact upon receiving countries, but also critically in reverse. Third, it has become necessary to think in terms of innovative ways of handing the development effort. All these responses have in common the need to grasp reality, as it were, for their basis, to develop concepts that will allow them to amass a "working capital" of ideas and even principles upon which to operate, to sort out the constant from the shifting, the relevant from the peripheral, the similar from the different—in a word, the need to compare.

Shifting to more academic concerns, it remains true that if the discipline of public administration is to have any respectability at all, it cannot be a discipline of administration in one country. One cannot assume that the administrative practices one finds in one's own country or even one's own neighborhood are identical with those elsewhere, nor that unfamiliar practices are either irrelevant or in some way wrong. If a discipline of public administration exists, it has to be a universal discipline, whose findings apply to Zambia as well as to France. The preliminary scientific step of *observation* may be undertaken in relation to phenomena in only one place, but if it is, the generalizations made from those observations usually lack more general validity and suffer from a lack of perspective (an awareness of where they stand in relation to those distilled from experience elsewhere).

Research without comparison does not lack veracity, but simply remains at the level of description.

Comparison is also necessary for the next step, that of *classification*. Without some order, perceived or in some measure imposed, the phenomena seen are just a jumble. The mind automatically sorts into categories, notes similarities and differences, categorizes into more or less, picks out the most salient features to form groups. The urge to classify is not simply instinctive; it is an essential precondition for making generalizations about behavior: this group of phenomena, identified by these features, behave in this way. Underlying classification is the crucial issue of *conceptualization and vocabulary*. Clearly groupings and the generalizations that depend on them are related to the criteria felt relevant by researchers. We may group administrative systems in a number of ways: size, complexity, economic context, political or constitutional framework, openness, societal function. The language we use to characterize what we see has a profound effect on the way we see it.

Within the framework we have chosen as appropriate, comparison is necessary for what many see as the major aim of any scientific discipline — *prediction*. In order to make hypotheses of any general validity, we have to compare more than one system: hypotheses on the basis of a single case carry little conviction — that particular case might have been influenced by particular circumstances: a number of similar cases allows firmer generalization. These considerations are even more apposite for a more advanced form of prediction, that of *theory building*. It is true that a theory may be advanced on the behavior of a single case, but it would be a theory that applied only to that one case. What even the most loosely scientific discipline requires is theories based on identifiable models. It is possible to derive such models entirely deductively, or out of imagination, and then interpret reality in their light, but most of us would reject such an approach and demand that models be built up from observation of the real world — through comparison again. The theories based on the predicted behavior of those models are similarly a result of comparison. Finally, the last and perhaps most important stage of scientific inquiry — *verification* — also requires comparison. The building up of knowledge involves a constant checking of ideas against the real world, and the adjustment of concepts, models, hypotheses, and theories in the light of new observations, involving once again the use of comparisons.

Such are the compelling reasons why comparative analysis will continue even if inevitably efforts fall well behind needs. Because CAG could not reach the critical mass does not mean that the critical mass is beyond reach. CAG brought the critical mass within reach. It mapped out the field, experimented with many different approaches, applied comparative analysis from other social sciences (systems, structural-functionalism, ecological, bureaucratic, institution building) and revealed the complex methodological problems involved in comparative analysis. These problems do not yield quick solutions and CAG experience is illustrative of the problems that continue to plague comparative administration.

Perennial Problems of Comparative Analysis

The first problem is that of level of generality. On the one hand, there is the search for overarching concepts and theories, embracing all disciplines, all societies and all time spans. Included in its assumptions are that the interrelatedness of all social phenomena preclude perception of "truth" at any lower level, that valid comparison requires universal concepts, which may be applied to all societies, and that there is available to us a conceptual framework, which will embrace observations across differing cultures, polities and economies. This approach is typified by a systems theory method of comparison, which shares the weaknesses of a general system approach to the social sciences. In terms of comparison, the level of abstraction required to cover the diversity of the phenomena, makes it impossible to operationalize, and the deductive nature of its theorizing involves the very risk of distorting data in the effort to squeeze it into the system.

In contrast to a general systems theory approach is the ecological approach, which roots each administrative system within its own ecology and stresses the impact of environmental factors upon it. Whereas the systems approach stresses the uniformity of social data and the applicability of general explanation in different contexts, an ecological approach stresses the uniqueness of the specific administrative system, the particularity of its administrative culture or administrative style deriving from sociocultural, historical and psychological factors that cannot be replicated exactly in any other place or time. In its extreme form, therefore, this approach would make comparison impossible for it allows no basis on which to compare. Clearly some kind of balance has to be found between abstraction and particularity, generality and uniqueness.

A second problem relates to the choosing of concepts applicable to a number of countries. Quite apart from the problem of level of generality, misleading conclusions may arise from the employment of concepts useful in one culture, but inapplicable to another. The result may be a false sense of superiority, a complete misjudgment of the authority structure or societal processes of another country, the mistaking of form for substance. This is the criticism applied to a comparative approach based on structures, or on visible institutions, and it becomes particularly acute where non-Western societies are compared with Western societies, particularly where the former possess a superstructure of Western institutions while retaining indigenous methods of societal maintenance and problem-solving. It applies to approaches that concentrate on the bureaucracy, particularly as a key to development and nation-building, and also to an institution-building approach, i.e., the assumption that change derives from institutions.

One way of avoiding the problem of culture-bound concepts based on structure has been to use concepts based on function. The relevance of function to comparison is that if all societies have to perform the same functions, whatever their level of sophistication in doing so, comparisons may be made of the ways in which they are carried out. The problem, however, does not go away: compelling as are the arguments set out by anthropologists and sociologists of the functions that are essential for society, these are still not analogous to the functions of the living body, still impose a direction and critique upon other societies, which may prevent the development of more suitable categories for them, and are sufficiently abstract to allow so many interpretations as to fragment them upon application. It is interesting in this connection that Almond and Powell were forced to resort to the concept of political culture to account for the uniqueness of systems, and to use it to span all functions on both input and output sides of the system. Further, they appeared to find no specific *administrative* function within the system, failing to differentiate it from political functions in general, a problem which has not been resolved in comparative politics (Almond and Powell 1971).

The question of function leads into the third problem of comparison, that of measurement. How much of any one function is essential for a society? How do we measure functions? More generally, comparison requires measurement of units along some kind of a scale, so that we can say one country has more of such a characteristic or less of another. Measurement does not necessarily have to be quantifiable; nor have we solved the problem of comparison by finding ways to measure things; nor is a single scale necessary which combines all submeasures as a means of ranking an administrative system. What might be called a "development approach" to comparison, however, does attempt precisely these three objectives. The results have not been impressive: the use of aggregate scores has tended to conceal more than it reveals; the assumption of unilinear progression of national development has resulted in narrowly based policy; the reliance upon quantification as the sole criterion of relevant data has led to the ignoring of qualitative problems or those not easily quantified; the shakiness of statistics, where these have been collected over a short period, demand expensive field research into inaccessible areas, incorporate political bias and dubious methodology, does not make for confidence in their use. A particular problem relates to the dynamic element in administration, and the difficulty of perceiving changes and their direction — let alone measuring them — as they are happening.

Finally, and related to all of these, there is a problem of defining and delimiting the area to be compared. What is administration and what does it cover? Is it the same in all societies? How may it be differentiated from other activities or processes? The temptation is to treat "administration" as a universal concept, and "culture" as a particularistic one. This may be misleading since there may be autonomous differences in administration from place to place, while "culture" is less an explanation than an expression of ignorance, or an admission that comparison is simply not viable.

Confronted with the problems of too much or too little abstraction, imposing order upon data or leaving data an unorganized jumble, steering a path between the universal and the unique, and being accused of too narrow an approach or letting the subject of study dissolve into its context, not surprisingly researchers opt for a "middle range" approach. Despite the apparent comfort of the Aristotelian maxim of the mean, and the admirable desire to come out just right, it is evident that if a middle range approach is to be more than an escapist mechanism, it too will involve both judgment and strategy. Researchers in comparative administration contemplating this approach have therefore to provide their own answers to the dilemmas outlined above, to decide what is germane to a truly comparative approach, and to outline a strategy which will incorporate these elements. If they are able to accomplish this, they will not have discovered *the* comparative approach, but may have found a useful way of handling the problem they have set out.

How does the comparative approach contribute to understanding in administration? Let us imagine an international conference of administrators called to discuss a particular problem. (Such conferences are all too often organized around papers presented by selected participants, which are circulated, discussed, and alas too often filed away.) We can imagine our conferees starting off with the simple question: *Do we all have the same problem?* What is its nature and dimensions? Which countries have more of a problem and which have less? At this point, when participants have agreed that they are talking about the same thing (with variations), they go on to a second question: *Why has this problem arisen?* Are the reasons similar? Can they be correlated to conditions that vary (variables) as between different countries? Are the reasons given the same or different? When did the problem begin? Has it changed over time? What have its consequences been? Are these the same in all contexts? Are they important? Finally, the conference moves on to discuss: *How do we deal with the problem?* What means have been used to cope with the problem? Have they worked? Which have been most successful? What general factors have resulted in persistence/success? What particular factors made a difference? What choices were open to us? How do we know if things are getting better or worse?

At all points, from beginning to end, we expect a good deal of dissension on definition of the problem no less than its solution. We expect that participants need to return to earlier stages of their discussion to redefine their terms, account for persistence of conditions, explain why form and substance conflict, or administrative effort fails to meet its goal. They need to go beyond their original frame of reference to discuss ultimate goals when their attention has been directed to processes, to encompass areas of study remote from their own specialization, to take a broad view of context instead of a narrow view of function. In finding a common language to describe and explain the phenomena they discuss, and in re-evaluating their own experiences in the light of others', it is expected that they gain a greater understanding of the world about them — which is after all the main aim of comparative study.

What is so difficult about applying similar comparative approaches beyond identifiable problems? Apparently, comparison is difficult for so little is done; that which is done is often demolished by methodological critics; and such treatment scares away those who might otherwise be tempted to try their hand at it. It is true that comparative analysis is probably the most difficult part of the study of public administration, that is, how administrative systems work and why they work differently. What does one focus on? Within what framework? Using what methods? To what level of generalization? It *is* difficult. Yet it is a fascinating challenge, forcing one to go outside one's own system as an outsider, not as an insider, using whatever reference points, definitions, classificatory frameworks, measurements and theories that are helpful from the vast array available from logic and scientific method. Anything can be compared providing that the things being compared are "capable of possessing the same attributes" (DeFelice 1980, p. 124; Niessen and Peschar 1982). The real stumbling block is not methodology so much as limited access to other administrative systems and inability to escape from one's own administrative system. The best work in comparative administration has been achieved by those who have been able to escape their own administrative system, the system most familiar to them, the system in which they were nurtured, the system they may personify to others, and who have had access to other administrative systems, systems they have experienced first hand, lived in and coped with, and come to appreciate as internationalists, rather than cultural imperialists.

The Revitalization of Comparative Administration

One thing certain about the future of comparative administration is that it has one. But what kind of future will it have? Looking back on CAG forecasters, one can see that they were wrong. The future is never a continuation of the present. The unexpected will occur. Perhaps an international body or a wealthy foundation will be convinced that comparative administration is still potentially rewarding, both intellectually and practically, and will fund on a generous scale empirical research and international networking. Perhaps international problems will become so compelling, that governments around the globe will join together in a concerted effort to seek feasible solutions from comparative studies. New trends and directions will be taken spontaneously by people in the field and sooner or later the academic world will catch up. One cannot tell beforehand what they will be but once taken, they will appear obvious and natural, the next logical step. Emphasis may switch from First World to Second World to Third World, even to an emerging Fourth World; it may switch from rural administration to urban administration to human service administration to the administration of robots; it may switch from the administrative state to regional administration to local government to not-for-profit organizations. New fads and fancies will intervene just as fashion changes from long to short hair styles for men and from short to long skirt lengths for women, and back again without logic or reason, just whim or passion. No one can tell what will be; only what they would like it to be.

In and Out of the Doldrums

Hopefully, the future of comparative administration will be better than the immediate past which has been rather depressing after the heady optimism of the early CAG years raised expectations so high. The letdown brought forth such a litany of hopelessness, recrimination and spite that many of the best brains fled the field altogether for more peaceful or inviting pastures elsewhere or they just moved to the sidelines to await developments. Their places have been only partially filled by a younger generation of scholars and practitioners, less ambitious, less flamboyant, less adventurous, mindful of the bitter criticisms (not wholly justified) leveled at previous work for being so abstract, inclusive, and shoddy, giving comparative administration a rundown, seedy look, past its prime and unlikely to be rejuvenated.

Comparative administration has been to some extent a victim of circumstances. It was borne along in the 1960s by the surge of interest in the emerging Third World bloc of less-developed countries, the Cold War competition to win the hearts and minds of the Third World peoples or at least their leaders through sizeable technical cooperation and aid programs, and attempts to speed up development in poor countries through modernization, institution-building and technology transfers. It was dashed in the 1970s by the energy crisis, the failure of the New International Economic Order to get off the ground, world trade depression, and the decline of international development efforts. Among the first casualties was funding for research and publications in comparative administration, followed not far behind by cutbacks in research projects, conferences and travel. Those bodies, like the United Nations family of organizations and the U.S. Agency for International Development, which had supported comparative studies, particularly in development administration, were forced to back off, while other international bodies, like the World Bank and the International Monetary Fund, which became more important, were just not interested at all in comparative studies or in comparative administration. Member states became more inward-looking, engrossed with new domestic problems. The revival of the Cold War reduced whatever access to the Eastern bloc had been achieved earlier while the Third World grew less and less enamored with the Western bloc and Western Europe diverged more from North America. International networks were imperiled.

Perhaps the most serious immediate threat to comparative administration was growing disillusionment with what had been its major component, development administration or rather "the developmental bureaucracy, as a spearhead of modernization . . . in the role of a Schumpeterian entrepreneur" (Dwivedi and Nef 1982, p. 60), led by take-charge technocrats waging war against poverty. Development aid and administration set out to modernize the administrative states of the Third World in the image of Western public administration—"professionally oriented, technically competent, politically and ideologically neutral bureaucratic machinery"—and generally to Westernize poor countries. Westernization turned out to be quite difficult at best, and impossible where countries did not want to be Westernized. An implementation gap soon appeared and widened. The induced administrative changes were largely symbolic and cosmetic, actually strengthening the traditional against the developmental, the authoritarian over the democratic, and therefore *antidevelopment* and pro-state terrorism when bureaucrats in uniform commanded bureaucrats without uniform. Clearly things had gone wrong in the field. Development administration was not so much the solution as the problem for developmental efforts. "A substantive criticism of administrative reform, planning and administrative development in general was that it did not produce change but rather modernized underdevelopment. Frustration with techniques combined with academicism had finally led to the abandonment of administrative tools. . . . Very soon development administration found itself with nothing 'tangible' to offer" (Nef and Dwivedi 1981, p. 64). With nothing to offer, soon there was little market for development administration products, except in public service training institutes around the world, which still clung either to the early ideology of development administration or to the technocratic benefits of managerial (administrative) development. Even so, this side of public administration was not mentioned at all in the accreditation guidelines drafted by the National Association of Schools of Public Affairs and Administration, a member of the International Association of Schools and Institutes of Administration. If this depressing trend went unchallenged, then soon there would be a dearth of new literature and materials, a general lack of interest (except by narrow, nonconceptual managerial trainers), and a generation of public administrators ignorant of comparative administration, comparative perspectives and alternative viewpoints on the administrative process.

Fortunately, the downward slide of comparative administration was arrested in the early 1980s, again rather fortuitously. The dearth in new materials meant that existing materials were becoming outdated and outmoded, and in the context of the rapidly changing world, possibly irrelevant and useless. Recent research needed to be incorporated and the subject presented in a more stimulating manner to attract a new audience. The new generation of public administrators might be tempted back to comparative administration if it could demonstrate that it was up-to-date, relevant and useful, which was not difficult to do if more recent research and theories were presented. This was especially true of the much maligned field of development administration, which had undergone a radical transformation in theory and practice. It had begun in the early 1970s with a conceptual shift from state-induced economic growth to the "basic needs" approach that stressed state intervention to affect the maldistributive outcomes of economic growth. This, in turn, led to a bypassing of the state itself for collective self-reliance and then a rejection of Westernization or Western notions of development altogether for alternative life-styles, in short, *"to create more options for more people"* (de Kadt 1985, p. 551), improve life chances and extend opportunities through popular participation, organization and mobilization, motives that originally fueled development administration and fed the (by now defunct) New Public Administration movement. These new modes of thinking about development were truly international (not just directed at the Third World or poor countries), comparative and creative, venturing into fundamental issues of administrative ends and means, and opening new lines of investigation quite appealing to the new generation of public administrators.

The Internationalization of Public Administration

The new generation of public administrators was also joined by a new generation of instructors and researchers of public administration who had been too young and inexperienced to participate in CAG and the earlier technical assistance projects. They had witnessed the revolt against traditional public administration by the New Public Administration movement and they were susceptible to new ways of looking at public administration. Furthermore, they were joined by counterparts around the world, mostly of non-American background even if they had received an American education. By the 1970s, American-educated scholars and administrators had returned in significant numbers to their home countries where they had assumed senior positions at universities, training institutes and government organizations. They were inevitably comparativists and they had begun to produce their own voluminous literature, sometimes imitative but often refreshing, new and insightful. Almost every important research center outside the United States started a scholarly journal of its own and where the articles were not published in English, French or Spanish, summaries were provided in those languages. In addition, and quite independently, other Western countries experienced a strong revival of public administrative studies, comparative studies, and development studies based on their own separate approaches. Indeed by the mid-1980s, the American dominance of comparative administration had long been eclipsed; it had been internationalized throughout the First and Third Worlds and with some thawing once again in Cold War rhetoric, even the Second World was breaking out of its Marxist-Leninist-Maoist confines and seeing what it might be able to borrow from the rest of comparative administration.

Already the Western stranglehold on comparative administration and comparative management had been broken by the challenge presented by Japan and several Third World countries, which had done remarkably well in economic development without copying Western public administration and Western business management methods. These had been able to modernize and develop and to beat the West at its own game. Naturally the Third World as a whole was curious to see how they had managed to preserve their indigenous culture (or how much of it had been Westernized) and whether they might be able to follow their own idiosyncratic paths to the future. The First World was also interested for it was losing out in head-to-head competition. It wanted to know the secrets of the Israeli kibbutz, Yugoslav self-management and Indian rural cooperatives.

The resurgence of interest in comparative administration was fueled in part by international and regional organizations that had at last begun to realize that traditional Western approaches were no longer adequate and might even be outmoded by world events. While the well-established organizations still maintained their research and grants, albeit at a reduced level, they had begun to be outbid by the World Bank, the Organization for Economic Cooperation and Development, the European Economic Community and the International Association of Schools and Institutes of Administration. It was all very well financing large development projects but the effort was largely wasted if those projects were ill-conceived, badly managed, and improperly maintained. The administrative side was probably just as important as the economic side. The need worldwide was for more competent policy analysis and more competent project management. The solutions would appear to come from new style comparative policy-making and comparative administration. And they were brought within reach by the ease of travel and the decline in real costs of air travel. It was no longer that expensive for researchers, trainers, consultants, evaluators, and even administrators themselves to join the jet set. By the mid-1980s, Mark Huddleston could remark with confidence that the level of activity was outstripping that of the heyday of CAG: "The difference now is that work in comparative administration is not identified as such. Instead, comparative analysis has begun to creep into the substantive subfields of public administration. . . . All . . . have been enriched in recent years by increased scholarly recognition of the importance and utility of comparative analysis" (Huddleston 1984). He was convinced that its spirit had pervaded and invigorated the rest of the discipline.

This revitalization of comparative administration could be illustrated by comparing the scope of comparative studies in the mid-1980s with that 20 years before. Then, comparative studies had concentrated on the nation-state, and the national bureaucracy. By the 1980s, international bureaucracies and world organizations could not be ignored. The International Monetary Fund had emerged as a potential world economic government and was virtually dictating to several Third World countries in economic difficulties, and the World Bank's influence had grown considerably as had that of world relief agencies and religious organizations. They, like the multinational business corporations, had created an influential superstructure, a transnational administrative system with a pervasive impact on rich and poor countries alike. Comparative administration had to go beyond public administration to take into account the delivery of public goods and services by nonpublic organizations and strange mixed public/private organizations at national and subnational level.

John Jun had predicted in the mid-1970s that comparative administration would have to go beyond the purely international and public administration to include the cross-institutional and "comparison of methods and strategies of organizational change and development in a cross-cultural context—or even in a domestic context" (Jun 1976, p. 645). He had also called for more comparative studies of the process of debureaucratization and the delivery of public goods and services through nonbureaucratic organizations, self-management and industrial democracy. Actually, such studies had long been underway, particularly in rural development in poor countries where governments had been unable to reach mass clienteles through public bureaucracies. The basic needs concept had brought government assisted traditional and interventionary administrative systems back into research focus together with new forms of constituency organization deliberately sponsored and supported by public authority (Esman 1978, p. 166–72). Comparative analysis of such constituency organizations in rural Asia was to bring Milton Esman to conclude that "constituency organization is a necessary condition for the effective design and delivery of nonroutine public services intended for socially and economically marginal mass publics—for those who need public services most" (p. 171). Other research recognized that local people who rejected the advice of outside experts often had good reasons; they had "indigenous technical knowledge" (ITK) and "folk management skills," which needed to be incorporated into project designs (see Honadle 1984, p. 174–79). Their findings confirmed the need for increased local participation in development administration, greater equity in distribution of public resources, and more emphasis on small scale, simple operations in implementing development projects. These results were rapidly being absorbed into public administration, organization theory and development literature, often without acknowledgment to the comparative studies on which they were based.

Thus recent comparative studies have broken the bounds of "national," "public" and "bureaucracy." They have also broken the bounds of "executive," "civil/public service" and "public enterprise." Most importantly, they have broken the bounds of "administration." Although the policy sciences had been conceived alongside comparative administration and comparative policies in the early 1950s, comparative policy-making (or public policy) was much slower to emerge as a field of study. It was still in its infancy when the American Political Science Association chose as the best publication for 1975 a book entitled *Comparative Public Policy* (Heidenheimer 1975).

Since then comparative policy-making has boomed with at least five journals devoted exclusively to comparative public policy (Hancock 1983, p. 283–308). It was motivated by the insularity and narrowness of public policy studies. It was intended to raise the sights of scholars, to get them to go beyond national and local policy formulation and implementation, to place research findings within the broader context in which policy actors operate, and to consider various policy options outside a given range of values and institutions (Cohen and Rackoff 1978, p. 319–27). Its early work was afflicted by exactly the same problems that had plagued early work in comparative administration, namely ambiguity in the use of major terms, disagreement over what and how to compare, and the matter of the competence of the researchers (cultural and ideological bias, inexperience, inaccuracy and over-simplification) (Feldman 1978, p. 319–27). Perhaps this is hardly surprising as relatively few of the pioneers in comparative policy studies came from comparative politics and/or comparative administration. Yet, they have continued to proceed largely in ignorance of the latter still although comparative administration has begun to take notice of the methodological, theoretical and research findings of comparative policy-making, particularly concerning the nature and size of governments, public actions in substantive public policy areas, performance of welfare states, explanations for social change, and policy implementation (intergovernmental relations, regulatory powers, human resource administration, urban planning). Although comparative policy-making, like CAG before it, has yet to discipline itself, to make priorities, to lessen its sights and to reduce "sharply divergent conceptualizations and research foci" (Hancock 1983, p. 293), its very stimulation pushes comparative administration into substantive policy issues and guides administrative practitioners perhaps not so much in what they should do and how they should behave as in what they should avoid doing.

A Research Agenda

The lesson to be drawn from comparative policy-making is that comparative studies have to be truly comparative. They have to go beyond description and analysis. Many have to go beyond one sample. They have to be matched by some common criteria of relevance that can be identified, defined, measured, evaluated, abstracted and hypothesized for further empirical testing. Much that poses as comparative administration is not. Much that is truly comparative is capable of being enlarged, tested and refined further. A good example of what can be done well without too much complication and invention is the theory testing and practical advice resulting from an insider's analysis of an agricultural extension service by David Leonard in *Reaching the Peasant Farmer: Organization Theory and Practice in Kenya* (1977), which takes public administration beyond folk wisdom and personal prejudice. Leonard's work supports Lee Sigelman's contention that: "What is immediately needed is not a new vocabulary or conceptual lens, but the availability of data series which would facilitate the testing of a myriad of previously untested speculations and the building of theory" (Sigelman 1976, p. 623).

In this vein, there are significant areas of public administration that have not yet been explored. Possibly the most obvious is the phenomenon of bureaucrats in uniform. Most regimes are military and where they are not the military and police between them constitute a sizeable portion of the public sector. In what ways do bureaucrats in uniform differ from bureaucrats without uniform? Another area ripe for comparative studies is the warfare state, which has not received anywhere near the attention that the welfare state has. Similarly, just as comparative public enterprises and comparative national planning have been studied, comparative economic policy and regulation have not yet been examined in depth from an administrative view. Several fairly universalistic government services have still to be studied comparatively — postal delivery, civil aviation, garbage collection, correctional centers, pollution abatement — activities often taken for granted because they are rarely newsworthy. There is no dearth of comparative material in public administration.

The real question is what should be done first. What ten areas of comparative administration should receive priority attention? The following suggestions are not in any order of importance, they are just areas ripe for comparative treatment.

THE CONFIGURATION OF THE ADMINISTRATIVE STATE. It would be desirable to know why the administrative state acts as it does and why different administrative states act differently. A theory of the administrative state, which would very much strengthen the disciplinary status of public administration, has yet to be formulated. One reason is that we lack sufficient empirical data about the administrative state, which would not be too difficult or costly to collect on the basis of what is already known and available about national administrative systems and national public bureaucracies. What is needed is a classificatory or mapping device that would tell at a glance the nature of any administrative state, its shape, its functions and services, its major organizational forms, the way it secures resources and disburses them, its financial, personnel and management systems, and the constraints imposed on it by the political, economic, social, legal and cultural contexts.

IDENTIFYING ADMINISTRATIVE CULTURES. Assuming that there really are distinctive administrative cultures, they need to be identified, their distinctive features revealed, and their impact on their members assessed. Is there a distinctive British or French or Thai administrative culture? If so, how and why does it differ from other administrative cultures? Why is it important to know the differences and similarities among administrative cultures? How are its members socialized into the administrative culture and how do they socialize the next generation of public employees? How are administrative cultures perpetuated? What are the consequences of failing to acclimatize to the prevailing administrative culture? What happens when administrative cultures conflict? What universals can be identified in all administrative cultures? These questions are not just applicable to cross-national data but also to intra-national data. For instance, different ethnic groups within a country may have quite different administrative cultures. Or the administrative culture of the bureaucrats in uniform may differ quite markedly from that of the bureaucrats without uniform and both often may contrast with the administrative cultures of business, academia, medicine, law and engineering. It may not be at all easy to move between one and another.

PUBLIC ENTREPRENEURSHIP. In the administrative state, government has taken on almost totalitarian proportions; seemingly nothing is beyond its reach if it is so inclined. Major initiatives in the community require government approval and often government support, subsidization and leadership. When things go wrong, the community looks to the government to put them right again, employing the machinery of the administrative state. Where no machinery exists to do what the government wants done, it has to create new machinery. This public entrepreneurship goes well beyond marketable goods and services, commercial ventures and public economic enterprise for it encompasses more than the purely economic well-being of the community. The entrepreneurial activities cannot be fitted well into the traditional machinery of government or into autonomous public agencies and quasi-governmental organizations (QANGOs) that sit uncomfortably at the edges of the traditional machinery of government. All around the globe, the entrepreneurial activities have given birth to curious creatures of government, not part of the traditional machinery yet not part of the business world or the legal system or political party organization. As they do not seem to fit into the traditional domain of public administration, they, like their commercial counterparts, have been neglected although comparative administration could shed much light on their origins, functions, forms, management and performance (Seidman 1983, p. 65–72). Their growing importance in the life of contemporary society requires that they be investigated according to governmental control, public responsibility and accountability, law-abidingness, competent management, openness, effectiveness and public participation.

COMPARATIVE PUBLIC FINANCE. The world debt crisis has revealed not just the poverty of nations but the poverty of comparative public finance. Public money has been mismanaged on a global scale. Orthodox budget practices have been abused. Traditional financial controls no longer work well or at all. Something is seriously wrong about current approaches to public finance in general, and the theories and practices of public budgeting in particular. The empirical studies undertaken by Naomi Caiden and Aaron Wildavsky (1974), which did so much to change thinking about planning and budgeting in poor countries, need to be repeated in the light of the momentous changes in public finance since then. Events move so quickly that several excellent comparative studies that have since appeared, have been outdated almost as soon as they were published (Goode 1984; Premchand 1983; Premchand and Burkhead 1984). Meantime, public authorities have adjusted to the monetary crisis with several budget innovations, such as program budgeting, program classification and performance measurement, which have been inadequately studied from a comparative perspective. In any event, "full-length studies of foreign systems of public budgeting are relatively rare" (Caiden 1974, p. 389), particularly outside North America and Western Europe, although "the study of comparative budget systems is a highly practical endeavor" (p. 395).

PUBLIC MALADMINISTRATION. For obvious reasons, researchers prefer to concentrate on the good side of public administration—its accomplishments and achievements, its routinization of innovation and creativity, its standardization of improved practices, its search for better performance, and its reform of inadequate administration. But there is also the bad side of public administration, which the mass media lampoon. The same scientific approach has not been applied to bad practices as to good practices. Yet possibly more is to be gained from correcting bad practices than from searching for better practices. Public administration would be considerably improved if public maladministration was diminished. While corruption has received more than its share of comparative treatment, other forms of public maladministration have rarely been approached from a comparative perspective. Clearly, there are universal forces that give rise to public malpractices and bureaupathologies, which in turn can be readily identified and classified, explained and evaluated. Careful analysis should result in practical prescriptions with predictive value.

PUBLIC SECTOR PRODUCTIVITY AND PERFORMANCE. It was once believed that public services could not be measured. Now we know differently. While some areas, such as foreign relations, are still difficult to measure, considerable progress has been made in many other areas in quantifying public sector productivity and evaluating programs, projects and performance. Given the poor public image of public bureaucracy and mass media distortions of public organizations and public employees, much more progress has to be made. Presumably, governments the world over are interested in improving public sector productivity and could learn much from one another's efforts. An international working group, similar to that sponsored by the International Institute of Administrative Sciences on comparative budgeting, is needed to encourage the internationalization of public sector productivity studies and to fill in the comparative framework provided in Robert Fried's *Performance in American Bureaucracy* (1976).

QUALITY PUBLIC EMPLOYEES. The early days of civil service reform were spent looking for qualified public employees. Now, the search is for quality public employees. Qualifications are only one measure, one requirement of competence and quality. What do comparative studies suggest are the most important factors attracting quality people into public employment? What do they suggest keeps quality people, once attracted, in public employment? What is meant by quality? How are such persons located and prepared for public service? What spirits them away? What is needed to maintain their quality? Is there any correlation between selection criteria and performance measurement? What do turnover figures really reveal about who leaves and why they leave? Does morale have any significance at all? Comparative studies of public personnel management generate much data but few attempt to answer these important questions.

URBAN PLANNING AND ADMINISTRATION. If any demonstration were needed that the quality and relevance of comparative administration has improved, one should compare one of the earliest studies, G. Montague Harris's *Comparative Local Government* (1949), with CAG-sponsored Richard Daland's *Comparative Urban Research* (1969), and two more recent works, Arne Leemans' *Changing Patterns of Local Government* (1979) and Robert Fried and Francine Rabinovitz's *Comparative Urban Politics: A Performance Approach* (1980). The latest studies are truly comparative. They provide sophisticated analytical tools, give detailed universalistic frameworks for comparative analysis with both theoretical and practical attributes, cover regions and countries often omitted for lack of access and reliable data, and aim to improve or raise urban planning and administration. With an increasing percentage of the world's population residing in cities, any improvement in urban planning and administration has an immediate impact on the quality of life and life chances of much of humanity.

ALTERNATIVE DELIVERY SYSTEMS. A mistake of comparative administration was to place so much faith on public bureaucracy, public management, and governmental delivery of public goods and services. Monopoly government organizations have the same virtues and vices as other monopolies. Institutional bureaucracies tend in time to exhibit crippling bureaupathologies that damage performance and client satisfaction. Governments have learned the lesson and have tended to experiment increasingly with novel forms of public service delivery outside the traditional public bureaucracy. They have not received much help from comparative administration. What is needed is another look at the traditional modes of public service delivery with a view to devising alternative modes where current mechanisms fail to satisfy. Public choice theory is helpful here but has rarely been the subject of comparative analysis. Debureaucratization experiments cry out for evaluation from a comparative perspective as do proposals for *democratic* administration, which go back to World War II.

EDUCATION AND TRAINING FOR PUBLIC SERVICE. Faith in the public bureaucracy has been backed by faith in public service education and training. The literature abounds in studies, many comparative, of curriculum development, teaching methods and instructional aids. What is needed more are comparative studies of the results of public service education and training. What happens once the trainees are placed on the job? Which parts of the curriculum turn out to be most useful in public service and organization management? What makes the difference? How does one enhance leadership and managerial skills? What should be taught and what is teachable? As Nef and Dwivedi (1985, p. 235–49) have pointed out, the education and training is for public *service,* not business management or organizational development or even administrative technology. Unfortunately, the academics and the trainers have too often been diverted from their mission to educate and train the next generation of public administrators by concentrating on pedagogy, isolating themselves from the real world of public administration, and finding themselves mistrusted by practitioners, thereby making much of their effort irrelevant. They generate ideas and teach ideals but they are insufficiently committed to see that what they preach is implemented. Meantime, the practitioners pressed by grave situations do not have the time and energy to listen to ideas unless they are immediately practicable, or practice ideals under critical conditions, especially when those ideas and ideals oppose their practices (Braun 1985). Consequently, faith in education and training has often been unjustified. It can be justified if comparative studies could give some practical answers to some real problems of practitioners.

Troubled Waters Require Good Steering

Nobody doubts that comparative administration suffers from methodological and conceptual ambiguities and that "the comparative analysis of administrative systems is inherently a difficult undertaking" (Aberbach and

Rockman 1985), but none of this is insurmountable. Comparative politics had succeeded in overcoming even worse difficulties. Comparative administration is well on the way to similar success. It lacks the institutional support of an International Political Science Association and a Prentice-Hall Contemporary Comparative Politics Series (edited by Joseph La Palombara). It lacks the financial support of a Ford Foundation or a World Bank. It lacks readily identifiable leadership. Yet, it has several advantages over its ill-fated CAG predecessor. It has a world-wide network of scholars and practitioners who meet often under various umbrella organizations, such as the International Institute of Administrative Sciences, the International Association of Schools and Institutes of Administration, the Section on International and Comparative Administration of the American Society for Public Administration, and the American Consortium for International Public Administration.

This network is attracting a new generation, a much younger generation, of devotees who have the energy, ambition and ability to go beyond the current state of the art. They are more realistic than CAG and know they have to be relevant and practical to appeal to the profession of public administration. They are probably more intellectually demanding than their predecessors. Like the historically oriented sociologists:

> They are now much more modest and sceptical with respect to general theories and complex conceptual systems. They strive for theories that are empirically founded and do justice to historical variations and subtle differences. Insofar as they make any use of theories that are further removed from empirical facts, they view them as guidelines rather than as the ultimate truth. In general, they prefer concepts derived from empirical research itself to those derived from a grand theory, and they tend to have a preference for generalizations based on thorough comparisons of developments in a limited number of societies rather than generalizations that combine a high degree of generality with a low level of information (Wilterdink 1985, p. 20).

Yet, the central dilemma remains. While comparative studies abound, comparative administration barely progresses. An inventory of comparative studies in progress reveals an amazing diversity. It would range from O.E.C.D.'s projects on European social policy and European policy-makers to W.H.O. and World Bank projects on community health services and public health administration, from USAID research on rural development projects to research on metropolitan rapid transit systems and airport management, from investigation of academic syllabuses to anticorruption tactics. While there is no lack of comparative scholarship, it is excessively diffused and particularistic. A field exists but few agree on its boundaries, function, paradigm (if indeed there is any such creature), practicality and fundamental values. Should some consensus on any of these matters emerge over the next decade, the future of comparative administration may look after itself.

References

Aberbach, Joel, and Rockman, Bert. "Methodological and Conceptual Ambiguities in the Comparative Study of Public Administration." Paper presented at the 13th World Congress of the International Political Science Association, Paris, July 1985.

Almond, G. A., and Powell, G. B. "A Developmental Approach to Political Systems: An Overview." In *Political Development and Social Change.* Edited by James Finkle and Richard Gable. New York: John Wiley, 1971, p. 51.

Braun, Juan. "Social Scientists: An Endangered Species." Paper presented at the 13th World Congress of the International Political Science Association, Paris, July 1985.

Caiden, Naomi. "Comparative Public Budgeting." *International Journal of Public Administration* 7, no. 4 (1985):375–401.

Caiden, N., and Wildavsky, A. *Planning and Budgeting in Poor Countries.* New York: John Wiley, 1974.

Cohen, Larry, and Rackoff, Robert. "Teaching the Contexts of Public Policy: The Need for a Comparative Perspective." *Policy Sciences Journal* 6 (Spring 1978):319–27.

Comparative Administration Group. *Newsletter,* May 1960 and May 1967.

Dahl, Robert. "The Science of Public Administration: Three Problems." *Public Administration Review* 7, no. 1 (1947):1–11.

DeFelice, Gene. "Comparison Misconceived Common Nonsense in Comparative Politics." *Comparative Politics* 13, no. 1 (Oct. 1980):124.

De Kadt, Emanuel. "Of Markets, Might and Mullahs: A Case for Equity, Pluralism and Tolerance in Development." *World Development* 13, no. 4 (1985):549–56.

Dwivedi, O. P., and Nef, J. "Crisis and Continuities in Development Theory and Administration: First and Third World Perspectives." *Public Administration and Development* 2 (1982):59–77.

Esman, Milton. "The CAG and the Study of Public Administration: A Mid-Term Appraisal." CAG Conference, University of Maryland, Apr. 1966, p. 3–4.

———. "Development Administration and Constituency Organization." *Public Administration Review* 38, no. 2 (Mar.–Apr. 1978):166–72.

Feldman, Elliot. "Comparative Public Policy: Field or Method." *Comparative Politics* Jan. 1978, p. 287–303.

Fried, Robert. *Performance in American Bureaucracy.* Boston: Little, Brown, 1976.

Gable, Richard. "The Teaching of Comparative/Development Administration: The Report of a Survey." CAG document, 1971.

Goode, Richard. *Government Finance in Developing Countries.* Washington, D.C.: Brookings Institution, 1984.

Hancock, Donald. "Comparative Public Policy: An Assessment." *Political Science: The State of the Discipline.* Edited by Ada W. Finifter. Washington, D.C.: American Political Science Association, 1983, p. 283–308.

Heady, Ferrel. *Public Administration: A Comparative Perspective.* Englewood Cliffs, N.J.: Prentice-Hall, 1966.

———. "Comparative Administration: A Sojourner's Outlook." *Public Administration Review* 38, no. 4 (July–Aug. 1978):358–65.

———. *Public Administration: A Comparative Perspective,* 3d ed. New York: Marcel Dekker, 1984.

Heady, Ferrel, and Stokes, Sybil, eds. *Papers in Comparative Public Administration.* Ann Arbor: University of Michigan, Institute of Public Administration, 1962.

Heidenheimer, Arnold, et al. *Comparative Public Policy: The Politics of Social Choice in Europe and America.* New York: St. Martin's Press, 1975.

Henderson, Keith. "Comparative Public Administration: The Identity Crisis." *Journal of Comparative Administration* 1, no. 1 (May 1969):69.

Honadle, Beth. *Public Administration in Rural Areas and Small Jurisdictions.* The Garland Reference Library of Social Science, 1984.

Honadle, George. "Development Administration in the Eighties: New Agendas or Old Perspectives." *Public Administration Review* 42, no. 2 (Mar.–Apr. 1982):174.

Huddleston, Mark. *Comparative Public Administration.* The Garland Reference Library of Social Science, 1984.

Ilchman, Warren. *Comparative Public Administration and "Conventional Wisdom."* Beverly Hills: Sage, 1971, p. 6.

Jun, John. "Renewing the Study of Comparative Administration: Some Reflections on the Current Possibilities." *Public Administration Review* 36, no. 6 (Nov.–Dec. 1976):645.

Kaufman, H., and Sayre, W. "A Research Design for a Pilot Study in Comparative Administration." American Political Science Association, Sept. 1953.

Landau, Martin. "Political and Administrative Development: General Commentary." In *Political and Administrative Development.* Edited by Ralph Braibanti. Durham, N.C.: Duke University Press, 1969, p. 332.

Leonard, David. *Reaching the Peasant Farmer: Organization Theory and Practice in Kenya.* Chicago: University of Chicago Press, 1977.

Loveman, Brian. "The Comparative Administration Group, Development Administration and Antidevelopment." *Public Administration Review* 36, no. 6 (Nov.–Dec. 1976):618.

Mayer, Lawrence. "Practicing What We Preach: Comparative Politics in the 1980's." *Comparative Political Studies* 16, no. 2 (July 1983):173–94.

Mievald, Robert. *The Bureaucratic State.* The Garland Reference Library of Social Science, 1984.

Mohapratra, Manindra. "Teaching of International and Comparative Public Administration in MPA Programmes in the United States." *Teaching Public Administration* 3, no. 2 (Autumn 1983):54–65.

Nath, Raghu. "A Methodological Review of Cross-Cultural Management Research." *International Social Science Journal* 20 (July 1968):35–62.

Nef, J., and Dwivedi, O. P. "Development Theory and Administration: A Fence Around an Empty Lot?" *The Indian Journal of Public Administration* 27, no. 1 (Jan.–Mar. 1981):42–66.

_____. "Training for Development Management: Reflections on Social Know-how as a Scientific and Technological System." *Public Administration and Development* 5, no. 3 (1985):235–49.

Niessen, Manfred, and Peschar, Jules. *International Comparative Research*. New York: Pergamon Press, 1982.

Peters, Guy. *The Politics of Bureaucracy*. New York: Longman, 1978, 1989.

Premchand, A. *Government Budgeting and Expenditure Controls: Theory and Practice*. Washington, D.C.: International Monetary Fund, 1983.

Premchand, A., and Burkhead, J., eds. *Comparative International Budgeting and Finance*. New Brunswick, N.J.: Transaction Books, 1984.

Raphaeli, Nimrod. *Readings in Comparative Public Administration*. Boston: Allyn and Bacon, 1967.

Riggs, Fred. *Administration in Developing Countries: The Theory of Prismatic Society*. Boston: Houghton Mifflin, 1964.

_____. "The Group and the Movement: Notes on Comparative and Development Administration." *Public Administration Review* 36, no. 6 (Nov.–Dec. 1976):649.

Savage, Peter. *CAG Newsletter,* June 1967, p. 12.

_____. "Optimism and Pessimism in Comparative Administration." *Public Administration Review* 36, no. 4 (July–Aug. 1976):415–23.

Schaffer, Bernard. "Comparisons, Administration and Development." *Political Studies* 19 (Sept. 1971):330.

Seidman, Harold. "Public Enterprise Autonomy: Need for a New Theory." *International Review of Administrative Sciences* 49, no. 1 (1983):65–72.

Siffin, William, ed. *Toward the Comparative Study of Public Administration*. Bloomington: Indiana University, Department of Government, 1957.

Sigelman, Lee. "In Search of Comparative Administration." *Public Administration Review* 36, no. 6 (Nov.–Dec. 1976):622.

Sigelman, Lee, and Gadbois, George. "Contemporary Comparative Politics: An Inventory and Assessment." *Comparative Political Studies* 16, no. 3 (Oct. 1983):275–305.

Udy, S. H. "The Comparative Analysis of Organizations." In *Handbook of Organizations*. Edited by James March. Chicago: Rand McNally, 1965, p. 678–709.

Waldo, Dwight. "Comparative Public Administration: Prologue, Problems and Promise." *Comparative Administration Group, Papers in Comparative Administration Special Series: No. 2*. Washington, D.C.: American Society for Public Administration, Feb. 1964, p. 7.

Wilterdink, N. "Comparative Historical Sociology in the Seventies." *The Netherlands' Journals of Sociology* 2 (1985):20.

Contributors

NAZIH N. AYUBI teaches at the Department of Politics, University of Exeter. A graduate of Cairo University, he obtained his doctorate from Oxford University. He taught at Cairo University from 1975 to 1979, and was Visiting Associate Professor of Political Science at the University of California, Los Angeles, from 1979 to 1983. In addition to the publication of scholarly articles in major international journals, he is the author of several books in Arabic as well as the author of *Bureaucracy and Politics in Contemporary Egypt,* and a contributing author to *Rich and Poor States in the Middle East, The Iran-Iraq War, The Middle East in the 1980s, The Arabian Peninsula, The Mediterranean Region,* and *Beyond Coercion: Durability of the Arab State.*

GERALD E. CAIDEN is Professor of Public Administration in the School of Public Administration at the University of Southern California. He received his B.S. in economics and Ph.D. from the University of London where he attended the London School of Economics and Political Science. Dr. Caiden has taught at universities in Canada, Australia and Israel, and has published over twenty-five books and monographs in public policy and management and comparative public administration.

NAOMI CAIDEN is Chair of the Department of Public Administration at California State University, San Bernardino. She is the author of numerous articles on comparative public budgeting and the coauthor, with Aaron Wildavsky, of *Planning and Budgeting in Poor Countries.*

ROSS CURNOW is Senior Lecturer in Government and Public Administration at the University of Sydney. Formerly editor of the *Australian Journal of Public Administration,* he is currently working on a bicentennial history of government administration in New South Wales.

WILLIE CURTIS is Associate Professor of Political Science at St. Cloud State University. He received his Ph.D. from the University of Delaware after completing an Agency for International Development/National Association for Schools of Public Affairs and Administration (NASPAA) internship in 1982.

ANDREW DUNSIRE is Professor of Politics at the University of York. A Scot, he graduated from Edinburgh in 1949 after war service, taught at the London School of Economics and Exeter, and was briefly a civil servant. He moved to York in 1964. His major books include *Administration, The Execution Process,* and, with C. C. Hood, *Bureaumetrics* and *Cutback Management in Public Bureaucracies.*

O. P. DWIVEDI is Chairman of the Political Studies Department of the University of Guelph, Canada. He has been policy consultant to the Ministry of State for Urban Affairs and the Public Service Commission of Canada. His international work includes assignments with WHO and the Criminal Justice Section of UNO, and he has worked as CIDA adviser to the Government of Papua New Guinea. His publications include *Resources and the Environment, Public Service Ethics, Administrative State in Canada,* and *India's Administrative State.* Dr. Dwivedi was elected president of the Canadian Political Science Association in 1986, and he was awarded the LL.D. by the University of Lethbridge, Canada, in 1988.

FERREL HEADY is Professor Emeritus, Public Administration and Political Science, University of New Mexico, and is a former president of the University as well as its Academic Vice President. He was formerly director of the Institute of Public Administration at the University of Michigan and has published extensively in the field of comparative public administration.

KEITH M. HENDERSON is Professor of Political Science, State University of New York College, Buffalo, and has served as department chair and chairman pro tem. He previously taught at the Graduate School of Public Administration, New York University. His publications include *The Study of Public Administration* and *Emerging Synthesis in American Public Administration.*

R. B. JAIN is Professor and Head of Political Science and Dean, Faculty of Social Science, at the University of Delhi. He holds an M.A. from Punjab University and his doctorate from the Indian School of International Studies (Jawaharlal Nehru University) in New Delhi. He has been a visiting professor at Carleton University, the University of Minnesota, Concordia University, and the University of Guelph, Canada, and was a Senior Fulbright Fellow at the School of Foreign Service at Georgetown University and a British Council Fellow at the London School of Economics and Political Science. He has published widely on political science and public administration.

JORGE NEF is Professor of Political Studies and International Development at the University of Guelph, Canada. He received his B.A. in public administration from the University of Chile and his Ph.D. from the University of California, Santa Barbara. Besides his experience in the Chilean civil service and his work as consultant and cooperant for Canadian and international agencies, he has taught in seven institutions in the United States, Mexico, Canada and Costa Rica. He has published over sixty articles on comparative administration, international development, comparative politics, and international relations in various journals and collections in Canada, the United States, India, Latin America and Europe.

CLAUDIUS DELE OLOWU teaches public administration in the University of Ife, Nigeria. He was a research associate and visiting scholar at Indiana University, Bloomington, during the 1985–86 academic year and served also as the International Union of Local Authorities 1986 Visiting Fellow. Dr. Olowu has written several articles on African and comparative public administration. He is coeditor of *Local Government in West Africa Since Independence* and author of *African Local Governments as Instruments of Economic and Social Development.*

WALTER OUMA OYUGI, a Kenyan, is Associate Professor and Chairman of the Department of Government, University of Nairobi. He received his B.A. in political science and M.A. in public administration from the University of California at Berkeley and a doctorate in government from the University of Nairobi. He joined the University of Nairobi in 1969 as an assistant lecturer. He has published many scholarly articles in journals and books, and is the author of *Rural Development Administration,* coeditor of *The Democratic Theory and Practice in Africa* and *The Crisis of Development Strategies in Eastern Africa,* and editor of *Teaching and Research in Political Science in Eastern Africa.* One of his latest works, *Bureaucracy and the Administration of Development in Africa,* is to be published by the University of California, Institute of International Studies.

RICHARD W. PHIDD is Professor of Political Science in the Department of Political Studies, University of Guelph, Canada. He received his doctorate from Queen's University, Kingston, Canada. He has taught public policy and public administration courses and has written the following books: *The Politics and Management of Canadian Economic Policy* and *Canadian Public Policy* (both with G. Bruce Doern). He has also contributed articles to other books dealing with Canadian public administration and public policy. He is currently writing a text on Canadian public administration.

JON S. T. QUAH is Acting Director of the Institute of Policy Studies in Singapore and Associate Professor of Political Science at the National University of Singapore. He is editor of the Public Administration in Asia Series for the Times Academic Press in Singapore; member, Advisory Board, *The Asian Journal of Public Administration;* and member, Board of Directors, International Institute of Comparative Government. He has published widely on Singapore politics and public administration in the ASEAN countries and his recent publications include *Government and Politics of Singapore* 2nd ed. (coeditor and contributor) and *Friends in Blue: The Police and the Public in Singapore.*

KU TASHIRO is a member of the International Civil Service Commission of the UN. He was a career executive of the Japanese Central Government and was given various overseas assignments including technical assistance on personnel administration to the Tanzania government and directorship at FAO of the UN. He also held senior executive positions in his home government.

GÉRARD TIMSIT is Professor, Vice-President of the Université de Paris I (Panthéon-Sorbonne); President of the Science Council of the European Institute for Public Administration; and Professor at the Collège d'Europe. He teaches the science of administration and comparative government and is the author and editor of a variety of books and numerous articles on public administration, including "La notion de fonction administrative," *L'Administration publique et le NOEI,* and "Théorie de l'administration."

ROGER WETTENHALL is College Fellow in Administrative Studies in the Canberra College of Advanced Education. He was consultant on statutory authorities to the Royal Commission on Australian Government Administration (1974–76), and has been Project Director of the Public Enterprise Working Group of the International Association of Schools and Institutes of Administration since 1982.

Index